MW01716486

Jesus in an Age of Terror

BibleWorld
Series Editor: Philip R. Davies and James G. Crossley, University of Sheffield

BibleWorld shares the fruits of modern (and postmodern) biblical scholarship not only among practitioners and students, but also with anyone interested in what academic study of the Bible means in the twenty-first century. It explores our ever-increasing knowledge and understanding of the social world that produced the biblical texts, but also analyses aspects of the bible's role in the history of our civilization and the many perspectives – not just religious and theological, but also cultural, political and aesthetic – which drive modern biblical scholarship.

Published:

Sodomy
A History of a Christian Biblical Myth
Michael Carden

Yours Faithfully: Virtual Letters from the Bible
Edited by Philip R. Davies

Israel's History and the History of Israel
Mario Liverani

The Apostle Paul and His Letters
Edwin D. Freed

The Origins of the 'Second' Temple: Persian Imperial Policy and the Rebuilding of Jerusalem
Diana Edelman

An Introduction to the Bible (Revised edition)
John Rogerson

The Morality of Paul's Converts
Edwin D. Freed

The Mythic Mind: Essays on Cosmology and Religion in Ugaritic and Old Testament Literature
Nick Wyatt

History, Literature and Theology in the Book of Chronicles
Ehud Ben Zvi

Women Healing/Healing Women: The Genderization of Healing in Early Christianity
Elaine M. Wainwright

Jonah's World: Social Science and the Reading of Prophetic Story
Lowell K. Handy

Symposia: Dialogues Concerning the History of Biblical Interpretation
Roland Boer

Sectarianism in Early Judaism
Edited by David J. Chalcraft

The Ontology of Space in Biblical Hebrew Narrative
Luke Gärtner-Brereton

Mark and its Subalterns : A Hermeneutical Paradigm for a Postcolonial Context
David Joy

Linguistic Dating of Biblical Texts: An Introduction to Approaches and Problems
Ian Young and Robert Rezetko

Redrawing the Boundaries
The Date of Early Christian Literature
J.V.M. Sturdy, edited by Jonathan Knight

Forthcoming:

Sex Working and the Bible
Avaren Ipsen

The Archaeology of Myth: Papers on Old Testament Tradition
N. Wyatt

Vive Memor Mortis
Thomas Bolin

The Bible Says So!: From Simple Answers to Insightful Understanding
Edwin D. Freed

The Joy of Kierkegaard : Essays on Kierkegaard as a Biblical Reader
Hugh Pyper

From Babylon to Eternity: The Exile Remembered and Constructed in Text and Tradition
Bob Becking, Alex Cannegieter, Wilfred van der Poll and Anne-Mareike Wetter

Charismatic Killers :Reading the Hebrew Bible's Violent Rhetoric in Film
Eric Christianson

On the Origins of Judaism
Philip R. Davies

Judaism, Jewish Identities and the Gospel Tradition
Edited by James G. Crossley

Jesus Beyond Nationalism: Constructing the Historical Jesus in a Period of Cultural Complexity
Edited by Ward Blanton, James G. Crossley and Halvor Moxnes

O Mother, Where Art Thou?
An Irigarayan Reading of the Book of Chronicles
Julie Kelso

A Compendium of Musical Instruments and Instrumental Terminology in the Bible
Yelena Kolyada

A Social History of the Phoenician City-States in the Achaemenid Empire
Vadim Jigoulov

JESUS IN AN AGE OF TERROR

Scholarly Projects for a New American Century

James G. Crossley

Routledge
Taylor & Francis Group
LONDON AND NEW YORK

First published 2008 by Equinox, an imprint of Acumen

Published 2014 by Routledge
2 Park Square, Milton Park, Abingdon, Oxon OX14 4RN
711 Third Avenue, New York, NY 10017, USA

Routledge is an imprint of the Taylor & Francis Group, an informa business

British Library Cataloguing-in-Publication Data

A catalogue record for this book is available from the British Library.

ISBN-13 978 1 84553 429 5 (hardback)
978 1 84553 430 1 (paperback)

Library of Congress Cataloging-in-Publication Data

Crossley, James G.
Jesus in an age of terror : scholarly projects for a new American century / James G. Crossley.
p. cm. — (Bibleworld)
Includes bibliographical references and index.
ISBN 978-1-84553-429-5 (hbk) — ISBN 978-1-84553-430-1 (pbk.) 1. Christianity—Origin. 2. Bible. N.T.—Criticism, interpretation, etc. I. Title.
BR129.C755 2008
270.072—dc22
2008013493

Typeset by S.J.I. Services, New Delhi

For Caroline and...

It is the responsibility of intellectuals to speak the truth and to expose lies. This, at least, may seem enough of a truism to pass over without comment. Not so, however. For the modern intellectual, it is not at all obvious.

N. Chomsky, "The Responsibility of Intellectuals"

CONTENTS

Acknowledgements

One of my mild worries about writing a book like this is that I might lose or offend friends and make plenty of enemies. Ultimately the importance of the subject matter had to override such concerns and I do not see how some of the outrageous claims made by certain scholars about others (e.g. Arabs) could be passed by without condemnation. Mike Bird, in particular, has been a friendly and entertaining debating partner for a while now and he does come in for some criticism in this book. He may or may not believe me but I think it is clear that his scholarship on Christian origins, unlike some of the critiques of scholarship in this book, has not been judged in any significant way: just some of his political statements. His career is growing at a dramatic rate in evangelical circles while he remains friendly and good natured.

Less defensively, I would like to thank Janet Joyce, Audrey Mann, and Philip Davies of Equinox for helping the publication of this book. Halvor Moxnes' Oslo-based group on Jesus and cultural complexity has proven to be particularly helpful in preparation for publication. In Oslo I was able to discuss Part III of this book in some detail. One Oslo participant, Bill Arnal, provided much inspiration for the ideas in Part III and gave much appreciated critical comments, while another, Ward Blanton, has shown new and significant ways of analysing the history of scholarship.

Similarly Burke Long's Social History of Biblical Scholarship group at the European Association of Biblical Studies has provided another outlet for discussion of aspects relating to Part III. Various figures associated with that group have helped me think about ways of analysing the discipline. In particular, discussions with my Sheffield colleague Hugh Pyper on antisemitism in nineteenth- and early twentieth-century scholarship have been particularly fruitful. I am also grateful for very helpful discussions at the universities of Exeter and Glasgow relating to Part II. Exeter's Francesca Stavrakopoulou has also given me important feedback on issues relating to antisemitism in scholarship and various issues surrounding faith-based scholarship.

Thanks as ever to my excellent colleagues in the Department of Biblical Studies at the University of Sheffield. There are very few institutions on the planet where such open debates on the politics of contemporary biblical studies could take place. As should become clear to the reader of the whole of this book, Keith Whitelam's work has probably been among the most influential book from biblical studies on this present work and regular discussions over the past few years led to the publication of this book. The regular departmental historiography group run by Diana Edelman has also been an important context for discussion.

In these and related contexts I should also mention the general inspiration and/or helpful discussions with and/or feedback from Jorunn Buckley, Wissam Magadley, David Horrell, Louise Lawrence, Reda Bouchami, John Lyons, Paul Nikkel, Rob Thorne and my Sheffield colleagues Jorunn Økland (oh, and hello Tora and Idun!) and Barry Matlock. A socio-intellectual colleague, Jacques Berlinerblau, has a fine knack of making discussions of secularism and politics seem like it might be worth doing biblical studies after all and even like we aren't doing biblical studies at all. Callum Millard has discussed politics with me for nearly 20 years now and should he be bothered to read this (or if I bother to give him a copy) he may well notice the development of these long-discussed ideas. Jim West and Steph Fisher both read an entire draft of the manuscript and provided important critical feedback. Jim West also supplied me with the latest media reporting of events relating to this book.

Particular thanks ought to be given to Todd Penner. In addition to much appreciated active support for the publication of this book, the more-regular-than-you-would-think serious conversations and Todd's published work on the history of scholarship have proven to be important for me.

As ever, Maurice Casey has been an important influence. I was introduced to his work on ideology, antisemitism and the history of scholarship at an early date, and at times during the embryonic period. It is difficult to think of too many who can rival his learning in several areas of Christian origins.

Getting more and more to the social side of things (several of the above ably straddle both sides), I have to thank people involved in the much needed aside of the sporting world. In particular, I should thank Paddy Maher, Sandra Eccles and Mick Jordan. Thanks also to the departmental six-a-side football/soccer team at Sheffield, Biblical Studies FC, and the valiant attempts to show that even with the most unlikely team name the players can actually play a bit.

Richard Crossley showed absolutely no interest in this book. His utter non-interest in academia has been much appreciated. Hello to Francis and Gill too.

Pamela Crossley (among a million and one things) kept me up-to-date with internet discussion groups and various media articles. Perhaps not entirely surprisingly for a parent, her views on politics and religion are eerily similar to mine. Good to know we're both right.

Finally, and in fear of sounding like a bad r'n'b album, let's thank the family Watt: Mike, Glennis, and Caroline. The first two have provided plenty of support over the years and for being living explanations of why Caroline is Caroline. Contrary to her own claims, Caroline *almost* read all of the manuscript. But *almost* all is better than *next to nothing*, right? And to be fair she has as sharp an eye for detail as anyone I know and sees nothing wrong with polemic far worse than I'm prepared to write (this book would have been far nastier if she had her way). And rather than let me sleep at night, she made me impregnate her.

Preface

This book will largely apply the writings of Noam Chomsky, Edward Herman, Edward Said and several others on international politics and the supportive role of the media, intellectuals and academics to Christian origins and New Testament scholarship since the not insignificant date of 1967. The major features of this book are to explain why two major developments in New Testament and Christian origins scholarship took place when and where they did and the ideology that keeps them buoyant. While numerous theorists could have been chosen to analyse intellectual culture (e.g. Gramsci, Foucault), Chomsky, Herman, Said and the others were chosen deliberately because they are ruthless in illustrating the harsh *contemporary* realities of the cultural contexts of elite culture, avoiding mere abstract presentations of hegemony. This is obviously particularly significant given my aims of a precise historical contextualization of scholarship and ideology.

The book will be set out in three parts, each containing two chapters. Part I will look at the ways in which New Testament and Christian origins scholarship has historically been influenced by its political and social settings over the past hundred years or so. Moving on to the present, I will then apply Edward Herman and Noam Chomsky's propaganda model of manufacturing consent in the mass media to the recent explosion of biblical scholars writing, often many times daily, on the internet, in particular scholars who have taken up "blogging." This is particularly important because it provides an outlet for scholars to talk politics as well as biblical scholarship. It is clear, I think, that political views conform strikingly to the emphases that come through in Herman and Chomsky's analysis of the mass media. The rest of the book will take up modified key areas of the propaganda model in more detail.

Part II will look at the Orientalist rhetoric of clashing civilizations and how this relates to the "war on terror" and the creation of Islam, Arabs, the Middle East, and so on, as the great enemy in the media and relevant intellectual thought since the 1970s and emboldened since September 11, 2001. I will then move on to show how this has had a highly noticeable impact on social sciences in New Testament and Christian origins scholarship, in particular the stark generalizations of Orientalist New Testament scholars, particularly some from the Context Group, using cultural/social anthropology based on studies of the Mediterranean and the Middle East. Regrettably some of this scholarship is grounded in outdated, nationalist, imperialist and, at times, plain racist social-sciences, some of which directly relate to Anglo-American foreign policy interests in the Middle East and beyond. Some of this Orientalist New Testament and Christian origins scholarship, consciously or unconsciously, makes some alarming and politically charged statements about "the Middle East" that cohere too closely with recent intellectual defences of indefensible actions in Iraq, Palestine and beyond.

Part III, will look at issues of Palestine and Israel in the media alongside Christian, secular and relevant intellectual thought since the "Six Day War" of 1967, focusing in particular on the dramatic shift towards massive and regularly uncritical support for Israeli state actions. I will then move on to show how this shift has had a profound impact on historical Jesus and Christian origins studies, particularly the strange emphasis on "Jewishness" and misplaced allegations of antisemitism since the 1970s.[1] I will also show that despite the shift in support of Israel this is rarely done for love of Jews, Judaism, Israel or Israelis because there remains a notable cultural and religious superiority. This too is strongly echoed in the scholarship of Christian origins where for all the emphasis on the "Jewishness" of Jesus and the first Christians, it is extremely common to find Jesus or the first Christians being better than Judaism or overriding key symbols of Judaism as constructed by scholarship. The end results of contemporary scholarship are not dramatically different from the results of the anti-Jewish and antisemitic scholarship of much of the twentieth century.

There are several underlying reasons for the writing of this book. On the broad historical level, the rhetoric of clashing civilizations and the "war on terror" is so prominent in the media and strands of intellectual thought that it seemed reasonable enough to think its impact would be found in biblical studies. In a previous book, I looked at the influence of the Cold War on scholarship and scholarly results and given that the rhetoric of "clash of civilizations," "war on terror" and so on are the direct heirs of Cold War rhetoric then it seemed doubly reasonable to think that there would be some kind of impact. Similarly, it became noticeable that more and more New Testament scholars were coming out with some hostile comments about Islam, the kinds of things, in fact, that were being said about Judaism by many New Testament scholars in the early- and mid-twentieth century. As it was clear that such earlier comments on Jews and Judaism were fuelled by European anti-Semitism, it again seemed reasonable to look for the reasons why Islam and Muslims were being negatively discussed by scholars of the New Testament and Christian origins.

Given that this book looks at contemporary scholarship in its historical and political contexts, it would be foolish to think that it was written without being influenced by recent history and politics. Some of the most famous examples are the escalation of violence in Israel and Palestine since the turn of the millennium, September 11, the invasions of Afghanistan and Iraq, Abu Ghraib, Guantánamo and the bombings in Bali, Madrid, and London. That these issues are frequently present in the book is, obviously, hardly a coincidence. I should also add that the US and its trusty UK sidekick have been at the forefront of the recent bloodbaths in Afghanistan and Iraq – not to mention plenty of less well publicized acts of aggressive foreign policy – and both, though particularly the US, have played central roles in the issues surrounding Israel and Palestine. This was the main reason behind the focus on Anglo-American scholarship, though results from German, Oceanic, Canadian and other "Western" countries are not dramatically different and will, on occasion, be referenced.

On the more personal level, politics – both national and international – has long been a major interest of mine and it sometimes puzzles me how I never ended up working in that area. I have been reader of works on the subject for at least as long as I have been reading works relating to biblical studies and so it was perhaps inevitable that the two would someday be combined. As it happens, my first ever public lecture was partly on one of the most explicitly political books ever written on biblical scholarship, namely Keith Whitelam's 1996 book, *The Invention of Ancient Israel: The Silencing of Palestinian History.*[2] The influence of Whitelam's book on ancient Israel scholarship on this particular book on Christian origins scholarship should be obvious.

Maurice Casey aptly refers to one aspect of New Testament scholarship (research on the hypothetical gospel source, "Q") as being in "a regrettably bureaucratized state."[3] Others (Casey included) could give plenty of other examples from scholarship where arguments descend into academic authorities declaring their opinion on a matter with little in the way of evidence and/or reliance on consensus (whether real or not) or friends, before expecting people to just agree because they said so.[4] This strikes me as a particularly unscholarly model of scholarship: refer to what is accepted as true and continually reference statements made by the good and the great, too often without reference to any kind of evidence, argument or counter argument. This scholarly "bureaucratization" hit me hard at an annual Society for Biblical Literature meeting where for once I decided to sit quietly at the back of sessions dominated by a given perspective, as a little private experiment to see how the arguments were conducted. I was taken aback and slightly depressed (relatively speaking) to see how arguments were at times deemed right or wrong by little more than rhetoric and group interests. My frustration with such scholars and scholarship has come through before in writing and it will come through again in this book but it was this kind of experience that led me to think further about the role of social context and the results of scholarship, given that evidence and argument are not always deemed significant enough.

Part I

Christian Origins and New Testament Studies in Ideologically and Historically Contaminated Contexts

Cultivated theory can bolster uncomplicated bigotry.

Amartya Sen[1]

There is however, a brighter side to the amount of energy and money that the establishment pours into the business of "managing" public opinion. It suggests a very real fear of public opinion. It suggests a persistent and valid worry that if people were to discover (and fully comprehend) the real nature of the things that are done in their name, they might act upon that knowledge. Powerful people know that ordinary people are not always reflexively ruthless and selfish. (When ordinary people weigh costs and benefits, something like an uneasy conscience could easily tip the scales.) For this reason, they must be guarded against reality, reared in a controlled climate, in an altered reality, like broiler chickens or pigs in a pen.

Arundhati Roy[2]

Chapter 1

Introduction: Reading the History of New Testament and Christian Origins Scholarship

Far from more or less accurate repetitions of an ancient object, modernity's depictions of original Christianity must be read as a working through of its own identity.

Ward Blanton[1]

This chapter will briefly introduce the ways in which New Testament and Christian origins scholarship have historically been embedded in their social, political and cultural contexts. The purpose of this chapter is to summarize some relatively non-controversial arguments made by several scholars, including myself, in order to provide a historical context whereby it can be seen clearly that scholarship is embroiled in the major political disputes of its day. The next chapter will provide a contemporary context where we will see scholars explicitly airing their political views. These first two chapters will be the foundation for the rest of the book because the subsequent chapters will then look at the more subtle ways in which politics and ideology continue to infiltrate New Testament and Christian origins scholarship.

Before we turn to a social history of New Testament and Christian origins scholarship, I will first look at a suitable model for analysing the role of politics and ideology among academics which will also form the basis for much of this book.

Manufacturing Consent: Christian Origins Scholarship in Context

Any group dominated by people with overarching similar interests will obviously have such interests reflected in its literary and rhetorical output. Edward Herman and Noam Chomsky showed this with reference to intellectuals and the mass media in their development of a "propaganda model."[2] The propaganda model shows that the press is not really an important tool of democracy and it is not really disagreeable, argumentative or subversive of political power, at least not in any significant sense. The function of the mass media is to provide support for the special interests that dominate the state and private activity. This is reflected in their choices, emphases, and omissions. It is the powerful who fix the assumptions of media discourse and decide what is allowed to be seen and heard, often with the support of academics. Disagreements reflect disagreements among the elites. Although individuals may hold very different views from the agenda of the mass media, these views will not be seriously reflected in the overall agenda or agendas. Fundamental dissent is largely missing from the press: it is more likely to be squeezed towards the back pages or left to some marginalized press. Censorship, then, effectively becomes self-censorship behind the rhetoric of free and open debate. Hence Herman and Chomsky borrow the loaded phrase "manufacturing consent."

As this analysis is focused on the media, I will apply and modify it in the next chapter on biblical scholars as bloggers. However, Herman and Chomsky's work is obviously applicable to a variety of areas, including scholarship, particularly as it analyses how dominant groups control the presentation of data. I have tried to do this elsewhere with reference to gospel scholarship and I have also analysed the ways in which the results of New Testament scholarship reflect the interests and ideology of the dominant participating groups.[3] Moreover, while Chomsky's work may have focused most heavily on the elite media, he has also shown that propagandistic tendencies are present in intellectual scholarship, even if those tendencies are more difficult to find.[4]

For example, echoing Gramsci on intellectuals as "experts in legitimation,"[5] Chomsky looks at the ways in which respectable scholarship either serves the needs of elite culture or avoids anything too critical of elite culture. Universities are dependent not just on tuition money but also on outside funding such as wealthy alumni, corporations, and the government, groups, in other words, with similar basic interests (see further Chapters 3, 4 and 5). Consequently, if universities stop serving such interests, there will be trouble. Chomsky is, of course, aware that things are not that simple and he does note that dissidents can be found but ultimately the problematic figures will be weeded out or made to conform. Chomsky regularly points to the contrast with the hard sciences. Basic scientific knowledge prevents scientists doing outdated science because scientific progress has been too great. This, Chomsky argues, is "very different from the social sciences and the humanities – you can tell falsehoods forever in those fields and nothing will ever stop you, like you don't have Mother Nature around keeping you honest."[6]

If there are going to be significant challenges to the political and economic system, there will likely be an attempt at marginalization, as seen in cruder forms such as purges in 1950s USA.[7] Chomsky gives explicit examples of academics told straight out not to publish on certain topics but the methods of control are more subtle and closely related to the subtle means of control in the propaganda model. The control of power can be done by denying or ignoring basic facts and by setting the agenda so that certain positions are "obviously" off-limits. Chomsky famously showed this in *American Power and the New Mandarins*, illustrating the ways in which academic historical analysis repeated the dominant liberal or anti-anarchist discourse when discussing the Spanish Civil War or how elite opinion in the US on foreign policy in South-East Asia was unquestioningly repeated by leading analysts.[8]

One major example is the early career of Norman Finkelstein – a perennial example of how the education system has functioned to exclude certain views – and his demolishment of Joan Peters' fraudulent and now infamous book, *From Time Immemorial*. Peters claimed, with the usual social scientific and scholarly paraphernalia, that Palestinians were in fact recent immigrants to the Jewish settled areas of former Palestine with the implication that there were really no Palestinians. The book got masses of positive reviews in the US where the issue of Israel/Palestine is particularly sensitive. However, Finkelstein noted that it was full of fraudulent detail and wrote an article demonstrating this. Yet after sending it off for publication no one bothered responding and it ended up in an obscure left wing journal.

Finkelstein was ostracized at Princeton and could get no support for his career. Finkelstein then followed up the details of Peters' book and found an exceptionally high level of fraudulent detail. Yet still he was being told not to bother following it up and continued to struggle to get the thesis published. When he finally did manage to get the book published, Chomsky sent it to major non-American journals, notably in the UK and in Israel. Though Finkelstein's work was not referenced, it did influence several such reviews which demolished Peters' book. As these non-American reviews were read by American academics, there was lots of scholarly backtracking.[9] Of course, since then we could go on to further mistreatments of Finkelstein, with de Paul's intellectually absurd but ideologically obvious denial of tenure to Finkelstein merely being the latest episode.

In terms of academia, Chomsky is scathing of certain academics presented as radical, particularly certain views associated with Marxist theory and strands of postmodernism. Marxism and Freudianism can be deemed intellectual fakery because they function as theology or organized religion, coming close to acting as if the figurehead is some kind of god who got virtually everything right. Instead, Chomsky argues, people should be asking which parts of say, Marx, are worth preserving and discussing further.[10] But as for areas of Marxism such as "dialectics," Chomsky says he simply does not understand them and suggests that overly complex intellectual language has more to do with creating an intellectual niche to preserve intellectual power. As Chomsky puts it more bitterly: "when words like 'dialectics' come along, or 'hermeneutics,' and all that stuff that is supposed to be profound, like Goering, 'I reach for my revolver.'"

Unsurprisingly, then, Chomsky is scathing of some leading postmodernist thinkers. He claims that when he reads Derrida, or Lacan, or Althusser, "I just don't understand it. It's like words passing in front of my eyes: I can't follow the arguments, I don't see the arguments, anything that looks like a description of a fact looks wrong to me... I think it's all fraud."[11] Intriguingly, Chomsky (who is extremely critical of the French intellectual scene) says of Lacan that he was a "conscious charlatan, and was simply playing games with the Paris intellectual community to see how much absurdity he could produce and still be taken seriously. I mean that quite literally. I knew him."[12]

Chomsky is partly hostile because he views such "radical" scholarship as a betrayal of popular movements and functioning as a kind of intellectual vanguard, hence the attraction of Leninism to many academics. Whatever we make of Chomsky's critique – and it would be very interesting to know how many sympathetic academics there are out there! – it should be noted that Chomsky adds an important function of unnecessarily complex "radical" scholarship for our present purposes: the higher education system can "get people to sell out even while they think they're doing exactly the right thing." It is possible to enter academia and be radical as long as the questions are framed correctly in order not to ask the right questions. The scholar may feel like they are not selling out by acting as, for instance, a Marxist economist, but in reality the individual has been neutralized.[13]

An analysis of the political control of higher education that complements Chomsky's analysis was developed by Edward Said and is particularly important because Said's critique of scholarship has regularly involved social-scientific study of the Middle East and Israel, areas of direct significance for the study of Christian origins and issues in contemporary Anglo-American foreign policy. As Said famously argued, the development of "Orientalism" was a way of studying Arabs, Asians or any kind of "other" as different, exotic, inferior, undemocratic, backward and so on, was tied in with Western imperialistic ambitions, from the British through to the contemporary US. As we will see, whatever the faults of Said's analysis, it is very clear that it has powerful explanatory force for analysing contemporary scholarship. Said also showed that Orientialism, which, as we will see, has a long history within biblical studies, is not "more biased than other social and humanistic science, it is simply as ideological and contaminated by the world as other disciplines."[14] Moreover, Said also showed that Orientalism – applicable to other culturally dominant motifs – is both implicit and explicit in all aspects of the culture studied, from film and advertising to politics and academia. In terms of the scholarship on Christian origins we may not always find explicit reference to the various themes to be discussed in this book but we should not be surprised if scholarly themes echo major themes elsewhere in contemporary culture.

These kinds of analyses have continued up to the present, including the present "war on terror." As Derek Gregory has shown, US centred colonialism is not simply reproduced though geopolitics, geoeconomics, foreign policy, corporate demands and so on but, crucially for present purposes, also through "mundane cultural forms and cultural practices that mark other people as irredeemably 'Other' and that licence the unleashing of exemplary violence against them...these imaginative geographies lodge many more of us in the same architectures of enmity." Gregory aptly adds that we should not allow the "spectacular violence" of recent times "to blind us to the *banality* of the colonial present and to our complicity in its horrors."[15] In a volume Gregory co-edited on "violent geographies," intellectual thought associated with specific "culture areas" and the "war on terror" are analysed in some depth.[16] This issue and that of imagined geographies will become important in Part II when we look at the ways the Mediterranean is used as a "culture area" in the anthropological study of Christian origins yet strangely merges into the "Middle East," accompanied by some outrageous stereotypes of "the Arab" and language also used in the Anglo-American political media right up to and including the "war on terror."

As the study of Christian origins does not always discuss *explicitly* the various key issues, it is necessary to infer or deduce such issues from context and see how similar trends and themes are found in what may seem to be different cultural contexts. This may mean in some cases – though certainly not all – that the study of Christian origins will produce watered-down versions of colonial trends and themes but they are, I hope to show, clear enough. This should be no surprise either as biblical studies is as every bit embedded in the cultural-political trends of its day as any other aspect of contemporary culture.

In objection to this, it might be countered that a great deal of recent scholarship has been dedicated to showing the radical nature of Christian origins and the New Testament. Jesus was a social revolutionary, Jesus *and* Paul challenged the power of the Roman Empire, Jesus did not like economic exploitation and neither should we, and so on. N. T. Wright even claims (wildly, it has to be said) that "in the real world...the tyrants and bullies (including intellectual and cultural tyrants and bullies) try to rule by force, only to discover that in order do so they have to quash all rumours of resurrection, rumours that would imply that their greatest weapons, death and deconstruction, are not after all omnipotent."[17]

One response to all this might legitimately be: so what? For a start, Hollywood has plenty of challenges to imperialism of the British or Roman variety. But even the radical Jesus or Paul or even Christian origins in general are hardly going to function as a major challenge to contemporary power structures. If everybody became active liberation theologians in Latin America or did a Schweitzer and went off and followed their results, *then* there might be a problem. But more often than not debates over early Christian radicals end up as an internal scholarly debate. Burton Mack's Jesus or Crossan's Jesus has only managed to wind up scholars and laity from different intellectual or theological persuasions or perhaps the odd media or church figure while N. T. Wright's Jesus has only managed to wind up people like me or some of the weird internet atheists. And, besides, how threatening *really* is a stress on resurrection? Maybe I am either naïve or cynical but I cannot see too many forceful tyrants and bullies of this world that Wright has criticized being remotely interested in issues of resurrection.

At best, some reconstructions of Jesus or Paul or a gospel writer (e.g. as social critics, proto-Marxists, opponents of the Iraq war etc.) can get ridiculed, rightly or wrongly, for being too anachronistic. None of this is the stuff anyone in a position of serious power would want to actually *ban* and has had minimal social impact beyond academia, at least in "the West." The façade of "radical" can be maintained but, as Chomsky pointed out, scholarship is effectively neutralized and prevented from having any serious insight into the ways in which power works.[18] To use a slightly exaggerated analogy, as Paul Weller is reported to have said of rock and pop music, if it really was such a threat to the establishment "they would have banned it years ago."[19]

One related example of this process in action involves people self-described as coming in from a position of relative radicalism yet peddling results congenial to Anglo-American hegemony involves the Context

Group. For example, Bruce Malina reviews the origins of Context Group-style approaches to the New Testament in a dedication to John Elliott:

> Jack Elliott takes pride in his career of liberal activism. In the 1960s, he protested the Vietnam War and marched in Selma, Alabama. Finding that he shared intellectual interests with a number of protesters – many of them from Berkeley – Elliott met with them off the streets to explore the intersection of politics and theology. They called themselves the Bay Area Seminar for Theology and Related Disciplines – BASTARDs. Searching for new theological perspectives to deal with the political situation, he began reading widely in sociology and political science. He asked many of the same questions as the liberation theologians active at the time, but he found that they were not systematic or rigorous enough in their analysis.[20]

The origins may be honourable but like many of that generation they have formed part of the establishment, particularly in Society of Biblical Literature circles. In turn, any troublesome radicalism gets filtered out, as perhaps the final sentence already implies (the genuinely dangerous radicals are, apparently, not sufficiently analytical). As we will see, the output of some prominent members of the Context Group has reproduced some of the most outrageous yet ideologically convenient stereotypes about Arabs and the Middle East (see Chapter 4). Additionally, Elliott has produced a major article on the term "Jew" and alternative translations relating to land and the land of Israel accompanied by explicit awareness of contemporary political ramifications, with concern for Palestinian claims being the conspicuous exception.[21]

Confessional Context of Christian Origins Scholarship

> *Strictly speaking Wycliffe Hall is a permanent private hall of the University of Oxford, rather than a full college. But the difference is pretty academic. Wycliffe has control over its admissions policy and those who graduate do so with a full Oxford University degree. Which is why the thought that Wycliffe has been taken over by Christian fundamentalists is ruffling senior common room feathers all over the university. For having a cell of religious extremists succeed in claiming one of its precious institutions does little to enhance Oxford's reputation. But can disgruntled dons do much about it? After all, Oxford was founded as a Christian institution and, for good or ill, Christianity is built into its DNA. Dominus Illuminatio Mea – the Lord is my light – is the university motto. It has a university church and university sermons; the colleges have chapels and chaplains. It's hardly a secular institution.*
>
> Giles Fraser[22]

New Testament and related studies have another crucial aspect which must be added to the Chomksy-Said approach. Such studies are heavily populated by *Christian* scholars who revere their sacred scriptures and have their own particular agendas. Maurice Casey has estimated that ninety per cent or more of applicants to the premier scholarly New Testament society, *Studiorum Novi Testamenti Societas*, are Protestant Christians.[23] Elsewhere I have pointed out that *academic* conferences have been known to open with prayers and pious praise – hardly the hallmark of secular academia – while much New Testament scholarship has one eye on contemporary Christian relevance, warnings about the potential dangers of certain approaches (e.g. social-scientific), and even learned arguments explaining how stories like the bodily resurrection of Jesus really did happen.[24]

Additionally, we might note that throughout the world there are countless theological and Bible colleges where New Testament studies is practised, providing a constant stream of academic and semi-academic posts for Christian scholars. In many cases, there is an additional party line at the colleges which openly restricts academic debate, and not simply involving the general Catholic and Protestant divide. At numerous colleges, academics cannot believe that Jesus was not God, that the "New Perspective" on Paul might be correct, that Paul did not write all the letters attributed to him, that homosexuality is acceptable, that the bodily resurrection of Jesus did not happen (as Gerd Lüdemann would unfortunately find out) and so on. Recently, Wycliffe Hall, Oxford, has been involved in some well publicized controversies over theological intimidation leading to resignations, with issues involving the usual church favourites: women and gays.[25] Of course, these colleges are usually designed to train people for church ministry but, whether we like it or not, it is simply a blunt fact that scholars from seminaries and Bible colleges make up a significant proportion of New Testament scholars.

There is an uneasy overlap with the universities too. The German university system contains Protestant and Catholic faculties for the academic study of theology. In the UK, the old theological colleges which gained university status in the 1990s are struggling to deal with the tensions between the ideal of openness in universities and their theological foundations, illustrated by Canterbury Christ Church's ban on civil ceremonies for gay couples on its campus due to "the ethos of the institution."[26] One of the most prominent biblical studies libraries and institutions in the world is the evangelical centre, Tyndale House. Tyndale House is not simply the equivalent of a seminary or Bible college because it includes joint appointments with the University of Cambridge, effectively guaranteeing an evangelical presence at a major university (imagine the uproar if the Humanist Society created a joint position with a major university!). Indeed, in a recent interview, the new warden of Tyndale House, Peter Williams, has suggested the possibility of "setting up more University appointments, not just in Cambridge, but also in other Universities in the UK." Williams, who had previously lectured in New Testament studies at the University of Aberdeen, has an unapologetic, hard evangelical line on university scholarship:

> I'd like to see confessional scholarship clearly outstripping non-confessional scholarship in its quality and rigor... All Christians in the academy must see themselves as serving the church and must make themselves accountable to the church. I don't think this means that all their writing should be aimed at typical church audiences. *Ultimately we should aim for all the academy to become church!*[27] (My italics.)

While the academy may not become evangelical overnight, the idea of a confessional discipline is a very real possibility. This is a notable point because such a theocratic notion of scholarship could not be done by law but it could be done by the kinds of mechanisms of the propaganda model whereby the interests of the group controlling knowledge, unconsciously or (as it would be in this case) consciously, manipulate the agenda.

Before we continue, let me make this absolutely clear so that I (hopefully) do not get misunderstood, as I often have been on issues relating to secularism in the discipline: I am *not* criticizing scholars for being Christian and I am *not* saying Christian scholars are somehow less intelligent or produce worse scholarship than non-Christian scholars. Issues of whether Christians or non-believers produce "better" scholarship hold absolutely no interest for me at present and are probably impossible issues to judge anyway. What does interest me is the brute fact that *most scholars are Christian and that this will almost inevitably be reflected in the results of scholarship.* If the majority of scholars in New Testament studies were, for instance, militant atheists then it would not be surprising to see their agendas filtering through. The day the discipline becomes overwhelmingly atheist, and assuming for one moment that I am not long dead if/when that day comes, I will happily analyse the results of the discipline. But if we really want to see why the results of scholarship are as they are, it makes sense to go for those who dominate a given discipline.[28]

This means that the propaganda model needs a slight tweaking when applied to the scholarship of Christian origins: it is not simply broader political and economic agendas that will be reflected in the rhetoric of the discipline. Religious agendas will be central and it will be no surprise that disputes will be disputes among Christian intellectuals with other non-Christian or non-confessional disputes largely put to one side.[29] As I argued elsewhere with reference to the study of the historical Jesus:

> As it stands presently NT scholarship will always get largely Christian results, be they the nineteenth century liberal lives of Jesus, the Bultmannian dominated neo-Lutheranism, or the results of smaller sub groups such as the social reformer/critic Cynic [-style] Jesus associated with the Jesus Seminar: all different but all recognisably Christian.[30]

Additionally, some of the perceived non-Christian views have been conspicuously ignored in the history of the discipline. A great deal of social-scientific scholarship not only defends itself against allegations that it is not 'reductionist' (despite virtually no-one actually reducing the texts to purely "social forces") and against the potential "dangers" of atheistic intellectual roots, but has also had a history of showing its theological usefulness in New Testament scholarship.[31]

I have elsewhere applied Herman and Chomsky's propaganda model to a less honourable and overtly "religious" theme, namely the Christology of Mark's gospel. Christology is an obviously useful area to analyse Christian scholarly agendas because the figure of Christ is, naturally, central to Christian distinctiveness, including distinctiveness over against Judaism. In Mark's gospel there are no explicit narrative indications that ought to be read as constructing Christology over against Judaism like the sort that could be read in John's gospel (e.g. Jn 5:16-18; 10:22-39) and there are no explicit narrative indications that it ought to be read as constructing an overtly Jewish identity like the sort that could be read in Matthew's gospel (e.g. Matthew 5–7). Yet much of Markan scholarship virtually *assumes* that Mark's Christology is significantly different from anything found in Judaism but, as I argued with reference to several of the key topics (e.g. "son of man," "son of God," "divinity," and so on), this can only be argued if contemporary Jewish evidence is ignored. What this shows is that the dominance of Christians in the discipline of New Testament studies fills the gaps and constructs a conveniently non-Jewish Christ of faith.

We might couple this with comments made by other scholars that are easily adaptable to the propaganda model as I previously have used it. Maurice Casey has regularly critiqued the ideological make-up of the discipline and the ways in which ideology dictates the results of scholarship. Among many other examples, Casey has argued that there have been constant attempts to show that Jesus and/or early Christians did not make mistaken predictions about end times, pointing out some elaborate and hugely unconvincing theories to deny the obvious. Casey also points out that there have been wide-ranging attempts to make the polemic against "the Jews" in John's gospel mean something other than a polemic against Jewish people as a distinct group which in turn ensures John's gospel is not implicated in the evils done to Jews over the centuries.[32] Notably, on this emotive issue for those who revere the New Testament, Casey – a prominent scholar writing for a prominent publisher – has been largely ignored, not even gaining a mention in a book of over 600 pages on anti-Judaism in John's gospel![33]

Such approaches have long been anticipated in feminist scholarship. It is now well established that a traditionally male dominated discipline has, almost by definition, excluded histories and stories of women in Christian origins or biblical texts. While far from perfect, things are certainly different now compared to what they were in the 1960s, with countless studies on women in the Bible or the ancient contexts. However, one aspect of feminist critique has been, more predictably, relatively ignored given the Christianized nature of the discipline: the critique of the validity of the biblical texts to say anything useful for contemporary life and the role of contemporary women.[34] Yet, relatively ignored by the mainstream though it may have been, this strand of feminist thought has opened the door for the equally marginalized critique of the religious dominance of the discipline. Perhaps the most famous example of this is the work of Elizabeth Cady Stanton and the publication of *The Woman's Bible* at the end of the nineteenth century which included criticisms of biblical texts, looking at the way they can encourage social control and manipulation of women.[35] Only in a qualified way (i.e. the Bible must remain relevant in some sense even if it has wrongly been used to control and manipulate) can such critiques become part of the mainstream.[36] Needless to say, a view which takes the Bible as wholly irrelevant and outdated is not going to endear itself to the mainstream of biblical studies. Rightly or wrongly (I make no judgment on the relevance of the Bible), it is hardly going too far to suggest that the present Christian dominance of the discipline means that approaches grounded in criticizing the context of their sacred text are not going to dominate scholarly agendas.

This brief survey should, hopefully, have shown beyond doubt that we must factor in religious agendas into any study of New Testament and Christian origins scholarship in historical and political contexts, not least the tendency toward a kind of theocratic model of scholarship.

The Dominance and Influence of Pre-war German New Testament Scholarship

Probably the one area where it is undeniable that scholarship has been influenced by cultural and political contexts involves the nineteenth-century liberal lives of Jesus, famously demolished by Albert Schweitzer at the turn of the twentieth century. It is worth noting that even Schweitzer himself, aided and abetted by his reconstruction of Jesus as an apocalyptic preacher of imminent end times, was far from immune from the influence of cultural context. As Ward Blanton has shown, Schweitzer's views on the apocalyptic Jesus and mysticism in Paul strongly reflect his philosophical background and a reaction to modernity.[37]

To the well-worn narrative of the liberal lives of Jesus in nineteenth-century scholarship we should add some recent developments on the impact of nineteenth-century debates about nationalism on the historical study of Christian origins. Here I will summarize two important recent studies by Halvor Moxnes and Todd Penner. Moxnes shows how Schleiermacher's interest in the historical Jesus involved writing a biography, a popular form in nineteenth-century bourgeois German circles, and the description of ideal figures who incorporated the values of society, values that were distinct from the more traditional power structures; in other words, the biographies of "Great Men." In particular Schleiermacher saw the individual in relation to people, land and nation, and, in terms of the study of the historical Jesus, to write the life of Jesus as a biography was to write it by using categories carrying meanings within an "imagined" German land, people and nation. Jesus represented a particularly great type of person who had influence over "all peoples and all ages," and so his relations to people, land and nation served as an ideal. Moxnes makes the more general and significant point that historical Jesus studies emerged at the same time as the growth of nationalism in Europe.[38] Anyone who has read Renan will notice the importance of Moxnes' claim here.

Todd Penner has shown how debates over Hellenistic Judaism, Palestinian Judaism and early Christianity are grounded in eighteenth- and nineteenth-century discussions of "the Jewish problem," and how to accommodate Jews and Judaism in the European model of the nation state or empire. Such discussions included major philological debates about how the language of a particular people is tied in with the essence of a nation. Such debates, which provide a convenient category with which to differentiate Christianity from Judaism while preserving its "purity" from the wider pagan world, are so embedded in the study of Christian origins and the New Testament that they continue to this day, peaking at the major reference point, Martin Hengel's *Judaism and Hellenism*.[39]

Another major historical and political issue affecting the study of Christian origins in the late nineteenth century and early twentieth century, and particularly in German liberal Protestant scholarship, was the dispute with the developing labour movement.[40] This should be no surprise. Marx and Engels had been establishing themselves as among the most influential thinkers of the nineteenth century while Karl Kautsky, the leading intellectual figure of the German Social Democratic Party, picked up the mantle for the next generation of Marx's followers. To blur the categories of religion, academic thought, and broader historical change, not only had Marx written on religion but Engels and Kautsky had written significant works on Christian origins.[41] The most significant development in this context was the Lutheran Evangelisch-sozialer Kongress in 1890 which included major scholars of Christian origins such as Adolf Deissmann and Adolf von Harnack.[42] One of the key functions of the Kongress was to stem the tide of support among the working classes for the Marxist Social Democratic Party, itself including major thinkers such as Kautsky. The plan included the development of a Lutheran social gospel for the masses, an idea reflected in speeches such as that given by Deissmann in Dessau, 1908, "Das Urchristentum und die unteren Schichten" ("Primitive Christianity and the Lower Classes"). Not only did this include attacks on Marxist figures such as Kautsky but the speech also strongly emphasized that Christianity must not be understood as a revolutionary proletarian movement aiming to restructure society. We also find such concerns reflected in Deissmann's scholarly work. Not only do Kautsky and Kalthoff come in for a harsh dismissal,[43] but Deissmann also argued that Christianity had its origins, to an extent, among the lower classes and writes some heavily romanticizing words on the subject.[44]

But there was, of course, another major development about to take place at this time: German nationalism would start feeding into German fascism and the rise of Hitler. It is becoming increasingly well known that parts of German New Testament scholarship were heavily influenced by outright fascism and antisemitism.[45] Probably the most famous example is Walter Grundmann, a member of the Nazi party and a supporting member of the SS, who pushed for an Aryan Jesus. Another highly prominent example is Gerhard Kittel who edited the still standard *Theological Dictionary of the New Testament* (*TDNT*), alongside writing the antisemitic pamphlet, *Die Judenfrage* ("The Jewish Question"), and writing for the official Nazi publication *Forschungen zur Judenfrage* ("Researches into the Jewish Question").[46]

The *TDNT* included several entries by Nazi scholars, most striking perhaps being K. G. Kuhn.[47] Kuhn joined the Nazi party in 1932 and developed research on "the Jewish question." In 1939, Kuhn wrote on "the Jewish question" as a problem for world history, which includes arguments such as Jew-hatred being ancient and arising from Judaism itself and chillingly ending with a hope that the Führer would finally solve the Jewish question.[48] As it happens, he also wrote a very faulty article in 1938 on terms relating to "Jew" (Ἰουδαῖος) in the *TDNT* and made the argument that even Jews did not like the term "Jew" (but cf. 2 Macc. 1:1!).[49] Ironically, for all the rejection of the Nazi past in New Testament scholarship in the previous 20 years and for all the emphasis on Jesus' "Jewishness," Kuhn's article still gets used uncritically and naively by major professors, without any consideration given to its ideologically skewed results.[50]

The stark example of fascism also shows how deeply embedded scholarship is in its broader cultural context, not least by showing how seemingly different areas of life are susceptible to the same kinds of influences. In a 2007 paper delivered at the European Association of Biblical Studies/International Society of Biblical Literature conference in Vienna, Hugh Pyper showed how cultural and political trends influenced the handling of Bruckner's symphonies.[51] Students revised Bruckner's symphonies in order to find the "authentic" version of the symphony, with Jewish elements removed. This quest for true origins reflects the kinds of things happening in biblical studies at the time, when form and source criticism were being vigorously developed with their own particular attempts to rid the "pure" form of biblical texts of any disagreeable (often Jewish) elements.

As I have argued elsewhere, it is in this context of antisemitic and anti-Jewish scholarship that we can partly explain why that ultimate quest for pure origins, "form criticism," developed in Germany, and was dominant for much of the twentieth century. Form criticism's failure to provide any serious social history and social context, despite its claims to analyse the "setting in life," meant that avoiding everyday Jewish contexts in the study of Christian origins suited the needs of German Christians and intellectuals.[52] Similarly, Maurice Casey has argued that form criticism's increasing shift away from the historical figure of Jesus toward the faith of the Church met the needs of German Christianity, and effectively ensured "that out from under the synoptic Gospels there could never crawl a Jewish man."[53] This quest for "pure" forms of belief is very precisely paralleled in the musical traditions analysed by Pyper, giving us a very good example of how scholarship, despite much rhetoric to the contrary, is no less liable to be tainted by cultural trends than any other cultural practice.

It is important to note how wide ranging the problem of antisemitism was in twentieth-century New Testament scholarship. Its influence can be found among scholars who were not Nazis and opponents of the Nazis. Much of Rudolf Bultmann's work, including work well beyond World War II, is riddled with ideas about Judaism being an inferior religion. In the 1960s, Ernst Käsemann was claiming that Paul was firing at "the hidden Jew in all of us, at the man who validates rights and demands over against God on the basis of God's past dealings with him and to this extent is serving not God but an illusion."[54] It was only with the work of E. P. Sanders and Geza Vermes in the 1970s that the depth of anti-Jewish and antisemitic views finally hit home, the reasons for which we will see in Part III.

The Cold War

While the Jewish social context of Christian origins was partly avoided due to anti-Jewish and antisemitic influence in mainstream New Testament scholarship, particularly the then powerful influence of German scholarship, there was another reason for the long-term decline of social history in the historical study of Christian origins: the Cold War. We have already seen the early twentieth-century disputes over the social context of Christian origins but by the 1930s social history and context had effectively dried up, with the "Chicago School" and the works of Shirley Jackson Case and F. C. Grant at the tail end of such scholarship. It was not until the 1970s that social history and social-scientific scholarship re-emerged in the study of the New Testament and Christian origins, with only rare exceptions in the interim.[55]

This gap is doubly puzzling when we look at what was happening in the study of history outside the study of Christian origins and New Testament studies in the mid-twentieth century. In France, the *Annales* school, peaking in the work of Braudel, was pioneering interdisciplinary approaches to history while the British Marxist historians (e.g. E. P. Thompson, Eric Hobsbawm, Rodney Hilton, Christopher Hill etc.) were also developing different approaches to social history, including "history from below." There were certainly Marxist analyses of Christian origins, including work by Friedrich Engels and Karl Kautsky, not to mention a strange tradition of work from behind the Iron Curtain, but this never came close to being accepted in the mainstream of New Testament studies.[56]

The reason for the absence of social history and social sciences in New Testament studies was due to the association with Marxism. Marxism was associated with atheism and atheistic Soviet Russia and this was not the kind of ideology that was compatible with the worldviews of Christian scholars (not to mention any thoughtful human being). Moreover, social sciences were being equated with Marxism as was (wrongly) the *Annales* school. It is little surprise that social sciences and social history were avoided in mid-twentieth century New Testament scholarship. Indeed, there are plenty of examples of hostility towards Marxism in New Testament scholarship, though sometimes the threat is more imaginary than real. For example, in the middle of a book on the historical Jesus, Günther Bornkamm presented what might seem to many of us an unusual parallel between Jesus and the Bolsheviks:

> these revolutionaries, when they wanted to claim Jesus as an ally in the struggle for a new world or social order, have had to learn again and again that they could not rely long on this ally, and that the kingdom of God which he proclaimed would not square with their own expectation. It is, therefore, not surprising that today this alliance, often enough attempted in revolutionary movements in the West, has apparently been definitely renounced, and that this completely secularised Marxist doctrine of salvation has replaced that of Jesus.[57]

Additionally, Bornkamm wrote an Appendix on the interpretation of the Sermon on the Mount and most of its space is given to dealing with Marxist interpretations, described as a "frequently horrible and grotesque misrepresentation of Jesus' person and message."[58] Little surprise then, that in the 1970s Gerd Theissen, who pioneered social-scientific approaches to Christian origins, still had to defend himself against allegations of "Marxism."[59]

Yet, clearly, Theissen *could* still pioneer social-scientific approaches in the 1970s. As it happens, the 1960s saw an end to the avoidance of social history and social-scientific approaches to Christian origins. The standard reasons given for this change of attitude include the influence of protest movements in the 1960s, the expansion of sociology in higher education, declining church attendance numbers, perception of secularization, and decolonialization. I would add that it is also significant that an explicitly non-Marxist social history was gaining prominence (particularly the work of Keith Thomas) alongside translations of Weber into English and developments in West German historiography, notably shifts away from the Nazi cult of the individual towards trends and themes. In Part II I will give further reasons for the shift towards social sciences, in particular anthropology, in New Testament and Christian origins scholarship, involving a new demonized "other" in Anglo-American thought: the Arab and/or the Muslim.

Conclusion

What I have hopefully shown in this chapter is that Christian origins scholarship has been deeply embedded in the social, cultural, economic, and political views of its time. The influence of nationalism, fascism, communism/anticommunism, and the social upheavals of the 1960s on Christian origins scholarship are clear in individual analyses but collectively make a powerful case for the ideologically and culturally contaminated nature of Christian origins scholarship. I should qualify this by saying that this is not to reduce scholarship merely to wider trends. In many cases it should be observed that I have made little judgment on whether the arguments are right or wrong (though I will). All I am saying for now is that various trends influence the way scholarly arguments are framed and debated. That does not make the results of arguments necessarily right or wrong.

Chapter 2

The Politics of the Biblioblogger

In a classic line from a Hollywood screwball comedy, the girl asks her boyfriend: "Do you want to marry me?" "No!" "Stop dodging the issue! Give me a straight answer!" In a way, the underlying logic is correct: the only acceptable straight answer for the girl is "Yes!" so anything else, including a straight "No!" counts as evasion. This underlying logic, of course, is again that of the forced choice: you're free to decide, on condition that you make the right choice.

Slavoj Žižek[1]

foreign policy itself is a meaning-making activity, and one that has helped frame our ideas of nationhood and national interest. Foreign policy statements and government actions become part of a larger discourse through their relation to other kinds of representation, including news and television accounts of current events, but also novels, films, museum exhibits, and advertising... Obviously the practice of foreign policymakers...works from a different set of assumptions and constraints that differs from that of filmmakers or television news producers. But foreign policy is a semiotic activity, not only because it is articulated and transmitted through texts but also because the policies themselves construct meanings.

Melani McAlister[2]

Rather than damn the entire enterprise because it is allegedly 'postmodernist,' some sort of rational argument might be preferable (This is what I dislike about Blogs and why they remins [sic] me so much of Talk Radio).

Jacques Berlinerblau[3]

Since the mid-1990s there has been a noticeable growth of academic New Testament studies and related areas on the internet. One of the first major developments involved the rise of email discussion groups dedicated to specific topics. These now include B-Greek, Biblical-languages, Corpus Paulinum, Biblical Studies, Ioudaios-L, Kata Markon, Synoptic-L, XTalk, and Christian Origins to name a few. Various informative websites have sprung up including well-known and extremely helpful websites like Mark Goodacre's NTGateway, April DeConick's homepage, Justin Meggitt's Resources for the Study of Christian Origins and Jim West's Biblical Studies Resource, again to name a few. The new millennium heralded the birth of blogging about biblical studies, with, as might be expected, the New Testament strongly represented, as are academic interpretations from across the secular-theological spectrum. Moreover, blogging has attracted people from different career stages, including famous scholars, research students and interested amateurs. While, as ever, diversity should always be noted, it seems that bloggers of biblical studies took on a collective self-identity through referencing and debating with one another. Indeed, these blogs were soon labelled "biblioblogs" by Classics blogger David Meadows.[4] Naturally enough, "biblioblogger(s)" and "biblioblogging" soon caught on. There is even a website (biblioblogs.com) which collects links to the various biblioblogs and has monthly interviews with the various biblio bloggers. Note the distinctive identity around the Bible as a whole (and this includes non-canonical material and early Judaism) rather than individual parts.[5]

Biblioblogs have increasingly become the morning reading for many scholars – at least they are according to conversations I have had with various scholars – who check the latest headlines, information and gossip. Some of it is very useful too. Biblioblogs such as James Davila's PaleoJudaica, April DeConick's The Forbidden Gospels, Mark Goodacre's NTGateway, John Lyons' The Reception of the Bible, Michael Pahl's Stuff of Earth, Jim West's Dr Jim West, and Sean Winter's Sean the Baptist provide plenty of helpful and up-to-date material about events, conferences, articles, books, ideas, controversies and so on. Book reviews are increasingly common, with publishers often sending books directly to the more regularly updated blogs. Most memorably, Chris Tilling gave a lengthy (28 part!), impressive and widely discussed series of advanced reviews of Richard Bauckham's major book, *Jesus and the Eyewitnesses*.[6] Paul Nikkel and Danny Zacharias' Deinde, Chris Heard's Higgaion, David Instone-Brewer's Tyndale Tech, and Tyler Williams' Codex, provide much helpful information of technological advances in the field. Several blogs are now discussing research in advance of or in light of publication. Stephen Carlson has also provided up-to-date information on the reception of his much discussed book, *The Gospel Hoax*, Mark Goodacre has posted detailed pre-publication ideas, while Aren Maeir has given updates straight from the Tell es-Safi/Gath excavations. Among the "purest" biblioblogs in terms of academic ideas are James Tabor's The Jesus Dynasty and Philip Harland's Religions of the Mediterranean, both of which have almost taken on the form of popular journal or online lectures.

There is also, unsurprisingly, plenty of opinion on the biblioblogs. Instead of celebrity gossip, there is chat about the top 10/20/25/50 biblical scholars, best books on x, y or z, and even an Evangelical Exegetes Hall of Fame.[7] The content of biblioblogging is far from restricted to things relating to biblical studies. There is plenty of opinion on just about anything from music, sport, and popular culture to personal work timetables, work desks, conference hotel rooms and book collections. Most crucially for present purposes, there is politics too.

Biblioblogging is important for the topic at hand for two main reasons. First, unlike academic books and articles, the blog format provides a medium whereby scholars can voice their political (and other) opinions *explicitly*. This makes it much easier to outline the ways in which contemporary ideologies impact contemporary biblical studies and form a basis for, and further support for, the subsequent analyses of contemporary scholarship in this book. Secondly, the internet format is arguably more closely related to Herman and Chomsky's propaganda model (see Chapter 1), and it is notable that numerous mainstream newspapers now run their own blogs, as do many mainstream journalists independently of the newspapers for whom they work. Consequently, we *might* expect biblibloggers to conform to the same kinds of patterns Chomsky and Herman found in their analysis of the mainstream media.

I should stress that there is nothing inevitable about blogging replicating the ideology of the mainstream media in the ways catalogued by Herman and Chomsky. Indeed, Chomsky is unsure about the role of the internet in relation to the propaganda model, adding

> my feeling is that the Internet is pretty much the same sort of phenomenon as radio and television were... Look, in most cases technology isn't predisposed to help or harm people...it just depends on who gets control of it...if it's put in the hands of private power, like T.V. and radio were, then we know exactly how it's going to turn out.[8]

We might also add that while small scale advertising does occur on the blogs, there is nothing like the demands of advertising on the mainstream media, a key feature of manufacturing consent in Herman and Chomsky's approach. This provides an important qualification and the lack of inevitability means that if there are similarities (which, as we will see, there undoubtedly are) then the possibility for a change in the views put forward is strengthened. Yet we should also recognize that we are back to one of the key features of the first chapter, that is, who gets control. In this context an empirical study of the bibilioblogging world should be able to reveal any underlying political agendas.

On the other hand, we should add that not only is the mainstream media tied in with blogging but blogging is intimately tied in with the world of the mainstream media, suggesting that it may well be replicating its patterns. More specifically, the biblioblogging world is intimately tied in with the world of the mainstream media. For a start, bibliobloggers have been cited in newspaper reporting, though not always fairly as James Davila found out.[9] It is noticeable that the biblioblogging world self-consciously takes on the role of the mainstream media. Most explicitly perhaps, Jim West and Chris Heard regularly report major and minor news stories with their own commentary. More significantly, perhaps, is the use of rhetoric that could either come from the mainstream media or ties in the biblioblogging world with the mainstream media, particularly the language of "holding to account." With reference to the birth-pangs at the start of the Jesus Project and its fellows, Mark Goodacre claims that "One of the strengths of the blogging community, all the more so when it is backed up by e-listers, is that it can hold public bodies to account; it can test misleading claims."[10] "Holding to account" is a classic media argument if ever there were one.[11] But then the media ought to watch out too because this kind of language can be turned on them, thereby keeping the close connections between the blogging world and the media world. With reference to the big media story concerning Jesus' "family tomb," Goodacre also claimed that one of the ways in which blogging is making a difference "is in the sheer range of expertise among the bloggers who are gathering to hold the media to account."[12]

Perhaps more than anyone, James Davila makes the most explicit ties with the media. In fact, Davila tries to recall, in an article on blogging, the reasons why he started:

> I don't remember the exact concerns that led me to open a blog. I think it was partly frustration with the carelessness and inaccuracy with which the mainstream media often treats specialist subjects such as my own, combined with being impressed with how often the major political blogs were able to catch the media in errors and sometimes get them to correct them… Having a blog gives me an international forum to give non-specialists a better perspective on the media reports they read about my field and to speak to them with something approaching my whole voice rather than just my scholarly voice.[13]

Davila goes on to list the places where he has shown the errors produced and these include several prominent media organizations (e.g. *Los Angeles Times*, London *Times*, *Guardian*, *Chicago Tribune*, *New York Times*, *Kansas City Star*). Davila even notes the role his blog has played running obituaries. Davila also criticizes ideology but virtually all such criticism involves the highlighting of Arab and Muslim sources, usually for antisemitic bias. We will return to Davila's blog in due course and its ideological significance but for now notice how Davila has focused most heavily on correcting basic facts and ideological problems with Arab and Muslim presentations. There is no concern to provide any kind of alternative media that would challenge the ideology of the Western media too much. On the contrary, as would be logically expected from his arguments, Davila appears to want to be part of it and strengthen it. Given the millions of blogs on the web Davila sees "the cumulative long-term effect of their criticisms is likely to be the steady erosion of the authority and credibility of the mainstream media, which should lead to the tightening up of standards in media treatment of specialized fields, hopefully with more consultation of experts."[14]

I should now confess that I have run a blog since the summer of 2005.[15] Like Davila, my main reason involved the media but, unlike Davila, my main reason also involved questioning the very basis of mainstream ideology of the Western media. What I noticed when reading the biblioblogs was that the general political views of bibliobloggers were very much akin to the political views reflected in the mass media. In an interview, I discussed why I started to blog. The reasons given were more tied in to academics but it equally applies to the mainstream media:

> One key reason was political, and in different senses of the phrase. It now seems naïve to me at least, but I once thought there were more politically radical people in scholarship, though I don't think that anymore. This disappointed me when it hit home and it disappointed me in terms of blogging because there, I thought, more than anywhere in biblical scholarship, would such views be found. The situation is quite the opposite, I think.[16]

In the rest of this chapter I want to show the reasons why I made such a statement with reference to some of the most prominent issues in international politics that will in turn be discussed in much more detail in the rest of this book. For now I want to focus in particular on the gaps in logic and evidence used by the bibliobloggers and how their arguments on international politics owe more to contemporary Anglo-American mainstream media agendas than simply a well-reasoned argument. I want to look at what kinds of detail their political arguments omit and why they might be omitted.

I would like to add that what follows is a critique of many people whom I regard as friends and some of whom I genuinely regard as impressive scholars in their particular sub-fields. I do not wish this to be taken as a personal attack on anyone and I hope that this chapter does not come across as too polemical. In most cases I do not think people are deliberately pushing political agendas; I think a lot of what is said and omitted is just representative of a broader cultural context, consciously, unconsciously, or subconsciously. In some cases I acknowledge that my arguments *are* very polemical, particularly in cases where I think the writer really ought to know better and is more likely to be deliberately avoiding basic facts.

Iraq, the Middle East, and the "War on Terror"

> *In three weeks of Foreign Office and other UK government briefings prior to taking up my post, there had been scarcely a mention of human rights and none of torture. The briefing I had been given put the emphasis first on FCO internal management procedure, second on Uzbekistan's supportive role in the War on Terror and third on Central Asia's economic and commercial potential in hydrocarbons, gold, cotton and agro-industry...nothing had prepared me for the reality of the War on Terror as I was about to encounter it... Chris received from London the report on the photos of the corpse of Mr Avazov. The pathology department of the University of Glasgow had prepared a brief but detailed report of their findings. The victim had died of immersion in boiling liquid. It was immersion rather than splashing because there was a clear tidemark around the upper torso and upper arms, with 100 per cent scalding underneath. Before he was boiled to death, his fingernails had been ripped out and he had been severely beaten around the face.*
>
> Craig Murray[17]

The issue of Iraq and the Middle East is probably the most important issue for US and UK foreign policy in the post-Cold War era, at least in terms of media coverage, a point to which we will return in more detail in the next chapter. For now, it can simply be noted that there is little doubt that the media have played an important part in endorsing the various actions in the Middle East over the past 15–20 years, the latest instalment of Orientalism as critiqued by Edward Said. So, in a geographical area intimately related to Christian origins and biblical studies as a whole, how have the biblibloggers reacted? The defence of, or at best the non-critical attitude toward, the Iraq war has been dominant among the biblibloggers.

There are bibliobloggers where this is no surprise given the explicit airing of their personal politics. Joseph Cathey – a Hebrew Bible/Old Testament specialist, who retired from biblioblogging in 2006 – is almost a clichéd right-wing, gun-toting, big-game hunting, Bible-thumping Texan (see Appendix). He had links on his now defunct blog to politically right-wing websites, including the unambiguous and ominous-sounding "Right Wing News" alongside various neo-conservative links. Most famously in the world of biblical studies, he regularly put pictures of guns on his blog and discussed which one was best (for what…?). It is perhaps no surprise that he unquestioningly endorsed the Iraq war and US imperialism in the Middle East, and he praised some weird fanatical blog entry, which, though he could not fully accept the argument, had a blanket condemnation of Muslims as terrorists, and which had called for a nuclear attack on Iran (see Chapter 3)! We even get some strange advice on how to react when the terrorists strike (get a rifle apparently) in a biblioblog entry helpfully entitled, "A Civil Service Message for Preparedness"! To the best of my knowledge this is not a joke:

> This is a public service announcement from you [*sic*] local conscience. Know I know that deep down in your soul you long for someone to stand in the gap when things go bump in the night. My only question to you is this – "when" (as the 9/11 commission report noted) the next terrorist event happens in the United States, and this time it is nuclear or biological, will you be prepared?[18]

Seriously.

There are others of an explicitly right-wing bent. Probably the most unflinching and detailed support for the "war on terror" and the Bush administration has come from the Old Testament/Hebrew Bible specialist Ken Ristau, someone who happily admits to being a strong Republican sympathizer and a political neo-conservative.[19] When Bush was re-elected in November 2004, Ristau informed us that "Bush now has a clear mandate that must be respected by the world" (the same reasoning did not apply to the election of Hamas)[20] and, just as alarmingly, "the American people have sent a clear message to Iraqis and Afghanis that we stand with them." Ristau's blog entry ends as follows:

> Imagine: Palestine and Israel on the road to peace and democracies in Afghanistan, Iraq, and Iran [??] by the end of Bush's term. I'm not just an idealist though; I am a realist too and so I know it may not happen so neatly or, in some of these things, at all. But, I'm thrilled that I can even imagine these things as possible in my lifetime let alone imagine them occurring with some justification over the next four years. Thank-you, W. Christians: It is time to pray![21]

While I can't help but counter-read that final line in a more desperate sense, it is not very easy to argue logically with such excessive devotion to the Glorious Leader that might seem a little over-the-top to some of us.. We are fortunate indeed, then, that Ristau has also given plenty of arguments with more concrete details.

Ristau, for example, fits in neatly to the presentation of the supposed broader threat Iraq posed beyond its borders. Some of the evidence of Saddam's threat in his final years has been so obviously fictitious that there is little attempt to defend the indefensible any longer, most spectacularly in the case of Weapons of Mass Destruction, the key reason given for going to war in 2003. Yet, in his own particular way, Ristau would not let this go and re-emphasizes the view that Saddam was a greater threat in the run-up to the 2003 war.[22] Ristau asks us if we remember those images released by Saddam before the invasion that were intended "to show to the world that Iraq's UAVs were crappier than your next door neighbour's cool remote controlled airplane? They looked like they were going to fall apart. He wasn't hiding anything in the sands of the Iraqi desert right?" Then he asks us to remember "how quickly opponents to the war pointed out that the Iraqi fighter aircraft had all flown to Iran in the wake of the first Persian Gulf War. Saddam had no ability to project force in the Middle East right?" Well, predictably enough, Ristau is about to prove such people wrong because sometime shortly after "the liberation of Iraq," Ristau received, "through a series of channels originating from someone in the USN," certain pictures. These were pictures of a MiG-25R Foxbat – "apparently the fastest combat jet in the world" – along with several other MiG-25s and Su-25s, all found in the sands near the al-Taqqadum Airbase in Iraq.

Initially, Ristau thought they might be a hoax or that something was amiss because of the lack of media coverage. Yet looking through the Department of Defence website he found his pictures confirmed. Ristau's email source said that these combat jets were equipped with "sophisticated electronic warfare devices" and "may" also be equipped with electronics sold by the French (who else?) and the Russians during the UN ban on selling arms to Iraq in the 1990s. The comments section on this post is also interesting, not least because it further shows how seriously Ristau takes these claims. "Pablo" countered, "Yeah but it's not like it's a weapon of mass destruction or anything, so what's your point?!?" to which Ristau responded, "You are being sarcastic, right?!?" Buying into the typical argument of "our" moral purity, "Johnny Gazelle" told us that Ristau's post was "pretty cool" before mentioning, seemingly without a hint of irony, that, "It is disturbing to see that the French & Russkies were selling stuff to Saddam but I cannot say I'm surprised. Both those countries are full of crooks."[23] No mention of the US previously selling "stuff" to Saddam, naturally.

The only real counter argument here is simple: if Ristau is right why hasn't his evidence been trumpeted by the American government and, especially, why was it not heralded by the British government who had staked so much on Saddam's threat as the main reason for going to war? It is difficult not to think that something else is going on here. But for now it makes quite clear the strange lengths one academic will go to defend Anglo-American foreign policy.

More significantly, again for present purposes, Ristau has also reproduced an email debate he had with an anonymous "American academic" on the issue of just war theory and the 2003 Iraq invasion.[24] What Ristau does is to repeat, with little if any qualification or questioning, the official US governmental line that the invasion of Iraq was strictly honourable (as if they or any state power would argue otherwise!). In fear of giving away too much of his argument in advance, Ristau believes (at least, presumably, he did so when this email debate was made public in 2005) that "Obviously, a reasonable hope for success existed" and indeed "considerable success" has been achieved at "obtaining peace and reconciliation between the warring parties."

Responding to the point that the US had supported Saddam in the 1980s, Ristau claimed that "rather than making the war disingenuous, it does quite the opposite." This previous support "further emphasizes why the U.S. had to bear the responsibility it owed to the people of Iraq and the world for keeping Saddam in power and providing him WMD, which he used to such destructive ends in 1989 in Halabja and earlier in the Iran-Iraq war." This is an interesting narrative. Not only does it maintain the fiction that the US government became pure of heart, but it now suggests that the US ought to act out of some kind of guilt for its past life. Indeed, I think a very good case could be made for saying that the US bears responsibility but it is not remotely likely that this has any bearing on the 2003 invasion of Iraq (see below). If we look at this from a certain angle, Ristau's logic is perverse. It is not far from implying that someone could have invaded the US when it was not-so-nice in order to stop support for figures like Saddam and prevent further human rights abuses and deaths. Should Ristau wish to accept that the US has continued supporting dictators the same logic could still be applied (or at least count as an argument against the Iraq invasion). In the wrong hands such kinds of logic are not only perverse, they are potentially deadly. And, as we will see, such kinds of logic have been used by bin Laden and his followers.

Building on the notion of purity of motive, Ristau argues, as other Christian just war advocates have done,[25] that the United States began to take a principled stand in Iraq post-1989 and now George W. Bush "has fundamentally changed American foreign policy so that it no longer proclaims freedom with one hand and supports tyrants with the other." He even claims that the Bush administration is "the first to promise its support to any country that desires freedom" and has "secured widespread international support for its campaign against terrorism." The narrative sounds good and functions to remove the present actions from any less-than-pure motives. In reality, however, it is difficult to establish whether Ristau is ignorant of basic facts or just an example of a confused academic basking in the glory of an illustrious leader and his posse, or a combination of the two. As for the United States taking a principled stand in post-1989 Iraq, the obvious response would be the economic sanctions on Iraq which were reported to have killed over 500,000 children, with the US knowing in advance of the potential for disease such sanctions would cause (see Chapter 3). As for the present Bush administration being such lovers of freedom which "no longer proclaims freedom with one hand and supports tyrants with the other," well that is contradicted by basic facts and has been heavily criticized by Chomsky and others. As Chomsky put it, referring to the Bush administration in 2004:

> the same policies are pursued today, without the slightest change. Is the US bringing democracy to Uzbekistan? Or to Equatorial Guinea, also ruled by a monster comparable to Saddam Hussein, but warmly welcomed by the Bush White House because he sits on a very large pool of oil. Take Paul Wolfowitz, described by the propaganda system as the leading "visionary" seeking democracy, whose "heart bleeds" for the suffering of poor Muslims. Presumably that explains why he was one of the leading apologists for General Suharto of Indonesia, one of the great mass murderers and torturers of the modern era, and continued to praise him well into 1997, just before he was overthrown by an internal revolt. It is all too easy to continue.[26]

Let's take the important recent example of Anglo-American support for Uzbekistan's brutal Stalinist dictator, Islam Karimov.[27] In October 2002, the British ambassador in Tashkent, Craig Murray, refused to do as he was told and gave a speech on some of the things happening in the US- and UK-backed Uzbek regime. Points raised by Murray included the following:

> disappointing progress in moving away from dictatorship; major political parties banned; between seven and ten thousand religious and political prisoners, many falsely accused, some had been human rights activists,

> many had been imprisoned on the basis of being Muslim, and there was even a trial of a Jehovah's Witness; torture in Uzbek prisons, including torturing to death by boiling (yes, *boiling*); a near 100% conviction rate in the criminal justice system.

As Murray pointed out, "if any of the Uzbeks present had made a speech like that they would have been straight into the torture chamber."[28] Yet prior to Murray's speech the US diplomat praised US-Uzbek relations and the progress made by Uzbekistan in democracy and human rights! Unsurprisingly the US and the UK governments were not supportive of Murray and it seems they made serious attempts to undermine him, not least through slurs and innuendo (see Chapter 3). But then this is perhaps no surprise. Murray's book on Uzbekistan gives some cheery pictures of a smiling George W. Bush with the Stalinist human boiler himself. There is also one of Donald Rumsfeld in such illustrious company that, should he wish, could be added to his picture taken with his once friend Saddam in the 1980s.

There were, of course, reasons to undermine Murray which were more significant than mere vanity. Uzbekistan, with its probably not insignificant rich reserves of oil and gas, was strategically important for the US-led coalition, providing airbases for attacks on Afghanistan. According to Amnesty International, Uzbekistan was able to use the "international war on terror" to "justify the clampdown on religious and political dissent."[29] According to Human Rights Watch, the Uzbek Minister of Defence Qodir Gulomov reportedly said that "his military had benefited from training and joint exercises with U.S. forces over the past several years and hinted that other types of aid might come in the future."[30] Indeed, in 2002 the US, who acknowledged the human rights abuses in Uzbekistan, provided $500m (£298m) in aid, "$79m of which was specifically for the same 'law enforcement and security services' they accuse of routine torture."[31] Yet when the US-Uzbek love affair came to an end and Karimov turned to Russian and China, a justifiably exasperated Murray exclaimed, "The US and UK governments discovered that – Shock! Horror! – this guy Karimov had been an awful dictator!"[32]

Ristau is important here because he is actually one of the most informed bibliobloggers on politics and he gives the appearance of attempting to deal with various positions fairly. Yet, at the same time, he still manages to allow masses of what might be deemed highly important contrary evidence to slip through his fingers, evidence which shows conclusively that the US government was not acting anywhere near as honourably as Ristau believes.

Ristau's online writing shows particularly well how the debate is framed to remove serious dissenting opinion.

The Myth of Unique Suffering

> *A propaganda system will constantly portray people abused in enemy states as worthy victims, whereas those treated with equal or greater severity by its own government or clients will be unworthy...the U.S. mass media's practical definitions of worth are political in the extreme and fit well the expectations of a propaganda model. While this differential treatment occurs on a large scale, the media, intellectuals, and public are able to remain unconscious of the fact and maintain a high moral and self-righteous tone. This is evidence of an extremely effective propaganda system.*
>
> Edward S. Herman and Noam Chomsky[33]

Ristau and Cathey could be dismissed as a couple of extreme neo-cons on the extreme wing of politics and biblioblogging. However, despite the lack of overt interest in the Iraq war on the biblioblogs, we should not be hasty in suggesting (should someone wish to do so) that there is no important ideological underpinnings relating to the "war on terror" in less politically extreme biblioblogging. In this light it is also notable that, with the exception of Jim West, the Iraq war is virtually ignored on the other biblioblogs, as indeed are Jim West's blog entries on Iraq. In the world of biblioblogging, as elsewhere in the mass media viewed through the propaganda model, what remains significant is that which is ignored and downplayed. One particularly important example is the London bombings of July 7, 2005, because biblioblogers were blogging on that very day.

There was, as might be expected, plenty of discussion with accompanying blessing, prayers and messages of goodwill, something which decent human beings are likely to do in the light of a very public act of cruel and indiscriminate murder that claimed 52 victims, all of whom were completely innocent. James Davila wrote, with an accompanying picture of the Union Flag, that "In the spirit of not permitting terrorist scum to disrupt our lives, blogging on ancient Judaism etc. will continue now as normally."[34] According to Mark Goodacre, "Tony Blair hit exactly the right note in his statement at lunchtime."[35] Michael Bird offered some vivid reflections on where he was and what he thinks, placing the bombings in a grand apocalyptic context:

> Last night I had some friends over for dinner and we were discussing some lovely topics, cricket, the weather, McKnight's book Jesus Creed,

> when the London terrorist attack beamed onto the TV. What can I say? So many feelings:
>
> > Bastards! Why, Why, Why? God, avenge us! Forgive them, for they know not what they do. How long O Lord how long!
> >
> > I think it is important that Muslims across the West are not persecuted for the actions of a small minority intent on exporting their violence in the service of destroying western democracies. I'm reminded of the words of an Arab publisher: "It is a certain fact that not all Muslims are terrorists, but it is equally certain, and exceptionally painful, that almost all terrorists are Muslims." From an article in the Telegraph called "Innocent religion is now a message of hate."
> >
> > What can we say, well turning to Revelation is always a source of hope and encouragment [*sic*] to me when times are tough. What do we find there, God's mercy triumphs over the most despicable of human evil in the end.
> >
> > Marantha![36]

(This biblioblog entry received one comment and that was from Scot McKnight himself, who simply commented, "My ears are burning"). The Aramaic and Dead Sea Scrolls scholar, Edward Cook, placed his thoughts on the July 7 murders in the context of global suffering and the mass bloodshed that was World War II:

> Our thoughts and prayers go out to the victims of the London bombings and their families.
>
> At times like these, I am often tempted to think, Why work? Why should I write, study, blog, catalog, parse verbs, or do research, when there is so much suffering in the world, so much of "real" importance to be done, besides which my activities pale into insignificance?
>
> I find C. S. Lewis's sermon "Learning in War-Time," delivered in Oxford as the Second World War broke out, a bracing tonic for these feelings. Read it all, if you can find it.[37]

In none of these cases was there any mention of UK foreign policy. In fact, the absurdly self-righteous yet chilling speech by the London bomber, Mohammad Sidique Khan, makes direct reference to Muslims killed in British foreign policy as part of his justification.[38] No matter how deluded and perverse this logic seems to many of us, it is unlikely he would have mentioned this had it not been a serious motivation or an issue which would resonate with at least some people. Given that we are dealing with murder it might be hoped that, like a criminal investigation, such motivations were investigated. Consequently, given what was mentioned on the biblioblogs (especially a positive mention of Blair and the emphasis on the "why" question) it might have made people think more about the underlying motivations, including the role of Blair's actions. As it happens, in a *Guardian*/ICM poll conducted shortly after the London bombings two-thirds of people felt that Blair's involvement in Iraq was "responsible" in some degree for the bombings (33% believed Blair bore "a lot" of responsibility; 31% "a little").[39] Yet despite foreign policy being a notable aspect for many British people and even a bomber himself, what was presented on the biblioblogs reflects the emphases of the British government, which refused to make a connection between Iraq and July 7.

Gilbert Achcar has argued with reference to contemporary US foreign policy that there is a powerful tendency in the media to dismiss any explanation of September 11 with reference to injustice in the world, often resorting to (false) accusations of justifying mass murder.[40] A cause-and-effect US foreign policy is to be dismissed. How often have we heard arguments claiming that "they" attacked because they hate "our freedoms" and so on?[41] September 11 became something effectively unparalleled, an act of absolute evil in the metaphysical sense. Achcar is extremely careful not to trivialize the September 11 act of mass murder but notes that it is important to contextualize it and compare it. He points out that compared to the scale of carnage for which the US government has been directly responsible, and for which it has never expressed any significant regret, the deaths of September 11 are not high:

> Is it forbidden to mention the 200,000 civilian victims of Hiroshima and Nagasaki, on the pretext that Osama bin Laden himself has made clever use of the argument? What about the three million Indochinese civilians who were victims of US aggression – whom bin Laden has mentioned much less, by contrast, because as the good anti-Communist fighter he was for so long he had to approve of that war? Do we need to keep silent, just because bin Laden has constantly referred to them?[42]

We could also mention, as Achcar does, that there were also the brutal 12-year sanctions on Iraq up to the invasion in 2003, which, it has been estimated, cost the lives of 500,000 children, or the victims in the Afghan war shortly after September 11 (see Chapter 3). Achcar then asks if a mass murder like September 11 took place somewhere outside the US, such as in a third world country, what would be the reaction then? The coverage of Grozny, Chechnya, which was razed to the ground by the Russians, gets little, if any, media attention. We might compare all this with the similar pre-September 11 chapter by Herman and Chomsky on "Worthy and Unworthy Victims" in the US media.[43]

Achcar calls this the exceptional intensity of emotions poured out after September 11, "narcissistic compassion." It is a form of compassion "evoked much more by calamities striking 'people like us,' much less by calamities striking people unlike us."[44] This explains why the European Union decreed a European day of mourning and three minutes silence for the victims of September 11 and why it did not observe so much as a one minute of silence for the seven thousand massacred in Srbrenica (presumably all "Europeans") or the hundreds of thousands of people massacred in Rwanda or those continually dying under sanctions in Iraq or those millions dying of AIDS in Sub-Saharan Africa despite ample Western resources to alleviate the suffering, and, sadly, so on and so on. Is there not something, as Achcar puts it, "deeply revolting" about deciding whose deaths are regarded meaningful? Yet this deciding has an important political function: justifying the present "war on terror."

This applies to the debates over July 7 among the bibliobloggers. We have already seen how mention of Blair and July 7 follow the mainstream media line and how they do not wholly reflect the views of the British public at the time. We have also seen how Edward Cook put July 7 in the context of global human suffering and Michael Bird located July 7 in a grand apocalyptic context. In both these cases, and for all the utter wrongdoing of July 7, the scale of deaths is not comparable to countless other mass murders around the world where such language might be more appropriate. *Something*, then, is going on.

Significantly, bibliobloggers have had relevant questions put directly to them and still the pattern Achcar highlighted comes through. One comment on Mark Goodacre's blog in response to his posting on July 7, 2005, said that Blair has "blood on his hands" but it was ignored. I brought up the issue of the use of white phosphorus and napalm in Falluja and Iraq in general in a couple of postings. The use of white phosphorus – which, incidentally, burns, including burning eyes and causes permanent damage – was confirmed by figures within the US military, caused more casualties than the London bombings, and yet was, as far as I am aware, ignored on the other biblioblogs, and Jim West was the only biblioblogger to comment in the hidden comments section.[45] Other things, such as the 500,000 plus Iraqi child deaths under UN sanctions and the continuing support of vicious dictators by the US and UK governments, have also been brought up in the biblioblogging world.[46] But these things too go ignored and unmentioned. In the abstract it might be fair to say that bibliobloggers are really there to discuss things related to biblical studies but bibliobloggers are not unconcerned with politics: various exotic politicized theologies and just basic comments dealing with the evil of terrorism are, as we will see, found on biblioblogs. And the result is entirely in line with the results of both Achcar and the propaganda model: suppress "our" aggression while highlight "their" aggression.

In fact, confronting bibliobloggers with various facts about US and UK foreign policy strongly highlights the distinct similarities with Herman and Chomsky's propaganda model. I once mentioned (negatively) US and UK involvement in the Middle East which led to 42 comments being made. This was largely an argument between myself and Ken Ristau. Ristau eventually accepted that the US and UK does support Stalinist and other brutal regimes, for example Karimov's Uzbekistan, but the best we get is the following, which seems exceptionally naïve in the light of what we have seen, though functions to make sure that our leaders are deep down, to paraphrase Tony Blair, pretty straight kind of guys: "Its present support for Uzbekistan and Pakistan is a concern certainly but I would *guess* [my italics] there are pragmatic strategic considerations, considering that it has been fairly consistent in its attitude towards other regimes."[47] One way to read the logic is this: the US government says it opposes dictators and so on but happens to support dictators. Therefore this must mean that the US government's rhetoric of hostility towards dictators must be true in reality because the US government says so. Basic facts to the contrary are irrelevant.

Ristau did concede (and he does not concede much) that the US and UK did make mistakes in the sanctions on Iraq. But look at the argument: "I'm willing to grant your point that the US shares some responsibility in the sanctions. They did, after all, approve both the sanctions and the Oil for Food program in the UNSCR. However, it would beg the question what in the world you'd tolerate the US having done in that situation?"[48] The argument about non-toleration of the sanctions involves the estimated deaths of 500,000 children and prior knowledge about the destruction and disease sanctions would cause. But worry is deemed extreme, hence the response which is worth reiterating: *what in the world you'd tolerate the US having done in that situation?* Any worry about thousands and thousands of deaths is shifted to a more administrative problem. But, again, look at the logic, if the basic facts of widespread suffering are taken into account: despite all this death and suffering, the US government *had* to do something, the US government *must* be correct. Otherwise, what? Is it me or is there not something utterly perverse about the reasoning here with the assumption that "their" lives are borderline meaningless? Of course, the reasoning is anything but perverse from the perspective of power.

Note throughout that Ristau did not *really* condemn those involved – at best the odd human error here and there – and he apparently still believes that western powers are acting with only kindness in their hearts. But with the propaganda model in mind, this begs the question, if he concedes wrongdoings then why can he not bring himself to condemn the wrongdoers or post comments on his blog, especially as he is arguably the most explicitly political biblioblogger?

This is has further significance because it implies that some of the bibliobloggers, particularly those who have read and commented on such political views, do not know what they are saying. To poach yet another argument from Chomsky, this time in response to Christopher Hitchens,[49] if such bloggers knew what they were saying many would have to be deemed as expressing terrible racist contempt because countless and largely uncounted lives of some people in some other country that major western powers have bombed, or the lives of those tortured under a western-backed dictator like Karimov, or the victims of white phosphorus and napalm, are of less value than the 52 innocent victims of the London bombings. Now none of the bloggers I know, and presumably almost certainly none of those I do not know, would ever accept that life is more important in the UK or US than it is in (say) Iraq or Uzbekistan. The Madeleine Albrights of this world aside, few people, I hope, would suggest that the loss of over *half a million* Iraqi children under the sanctions was a price worth paying, though Ristau's logic comes terrifyingly close.[50] But it would follow logically that the emphasis on one set of deaths over against another has to reach the conclusion that such lives are of less value.[51] This problem exists, I think, because the problem is a broader cultural one and *not* a personal one. Individually the bibliobloggers, like most journalists, are probably all perfectly decent human beings; certainly the ones I know are.[52] Yet the bibliobloggers, however unintentionally, show clear signs of sympathy with "those like us" and not "those unlike us." It would seem that they have also inherited, unwittingly, the mechanisms of Chomsky and Herman's propaganda model from the mass media leading to some dubious omissions and inclusions.

Some of my Best Friends Are...

> *In the films and television the Arab is associated either with lechery or bloodthirsty dishonestly. He appears oversexed, degenerate, capable, it is true, of cleverly devious intrigues, but essentially sadistic, treacherous, low... The Arab leader...can often be seen snarling at the captured Western*

hero and the blond girl... In newsreels or newsphotos, the Arab is always shown in large numbers. No individuality, no personal characteristics or experiences... Lurking behind all of these images is the menace of jihad. *Consequence: a fear that the Muslims (or Arabs) will take over the world.*

Edward W. Said[53]

First, people can you say with me JIHAD? Theologically, the Islamic terrorists are driven by their warped sense of eschatology. They are not going to be happy and nice once we are out of Iraq or Afghanistan. Do you who are so negative of the President even READ what is being put out in the Middle East? Do you monitor Al-Jezera [sic] and listen or read WITH YOUR OWN EYES that Islamic fascists will not be satisfied until the Islamic Caliph is once again from sea to shining sea?... Second, death is acceptable Islamic terrorists! They are happy to kill you here in the streets, overseas in Europe, anywhere they can find you...they have moved their theology worldwide now. It is about either converting or dying for the cause of Islam. Islamic groups in the United States have said that they will not be satisfied until the US is under the leadership of the Koran and an Islamic Caliph is in control... Third, DO YOU REALLY WANT THIS TO HAPPEN IN THE US? If you do then fine – complain all you want but when they start killing your family don't come crying to we who told you this was going to happen. When your wives are made to wear the Burka and Chaddar don't wine [sic] and complain that "this isn't what you wanted."

Joseph Cathey[54]

There may be one reason in particular why the propaganda model has much to say about biblioblogging, namely the fact that Islam happens to be the major religion of the Middle East, the area where the interests of Anglo-American foreign policy, biblical studies, and certain Christians meet. Unsurprisingly, there is a notable hostility towards Islam among the Christian biblioblogers: Islam is, after all, a historic rival. While there are plenty of Christians with positive views of Islam there is almost no end to the Christian material with some extremely hostile things to say about Islam. Likewise, there is plenty of secular hostility toward Islam. Muslims, it is regularly argued (e.g. Sam Harris), are so *obviously* violent and so *obviously* deluded that something must be wrong with this religion in particular.[55] Similarly, as we will see, such views are also found in the biblioblogging world. As we will also see in detail in Chapter 3, this hostility – whether religious or secular – toward Islam is prominent in the media and intellectual thought with almost no end to the material on the subject of the clash of civilization, with the emphasis on, naturally, the superiority of Christian and "western" values and the inferiority of "Muslim" or "Arab" values. Again, we are back to Said.

Anti-Islamic sentiment in some form or other is bountiful in the biblioblogging world. Cathey – and note the assumption of the audience's gender – finds it "mildly ironic that academics [unnamed] don't get the WWII analogy that President Bush is making" about militant Islam and Iraq and warns us that if we don't face up to this threat they'll "start killing your family...your wives will be made to wear the Burka and Chaddar."[56] Such (unnamed) people should realize this is a war against evil like we have not seen since Nazi fascism. These certain (unnamed) people have to get on the "program or get out of the way" and, when all comes to pass, they shouldn't "wine [*sic*] and complain that 'this isn't what you wanted' " Got that? Well, if not, it is probably no surprise as people unlikely to understand Cathey are unlikely to be as well-versed as he is in Islamic history:

> Do you monitor Al-Jezera [*sic*] and listen or read WITH YOUR OWN EYES that Islamic fascists will not be satisfied until the Islamic Caliph is once again from sea to shining sea? Do you even know what a Caliph is and how it relates to the WAR on terror? Sadly, most of those who are criticizing the president have neither read Islamic history nor do they care to – it would dispel their ignorance.

No evidence for Saddam being an Islamic extremist is given, no names of any of those opponents who criticize the president yet do not know Islamic history, no discussion of the implied people who *do* know Islamic history and criticize the "war on terror" and why their ignorance has not been dispelled, and, frankly, no sense of proportion: really, what are the chances of the US being run by Muslims of any persuasion any time soon? And when you have this kind of logic there is only one obvious conclusion and one which sounds profoundly undemocratic and downright creepy, if not plain Stalinist, if not a touch ironic given the Nazi comparison: "By your tone and actions you are siding with the enemy." This is pretty naked scaremongering propaganda aimed at unnamed people and backed up, not with any significant facts, just the apparent knowledge that this scholar of the Old Testament/Hebrew Bible knows Islamic history and so he just *knows*.

We could waste a lot more energy on Cathey but, in terms of the propaganda model, it is probably more fruitful to look at the more reserved and thoughtful Michael Bird (most Muslims are "probably" peaceful) because despite his more moderate outlook his claims effectively reveal the underlying metaphysical assumption: "the radicals are not the victims of US foreign policy or merely standing up to US imperialism, they [are] just insidiously evil."[57] Look at the logic here if followed to its natural conclusion: something *must* be unusually wrong with certain Muslims or part of Islam. Do large numbers of Muslims have mental defaults or are they sub-human? Clearly that would be absurd. As for sub-human, that cannot be the case anyway because Muslims are, after all, potential converts. So is it something in their religion? This is, unsurprisingly, an answer among the biblioblogger. Ken Ristau, for example, claims: "From the beginning Islam's history is wedded to the sword."[58]

This sort of reasoning is also heavily implied by Bird who quotes an "Arab/Muslim perspective" (as noted earlier):

> I think it is important that Muslims across the West are not persecuted for the actions of a small minority intent on exporting their violence in the service of destroying western democracies. I'm reminded of the words of an Arab publisher: "It is a certain fact that not all Muslims are terrorists, but it is equally certain, and exceptionally painful, that almost all terrorists are Muslims." From an article in the Telegraph bearing the title, "Innocent religion is now a message of hate." It is a good read from an Arab/Muslim perspective.[59]

Bird should have checked his source. The *Telegraph*, as we will see again in Chapter 3, has published some of the most extreme anti-Muslim and anti-Arab views in the British press. That aside, Bird uses this "Arab/Muslim perspective" as an argument for something being wrong with Islam but he does not address some logical problems: if this were a true generalization, how did the situation arise when Islam could be used for such hate? Might there not just be a role for various present day situations? We will see in Chapter 3 that there were numerous issues underlying violence in the name of Islam such as population growth and slums, oil economies, western-backed dictators, the peculiarities of Wahhabism and Saudi Arabia (from where the majority of the September 11 hijackers came), Israel/Palestine, and the decline of secular nationalism. When pressed, however, Michael Bird did acknowledge a major role of western intervention, although he could not remove himself from the view that there was a problem with Islam: "I don't wish to invoke animosity against Muslims, [wait for it...] but the fact is many Muslims commit acts that are despicable and do not happen in Western countries!"[60] Of course, there is no mention by Bird of the acts committed by Christian leaders in the West (e.g. Thatcher, Reagan, Bush, and Blair) and how they might have been involved in the despicable acts that occur in non-Western countries.

Moreover, some kind of "problem with Islam" comes through in his later handling of violence where there is asymmetry in his division of "sides" (ultimately Muslims are worse), and presented in the dubious dress of "some of my best friends are...but..."

> I live next to a Muslim family here in Dingwall, who are very friendly and amiable, and I get on well with them. I imagine that they, like most Muslims living in the West or in the East, simply want to live and enjoy a happy life and feel free to practice their religion in peace with people of other religions. But how is the West to respond to Islamic extremists, institutions and governments who believe that the West must either convert to Islam or be annihilated? I'm not afraid of an American President, however inept, who can launch 1000 ICBM nuclear warheads – but I am afraid of a [*sic*] extremist who wants only one nuclear device! Will it come to this, who nukes who first? Let us pray that it is not!!![61]

Notice the rhetoric of an overarching western power over against a Muslim other. While obviously not wanting a nuclear device in the hand of a violent Muslim intent on destruction, we should not forget which country has unleashed a nuclear device and we should not forget the amount of death and human suffering this country has caused, not least in Muslim and Arab countries. We should also remember that American presidents have been present for the hideous economic sanctions on Iraq, the use of cluster bombs and the use of depleted uranium. Some of this is very well known but it is simply ignored. Muslims, and not "us," are the ones who do the *really* bad things.

One of the most interesting examples of Islam and its apparent deficiencies among the biblioblogers is Loren Rosson. Rosson is interesting not only because he has written several blog entries on issues relating to Islam but also because he explicitly comes in from a liberal secular perspective – so it is not so easy to dismiss his arguments as those of a religious rival – and comes close to being a pacifist – so he cannot be dismissed as some right-wing warmonger. Consequently, Rosson attempts to give more academic and social scientific explanations for the problems with Islam. Rosson will be discussed in detail in Chapter 4 because his outlook on Islam is motivated by the honour-shame approach to the Mediterranean and the Middle East, a critique of which will be the primary focus of that chapter. But for now we can mention one example, namely Rosson's claim that after the Crusades, Islam became "over-sensitive, defensive, intolerant, sterile," attitudes that "grew steadily worse." This "stagnation" was due to "the *jihad* revival" which was "in reaction to the success of the First Crusade (1099)."[62]

Note again the deep roots of the "problem with Islam," grounded in the depths of long past history. This does raise the possibility that the problem has nothing to do with "us." This by itself does not make the argument wrong but there are specific issues that suggest it is at the very least problematic. There is no interaction with US foreign policy, no mention of any social or economic issues affecting parts of the Muslim world, no mention of the twentieth century ideological developments in Islam, arguments that are regularly made by scholars of Islam and ones that will be developed in Chapter 3. Rosson gives little in the way of detail – precisely what does he mean by "stagnation" and "sterile" and how are they measured? Is there not a problem of making such loaded generalizations for masses of people over vast geographical areas? Furthermore, the idea of centuries of decline is an idea Edward Said denounced as "preposterous" for similar reasons given here: it is part of the popular re-cycling of "the same unverifiable fictions and vast generalizations so as to stir up 'America' against the foreign devil."[63] I will return to a more detailed refutation of Rosson's ideas in Chapter 4 but for now it is clear that, once again, we are dealing with reliance on ideology rather than fact.

Israel/Palestine

> *if the Arab occupies space enough for attention, it is as a negative value. He is seen as the disrupter of Israel's and the West's existence...the Arab is conceived of now as a shadow that dogs the Jew.*
>
> Edward Said[64]

Issues relating to Muslims and Arabs soon dovetail into issues relating to Israel and Palestine, an issue which has been a major area developed by Chomsky with reference to the propaganda model and how the media and established academics have played a crucial role in support for Israeli policies against Palestinians. This is supported by research which will be discussed in Chapter 5 where some detailed empirical work has shown that there is an overwhelming bias in the Anglo-American media, from popular culture to news coverage, in favour, though in a patronizing way, of Israel over against Palestinians, particularly since 1967.[65] This pattern of overwhelming bias is paralleled in the biblioblogs.

An excellent example of the overlapping issues of Muslims, Arabs, Israel, and Palestine is James Davila's blog. As we have seen, Davila is probably the biblioblogger most aware of blogging and its relationship to the mass media and so he makes a particularly significant example. As already noted above, in his essay on biblioblogging he makes it clear that he will criticize misinformation in the media and he will criticize the abuse of ideology but particularly when it comes to Arabs and Muslims. For example,

> My previous impression of media carelessness and distortion has been fully borne out. This is not merely a matter of predictable biases and distortions in media outlets that have a particular axe to grind, such as Al Jazeerah's use of anti-Semitic propaganda about the Talmud or Jihad Unspun's bizarre transmogrification of the story of the Iraqi Jewish archive recovered during the Iraq war... It is regrettable, but not surprising, that some anti-Semitic sources in the Middle East deny that a Jewish temple ever stood on the Temple Mount in Jerusalem.[66]

Note the clear emphasis on Arab and Muslim media. This is not to say Davila is factually inaccurate and this is not to say that he has not picked up on anything important. What is significant is the *focus*: it is regularly on *Islamic* or *Arab* distortions. Now, it could be argued that as Davila's blog is on early Judaism then why should he focus on misrepresentations of anything Arab or Muslim? Yet such issues do appear on his biblioblogging radar. For example, while referencing an outrageously anti-Islamic rant (see Chapter 3), which was supposed to be a review of Nadia Abu el-Haj's critique of Israeli archaeology by someone apparently called "Hugh Fitzgerald," Davila made no comment, simply saying "I haven't read the book, so I won't comment further."[67]

In the abstract that might still be fair enough but then, it could be said, why report on the political side of things? Why not simply stick to reporting about conferences, discoveries and academic gossip relating to early Judaism? Why have regular links to Solomonia, an extremely well-run and well-sponsored blog with openly right-wing, neo-conservative (and friends with a blogger known as "neo-neocon"), anti-Muslim and ultra-Zionist values, dedicated to seeing off liberals, radicals, Chomsky, Said, and anyone mildly critical of the state of Israel?[68] Why does Davila follow controversies surrounding Joel Beinin? Why follow the issues surrounding academic boycotts of Israeli academics, no matter how wrong a boycott would undoubtedly have been and no matter how agreeable some of Davila's points certainly are? Why does Davila look at *contemporary* politics, often involving antisemitism, elsewhere on his blog? Indeed, he says that Temple denial among Palestinians, Arabs and Muslims is "Palestinian propaganda" which is "widespread in the Islamic world."[69] He further suggests that "these bogus notions are coming from PA leaders and Muslim clerics employed by the PA. They seem to be mainstream positions among Palestinians and widely in the Arab world. They need to be replied to even though they are bogus."[70] Again, if true, this is fair enough, but as Nadia Abu el-Haj has shown with reference to Israeli archaeological practice and Keith Whitelam with more reference to Old Testament/Hebrew Bible studies, archaeology and exegetical work in relation to the creation of Israeli identity is hardly without its political dangers, particularly in relation to the Palestinians.[71] So why not discuss these kinds of issues in the same depth? Davila has also claimed the following: "I take time to refute Palestinian Jewish-Temple denial not because it has merit, but because the PA and others use it as a political tool."[72] But does not the political tool cut both ways, particularly when it comes to the ideological (not to mention physical) treatment of Palestinians by the Israeli government?

Davila has also run a series on Temple Mount Watch which regularly links to stories about Waqf activities on the Temple Mount in Jerusalem. Davila often gives his own commentary and it is damning of the Waqf. Again, as a historian of early Judaism, this is unsurprising but, again, there have been allegations made the other way, so to speak. Abu el-Haj has made allegations of Israeli malpractice with archaeological remains of different cultures, including Arab. Davila has followed the controversy surrounding her allegations and he has mentioned that he has not yet completed her book (he has now – see Chapter 5) and he remains concerned, being "quite sympathetic" with the worries of people such as Campus Watch (see Chapter 3) founder Daniel Pipes, but carefully qualifies this with, "based on what I've heard about it."[73] Yet, significantly, when the allegations of Israeli archaeological demolitions are made elsewhere, we get the following response from Davila:

> The accusation that Israeli archaeologists "have destroyed many strata of other periods" is bizarre. Archaeological excavation involves the "destruction" of the excavated parts of the site, which is why it is always accompanied by careful documentation of any strata excavated. This is elementary.[74]

Davila knows of Abu el-Haj's claims but when something similar to her claims is reported, it is dismissed out of hand as being self-evidently wrong. Abu el-Haj may or may not be right but there is, clearly, an imbalance in the reporting here.

In fact, Davila even comes close to taking Temple denial to a whole new emotional level. Commenting on reports that Gabriel Barkai claimed that Temple denial is just as serious as Holocaust denial, Davila remarked: "I think it's an overstatement to say this is worse than or as serious as Holocaust denial, but it's still vile."[75] I cannot help but wonder, for all the problems with Temple denial, and with the clear qualifications made by Davila, if it is really fair to mention it even in the same breath as Holocaust denial? As an aside, precisely why should Temple denial be mentioned in the same breath as Holocaust denial? Does that not suggest something ideologically at work in Davila's source?

Elsewhere Davila makes some exaggerated comments concerning the apparent influence of Temple denial. Thanks to a report from the Committee for Accuracy in Middle East Reporting in America (CAMERA), Davila speaks about "two incidents of pandering to the Jewish-temple deniers in major media outlets."[76] These incidents are: "*Jews say* [Davila's emphasis] a biblical Jewish temple was razed by the Romans in 70 A.D." (Reuters) and "*Jews believe* [Davila's emphasis] that the site, also known as the Temple Mount, housed the second temple, which was destroyed by the Romans in A.D. 70" (*New York Times*). Is this really *pandering* to the Temple deniers? It seems a little far-fetched to think that the mainstream American media would have pandered to such views on Temple denial. Indeed, the *New York Times* version made changes in a subsequent report on the Temple, as noted by CAMERA.[77] More likely, I suspect, is that this reporting reflects basic ignorance of history (as often pointed out by bibliobloggers like Davila) and the fairly typical patronizing language found in newspapers when trying to explain religious belief.

It may well be significant that those bibliobloggers who comment on Israel (ancient and modern) are almost always specialists in Hebrew Bible/Old Testament or early Judaism. New Testament bibliobloggers *tend* to leave the subject alone. Naturally, exceptions will be found, though we will see how New Testament and Christian origins scholarship has reflected issues surrounding Israel and Palestine.

There are notable exceptions to the general stance of over-sensitivity toward Israel and the downgrading of Palestinians. Paul Nikkel has produced some short, sporadic and completely ignored critiques of the portrayal of the Israel-Palestinian situation, despite reference to other bibliobloggers.[78] The major exception is Jim West. West has been critical of Israeli state aggression against the Palestinians (and has been denounced for this). But controversies also come through in his handling of ancient history. For example, West is not entirely convinced by the argument that there was an extensive first Temple in Jerusalem. Following such suggestions by West, there were open attempts to marginalize his views after a particularly fierce exchange between West and Davila, a heavyweight biblioblogging duel if ever there were one. West claimed that there needs to be hard evidence of an extensive first Temple and he then said that Davila replied that it ought to be in a peer reviewed journal before it could be taken seriously.[79]

Davila was furious when West reported this and accused West of misleading everyone as Davila pointed out that he has in fact discussed non-peer reviewed material. Davila demanded an apology and retraction and advised his readers to ignore anything West says about him and that he will not reply to anything more West says. And then bibliobloggers weighed in with their say, all, as far as I am aware, in favour of Davila: Cook, Ristau, Cathey and others.[80] No-one, as far as I am aware, supported Jim West. For present purposes, allegations of misrepresentation and talking past each other are beside the point. More importantly, issues that ran throughout the dispute included contemporary Israeli politics, Jim West's critique of a "hawkish" Israeli position, and the explicit linking of the ancient issues with contemporary Israel/Palestine issues. As Davila said in response to West, "I take time to refute Palestinian Jewish-Temple denial not because it has merit, but because the PA and others use it as a political tool."[81] Quite clearly, anything sounding like a critique of modern Israel makes the situation particularly sensitive.

Chris Tilling is a significant example here because he is obviously a thoughtful Christian critical of Christian Zionism with an obvious skill for constructive debate. In fact he sees "Christian Zionism" as "highly problematic," though stops short of calling it heretical.[82] Tilling also ran a nine-part series on Christian Zionism.[83] While much of this is an attempt to critique the theology and interpretative value of Christian Zionism, he promised that in "a later post in this series" he would show, rightly many would add, why this is not just merely a "theological curiosity" that should be left alone but that it "impacts world politics" (see also Chapter 5). Consequently, we are in a position whereby a major political issue could be discussed on the biblioblogs. However, while Tilling's intentions are certainly honourable, I would suggest that his series runs into the difficulties encountered in the mainstream media when critical of Israeli and US governmental action in that any dissenting voices are marginalized in line with widespread ideological tendencies.

C. Stirling Bartholomew started things off in response to Tilling's opening introductory post by claiming that "the problem with a lot of you Zionist bashers is that you haven't read the Zionists," despite (as a couple of not-particularly-hostile comments pointed out) Tilling not giving his opinion on Zionism and no one yet making a comment on Zionism at this point in the comments.[84] Bartholomew later moved on to speak of "35 year [*sic*] of hearing Israel Lovers bashed by the left wing of the church, my old buddies who read Sojourners and used to talk about Marx and Jesus and all that rot" [aside: this is an odd way to describe Jesus, is it not?]. The following comments became increasingly political focusing on the Israelis and Palestinians. There were attempts at putting different political views across but they were met with putdowns. For example, the killing of Palestinians was brought up along with a reference to Chomsky. The response by "shrewsfan" included reference to more and more pro-Israeli state actions concerning the Palestinians and some weird and factually useless anti-Chomsky website full of rants minus any evidence or interaction. This was the last word on Part 1 of Tilling's series.

In the other comments on the following posts, there is little in the way of politics. By the time we get to Part 5 anything deemed an attempt (there was virtually nothing, significantly enough) to discuss the plight of the Palestinians or criticize Israeli governmental actions was put down. For example, the other key example was a newcomer to the debate called "Sam" who had just introduced himself to the debate.[85] Sam happened to write blog entries elsewhere which were critical of some Israeli governmental actions (but more scriptural and theological discussion than anything else), though said nothing of this initially in the comments section. James Mendelsohn responded by informing "Sam" that he was a "Messianic Jew based in the UK" and recommended the old favourite, Dershowitz's *The Case for Israel*, claiming that it "is the best resource I know setting out the case for Israel's right to exist and defend herself, and it comprehensively dismantles much of the ubiquitous anti-Israel propaganda which is in circulation – from which, sadly, Christians are not always immune."

Despite this claim, no-one was denying Israel's right to exist and no-one was denying that Israel had no right to "defend herself" but the debate was spuriously framed in such a way, presumably to avoid disagreements that pose more serious problems. I might add that I have never come across a single biblical studies scholar, biblioblogger or biblical studies student who has denied that Israel has a right to exist or "defend herself" which again begs the question, why was the debate framed in such a spurious way? In any event, Sam was hooked in and responded politely saying that he had not read Dershowitz's book and that he was not against the state of Israel and that he does not deny "the right to defend on the basis of a carefully argued application of Romans 13 to international politics. I would probably agree with Dershowitz if he argues on this basis." The focus was shifted even further to the theological when Sam said, "My concern is to show that the theological justification of a special political status for Israel (and a blanket approval of any political action) is not tenable, since God's kingdom, inaugurated by Yeshua, is fundamentally non-nationalist. My strong tone reflects my distaste for militant nationalism, and not a desire to single out any particular nation."

Mendelsohn replied by informing Sam that Dershowitz does exactly that: he "compellingly weighs many of the various accusations made against Israel in the light of international law" and that he does "not give blanket support for every Israeli action," before adding that one Christian Zionist writer says Israel's actions need to be weighed against biblical principles. Notice how the debate has also shifted well away from any concerns about the Palestinians and on to the role of Israel and the high standards required and, we are told, usually met. Mendelsohn was eventually given the space for a guest posting on Tilling's blog.

In the immediately following part, Tilling gets to pause for clarification and summary (Part 6 of 9). And after plenty of emails and comments, politics is definitely off the agenda:

> I need to point out again, this discussion concerns not first and foremost the political issues of Land and other interesting matters that have been discussed (and rightly so) in many of the comments to my posts above, but the specific issue: the use of Scripture in Christian Zionism. In other words, my focus concerns hermeneutics. This is why I'm pursuing the question as to how the early Church uses the OT, to shed light on their hermeneutical strategies, even if my presentation will naturally be selective given the amount of relevant material.[86]

From then on, the remaining three posts and the comments were all heavily theological and exegetical with politics firmly on the backburner. It is worth comparing this with Part 1 of Tilling's series and his discussions of definitions of Christian Zionism. He made reference to some overtly political definitions relating to claims about "the land of British Mandate Israel," biblical prophecy and "the establishment of the State of Israel in 1948," and "defenders of, and apologists for, the state of Israel" with biblical support for Israel's "occupation and settlement of the West Bank, Golan and Gaza" and opposition to "those deemed to be critical of, or hostile towards Israel."[87] Given this and given that there are massive issues with the plight of the Palestinians tied in with biblical justification and that the Christian Zionists, particularly in the US, carry some influence on these matters (see Chapter 5), we might reasonably expect some more engagement with the political side of things too, particularly as they were promised. It seems, however, that for all the genuine interest he has in this issue, Tilling soon felt the pressure to conform to the limits of this debate and to what could and could not be discussed.

There is another important element that needs to be added to the mix: Palestinian Christians. Given their religious affiliation, they have the potential not to be wholly ignored. Michael Bird wrote of an instance where an "Arab Christian from Israel, specifically, the Galilee" was a guest speaker at a missions prayer lunch at Highland Theological College.[88] Bird gave a moving account of the talk:

> Our speaker told the story of how Israeli troops forcibly expelled whole villages and simply told them to go Lebanon. These were Christian villages that have never resisted Israeli rule/occupation (delete as preferred) or fired a shot in anger. His attitude towards Israel was one of frustration rather than hatred and he just wanted a fair deal, a place to live, and some political rights for Arab Christians. He talked about how Christians largely run the education and health care system in the Galilee and the ministry that they have there.

Bird then gives his own judgment:

> Personally, I remain perplexed as to why certain Christians, predominantly Americans, feel a closer degree of affinity with the secular state of Israel than they do with Palestinian Christians! I'm not anti-Israel (I think that the President of Iran, Ahmydinnerjacket [Bird's *sic*!], has more fruit cakes in his head than an Aussie Christmas party) but we should support the plight of our Christian and brothers and sisters in the land of Palestine and object when they are boxed into ghettos.

On one level this is an important point (though it is odd that Bird has to distance his views from those of Ahmadinejad, of all people, when defending his attitude towards Israel: the two views are barely comparable). Yet we should not lose sight of the fact that compassion is only shown to *Christian* Palestinians. We should recall that non-Christian Palestinians also live in such conditions, including those have behaved with a sense of social justice towards those in need. (Indeed this is one of the standard reasons given for Hamas' popularity and their electoral victory!) Bird may well have such sympathies with Muslim and non-Christian Palestinians but, if he does, it is significant that such views do not filter through. Whatever, in the case of Bird we have a particularly useful example of the Christian impact on my use of the propaganda model discussed in Chapter 1.[89]

Politics and Constructing Biblical Studies

> *The amount of books that N. T. Wright puts out in a year is quite remarkable, if not amazing. Does anyone have a rough idea of how*

much time he spends reading or writing in an average "work" day? I'm presently completing my undergrad in theology. Just doing the course work for this is sometimes daunting. I hope Wright's work-ethic will inspire us all to keep doing what we're doing, and work hard for the Kingdom.

A message from the internet discussion group, "Wrightsaid," dedicated to the work of N. T. Wright[90]

What is also notable is how politics spills over into biblioblogger's views of the discipline of biblical studies. Sean du Toit, a devout N. T. Wrightian, provides a spoof scenario of the world in the year 3742 where very few historical records survived and historians attempt to reconstruct the past.[91] On a TV show "History Tomorrow" they look at "a popular but enigmatic 21st century figure," the historical George Bush, and show a televised debate between Harvard professor Nathan Wright (obviously the arch-conservative scholar and Bishop of Durham, N. T. Wright), a defender of the traditional history of Bush, and Phonias J. Futz from the controversial Bush Seminar (obviously the arch-liberal North American Jesus Seminar). To cut a long and not very exciting story short, Futz is a Robert Funk-style figure who does not believe Bush was ever president but was instead a social critic whereas Nathan Wright obviously knows the truth and gets everything correct. Futz is stupid and cannot assess evidence while Wright is a sober, careful scholar who we just *have* to agree with. Interestingly enough, Bush is presented as a remarkable historical figure – Jesus-like no less! – whose name, as Nathan Wright tells us, should not be slurred and neither should the history of the United States by denying his greatness. Even if the Jesus analogy cannot be pushed too far, Bush remains a great figure: he is given (according to Wright and in a document that is supposed to be parallel to Luke's gospel and so, therefore, presumably "true") "one of the greatest send offs in history and a national day of mourning." The Futz version of history is deemed trendy (in the very negative sense) and, like the Jesus Seminar's apparent discomfort with "traditional" and conservative images of Jesus today, so Futz's version acknowledges that Bush's patriotism and conservative politics may make people feel uncomfortable. Consequently, Futz had to invent a more "culturally relevant" Bush. In fact, Futz says, the "traditional image of Bush is then used as an icon by certain out-of-date politicians who want to turn America back into a democratic free market society!" Theologian, Milton expert and blogger Benjamin Myers thought this story was "hilarious stuff!" while Chris Tilling settled for "funny!"

The underlying ideology does not need spelling out. An important aside, however: it is significant that N. T. Wright has been a fierce critic of George

W. Bush.[92] In fact this Wright who opposes the war in Iraq has caused some heartbreak among US evangelicals, Wright's true "base." One Robert Osburn, Executive Director of the conservative Christian Maclaurin Institute, heaped praise after praise on Wright, even suggesting that the "gloriously gifted Bishop of Durham" should become Archbishop of Canterbury (incidentally, we are away from fiction now). Then he stumbled upon the serious problem that Wright opposed the invasion of Iraq. Here Wright finally becomes fallible, and this may be the *only* area where he is fallible for his devoted US evangelical following. For all his reason and intellectual strength, Wright is unfortunately unaware that most US citizens, apparently (no evidence cited), "know…that the approach to war in Iraq was not a rush, but, in some real sense, a measured, calculated decision grounded, to some extent at least, in just war theory (see Jean Bethke Elshtain's newest book by that title…)." Unfortunately, American Christians do not appreciate "a nearly-universal European dislike for American unilateralism" which may be due to a brutal European history of wars and unilateralists like Hitler. Consequently, and without a hint of irony, Europeans "probably don't appreciate the reasoned, cautious approach cultivated within the Bush White House."

It is difficult to know where to begin on all this. We might question the generalization about American Christians and support for the war, though possibly Osburn thinks his kind of evangelicals are the only true Christians. Naturally, we are just told that the decision to go to war was reasoned and rational because, presumably, Osburn was told so. No mention is made over what might reasonably be called confusion over reasons for going: was it over weapons of mass destruction? Was it to remove Saddam? Was it because of some link between Saddam and terrorism? Was it to carve Iraq up for the respective corporations? Did the White House carefully plan for the subsequent chaos in Iraq? Was the Iraq war measured and calculated before September 11 and in the immediate aftermath of September 11 and if so is this not reason for scepticism? Did Rumsfeld carefully plan to ruin his political career?

And, of course, there is the obligatory non-mention of recent US foreign policy disasters (for the recipients in particular), and no mention of Europeans (or Americans) who thought they were being lied to, who believed that this was an imperialistic venture and so on. More on all this in subsequent chapters: the point for now is that Wright has to be filtered though the system to make him suitable for his audience. In this context we can see something similar, though in a different way obviously, happening with du Toit's presentation of Wright. Wright, in both instances, gets filtered through the biblioblogging world and a suitable ideological make-over for the amateur Christian media.

Comments on du Toit's funniness in his reconstruction of hypothetical history in the future were forthcoming from biblioblogger but the spawning of a gushing imitator was the ultimate praise. Ken Ristau provided the Hebrew Bible/Old Testament version of the Quest for the Historical Bush by turning it into the fierce minimalist-maximalist debate over the history of ancient Israel.[93] Ristau's stupid scholar is Benard Sauvant (obviously BS) of the Free University of Central Kansas (obviously FUCK) who offers thanks to the Langford Institute of Early Studies (obviously LIES – by the way, does this mean Ristau thinks certain scholars are *lying*?).

Ristau effectively equates maximalism with historical truth and (positively) with the Bush administration. Ristau's development of this story of dubious hilarity turns into a debate about George W. Bush's period of office. Mischievous scholars have said that Bush was never in office and that in reality Clinton was the great leader who liberated Iraq. History ends this way: "It is clear now that it must have been the Republicans who were on the wrong side of history and that it was Bill Clinton and Al Gore who, taking over from the inept George H. Bush administration, finished the Iraq war and introduced the policy of democratization that ultimately delivered the Middle East from its tyrannical governments." Once again, praise was forthcoming: "funny!" exclaimed "Pablo." "An excellent post!!!" remarked Joseph Cathey, who saw fit to give it three exclamation marks.[94] Whereas Bush became the equivalent of Jesus for du Toit, the Bush administration becomes the equivalent of ancient "biblical Israel" in all its glory. The fact that Ristau is so pro-Bush and anti-Clinton matters little: the assumption is that the Iraq war needed to be finished and, despite supporting countless tyrannical regimes and undermining democracy around the world (see above), the US government is really interested in delivering the Middle East from tyrannical governments and introducing democracy. Once again, the correct ideology shines through and contrary facts disappear as if they were never there.

Conclusions

In the previous chapter we saw how *historically* New Testament and Christian origins scholarship has been tied in with the political and ideological issues of its day and how scholarly results, quite naturally, reflected the beliefs of scholars. In this chapter, we have now seen how *contemporary* New Testament and Christian origins scholarship, though in the broader context of biblical studies scholarship, is also tied in with some of the key political issues in the Anglo-American mainstream media. The decision to focus on blogging was deliberate because here we have the perfect medium for scholars to air their opinions *explicitly*. It is clear that the views of New Testament and Christian origins scholars on the internet are in many ways self-censoring, pushing anything too dissenting away from the spotlight, and tend to match effortlessly the agenda of Anglo-American foreign policy.

This now gives us a firmer foundation upon which to analyse the *implicit* assumptions of scholarship in the more conventional printed form (books, journal articles etc.). Throughout this chapter there has been reference to future chapters. This is particularly so in instances where there has been gaps in arguments that ought not to be there if as much evidence as possible were genuinely being discussed. So before we look at New Testament and Christian origins scholarship in more detail we need to examine in further depth the kinds of broad political and intellectual currents that dictate the gap-making in scholarship, how they are seriously problematic, and how they are intimately tied in with the agendas of mainstream intellectual, political and cultural power.

Appendix: Selected Unedited Excerpts from the Now Defunct *Dr Cathey's Blog* for Purposes of Reference

Joseph Cathey, "War on Terror, President Bush, and World War II" (August 31, 2005)

I find it mildly ironic that academics don't get the WWII analogy that President Bush is making. I have blogged on this way too often to offer hyperlinks so if you want to search the blog do so. However, I will take a bit of time to once again put things into perspective.

First, people can you say with me JIHAD? Theologically, the Islamic terrorists are driven by their warped sense of eschatology. They are not going to be happy and nice once we are out of Iraq or Afghanistan. Do you who are so negative of the President even READ what is being put out in the Middle East? Do you monitor Al-Jezera and listen or read WITH YOUR OWN EYES that Islamic fascists will not be satisfied until the Islamic Caliph is once again from sea to shining sea? Do you even know what a Caliph is and how it relates to the WAR on terror? Sadly, most of those who are criticizing the president have neither read Islamic history nor do they care to – it would dispel their ignorance.

Second, death is acceptable to Islamic terrorists! They are happy to kill you here in the streets, overseas in Europe, anywhere they can find you. It is NOT ABOUT OIL anymore – they have moved their theology worldwide now. It is about either converting or dying for the cause of Islam. Islamic groups in the United States have said that they will not be satisfied until the US is under the leadership of the Koran and an Islamic Caliph is in control.

Third, DO YOU REALLY WANT THIS TO HAPPEN IN THE US? If you do then fine – complain all you want but when they start killing your family don't come crying to we who told you this was going to happen. When your wives are made to wear the Burka and Chaddar don't wine and complain that "this isn't what you wanted." By your tone and actions you are siding with the enemy. We are engaged in a WAR against evil that hasn't been seen since the likes of Nazi fascism. Get with the program or get out of the way.

Joseph Cathey, "Guns Not Evil!" (August 30, 2005)

I could not help but notice this blurb in an AP Wire story on the destruction in New Orleans. The story was about the hospitals which are still continuing to function under such a strain. One of the workers went out and tried to check his home. This is a direct quote from him: "It looks like a Steven Spielberg movie set out there," he said. "The only people you see are people with ***shotguns*** protecting their property."

So, you see those who decry the use of firearms really have not thought their statements through now have they? If, as some suggest, that only the law enforcement and military have firearms do you think the criminal element would give up their weapons? I can tell you for a fact (having lived in Africa where it is virtually impossible to get a firearm) that criminals will ***always always always*** be well armed. Who is going to protect you when tragic circumstances come and the police simply turn their heads when the looters strip your home bear?

Joseph Cathey, "A Civil Service Message for Preparedness!" (November 4, 2005)

[This was accompanied by a picture of an "ordinary" woman with her back turned and a rifle strapped to her back. The picture had the words, "After the hurricane, looters stayed out of her neighbourhood. Would they stay out of yours?"]

This is a public service announcement from your local conscience. Know I know that deep down in your soul you long for someone to stand in the gap when things go bump in the night. My only question to you is this – "when" (as the 9/11 commission report noted) the next terrorist event happens in the United States, and this time it is nuclear or biological, will you be prepared?

Joseph Cathey, "Children and Firearms!" (November 4, 2005)

[This was accompanied by a photograph of a smiling young girl (approximately five-six years old) with a parent's upper legs and stomach section visible behind her with hands placed on the daughter's shoulder. A gun was visible in the parent's holster. The picture had the words, "KIDS TRUST PARENTS TO KEEP THEM SAFE. HONOR THEIR TRUST."]

My child expects me to protect her from evil. I do this in two ways - first I pray for her everyday and read to her the Scriptures of the Old and New Testaments. I take her to church and let her know that mommy and daddy love Christ with all their heart. However, I also protect her from evil incarnate on earth. I carry two pistols whenever I am off campus. I carry a S&W 38 340PD as well as a Kimber Tac Pro II in the ole 45 ACP. My back pocket contains my CRT lockblade.

Now my question to all my naysayers is what are you going to do when a carjacker comes and takes your car with your daughter or son in the backseat? What are you going to do when someone sticks you up at the mall when you are getting in your car? It seems to me that platitudes are of little use in defeating evil.

Part II

Neo-Orientalism: Orientalism, Hideously Emboldened

Orientalism is abroad again, revivified and hideously emboldened.

Derek Gregory[1]

It is surely one of the intellectual catastrophes of history that an imperialist war confected by a small group of unelected US officials...was waged against a devastated Third World dictatorship on thoroughly ideological grounds...but disguised for its true intent, hastened and reasoned for by Orientalists who betrayed their calling as scholars. The major influences on George W. Bush's Pentagon and National Security Council were men such as Bernard Lewis and Fouad Ajami, experts on the Arab and Islamic world who helped the American hawks to think about such preposterous phenomena as the Arab mind and centuries-old Islamic decline... Today bookstores in the US are filled with shabby screeds bearing screaming headlines about Islam and terror, Islam exposed, the Arab threat and the Muslim menace...the omnipresent CNNs and Foxs of this world, plus myriad numbers of evangelical and right-wing radio hosts, plus innumerable tabloids and even middle-brow journalists, all of them re-cycling the same unverifiable fictions and vast generalizations so as to stir up "America" against the foreign devil.

Edward W. Said[2]

Chapter 3

The Context: A Clash of Civilizations?

I am again tempted to conduct a simple mental experiment: let us imagine an Arab newspaper making the case for the torture of American prisoners – and the explosion of comments about fundamentalist barbarism and disrespect for human rights this would provoke!

Slavoj Žižek[1]

Introduction: Clashing Civilizations, a New Threat, and Christian Origins

In Chapter 1 I referred to my argument that social sciences in the study of the New Testament and Christian origins were virtually non-existent between (approximately) the 1930s and the 1970s. Key reasons for this included the not wholly unjustified association between social sciences and atheistic Marxism and, by implication, Communism. The usual social reasons for the shift toward social-scientific criticism in the 1970s include the prominence of 1960s protest movements, the impact of 1968, the increasing influence of sociology in the universities, declining church numbers, the perception of secularism, and the impact of decolonialization. I have added several other reasons, including the development of an explicitly non-Marxist (and therefore more palatable) social-scientific/anthropological approach (e.g. Keith Thomas on magic), translations of Weber into English, and overt shifts in West German historiography away from the Nazi cult of the individual toward trends and themes.[2]

There is another important argument that now needs to be added to this explanation, particularly given the controversial events of the late 1960s onward taking place in the portrayal of world history and corporate interest. In 1967, Israel had established itself as a major player in the Middle East, one not easily messed with. We will return to the impact of the events in 1967 and beyond in the next major part of this book, but for now we can see the dramatic emergence of a new "other" in the US and western media:

the Arab. Furthermore, Edward Said noted that from the early/mid 1970s, and after the Arab-Israeli wars in particular, "the Arab" and/or "the Muslim" had become a figure in American popular culture, the academic world, the cultural world, the policy planner's world and the business world. After the 1973 war, the image of the Arab appeared regularly: cartoons frequently depicted an Arab sheik by a gasoline/petrol pump with strongly "Semitic" features (hooked noses, moustachioed leer etc.) and the function of transferring antisemitism from Jew to Arab. Arabs became "the shadow that dogs the Jew" (especially in Israel) and the oil supplier *par excellence.* In the news, the Arab turns up regularly in large numbers, perhaps in a scene of mass rage with strange gestures, minus individuality and personal characteristics, the kinds of people that might want to take over the world. And they are the mild images.[3] Said's analysis has subsequently been reinforced, though certainly not without nuance, with further reference to film, media and popular culture.[4]

Such concerns with things Arab and Islamic were heavily reinforced with the Iranian revolution and the fall of the Shah in 1979, tied in with an anti-American fuelled Ayatollah Khomeini as the figurehead dominating the media and an order designated Islamic. At the end of a decade of energy crises, the media and intellectuals in the US would never avoid reporting a revolution in a major oil supplying country. To cap things off, in November 1979 there was the capturing of the US embassy and the accompanying months long hostage crisis. In reaction the American and western media could provide analyses of, for instance, "the Persian" psyche or national character to help, apparently, understand what was going on, and often avoid any underlying reasons for hostile attitudes toward "us," "America" or "the West."[5] Add to this the strategically significant Iran-Iraq war, the Lebanese conflicts, airline hijackings, the emergence of Hamas and Hizbollah, the Algerian civil war, the Salman Rushdie affair, bombing outrages in Israel, and further hostage situations in the 1970s and 1980s "Arab and Muslim world," and the media and intellectual opinion would inevitably be reeling off things to say about and portray this "other" threatening "our" way of life.

In the 1970s, a group of people portrayed collectively and stereotypically and in direct relation to Israel – the central geographical place in biblical and Christian stories – were becoming culturally prominent thanks to their relation to developing markets in the Middle East. These broader political and cultural developments, I would suggest, paved the way for the use of anthropology in the study of the New Testament and Christian origins, particularly of the variety of national or pan-national character and psychology, buoyed along by the cultural shift to a new symbolic geography very relevant for the study of Christian origins and its geographical place of origins. Given what we have seen on the impact of major political and cultural trends in Chapter 1, it would be remarkable if such issues did not get reflected in the study of the New Testament and Christian origins.[6]

I will discuss the connections with the study of Christian origins in more detail in the next chapter but as this present chapter is largely focused on the political and cultural contexts of Christian origins scholarship it is worth providing a more specific outline of the kinds of scholarship I have in mind for the next chapter. The most significant development in this context has been the emergence of anthropology as used by the Context Group. The Context Group define themselves as "a project on the Bible in its socio-cultural context" and "a working group of international scholars committed to the use of the social sciences in biblical interpretation." The group emerged in the 1980s from the Society of Biblical Literature and Catholic Biblical Association meetings and formed a distinct identity in its own right. The work of Bruce Malina has proven to be of huge importance for the Context Group, providing many of the anthropological models which have been consequently employed by Context Group associates. The Context Group has included plenty of other big names in New Testament scholarship, such as Philip Esler, Jerome Neyrey, and John Pilch. Members meet annually, work collaboratively, and peer review one another's work. Although an international group, the base is very much North American and dominates social-science sessions such as those at the annual (North American) Society of Biblical Literature meetings.

Central to the work of the Context Group are generalizations about, and pivotal values of, "the Mediterranean" (which, as we will see, often drift into generalizations about "the Middle East"). Probably the pivotal feature of the Mediterranean, according to several members of the Context Group, has been that of "honour and shame," where attempts at gaining honour and avoiding shame were/are publicly played out in games of challenge and riposte.[7] This modelling may sound too general and too historically distant for the tastes of some but several Context Group members have also argued that these models should not be taken too literally and they serve more as heuristic tools and not a precise like-for-like fit for the ancient world. Avoidance of ethnocentrism is an important and related goal of the group, including attempts to show how the Mediterranean is different from the contemporary USA, often by listing or tabulating key differences.

By the mid-1990s, more and more publications on social/cultural anthropology, particularly by the extremely productive Context Group, were being put out and were having a notable influence on the scholarship of Christian origins. A decade later the influence of anthropology on New Testament and Christian origins study is much clearer and deeply embedded. At the turn of the millennium, Burton Mack, via Jonathan Z. Smith, was developing new approaches to Christian origins heavily and self-consciously grounded in cultural anthropology.[8] This was developed and taken up by a group of like-minded scholars, resulting in the recent book edited by Ron Cameron and Merrill Miller, *Redescribing Christian Origins*.[9] There have been other major anthropological perspectives on Christian origins, including anthropological perspectives in the previously neglected area (in terms of anthropological approaches, not scholarly attention) of historical Jesus research. Not only did John Dominic Crossan write a much discussed anthropologically grounded book on the historical Jesus but he also followed it up with another anthropologically grounded book on the birth of Christianity.[10] William Herzog has provided further significant historical Jesus work through the use of anthropology, culminating in an important introduction to historical Jesus studies.[11]

Similarly, if the significance of Context Group-style social sciences has not quite penetrated into the heart of mainstream, middle-of-the-road historical Jesus studies, its importance has at least been noted, most notably by scholars who do not use social sciences in any thoroughgoing way. John P. Meier's first instalment of his heavily fact-orientated, *A Marginal Jew*, acknowledges, with reference to Neyrey, the importance of "sociological analysis" or "the cross-cultural analysis of anthropology," though he warns readers that while sociological analysis might be applied to the material in the book, he insists on "one step at a time."[12] N. T. Wright tells us that "no one should doubt the great value of social anthropology as part of the equipment of the historian" and that "it is a way of avoiding anachronisms by recognizing that different societies operate with different worldviews and social norms." Wright then proceeds, with reference to Malina and Neyrey, to tell us in typical Wright fashion that, through the use of social anthropology, passages such as Luke 10:38-42 show how, despite no textual indications, the Jesus tradition subverts (read: is better than) its "Palestinian village" context.[13]

We should not underestimate the impact of September 11 and the subsequent "war on terror" on the use of anthropology in New Testament and Christian origins studies, not least because the rhetoric involved in both New Testament studies and things relating to the "war on terror" profess to have an interest in the "other." This impact is made quite clear in one of the most important and sophisticated recent works on anthropological approaches to the New Testament:

> To understand the "other" not as a "native" or "stranger" but as a fellow human being, born into a different social situation, also provides salutary reading for understanding cultural differences in our contemporary situation. Not least, since the world was rocked by the events of September 11th 2001. To understand the value and "honour" of another is central if we are to understand the assumptions that underlie and inform their actions. The study of people (ethnography) and their values may therefore hold promise for development far beyond the parameters of this particular study, and the social-scientific programme that informs it.[14]

As I said, I will attempt to show the social, cultural and political connections in more detail later but, to anticipate later conclusions, in general terms it is difficult not to see broader social and ideological reasons for this shift in the study of Christian origins embedded as it is in popular and intellectual culture.

Other recent historical events also helped pave the way for more anthropology and generalizing of the Middle Eastern "other." The fall of the Berlin Wall and the end of the Cold War meant that "Islam" and the "Arab world" were able to replace the Soviet Union as the virtually unchallenged Great Threat to Civilization. Such ideas gained intellectual credibility in Samuel Huntington's much discussed article, "The Clash of Civilizations?", itself owing something of a debt to another influential article, Bernard Lewis' "The Roots of Muslim Rage."[15] For Huntington, the cultural differences between civilizations would become increasingly important. Huntington identified several civilizations (Western, Confucian, Japanese, Islamic, Hindu, Slavic-Orthodox, Latin American and possibly African) which are differentiated from one another by history, language, culture, tradition, and, most importantly, religion. The differences were expanded further and the paramount axis of world politics would be, Huntington predicted, between "the West and the Rest." Western ideas such as individualism, liberalism, human rights, equality, liberty, democracy, free markets, and so on are not found in other civilizations. On the other side, "Islam" would take on a more prominent oppositional role to "the West" with its apparently violent tendencies:

> In Eurasia the great historic fault lines between civilizations are once more aflame. This is particularly true along the boundaries of the crescent-shaped Islamic bloc of nations from the bulge of Africa to

> central Asia. Violence also occurs between Muslims, on the one hand, and Orthodox Serbs in the Balkans, Jews in Israel, Hindus in India, Buddhists in Burma and Catholics in the Philippines. Islam has bloody borders.[16]

On the issue of Islam versus the West, Huntington was more explicit and starker in his subsequent book where Islam is treated extensively and is the most prominent "civilization" in opposition to the West.[17]

While there are serious problems (as we will see) with such stark generalizations about millions and millions of people, it is significant that the rhetoric of the clash of civilizations, for all its critics, has become increasingly prominent in popular and intellectual culture (again, as we will see). Harking back to the first chapter, there are broader historical contexts which suggest that this rhetoric of cultural generalization is embedded in imperialist agendas. David Harvey, building on a long intellectual tradition, has recently shown the close links between nationalism, imperialism and national and/or ethnic superiority and differentiation underlying present day US power. Indeed, the creation of some "other" or some sort of "outside" plays a significant role in the perpetuation of the capitalist system, often taking the form of violent dispossession.[18] The emergence of competing imperialisms grounded in European nations seeking new geographical areas for surplus capital went hand-in-hand with ideas of racial superiority and aggressive exploitation of the colonies. In Europe, trends relating to nation-based imperialism and racial superiority culminated hideously in the rise of Nazism and the Holocaust. US imperialism had its own distinctive spin. There has been the dramatic post-Civil War economic growth, potential for wide internal expansion, a governmental system reflective of corporate and industrial class interests lacking in an aristocratic or feudal past, an ideology of individualism and private property.

However, the US was also a multi-ethnic society which prevented the European approach of hard ethnic nationalism so instead there was a kind of internal racism (indigenous, blacks), paralleled in an external hostility toward anything deemed non-Caucasian and neighbouring territories (Mexico, Caribbean). Despite strong isolationist tendencies in US politics, there were still signs of tendencies that may generally be labelled imperialistic. Inspired by the Monroe Doctrine, the US attempted to dominate and coerce Latin America and many other parts of the world by privilege, trade relations, intimidation and force. In terms of political rhetoric at least, American universalist values as the global leader of the "free world" replaced territorial expansionism.

As mentioned, Harvey also points out, as many others have, that American politics has been dominated by a constant fear of some "other," for example socialism, anarchism, China, Chinese immigrants, even general "outside agitators" and, most significantly, Communism and the Soviet Union.[19] Internally, this was seen most famously in McCarthyism and more recently in the reception, interpretation and re-interpretation of Leo Strauss in neo-conservative thought. In the past 20 years, Saddam and Saddam's Iraq have been fitted into one of the key roles of "dangerous threat" and hindsight shows just how manufactured and absurd this threat was. Chomsky, for example, recalls that during the first Gulf war he and others like him went to some of the most reactionary parts of the US and found people absolutely terrified of Saddam. In rural, isolated Chico State, California, he found that the airport was surrounded with yellow police tape to protect the people from "Arab terrorists" and people "walking around in army fatigues and wearing yellow ribbons, saying 'If Saddam comes, we're going to fight to the death!'" As it was easy enough to persuade people that the threat was absurd with basic facts, there can be little doubt that the media propaganda machine had done their job in massively exaggerating the threat and consequently paved the way for the bombing of Iraq.[20]

In the past 30 years, the UK has increasingly taken on the role as America's "attack dog."[21] Consequently, it should be of little surprise that the same kind of demonizing has taken place in the UK. We might add one of the ways in which the UK in particular drilled up support for the 2003 invasion of Iraq: the infamous, and seemingly non-existent, Weapons of Mass Destruction (WMD). In the UK, one fraudulent 2002 government document on Iraq's WMD threat was prefaced by the then Prime Minister Tony Blair with the following attempt to persuade people of the threat of Saddam:

> in light of the debate about Iraq and Weapons of Mass Destruction (WMD), I wanted to share with the British public the reasons why I believe this issue to be a current and serious threat to the UK national interest.
>
> In recent months, I have been increasingly alarmed by the evidence from inside Iraq that...Saddam Hussein is continuing to develop WMD, and with them the ability to inflict real damage upon the region, and the stability of the world.
>
> What I believe the assessed intelligence has established beyond doubt is that Saddam has continued to produce chemical and biological weapons, that he continues in his efforts to develop nuclear weapons,

> and that he has been able to extend the range of his ballistic missile programme
>
> ...*his [Saddam's] military planning* allows for some of the WMD to be ready within 45 minutes of an order to use them *[my italics].*
>
> In today's inter-dependent world, a major regional conflict does not stay confined to the region in question. Faced with someone who has shown himself capable of using WMD, I believe the international community has to stand up for itself and ensure its authority is upheld.
>
> The threat posed to international peace and security, when WMD are in the hands of a brutal and aggressive regime like Saddam's, is real. Unless we face up to the threat, not only do we risk undermining the authority of the UN, whose resolutions he defies, but more importantly and in the longer term, we place at risk the lives and prosperity of our own people.[22]

For all Saddam's crimes against humanity, it is now famously clear that Blair's assessment was inaccurate in this instance and it ought to be regarded as a classic example of whipping up hostility to be aimed at the latest convenient devil, presumably (given the high degree of deceit about threats and the fact that corporate interests in Iraq have long been noted) in the service of long-term geopolitical aims in the Middle East. Even though the dossier did not claim that Britons were 45 minutes away from a chemical attack, the British press, true to form, were more than happy to amplify some fictitious claims of such a threat and the British government did nothing to counter such claims (though acted swiftly and mercilessly when accused of "sexing up" the intelligence):

> 45 MINUTES FROM ATTACK: dossier reveals Saddam is ready to launch chemical war strikes.
>
> London Evening Standard[23]
>
> BRITS 45mins FROM DOOM: Cyprus within missile range.
>
> The Sun[24]
>
> MAD SADDAM READY TO ATTACK: 45minutes from a chemical war.
>
> Star[25]

Following Harvey and others, if nationalism coupled with imperialism almost inevitably leads to racism, then little surprise that Muslims and Arabs in the US and UK (not to mention much of Europe) are effectively Public Enemy Number One in the present "war on terror" and here we are close to where we began: Said on Orientalism, Islam and Arabs. But now this neo-Orientalism is, as Gregory might put it, Orientalism, hideously emboldened. The rest of this section will look at this hideously emboldened Orientalism and further show how the ever developing polarization of the clash of civilizations is profoundly embedded in Anglo-American intellectual thought and increasingly amplified with the decline of the Soviet Union. We will then be in a position to see how the use of anthropology in studies of the New Testament and Christian origins is strongly tied in with the contemporary rhetoric of clashing civilizations and how this is potentially dangerous, based on seriously problematic and sometimes racist scholarship and assumptions, and how it is carried along by ideas underlying the "war on terror." We can then see that some significant *detailed, empirical* analysis ought to take place when using such approaches.

The Dominant, Influential and Problematic Ideology of Clashing Civilizations

> *The United States is no longer just a nation. It is now a religion. Its soldiers have entered Iraq to liberate its people not only from their dictator, their oil and their sovereignty, but also from their darkness. As George Bush told his troops on the day he announced victory: "Wherever you go, you carry a message of hope – a message that is ancient and ever new. In the words of the prophet Isaiah, 'To the captives, "come out," and to those in darkness, "be free." ' " So American soldiers are no longer merely terrestrial combatants; they have become missionaries. They are no longer simply killing enemies; they are casting out demons... Like all those who send missionaries abroad, the high priests of America cannot conceive that the infidels might resist through their own free will; if they refuse to convert, it is the work of the devil, in his current guise as the former dictator of Iraq... The United States of America no longer needs to call upon God; it is God, and those who go abroad to spread the light do so in the name of a celestial domain. The flag has become as sacred as the Bible; the name of the nation as holy as the name of God. The presidency is turning into a priesthood. So those who question George Bush's foreign policy are no longer merely critics; they are blasphemers, or "anti-Americans." Those foreign states which seek to change this policy are wasting their time: you can negotiate with politicians; you cannot negotiate with priests... The dangers of national divinity scarcely require explanation. Japan went to war in the 1930s convinced, like George Bush, that it possessed a heaven-sent mission to "liberate" Asia and extend the realm of its divine imperium.*
>
> George Monbiot[26]

> *What was it about our Lilliputian leaders that they dared to trivialise the massive sacrifice of the Second World War for their squalid conflict against Iraq, elevating Saddam's tinpot dictatorship into the epic tragedy of the 1939–1945 war?*
>
> Robert Fisk[27]

Pick just about any imperial force (and many less powerful groups) and the highly general "us"/"them" dichotomy will usually lie at the heart of the construction of the Enemy, with convenient details slotted in when required. In the present "war on terror," such language consistently invokes apocalyptic or primordial imagery of good versus evil, angelic versus demonic, alongside the presentation of the stark absolutes of "civilization" and "barbarism."[28] Close to the heart of power, there has been relentless rhetoric about "confronting evil" from the Bush and Blair (and consequently Brown) administrations. Most infamous has been Bush's "axis of evil," made up of *uncivilized* states like Iraq along with Iran, North Korea and their "terrorist allies," "arming to threaten the peace of the world."[29] What kind of human being would possibly oppose good or an angel to side with evil or a demon! Little wonder that the stark and deliberately intimidating phrase, "for us or against us," stuck.

Unable to push the Nazi analogy too far on the eve of the 2003 Iraq war, Blair was forced to resort to primordial generalizations of chaotic evil to describe the enemy: "The threat today is not that of the 1930s...the world is ever more interdependent... The key today is stability and order. The threat is chaos and disorder – and there are two begetters of chaos: tyrannical regimes with weapons of mass destruction and extreme terrorist groups who profess a perverted and false view of Islam."[30] To this we could add, as already hinted, the frequent and equally absurd language of World War II in the buildup to the Iraq war. Notably Churchill (=Bush/Blair) versus Hitler (=Saddam) were cast as the epitome of good versus evil and the war apparently functioned as some kind of blueprint for how action should be taken.[31] What kind of human being would possibly come close to siding with the new Hitler!

The rhetoric of a clash of civilizations reflects the dominant underlying ideology of the media and intellectuals when discussing anything to do with war, terrorism and/or Muslims and Arabs. Islam, Muslims and Arabs come under grand classifications that merge race and religion effortlessly and which in some form or other tends to constitute the content of the grand dichotomy. As Amartya Sen has stressed, this rhetoric is deeply embedded in contemporary thought, whether that thought is academic (including, crucially, social-theoretical), popularist, or party political, all mutually reinforcing, and heavily developed since September 11, rightly adding (see also above) that, "Cultivated theory can bolster uncomplicated bigotry."[32] The overarching rhetoric will be familiar to most. "True Islam" is a religion of peace (therefore "false Islam" is the enemy), the concept of "moderate" Islam (likewise, "extreme" Islam is the enemy), Islam itself has an inherently violent streak, Muslim values are authoritarian and illiberal in contrast to Western traditions of freedom, democracy and liberty, and so on. Islam (in whatever form chosen) *is* x, y or z. But whatever it is, its worst side (though for some commentators *all* Islam or even "the Arab world" does the job) is, at best, another "civilization" or, at the worst end of the worst side, the enemy of "civilization."

Lest my argument itself sounds too generalizing, let us look at some of the evidence. In a recent (2006) *Washington Post* poll, 46% had a "generally unfavourable" view of Islam (43% generally favourable), 33% believed that "*mainstream* Islam" (my italics) encourages violence against non-Muslims, 58% believed that there are more violent extremists in Islam than in other religions, and 34% had heard someone recently "say prejudiced things" against Muslims.[33] In a recent BBC poll covering 27 countries and on the "relationship between Muslim and Western cultures" an average of 56% said they saw positive links "between the cultures" while 28% thought violent conflict was inevitable.[34] Now, there are plenty of other polls with all kinds of variations but the kinds of questions and their assumptions are just as significant (and consistent). They can assume a cultural context whereby these questions concerning sweeping cultural differences can be asked without blinking an eyelid.

On the extreme (and weirdest) wing, shock columnists can barely conceal their delight/racism, as in the case of Ann Coulter, who effectively goes as far as having the US versus the rest of the world as two distinct civilizations (if we non-Americans don't watch it) in an article bearing the telling title "Why We Hate Them":

> Gore also complained that Bush has made the "rest of the world" angry at us. Boo hoo hoo... Good. They hate us? We hate them. Americans don't want to make Islamic fanatics love us. We want to make them die...wait until they see American anger. Japanese kamikaze pilots hated us once too. A couple of well-aimed nuclear weapons, and now they are gentle little lambs. That got their attention... Alas the Germans hate us... Perhaps we could get Djibouti to like us if we legalized clitorectomies for little girls. America is fighting for its survival and the Democrats are obsessing over why barbarians hate us... Instead of obsessing over why angry primitives hate Americans... [etc. etc. etc.][35]

Of course, Coulter has said lots of bizarre things relating to this general topic. After September 11 she acknowledged that it "is preposterous to assume every passenger is a potential crazed homicidal maniac" but "we know who the homicidal maniacs are. They are the ones cheering and dancing right now." Consequently, "We should invade their countries, kill their leaders and convert them to Christianity... We carpet-bombed German cities; we killed civilians. That's war. And this is war."[36] Obviously, these crude generalizations completely avoid any serious historical contextualization and, to put it mildly, the underlying racism is not too difficult to detect. The very fact that Coulter is happily advocating the forced conversion and, presumably, the bombing (perhaps, given the Japanese analogy, nuclear bombing?) of third world countries with some of the *poorest civilians on the planet*, many of which have little to thank the US for, already says far more about Coulter, the underlying ideology, and her cultural context than solutions to world problems.

Other articles from the same mindset but with an intellectualizing overlay, and which do attempt some historical contextualization, are also significant for their basic factual errors. With more detail, but with no less imperialistic zeal, Will Cummins, in the London *Telegraph*, spoke of "the fact" (!) that "Christians are the original inhabitants [*sic*] and rightful owners [*sic*] of almost every Muslim land, and behave with a humility quite unlike the menacing behaviour we have come to expect from the Muslims who have forced themselves on Christendom." Cummins adds that the "indigenous non-Muslims were either exterminated (the fate of the Christians of North Africa), or reduced to the status of third-class citizens in their own countries, their fate to this day."[37] Yet as Hugh Goddard points out in response to Cummins, "tolerance usually extended to Christians and Jews in the early Islamic empire was in marked contrast to the treatment which Jews generally received in the medieval Christian world." Goddard then adds, "how...does the author explain the fact that there are still sizeable Christian communities in Egypt, where they make up perhaps 10 or even 15% of the population, and Lebanon, where they are probably at least 40% of the country's inhabitants?"[38] It would seem that Cummins is either lying or ignorant – either way, the publication of his piece is telling us something significant about present ideological, cultural and political contexts. Without wishing to state the obvious, something else is going on other than pious warnings to an apparently gullible public.

Countless such examples of the clash of civilizations rhetoric, with particular reference to Islam and Arabs, can be found on a regular basis. For the self-proclaimed conservative writer, Peter Hitchens (brother of

Christopher), "Islam – yes, even 'moderate' Islam – threatens our freedom and civilisation."[39] The generalizing attitude concerning a Muslim or Arab "other" is hardly restricted to the "conservative" tradition. From the more "liberal" tradition, Will Hutton, a journalist for the centre-left *Observer*, claims that "radical Islam" represents the "biggest challenge to Western civilisation since the demise of fascism and communism." Yet, for Hutton, there are not only problems with "radical Islam." While recognizing that "there are broader strains within Islam that do offer a pluralist moral code," it is also "at the moment predominantly sexist and pre-Enlightenment – and that is the core of the problem both within the Islamic world and in its relationship with the West."[40]

While, as we will see, I am not going to downplay any threats in the name of Islam, sentiments such as those outlined above can be turned around to show their problematic or uncomfortable nature concerning the construction of identity. "Radical Christianity" of the extreme American right threatens plenty of "civilizations," including "our" own, if we take the Huntington definition of civilization. To make matters worse, such Christians are hardly a fringe movement. We will later see just how outlandish and dangerous the views of the Christian Zionists can be but a couple of points are worth noting for now. Christian Zionists have been taken seriously enough for Karl Rove to seek out their support for the Republican Party and we will see how their aggressively anti-Muslim and anti-Arab views have a notable influence on policies relating to Israel. Furthermore, Reagan and George W. Bush were/are part of their ranks.

Or again, if we want to find extremism on "our" side, any look at some fairly mainstream internet discussion groups and forums will show some frightening sentiments from various well-to-do individuals typing away from the analytical eyes of much of the Western mainstream media and academics. Frightening sentiments can, of course, also be found around the blogs. The following example, from someone going by the name of Doc Russia on his aptly named blog, Bloodletting, is, as we will shortly see, particularly relevant:

> The simple fact of the matter is that muslims are out to destroy western civilization. I intentionally didn't say "extremist muslims are out to destroy western civilization" because that is a mythical group. Extremist muslims are like extremist Christians, only with reversed ratios. What I mean by that is that while there is the rare Jim Jones out there for the christians, the most of them are pretty decent, honest, and simple folk who abhor violence...you have the rare, tolerant muslim, but the most

> of them are extremists, and when the extremists become the norm, there are no more extremists.
>
> We are in the impossible situation of being expected to avoid civilian casualties while still being chastised as morally inferior to the terrorists because they are fighting for "root causes." There is no way that a society so terminally entrenched will ever change their mind. So, as CPL Keeney used to say, "since they won't let us win their hearts and minds, it's time to burn their fucking village down."
>
> So, my dear readers, I am advocating the implementation of what I call the "Ripley Strategy." The "Ripley Strategy" is named for the "Ripley" character played by Sigourney Weaver in the movie "Aliens." Ripley is iinterrogated, given her prior experience with the Aliens, as to what she thinks the best course of action is. Her reponse is the most pure of American simplicity.
>
> Nuke it from orbit; it's the only way to be sure
>
> NUKE IRAN.
>
> No UN security council, No mulit-bi-uni-lateral talks. No threats, no negotiating. Iran is the prime mover behind muslim terrorists, and muslim terrorists are the prime causes of violence on this planet in our day, so I say that, we Nuke Iran first, and then instead of our usual policy of asking permission, we instead ask for forgiveness for making Lake Tehran with it's radioactive glass shores. [All typos original][41]

Now obviously anyone can find, with great ease, material on the internet advocating such extreme fundamentalist violence and if similar sentiments had come from a Muslim it could, with some justification, be associated with those associated with bin Laden and al-Qaeda. However, what is particularly significant about this example is that a Christian biblical scholar, Joseph Cathey, said the following of Doc Russia's post (and later qualified that he did not agree with suggestions about how to deal with Iran – well, it's a start, I suppose):

> Doc Russia has a very good post here – and to top it off he has a great quote from one of my all time favorite movies – Aliens. You may not agree with him – but you can't beat his logic![42]

No, honestly.

If we want to construct "moderate" Christianity and the dangers "moderate" Christianity brings, why not use Tony Blair? Unlike some of his American allies, he is comfortable around homosexuals and does have a liberal view toward women but he shares with some of his American friends a public portrayal of a profoundly religious man. Blair's speeches often show a staggering degree of messianic zeal. Compare the following example from the September 2001 Labour Party conference (it really has to be seen and heard to take in the full scale of the manufactured emotion):

> In retrospect, the Millennium marked only a moment in time. It was the events of September 11 that marked a turning point in history, where we confront the dangers of the future and assess the choices facing humankind. It was a tragedy. An act of evil... We [the British nation] were with you [the American people] at the first. We will stay with you to the last... It is that out of the shadow of this evil, should emerge lasting good: destruction of the machinery of terrorism wherever it is found; hope amongst all nations of a new beginning where we seek to resolve differences in a calm and ordered way; greater understanding between nations and between faiths; and above all justice and prosperity for the poor and dispossessed, so that people everywhere can see the chance of a better future through the hard work and creative power of the free citizen, not the violence and savagery of the fanatic. I know that here in Britain people are anxious, even a little frightened. I understand that... Don't kill innocent people. We are not the ones who waged war on the innocent. We seek the guilty... Today the threat is chaos... The starving, the wretched, the dispossessed, the ignorant, those living in want and squalor from the deserts of Northern Africa to the slums of Gaza, to the mountain ranges of Afghanistan: they too are our cause. This is a moment to seize. The kaleidoscope has been shaken. The pieces are in flux. Soon they will settle again. Before they do, let us re-order this world around us.[43]

In retrospect, these comments now sound creepily deceitful with the liberal-Messianic rhetoric hiding what horrific damage was subsequently done – we could point to cluster bombs, torture, mass deaths and casualties, damaged state infrastructure, support for Uzbekistan's opponent-boiling leader Islam Karimov, and so on – in the name of those murdered on September 11.

On the intellectual wing of the churches, Charles Reed – who has a background in international relations, who has been a political advisor to the Church of England's Public Affairs Unit, and who has taught ethics and international relations at Sarum College, Salisbury – wrote an entire book supposedly showing how actions in Iraq and Afghanistan – where thousands upon thousands of innocent people have died, and have been locked away and tortured – were "just" actions. Reed disgracefully ignored masses of related detail readily available to him, most notably his historically bizarre, but ideologically convenient, claim that America has been a benevolent force post-Vietnam (see further below).[44] What we have here is a "reasonable" and "rational" figure of religious significance in the UK providing intellectually "credible" justifications for Anglo-American violence, so long as evidence to the contrary is ignored. If we take the logic applied to some of the views on Islam and Muslims as seen above, this could lead to the conclusion that "moderate Christianity" is no different from violent, "extremist Christianity." But of course, the argument does not work like that because there is, presumably, the tacit understanding that God is *really* on "our" side.

The purpose of this game of role-reversals is not to engage with some kind of "moral equivalence" (a dubious allegation sometimes made, as we will later see) but, by applying such arguments and statements to "ourselves," to show how *bad* such arguments and statements are, not to mention downright hypocritical. Consequently, on the analogy that the above construction of Christianity as a religion of violence is a gross caricature of Christianity, a closer analysis of the obsession with the constructing of, and finding solutions to, "radical" or "moderate" Islam, might actually suggest that problem solving may involve far more than what is wrong with "them." And such self-righteous "just war" theories powerfully highlight the deep, deep roots that the clash of civilizations theory has in contemporary imaginations and how lack of detail shows the discrepancies between rhetoric and reality. Ideology bulldozes its way through any facts that may dare stand in its way.

Countless articles in the western media have also provided "expert analyses" on the differences between the secular or Christian West and the Islamic East and take up some exceptionally outdated Orientalist themes. Sir John Keegan, the military analyst for the London *Telegraph*, has provided a series of articles on how Afghans, Arabs, and/or Muslims can be defeated in the "war on terror" or related issues. And they are packed to the brim with cultural and pseudo-anthropological differentiation of an "us" (US, UK, West etc.) and "them" (Muslims, Arabs etc.) variety and happily name check Samuel Huntington and his clash of civilizations theory.[45] As we will see, the rhetoric is hardly a million miles away from that used by some of those using anthropology in New Testament studies in its use of generalizing differentiation lists and, of course, that word "honour." In fact Keegan's rhetoric is so startling, so unbelievably outdated and so packed with falsehoods that it deserves an extensive quotation. Not to give too much away, but you do not need me to remind you of the dominant method of fierce air strikes by the US-led attacks or the fact that surprise attacks are carried about by Western powers:

> A harsh, instantaneous attack may be the response most likely to impress the Islamic mind. Surprise has traditionally been a favoured Islamic military method. The use of overwhelming force is, however,

> alien to the Islamic military tradition. The combination of the two is certainly designed to unsettle America's current enemy and probably will... If I thought Huntington's view had a defect, it was that he did not discuss what I think the crucial ingredient of any Western-Islamic conflict, their quite distinctively different ways of making war. Westerners fight face to face, in stand-up battle, and go on until one side or the other gives in. They choose the crudest weapons available, and use them with appalling violence, but observe what, to non-Westerners may well seem curious rules of honour. Orientals, by contrast, shrink from pitched battle, which they often deride as a sort of game, preferring ambush, surprise, treachery and deceit as the best way to overcome an enemy... Relentlessness, as opposed to surprise and sensation, is the Western way of warfare. It is deeply injurious to the Oriental style and rhetoric of war-making. Oriental war-makers, today terrorists, expect ambushes and raids to destabilise their opponents, allowing them to win further victories by horrifying outrages at a later stage. Westerners have learned, by harsh experience, that the proper response is not to take fright but to marshal their forces, to launch massive retaliation and to persist relentlessly until the raiders have either been eliminated or so cowed by the violence inflicted that they relapse into inactivity... This war belongs within the much larger spectrum of a far older conflict between settled, creative productive Westerners and predatory, destructive Orientals.[46]

The crude (to put it mildly) generalizations made by Keegan hardly need to be illustrated much further. Admittedly, a newspaper article is hardly going to be able to provide masses of detail but it might be expected that some mention of massive military inequality might explain some differences, or that there might be major differences in practices when looking at the details of, for instance, Vietnamese warfare (which Keegan cites as a modern-day example) as compared to, for instance, Afghan warfare, not to mention non-nationalized constructions of military tactics. Keegan is aware of such potential criticisms and, with one eye on historical-anthropological generalisations, responds by effectively reaffirming his position:

> This is not to stereotype Afghans, Arabs, Chechens or any other Islamic nationality traditionally hostile to the West as devious or underhand, nor is it to stereotype Islam in its military manifestation. The difference in styles of warfare is borne out by the fact of military history. Western warfare had its origins in the conflicts of the citizens of the Greek city states who fought to defend the strictly defined borders of their small political units. Beyond their world the significant military powers, however, were nomads, whose chosen method was the raid and the surprise attack. Once they acquired a superior means of mobility, in the

> riding horse, they developed a style of warfare which settled people found almost impossible to resist... It is no good pretending that the peoples of the desert and the empty spaces exist on the same level of civilisation as those who farm and manufacture. They do not.

In this case, and many others, the sentiment is little more than scaremongering and a weird kind of antiquated imperialism with little in the way of supporting evidence. This in itself is significant: clearly the polar opposition – and *not* basic fact and detail – dominates. Given the billion-plus Muslims and Arabs spread out across the world, citing either no examples or the occasional example to support a generalized case is hugely problematical. As ever, something else is going on. *What* details are being omitted and *why* are details being omitted?

As some of these examples show, it should be obvious, but for some it clearly is not, that such sweeping classifications can be seriously unhelpful. But we do not have to think in the abstract. Empirically, studies of people who happen to be Muslim throw up a massive range of behaviour and identities are utterly diverse, as ought to be expected, crossing all kinds of political, cultural, ethnic, gender, intellectual and class divides. India, despite the rhetoric of the Hindu nationalists, is not simply a Hindu country, and nor could it be with 145 million Muslims. Yet the number of those identifying in someway as Hindu (800 plus million) – not to mention those identifying as Sikh or Buddhist among others – shows that "the Muslim world" and "the Islamic world" are problematic categories. Then again, why should I or anyone else be defining along religious lines? There are plenty of figures in Indian arts and culture who happen to be Muslim or Hindu and happen to be respected by Hindus and Muslims.[47]

We could take countless other examples of messy or (for some) surprising identities and of religion or being Muslim having little to do with everyday life for some Muslims in different parts of the world. One that has been particularly memorable for me is that of the Meskhetian Turks in southern Russia who, as Kathryn Tomlinson points out, do not necessarily foreground religion as part of their identity. Indeed Tomlinson, who carried out fieldwork among Meskhetian Turks, discusses various aspects of Meskhetian Turk identity, including being Turkish, being Soviet, and being Muslim. She also points to aspects of Meskhetian Turk life which may not seem typically "Muslim" by the standards of the Anglo-American media. For example: there was a banning of drinking vodka during Ramadan (or, Ramazan); while at prayer, one girl accidentally washed her nose rather than ears and so giggled and asked her ears for forgiveness; and questions about religion are often met with a laugh and a response along the lines of

"Ask a mullah!"[48] Such examples of non-typical (by certain standards) behaviour ought to highlight what ought to be an obvious point: Muslim (or indeed any other "religious") behaviour is massively diverse, not necessarily at the fore of everyday life and, if noted, resists dubiously imposed generalizations.

The broader historical context also shows the problems with the clash of civilizations rhetoric. As is being increasingly acknowledged, numerous scientific, engineering, mathematical, and philosophical advances have come to "the West" via centuries of Arab, Iranian, Chinese, Muslim, Indian, and so on, influences. The preservation of classical Greek texts – which, despite all the differing cultural connections, have now become the cornerstone of the "Western" tradition – was assisted in no small part by Arabic translations. Similarly, classical Greek democratic developments have been hijacked and placed in the "Western" tradition, despite connections with, for instance, Persians and Egyptians (and not too many connections with "western" Europe!). "Democratic" rhetoric could be found, for instance, in a major ancient Iranian city like Susa for several centuries. Public discussion, political participation and religious tolerance have been a historic feature of political thought in Middle Eastern and Islamic traditions, from Cairo to Córdoba, from Baghdad to Istanbul.[49]

What we are now starting to see is that Islamic, Arab, Middle Eastern, and so on, identities are being generalized and constructed with little attention to contrary facts and all fulfilling the needs of a certain ideology. We can now turn to the role these generalizations play in US foreign policy, including the "war on terror" where this neo-Orientalism has become "hideously emboldened."

"War on Terror" and Ignoring the Details I: "The Geraldo Rivera of the NYT" and the Complexities of Arab, Muslim and Islamic Violence

> *In discussion of international relations, the fundamental principle is that "we are good" – "we" being the government, on the totalitarian principle that state and people are one. "We" are benevolent, seeking peace and justice, though there may be errors in practice. "We" are foiled by villains who can't rise to our exalted level.*
>
> Noam Chomsky[50]

Intentionally or unintentionally, the simplifying, generalizing and imposing of broad identities we have seen are bolstered, legitimized and influenced by, not to mention fed into, the very real desires of US foreign policy and US attitudes toward terrorism.[51] Indeed, the whole history of the recent conflicts in Afghanistan, Iraq, Israel and Palestine are hardly reducible to "al-Qaeda," "Islamic fundamentalism," or "Islamic terrorism," given the range of complex individual, local, regional, and imperial histories.[52] Even the great enemy al-Qaeda appears to be more fragmentary – more a lethal series of networks than a monolithic entity – than is presented across the media.[53]

Again, as ever, countless examples of ideological generalizations concerning Islamic violence could be given but one more will have to suffice before we move on to a detailed example. Beyond the favoured imagined geography of the enemy, Jim Glassman, with reference to a range of empirical data and secondary literature, shows that, for all the political diversity in the Philippines, Indonesia, and Thailand, the Bush administration and the "war on terror" has rendered these different lands a collective area of Islamic terrorist threat. However, Glassman adds that the diversity in Southeast Asia would suggest that this is more of an ideological feat. The simplifying, generalizing and imposing of an overarching identity would, once again, suggest that something else is going on and, with reference to (among others) the neo-conservative pressure group, the Project for a New American Century, a similar agenda and interest in Southeast Asia is clearly discernable prior to September 11 and independent of alleged Islamic terrorists threats.[54]

Predictably, journalists – liberal and illiberal – have followed the ideological generalizations effortlessly in the promotion of US foreign policy and the "war on terror." The Pulitzer Prize winning *New York Times* journalist, Thomas Friedman speaks of the "terrorism bubble," a dangerous fantasy believed by "way too many people in the Middle East," said that "it was OK to plow airplanes into the World Trade Center, commit suicide in Israeli pizza parlors, praise people who do these things as 'martyrs,' and donate money to them through religious charities." Friedman said this bubble had to be burst "and the only way to do it was to go right into the heart of the Arab world and smash something – to let everyone know that we, too, are ready to fight and die to preserve our open society."[55] The various cases of generalizing we have seen buy in to the all-too-common rhetoric of how "they" must change and that "we" ought to change "our" often too kindly ways towards "them." With the Friedman example we can see that this is seriously problematical and ignores some of crucial historical contexts, especially in his insistence that the only way "we" need to change is to go get "them."[56] The realities of terrorism in "the Middle East" and beyond are far more complex and should be outlined in a little more detail.

One key reason for the rise of a more widespread militant Islam or widespread support for militant Islam in the Middle East involves the decline of secular nationalism, embodied by figures such as Nasser, since the 1970s in North Africa and the Middle East, with militant Islam filling the void and becoming the main viable option of anti-US protest, though not infrequently being previously supported by the US.[57] There has also been the issue of oil and the widespread wealth it could have created. Yet oil economies, which in many ways underlined the importance of many Muslim states for the US and allies, have proven to be profoundly corrupt, socially unjust, economically underdeveloped, highly oppressive, with the extreme wealth ending up in the hands of the few, and invariably backed or tampered with by Western powers.

In addition to these serious enough problems, the Muslim and Arab countries in North Africa and the Middle East have endured serious problems of overpopulation.[58] Michael Watts points to the increasingly high percentage of people living in slums, an unprecedented development. Outside India, half of the population in the ten most populous Muslim states are urban dwellers, a figure expected to rise beyond two-thirds by 2015. This slum-dwelling population is mostly under 30 years of age and often literate and educated. Watts comments:

> One might say that the historical agent of the contemporary Muslim city is the young, part or wholly-educated, unemployed male scraping a marginal living of the shambolic economy of Jakarta's *kampungs*, Istanbul's *gecekondus*, Khartoum's *shammasas*, and Cairo's *baladis*. It is from this incendiary milieu that the fire of political Islam has spread and where the crisis of secular nationalism is most palpable.[59]

He adds that with the shifting of vast dollar resources to Saudi Arabia and the Gulf came millions of migrant workers from an array of ethnic and national backgrounds, opened them up to some of the radical doctrines (notably Wahhabism), and opened up wide-ranging networks. The bust inevitably followed the boom and in the 1980s the various Muslim-dominated cities felt the full force of the petro-crash. It would not be too difficult to make a compelling theological case for society being morally depraved in this context with some kind of accompanying theological reaction. And the oil revenues also cultivated new leaders and backers for any Muslim response.

Then throw into the mix several key US foreign policy decisions: the centrality of oil, unflinching support for Israel, support and tampering with politics in North Africa and the Middle East, the highly provocative bases near Mecca (and, recall, that 15 of the 19 September 11 hijackers were Saudis), and the encouragement of an uprising in southern Iraq in 1991 only for support to be withdrawn before Saddam's slaughter commenced.

One of the most disastrous – on many levels – foreign policy decisions was the horrific sanctions imposed on Iraq in the 1990s which were estimated to have claimed the lives of around 500,000 children. This outraged former UN humanitarian coordinators for Iraq, Hans von Sponeck (1998–2000) and Denis Halliday (1997–98) who resigned from their posts in disgust:

> The current policy of economic sanctions has destroyed society in Iraq and caused the death of thousands, young and old. There is evidence of that daily in reports from reputable international organisations such as Caritas, Unicef and Save the Children... The UK and the US, as permanent members of the council, are fully aware that the UN embargo operates in breach of the UN covenants on human rights, the Geneva and Hague conventions and other international laws... The death of some 5-6,000 children a month is mostly due to contaminated water, lack of medicines and malnutrition. The US and UK governments' delayed clearance of equipment and materials is responsible for this tragedy, not Baghdad... What we describe is not conjecture. These are undeniable facts known to us as two former insiders. We are outraged that the Iraqi people continue to be made to pay the price for the lucrative arms trade and power politics.[60]

We now know that the US government knew of the kind of impact these sanctions would have. Defence Intelligence Agency documents now available, thanks in particular to Thomas Nagy,[61] show that there was expectation of a degrading of Iraq's water system, widespread food and water shortages, lack of medicine, and the spread of diseases and epidemics.[62] Yet despite this, there was also a concern in these documents that public health services and shortages of medical supplies would be used by Saddam's regime "to keep public opinion firmly against the U.S. and its Coalition allies" and that it would "exploit disease incidence data for its own political purposes."[63] Read another way, and in fear of understatement, the sanctions had the potential to intensify the hostilities. Furthermore, the impact of the sanctions on Islamic terrorism should not be underestimated. We will see shortly how the sanctions, with the deaths of children sometimes being exaggerated well beyond their already gruesomely high level, have been used by bin Laden, al-Zawahiri and their admirers.

In answer to Friedman, then, it might be said that the US has already gone into the heart of the Arab world and smashed things, many, many times.

We might also add the point that much of the rise of Islamic violence was assisted by Western support. The US has also supported various brands of highly conservative Islam such as its old allies, the Saudis. We should not forget the US support for the Mujahideen against the Soviet Union, providing a battle-hardened group ready for further combat, and initial support for the Taliban as they rose to power.[64] We could also add some of the decisions made by Israel, particularly in reaction to secular nationalism in its nurturing and encouragement of Hamas, now an arch enemy for Israel and the US, to undermine Arafat and the PLO, through support for mosques, social services, and education.

On the subject of the central issue of Israel and Palestine, the failure and fallout from the US-backed Oslo Accords led to a wave of Palestinian grievances, not to mention hostility toward Arafat and the PLO for selling the Palestinians short. Moreover, the population growth rate among Palestinians was among the highest in the world which, coupled with lacking economic resources, contributed an increase in frustrated and angry young people, especially in refugee camps including those of Palestinian families removed under the 1948 borders. There were also those less marginalized but who were not part of the Arafat clique who were also among the pool of the resentful. In this context, Arafat had to compete with the politicized Islamic groups (Hamas, Islamic Jihad) for the attentions of the Palestinian youth bringing religion further to the fore.[65]

The election victory of Ariel Sharon, the man who can count overseeing the Sabra and Shatila massacres in 1982 among his life's notorieties,[66] intensified the hostilities, as did the support for the infamous "man of peace" by George W. Bush. In 2001 horrific suicide attacks were carried out on civilians in Israel. The perception of the "success" of suicide bombing was boosted by a perception, real or otherwise, of Hezbollah's success in driving Israel out of southern Lebanon in 2000 after 22 years. If Hezbollah could succeed, so one argument went, then why not other such attempts by Palestinians? And with the standards of living between Israel and Arab territories such as Palestine and parts of Lebanon being starkly different, then would not the taste for death and danger be starkly different on both sides? Support for acts of grotesque violence grew, seen as the only way to deal with Israel's military superiority, notably among the radicalized youth, for groups like Hamas and Islamic Jihad who could now be seen in stark contrast to Arafat and his circle. If no nation could possibly support such actions, individuals and groups, those like bin Laden and al-Qaeda certainly could.

The above is a regrettably brief sketch of the kinds of issues underlying various aspects of terror and violence associated with Islam and "the Arab world." With these thoughts in mind, it ought to be clear not only that Friedman's solution would hardly help matters (if anything it would greatly amplify the already terrible problem) but his kind of rhetoric, which is common, also assists in the covering up of the various messy issues underlying the rise of violent militancy attached to Islam, including a high degree of culpability on "our" side. What is crucial for present purposes is that the generalizing "us" versus "them" rhetoric drives all analysis and effectively covers up any complicity or failure in the global economic system. Yet the situation is anything but a simple one of "them" having to change "their" ways. It is far more deadly, terrifying and complex than that.

"War on Terror" and Ignoring the Details II: The Ideologically Convenient Atheism of Sam Harris

We are at war with Islam

Sam Harris[67]

The past ten years have not only seen another revival of American conservative Christianity but a notable reaction: aggressively anti-religious atheism (cf. Chapter 1). For what it is worth, both, in my view, are dangerous, both are partly driven by the clashing civilizations thesis, and both, consequently, have a notable dislike/hatred of Islam. Both are also significant for present purposes because both, as we saw in Chapter 1, have had a notable impact on biblical studies in the past decade and individuals of both persuasions are known to be dabbling with anthropology and cultural generalizations in the study of Christian origins. Christian views have been seen throughout this section, and will be seen in the next section, and consequently certain hard secular views now need to be shown and particularly how they too are driven by a similar underlying ideology as that which drives anti-Islamic Christianity.

One of the most prominent contemporary anti-religious atheistic writers is Sam Harris. Harris is important because he brings together several popular arguments against those who do not see a near-essentialized view of Islam as the heart of the world's conflicts. He is further important because he writes in an area overlapping with biblical and religious studies and he tries to engage with some of the details of US foreign policy and morality. Yet while Harris is ignorant of several mainstream arguments concerning religion, Islam and violence, his hard secular views effectively take the dehumanizing views discussed above to their logical conclusion and reveal the naked brutality covered up by so many intellectual views in the US and UK media.

Harris is keen to make distinctions between religious believers and this is crucial because Islam gets conveniently highlighted with his rhetoric slipping easily into that relating to the contemporary "war on terror." "There is a reason," he says, "why we must now confront Muslim, rather than Jain terrorists, in every corner of the world." Muslims, he informs us, have their fair share of "bad beliefs," even if positives can be cited. Harris is aware of the social, political and economic "roots of Muslim violence" (cf. Bernard Lewis' infamous "The Roots of Islamic Rage," an authority Harris likes to cite) and points to Israeli action in Gaza and the West Bank, Western collusion with brutal dictatorships, poverty and lack of economic opportunity in the Arab world. However, we can ignore these arguments because there are similar things going on all over the world with recipients who do not and will not commit terrorism "of the sort that has become so commonplace among Muslims." Islam is not really peaceful because the Qur'an and hadith prescribe a vision of life to all Muslims that is all violence, conquering, converting, dominating, and death for apostates and assimilators to modernity. And so a future in which "Islam and the West" do not stand "on the brink of mutual annihilation" is a future in which "most Muslims" have learned to ignore most of their '"canon," something hardly guaranteed. Moderate Islam ("*really* moderate, *really* critical of Muslim irrationality") barely exists.[68] Harris gives lots of quotations and statistics showing how strongly Muslims endorse suicide bombing and killing. Ultimately, then,

> In our dialogue with the Muslim world, we are confronted by people who hold beliefs for which there is no rational justification and which therefore cannot even be discussed, and yet these are the very beliefs that underlie many of the demands they are likely to make upon us.[69]

That alone should be some indication of Harris' aggressively secular rhetoric buying into US imperialism but then he gets all overtly political. While not uncritical, he sees a lot of good in Samuel Huntington's clash of civilizations thesis, he certainly likes Bernard Lewis, and he describes *New York Times* journalist, Thomas Friedman, as "a tireless surveyor of the world's discontents."[70] Indeed, in true Friedman style, while acknowledging that the failure to support the encouraged uprisings against Saddam in 1991 was highly unethical, Harris tells us that "were democracy to suddenly come to these countries, it would be little more than a gangplank to theocracy...the only thing that currently stands between us and the rolling ocean of Muslim unreason is a wall of tyranny and human rights abuses that we have helped to create." Then we find the key argument behind this logic: religion, especially Islam, is backward and *pre-modern*: "we cannot merely force Muslim dictators from power and open the polls. It would be like opening the polls to the Christians of the fourteenth century."[71]

This leads on directly to Harris' analysis of the details concerning US foreign policy, economics and Islamic reactions. Harris acknowledges that poverty and lack of education play their part. The "Arab world" is "economically and intellectually stagnant" with a shocking degree of "insularity and backwardness." But this does not tell us very much, Harris argues. Muslim terrorists notably bin Laden, "have not tended to come from the ranks of the uneducated poor": many have been "middle class, educated, and without any obvious dysfunction in their lives." Such facts suggest that "even if every Muslim enjoyed a standard of living comparable to that of the average middle-class American, the West might still be in profound danger of colliding with Islam." In fact, in true scaremongering style, Harris suggests that "If Muslim orthodoxy [which is...?] were as economically and technologically viable as Western liberalism, we would probably be doomed to witness the Islamification of the earth." Muslim discourse, he adds "*is* [my italics] currently a tissue of myths, conspiracy theories, and exhortations to recapture the glories of the seventh century. There is no reason to believe that economic and political improvements in the Muslim world, in and of themselves, would remedy this."[72]

None of Harris' arguments are useful, and some are just aggressive slurs.[73] On his critique of economic conditions (a very common argument),[74] let me give one parallel theory that has sometimes been borrowed by scholars of Christian origins: leadership in social upheaval. There has long been discussion, particularly in Marxist circles, over the role of outside leadership of class-based uprisings, with an influential view claiming that peasant and lower class uprisings are frequently led by outsiders, those with resources, background and connections to help uprisings spread beyond their localized origins.[75] I am not suggesting this approach is necessarily correct and I am not suggesting that this approach necessarily has anything to do with bin Laden but what I am suggesting is that the idea that the wealthy being involved in violent reactions is ancient and does not by itself disprove that issues surrounding harsh socioeconomic conditions are an underlying factor in violent reactions.

As it turns out we can provide some more concrete examples of the rich appealing to socioeconomic circumstances for support. The disastrous results of the economic sanctions in Iraq, which, as noted above, have been estimated to have killed approximately 500,000 children through, for instance, malnutrition and lack of medical supplies, has been exploited by bin Laden and his associates who have made claims such as the exaggerated figure of 1,000,000 children dying. Footage of people using such language has been filmed and is readily available on the internet. Consequently, as David Leigh and James Wilson point out, "it seems chillingly clear that, in the training camps and round the campfires, Bin Laden's young Muslims have it dinned into them again and again that the Americans kill babies."[76] Why? Or again, the preface to the video speech by the London bomber, Mohammad Sidique Khan, contains speeches by al-Zawahiri and bin Laden, footage of September 11 and July 7, and numerous mentions of events in Chechnya, Iraq (including the sanctions), Afghanistan, and Palestine, with reference to policies of Bush and Blair, as well as the standard religious rhetoric.[77] Presumably these things are said for reasons and presumably these reasons include emotional impact to whip up hostility against the US and UK and they perform the function of recruiting sergeant, particularly among the non-Saudi pool of potential recruits and followers.[78] Otherwise, why don't bin Laden and co just say that Islam demands the killing of infidels and nothing more? The obvious answer would be that few would follow such murderous demands. This is hardly the most difficult concept to grasp and the perception – real or otherwise – of suffering has been extremely common and widespread in recruiting people to kill other people they do not know, from wars to terrorism. Consequently, we should not be looking at such stunningly simplistic and ideologically convenient answers like those of Harris and we should be looking more widely – and, I would add, far more responsibly – at the serious problems that allow bin Laden and al-Zawahiri to recruit people to become brutal, cruel and indiscriminate murderers.

We might also look more broadly at the issue of the July 7 bombings in the UK. In a 2005 *Guardian*/ICM poll among British Muslims, despite strong condemnation of the bombers themselves, only 10% thought Tony Blair bore no responsibility for the London bombings.[79] Or again, in a 2006 *Sunday Telegraph*/ICM poll, 20% of Muslims, irrespective of whether they approved of the bombings, had sympathy with the "feelings and motives" of the July 7 attackers, but 1% thought the bombers were right to carrying out the attack.[80] What is going on here? Does this not say something about the way Muslims feel and that their religion does not necessarily lead to supporting violence? I mean, they should know, shouldn't they? Or did they just lie to the pollsters?

Like the middle-class outrage of many commentators, Harris also appears to assume that socioeconomic explanations somehow do not affect the middle classes and that without "dysfunction in their lives" how could they possibly believe such strange things! This sort of assumption is not only wrong it also avoids arguments that have long been made about Islamic violence, including arguments already seen and arguments made by prominent commentators such as Gilbert Achcar. Achcar, with explicit Marxist leanings, has argued that with the failure or elimination of nationalist, anti-imperialist, socialist and so on dimensions in Arab and Islamic contexts, "radical, anti-Western Islamic fundamentalism is a distorted, reactionary expression of the middle classes' and plebeian layers' resentment against distorted capitalist development and Western domination, often exacerbated by a despotic local state."[81] Obviously, there is much more to Achcar's argument than a mere quotation can convey but the point is not necessarily whether Achcar is right or wrong but the fact that a range of shifting socioeconomic reasons can be, and have been, given to explain the rise of Islamic violence, without relying on that old caricature that reaction must only come in light of things that happen to the poor. More generally, given the countless Marxist analyses of bourgeois revolutions and revolts, it seems quite strange that this passes Harris by. Strange, unless we acknowledge that his view of history and change is dictated by a mysterious kind of evolution of moral thought.

Clearly, there is much more significant influence of social, political and economic factors underlying Islamic violence than Harris' oversimplifications allow. Yet, to be fair, there is something connected with Islam that has given justification to acts of terror. We have already noted the various specific social, economic, political, cultural, and geographical factors underlying violent Islam. But there are other important reasons that ought to be noted because, contrary to Harris' stress on the non-modern nature of religious and specifically Islamic violence, the revolutionary or highly politicized sorts of Islam from the Iranian revolutionaries to al-Qaeda are in many ways, though not unprecedented, thoroughly *modern*, developing throughout the twentieth century and associated with pivotal figures such as Hassan al-Banna (1906–1949), Sayyid Abul Ala Maududii (1903–1979) and Sayyid Qutb (c. 1906–1966) and movements such as the Muslim Brotherhood. As is often pointed out, underlying the Qur'anic and general Islamic rhetoric are clear influences from strands of Marxism (e.g. revolutionary vanguard, anti-imperialism, terror, internationalism, and popular justice – even the aggressive splintering and internecine disputes so often associated with Marxist groups), hardly a surprise given the prominence of intellectual Marxism in universities and the nationalist and socialist movements in colonial, postcolonial and neo-colonial contexts, including the Middle East, India and North Africa. Communist and fascist totalitarianism would also feature as a notably modern influence. Furthermore, this heavily politicized Islam had an appeal well beyond the universities as it began to flourish among the urban lower classes in North Africa and parts of Asia and so, just as we find in left-wing and even hard-right thought, there is an attempt, crucially, to deal with serious socioeconomic problems, with further reference to cultural, spiritual and moral issues.[82]

There is, obviously, far more to be said about the ideological roots of Islamic violence but this brief sketch should hopefully have shown how seriously simplified Harris' view of religion and Islam actually is. The fact that the kind of Islam Harris fires at is, as it turns out, a *modern* movement, and one partially influenced by secular worldviews and secular failings and wider historical trends (nationalism, overpopulation, slums, oil, colonialism etc.), ought to suggest that Harris has got religion very wrong in this instance. And if his view is taken further, it can only contribute more to a hideous misunderstanding of a terrible, terrible problem.

After a dubious account of Israeli human rights toward Palestinians, based on Alan Dershowitz's, *The Case for Israel*, and the hardly difficult debunking of the view that Israelis are to be compared with the Nazis, Harris gives the following, and frankly perverse, example:

> Ask yourself, what are the chances that the Palestinians would show the same restraint [as the Israelis] in killing Jews if the Jews were a powerless minority living under their occupation and disposed to acts of suicidal terrorism? It would be no more likely than Muhammad's flying to heaven on a winged horse.

Palestinians? Including Palestinian *Christians*? Not simply *Muslims*? But, then, the comparison with Muhammad drags us into simplicity. Again, it is noticeable that the structural divide at the heart of the clash of civilizations is carelessly dictating Harris' argument. And again, this massive generalizing theory means avoidance of some important details. For a start, Arafat and the PLO have their origins in secular nationalism and Hamas were, as mentioned above, initially encouraged and nurtured as a counter secular nationalism! Harris' attempt to analyse Palestinians is another grotesque handling of a serious issue and, after glibly passing over issues that might relate to settlements, bombings, water resources, and so on, has managed to justify actions against the Palestinians by telling us that the Palestinians would be far, far worse if they were in charge with evidence amounting to nothing more than a rhetorical flourish.

Harris does at least attempt to deal with prominent opponents of US actions in Muslim countries, figures routinely ignored in the mainstream. Noam Chomsky, for instance, is denounced as an "exquisitely moral man whose political views prevent him from making the most basic moral distinctions – between types of violence, and the variety of human responses that give rise to them." He points to Chomsky's much misunderstood mention, in the aftermath of September 11, of the 1998 bombing of the al-Shifa pharmaceuticals plant in Sudan which could have contributed to the deaths of (literally) countless Sudanese, accusing Chomsky of drawing "moral equivalences" between US actions and actions of those such as al-Qaeda, which no "honest" [so are Harris' supposed opponents *lying* or *dishonest*?] observation of current events could possibly claim.

Harris thinks this is dubious because it ignores motivation and intention: there was no intention to kill as many Sudanese as possible. The followers of al-Qaeda and Saddam Hussein are in a "different moral universe entirely" to Bush and Blair and so the comparisons between Bush and Saddam (or any other dictator) by Chomsky, and in classrooms throughout the "free world," are facile. While acknowledging US foreign policy disasters, Harris believes the US is a "well-intentioned giant" and finds it is astonishing that people like Chomsky and Arundhati Roy do not see this. Bush would not target innocents if he had a "perfect weapon" whereas bin Laden or Saddam would because places like the US are much more morally developed than many other (Muslim) cultures. For all the bad things done, at least there is outrage at violence to distinguish "us" from many of our enemies. After all, makers of cars and hockey sticks know people will get hurt and die but at least that was never the intention.[83] So that's ok then, right?

Chomsky and Roy are capable of fighting their own battles but some objections do need to be raised against Harris' thoroughgoing caricature of Chomsky because here we see how Harris' overall argument buys into the classical imperialism of the enlightened "us" and the backward natives riddled with superstition who could not possibly be trusted to be democratic. He is wrong on Chomsky and "moral equivalence" (incidentally, how is "morality" measured in order to get "equivalence"?). It should be immediately striking that he cites *not one single reference* from Chomsky on moral equivalence (he only discusses Chomsky's very short book on September 11 anyway) which is particularly dubious given that Chomsky has actually discussed the subject (incidentally, Harris gives no example from classrooms either). As Chomsky has put it:

> The term moral equivalence is an interesting one, it was invented I think by Jeane Kirkpatrick as a method of trying to prevent criticism of foreign policy and state decisions. It has a meaningless notion, there is no moral equivalence what so ever.[84]
>
> ...moral equivalence. There is no such notion. There are many different dimensions and criteria. For example, there's no moral equivalence between the bombing of the World Trade Center and the destruction of Nicaragua or of El Salvador, of Guatemala. The latter were far worse, by any criterion. So there's no moral equivalence. Furthermore, they were done for different reasons and they were done in different ways. There's all sorts of dimensions...[85]
>
> Hitchens condemns the claim of "facile 'moral equivalence' between the two crimes." Fair enough, but since he fabricated the claim out of thin air, I feel no need to comment.[86]

We might also notice that, once again, Harris has shifted the issue onto personal morality and away from any systematic and medium/long-term sociopolitical issues. It is unlikely that the recipients of carpet bombing in Cambodia, the countless dead in Iraq as a result of US-led actions, or the recipients of white phosphorus in Falluja, will be grateful for Harris' explanation that innocents would not have been killed in an ideal situation. Perhaps the recipients of bombs will be relieved to know that the bombs were presumably made as innocently as hockey sticks. Following Harris' arguments through to their logical conclusion would hardly provide the best means of preventing acts of terror in the future and it might explain why some people around the world are not overwhelmed by arguments about the supposed moral superiority of "the West."

It ought to be stated bluntly: Harris' demonizing of Islamic thought ends up being an act of defending the indefensible, apparently in the name of showing how rotten religion is. Gone is the evil of some race. In its place, a certain religion is rotten to the core and must be segregated, oppressed, and even killed. Not because "we" want to, mind, – because "we" are good at heart – but because "they" are inferior and are morally less evolved than "us." On the other hand, and to be fair to Harris, it might be said that Harris is only making explicit a widespread intellectual/media-intellectual assumption.

Related Scholarship and the Language of Cultural Difference

> *In 1970 there were 15,000 Muslims in the Netherlands. There are now one million. They are causing now, and they have caused, a situation for the indigenous Dutch (and of course for other, but non-Muslim immigrants...), that is far more unpleasant, expensive, and physically dangerous than it would be without that quite unwelcome, quite unnecessary, and deeply dangerous Muslim presence. That presence is one that the Muslims themselves recognize as being one behind what they are taught to regard, and most do regard, as enemy lines, the lines of the Infidels.*
>
> *...Western tolerance is based on the Western enshrinement of individual rights. That does not include tolerating those who cling tenaciously to a doubly totalitarian Belief System, that offers a Complete Regulation of Life, and a geopolitical plan that justifies, by any instruments available and effective (and not merely qitaal, or combat, or its variant "terrorism"), the removal of all obstacles to the spread and dominance of Islam everywhere, and everywhere a situation where Muslims rule.*
>
> *Benes and Masaryk were wise, tolerant, advanced statesmen, two who belonged to an older and better educated generation. They had no hesitation in implementing the Benes Decree(s) of 1946, and in banishing the Sudeten Germans who had proved to be such a threat. For them, for the Czechs, Germany lay prostrate, but they were not about to take another chance. And no one at the time, and no one since, has thought what the Czechs then did was immoral – save for a handful of German revanchists and those who have a particular soft-spot, one that deserves to be examined, for the treatment of Germans after the war.*
>
> *Why should the Netherlands, Denmark, Italy, and the other countries of Europe not recognize a similar permanent danger in their midst, in the presence of jihadists and Sharia supremacists? And if Germany was prostrate in 1946, the world of Islam is hardly prostrate today. Rather, it feels itself stronger than ever.*
>
> "Hugh Fitzgerald" (Campus Watch)[87]

We have seen some of the broad interests of various western elites relating to defining Enemy Number One. We have also seen broad interests reflected in areas close to biblical and religious studies (Sam Harris). We can now focus on another important context for understanding the professorial class in biblical studies, namely issues relating to universities. In areas close to New Testament studies the rhetoric of civilization is being declared loud and clear. There is the notorious case of the events in 2002 at the University of North Carolina (UNC) in Chapel Hill and the use of Michael Sells' book, *Approaching the Qur'an: The Early Revelations* as a core text to read in preparation for university level study. There was even a provision for students and/or their families who might be offended to not read the book, so long as they gave their reasons why in their written assignment. However, there was a backlash. One conservative group initiated a lawsuit and claimed that this reading infringed the separation between Church and State, that it was an attempt to convert students to Islam and that it was not presenting Islam fairly because violent verses from the Qur'an were not included.[88]

Some, though certainly not all, of the media reaction has been aggressive toward UNC.[89] William Buckley, presumably not having read Sells' collection, informs his readers that "*Time* magazine reports [so no attempt to read the source?] that the bowdlerizers at the University of North Carolina have got out a special edition [*sic*!] of the Koran (political correctness: the Qur'an)... This edition is exorcised of any sentiments such as might have impelled the knights of 9/11 to plunge themselves and their steeds into live Americans, innocent of any infidelity to Islam, this side of not adhering to it." For good measure Buckley posed the following: "When we conquered Hitler, we denied the Germans the right to buy a copy of *Mein Kampf*. Should we ask the Muslim leaders to circulate only the University of North Carolina edition of the Qur'an?"[90]

The *Jerusalem Post* saw fit to write an editorial on the matter, "Sanitizing Islam." Sells' book is again put into a much broader context. The editorial opens as follows:

> In Funtua, Nigeria, last week, a 30-year-old mother named Amina Lawal was sentenced to death by stoning by an Islamic court for "adultery," although in her case this means only having sex out of wedlock. The sentence, which Lawal has accepted as "the will of God," will be applied as soon as she is through breast-feeding. Around the same time, CNN aired an al-Qaida videotape showing a dog, in excruciating pain, succumbing to poison gas. Meanwhile, the Fourth US Circuit Court of Appeals has upheld the right of the University of North Carolina at Chapel Hill to require this year's 3,500 freshmen to read Approaching the Koran.

After recommending Bernard Lewis on Islam as a healthy alternative, the editorial ends as follows:

> Today, every military regime in the world but one is in a Muslim country. Two-thirds of the world's political prisoners are held in Muslim countries. Eighty percent of executions carried out each year take place in Muslim countries. No Muslim countries save Turkey and Bangladesh are democratic. There is an urgent need in the West to understand why all this is, and universities could have a vital role to play in achieving it. By assigning Sells's book, all that Chapel Hill has managed to do is whitewash

reality in the name of raising awareness. For the likes of an Amina Lawal, this will offer little solace.[91]

A justifiably angry Sells responded, highlighting the ways in which Islam is generalized from particulars and contrasted with a more civilized world. He points out that the title of the *Jerusalem Post* article sets the tone ("What needs to be sanitized: privies and infected areas") and the article is littered with hate speech: "people [are] dehumanized on account of their race, religion, or nationality, are compared to something filthy or to an infection or cancer." The reference to the atrocity in Nigeria is then somehow tied into the essence of Islam and Muslims. Sells, incidentally, parallels this with antisemitism in the Arab world where individual acts (e.g. Sharon's actions in Sabra and Shatila in 1982) are generalized as typical of Jews and Judaism.[92] With reference to the end of the editorial, we might, again, add that there is no mention of the various issues relating to colonialism, western interference, the decline of secular nationalism, the issue of over-population, and arms sales, not to mention localized particularities in Muslim countries. The situation is far less one-dimensional than the editorial suggests, despite its apparent concern "to understand."

Closer still to New Testament studies and Christian origins, and of direct relevance for social sciences in biblical studies, is one of the many recent attacks on the work of Nadia Abu el-Haj who wrote a critique of archaeological practice and its relation to Israeli nationalism.[93] In his highly polemical and academically pointless "review" (it is difficult to find details of the book, easy to find details of the reviewer's opinions), "Hugh Fitzgerald"[94] strays off topic and descends into an anti-Islamic rant, making major generalizations about the Islamic world and "their" lack of concern for the history of others:

> As is well known, in Islam there has been an almost total indifference to the non-Islamic or pre-Islamic world. Many of the artifacts of that world have been destroyed over 1350 years of Muslim conquest and subjugation of Christians, Jews, Zoroastrians, Hindus, Buddhists. In India, the Muslim conquerors destroyed as much of the Buddhist and Hindu heritage as they could, sometimes in order to quarry the stone, sometimes to destroy statuary. The Indian historian K. S. Lal has provided a meticulous list of tens of thousands of identified Hindu temples destroyed by the Muslim invaders, for example.
>
> In Egypt, members of the Muslim Brotherhood even muttered about destroying the Pyramids, but cooler heads prevailed. It was not out of Egyptian nationalism, save among the Copts and a small sliver of the Egyptian elite, nor out of any respect for the pre-Islamic past, but rather the fact that too many Egyptians depend for their livelihood on tourist

dollars, that managed to prevent attacks. Similarly, the tourist attraction of Petra seems safe, precisely because it is a money-maker, not out of some deep conviction that these Roman-era ruins are otherwise of note.

In Iraq, the old Sunni elites, trained by Gertrude Bell and others, did acquire a certain taste for preserving the pre-Islamic artifacts, and that seems to be the one exception – and an exception only among a very small sliver of Iraqi society – to the general indifference to any artifacts except those representing the time of Islam, not that of the pre-Islamic Jahiliyya.[95]

There is no concern for any serious arguments to the contrary. We can simply take the illogic of his own argument: there is no worry that the pyramids and Petra have managed to survive a *very* long time surrounded by Muslims and no worry that the works of classical (and, of course, pagan) philosophy did not, for some reason, undergo systematic burning. Despite this, "Fitzgerald" then contrasts Israeli (and presumably Western?) concerns which are, of course, notably different:

Israeli archeologists have, often with foreign colleagues, discovered Roman coins and mosaic floors and temples, have uncovered Byzantine artifacts, and those of the Islamic conquest, both of the Arab period, and of the period of Ottoman rule. Many of the Islamic artifacts have, in fact, been meticulously and scrupulously catalogued, studied, and preserved – all serious students know about the Islamic Museum in Jerusalem and its exceptional collection.

It is significant that this nasty anti-Muslim rant was published by Campus Watch, a group to which will return in Chapter 5.[96] Campus Watch is an aggressively neo-conservative and ultra-Zionist group of academics which sweats McCarthyism. Or, in its own words, "a project of the Middle East Forum, reviews and critiques Middle East studies in North America with an aim to improving them." The project's main concerns are to counter the supposed pro-Islamic bias in North American universities, more specifically, "analytical failures, the mixing of politics with scholarship [*sic*!], intolerance of alternative views [*sic*!], apologetics [*sic*!], and the abuse of power over students." On its explanatory webpage, the contemporary political context remains prominent: "Middle East studies have a special importance due to its many subjects at the heart of the public debate, such as the war on terror, militant Islam, the Arab-Israeli conflict, Iraq, Saudi Arabia, and others specialists have an extensive but subtle influence on the way North Americans see this range of topics."[97] The emergence of Campus Watch in 2002 is hardly coincidental. It entered the scene with a bang, naming US professors who were critical of US foreign policy and Israeli actions toward Palestine, following in the wake of scaremongering tactics against US professors elsewhere in American politics.[98]

"Fitzgerald" is described as a "noted commentator on the Middle East and Islam" and he is a major Campus Watch contributor. Given the aims of Campus Watch, and the unpleasant agenda of "Fitzgerald," it is no surprise that "Fitzgerald" accuses Abu el-Haj of "shabby or pseudo or nonexistent scholarship" which "disguises a naked political assault." Would it be going too far to suggest that "Fitzgerald" and Campus Watch might try a little self-analysis on such an issue? Whatever, "Fitzgerald" and Campus Watch provide excellent examples of how issues relating to the "war on terror," clashing civilizations, and cultural stereotyping overlap with social-scientific concerns in biblical studies with specific reference to the context of American academia.

"If We Step on an Ant While Walking, We Have Not Purposely Killed It": Some Gruesome Results of Stereotyping and Dehumanizing

> *It is acceptable to report the "collateral damage" by bombing error, the inadvertent and inevitable cost of war, but not the conscious and deliberate destruction of Afghans who will die in silence, invisibly – not by design, but because it doesn't matter, a deeper level of moral depravity; if we step on an ant while walking, we have not purposely killed it.*
>
> Noam Chomsky[99]

> *Still, it was with some surprise that I found myself reacting to THAT photograph — Specialist Lynndie England, aged 21, looking almost wistfully at a naked man on a leash, the end of which she just happened to be holding — with the following thought: "Gosh, what a change to see a WOMAN treating a MAN like a dog in a Muslim country, rather than the other way around!"... I see the snaps of our young Yankee allies taking their low, lonesome revenge at Abu Ghraib — for all the times their fresh-faced, well-meaning comrades have been butchered, blown up, pulled through the streets barely dead by people of the very nationality they gave up their lives to help — and I see, in the very exposure of those photographs, a good part of the reason why we are fighting, and why we are better. At last in Iraq there is a regime under which "torture" is NOT the norm, but something which has even that regime's supporters running around screaming like hairdressers for it to be stopped, right now! Now that's progress...would anyone bar a cretin claim that the wholesale rape of German women by Soviet boys invalidated the Allied victory, or made the Red Army's contribution less cherishable? Soldiers are never saints — unlike we hacks, they never claim to be! – but thank goodness we have them there to protect our sissy ways... God forbid an unrepentant*

Zionist like me should bring up the uncomfortable fact that there are on Earth 22 MUSLIM NATIONS, NOT ONE A DEMOCRACY! as I do all the time on internet talkboards; do that, and you're "just playing on racial stereotypes." But it's 22 NATIONS! – how can it be a coincidence that not ONE of them trusts their people enough to give them the vote?

Julie Burchill[100]

From the moment I knocked on the front door of Daoud Mousa al-Maliki's home in Basra, I knew something had gone terribly wrong in the British Army in southern Iraq... Baha Mousa, Daoud's son, had died from the injuries he received in British custody, a young, decent man whose father was a cop, who did nothing worse than work as a receptionist in a Basra hotel. Then I went to see Kifah Taha, who had been so badly beaten by British troops in the presence of Baha Mousa that he had terrible wounds in the groin. He told me how the soldiers would call their Iraqi prisoners by the names of football stars – Beckham was one name they used – before kicking them around the detention headquarters in Basra. There were stories of Iraqi prisoners being forced to kneel on sharp stones, of being kicked and punched in the groin, the kidneys, the back, shoulders, forced to sit with their heads down lavatory holes... What culture created these young men who treated their civilian prisoners with such contempt, cursing them and - if the documents are accurate - calling them "shit" and treating them like animals? Did it come from Glasgow or Cardiff or London or from some prison - yes, quite a lot of British soldiers are ex-prisoners themselves, former guests of Her Majesty who know all about prison rules and prison abuse. How come the Americans tortured men at Abu Ghraib - officially permitted to do so, as we now know - without realising that they were breaking the rules of ordinary humanity?

Robert Fisk[101]

In 2003, Baha Mousa, a hotel receptionist, was killed in the custody of British troops in Basra while other prisoners were horribly beaten. In 2007, six British soldiers of the then Queen's Lancashire regiment (now the Duke of Lancaster Regiment) pleaded not guilty to charges related to Baha Mousa's death and were acquitted. One soldier, Corporal Donald Payne, admitted inhumane treatment of persons but pleaded not guilty to the manslaughter of Baha Mousa.[102]

Robert Fisk, the British journalist who investigated this story in Basra from the start, spoke of the indignation of Baha Mousa's father, Daoud, at the failure of the British courts martial to convict anyone for murder, calling it "a moving cry for justice from a good man in Iraq who expected British troops to protect his family, not kill his son," before adding the critical question, *What culture created these young men who treated their civilian prisoners with such contempt?*[103] As in the 2007 article, Fisk gave a plausible explanation three years earlier. He even asked why we are surprised at the racism, brutality and sheer callousness aimed toward Arabs. The American soldiers in Abu Ghraib and the British soldiers in Basra "came – as soldiers often come – from towns and cities where race hatred has a home: Tennessee and Lancashire." Fisk broadens out the cultural context of Anglo-American dehumanization and racism in Iraq, showing how Arabs are negatively depicted in film because they are "fair game." As "potential terrorists" and "a lesser breed" of human being, "they must be 'softened up,' 'prepared,' humiliated, beaten, tortured.[104]

It is easy enough to lay the blame on supposedly ignorant soldiers like Lynndie England who for a while become almost synonymous with Abu Ghraib, a generation from deprived backgrounds, "fleeing from dead-end McJobs," as Naomi Klein put it, to get a "strings attached" paid education with the army.[105] It is easy enough to look to the prejudices on social and geographical locations of soldiers. Yet, as Fisk implies, we should note the massive and influential role played by the more privileged classes in the dehumanization of the enemy. Just look at the Burchill quotation at the beginning of this section or just recall any number of those outrageous intellectual generalizations about Arabs and Muslims in this chapter. We can also see the potentially hideous effects of such stark differences and demonizing when pushed to one gruesomely logical extreme in contemporary Anglo-American culture through the handling of the deaths or sufferings of different groups in recent attacks carried out by US and British governments, right up to and including the present "war on terror." Unfortunately, there are a depressingly high number of obvious examples for the dehumanization of the enemy.

For example, let's once again recall the sanctions on Iraq after the first Gulf War reported to have cost the lives of 500,000 children about which Madeleine Albright infamously managed to say that it was a price worth paying.[106] Are "our" lives more valuable than "their" pitiful lives? In this context we should wonder how deep such attitudes ran. Here we can recall the Defence Intelligence Agency documents mentioned above which in 1991 predicted the impact of sanctions. As Thomas Nagy, who has tried to bring these documents to wider attention, put it, "For more than ten years, the United States has deliberately pursued a policy of destroying the water treatment system of Iraq, knowing full well the cost in Iraqi lives... No one can say that the United States didn't know what it was doing."[107] Again, are we dealing with a hierarchy of life value?

More recently in the war in Afghanistan, several commentators have pointed to the secrecy surrounding massacres of thousands of Taliban captives by the US, UK and Northern Alliance in contrast to swift investigations in the deaths of coalition troops by "friendly fire."[108] Or again, we might point to a reluctance to investigate properly the death tolls in Iraq and Afghanistan. Or again, we might point to the high profile media reporting of western victims of terrorism or soldiers killed in the field with the almost bland reporting of a sickening high number of people dying week by week in Iraq, a situation directly relating to US and UK actions. Or yet again, we might point to the largely forgotten people who survive the immediate impact of bombing in (say) Afghanistan and Iraq but consequently suffer or starve due to the destruction of infrastructure. We might follow Gilbert Achcar and ask why there was such widespread official mourning in the European Union for the September 11 victims of mass murder and no comparable concern for the thousands massacred in Srbrenica, Chechnya, Rwanda, or the countless victims of US governmental crimes?[109] And so on, and so on. Are some lives just not worth bothering about? How can this be culturally acceptable?

But we should also be aware of what can happen when a cultural context dehumanizes human beings, or if extraordinary racial contempt becomes too mainstream. Questions concerning the disinterested killing of human beings were addressed by Christopher Browning and his study of a group of middle-aged, largely working class, family men who formed the Reserve Police Battalion 101 in occupied Poland during the Second World War. These men were not particularly frightened individuals worried about the consequences of disobeying orders, they were not particularly suited for the job – they were not keen political sympathizers or known mass killers – and they were not forcibly drafted. Yet 80-90% of the men carried out their job of killing Jews face-to-face. Browning suggests a combination of reasons such as fear of isolation in a tight-knit group stationed among a hostile population, peer pressure, not wanting to leave the "dirty work," along with more ideological factors such as antisemitic propaganda, negative racial stereotypes and distancing and dehumanizing of the "other" in German society.[110]

This should be no surprise. One of the classic problems in the history of warfare is that human beings are not generally automatic killing machines. For human beings to become killers requires some change of social and psychological conditions. Historical, psychological, and social-scientific studies, many of which are employed by Browning, have shown that in warfare and related situations it becomes disturbingly easy for human beings to act in ways that would usually horrify and this change is due to brutalization and other general social circumstances of clear significance for our present purposes, for example, peer pressure, group coherence, propaganda, dehumanization of the other, exaggerated differences between groups and racial stereotyping.[111] The My Lai massacre did not happen because there were a collection of soldiers who were all just evil.

Issues surrounding immediate peer pressure help explain why soldiers have carried out tortures, beatings, humiliations and killings in Afghanistan and Iraq. So, too, does the general context of stereotyping and dehumanizing of Arabs and Muslims by the media and in popular and intellectual culture. We might also add that the ant-like distance and the bureaucratic distancing of the recipients of sanctions and bombings further helps explain why sanctions and bombings are carried out without a second thought. After all, repeated pictures on the front of the newspapers and continual filming on the television news of what happens on the ground would hardly have drummed up support for, say, the recent wars or the sanctions on Iraq. Repeated stereotyping of Arabs and Muslims is much more helpful. Little wonder that there is a price to pay when reporters or ambassadors disobey their calling and highlight suffering and injustices that "we" carry out.

Craig Murray, the former British ambassador in Uzbekistan found this out the hard way. When he dared to criticize the profoundly anti-democratic nature of the Uzbek regime, refusal to distinguish between peaceful Muslims and Muslim terrorists, widespread torture and other human rights abuses, most notoriously the boiling of opponents, the establishment took steps to discredit him.[112] Murray was accused of petty misbehaviour, such as being drunk and disorderly, and threatened with dismissal. It has even been reported that a foreign office source claimed Murray was put under pressure to stop his repeated criticisms of the Karimov regime and that the pressure was partly "exercised on the orders of No 10," which did not take kindly to such criticisms in the buildup to the Iraq war, something Murray himself has also claimed. Murray was also treated for depression which, as a foreign office source is reported as saying, was preceded by "a campaign of systematic undermining."[113] Presumably, concern for human rights and suffering are only significant when the leader (in this case Tony Blair) wants to take a country to war against a chosen country. They certainly do not matter when it comes to "our" allies. If this was widely known, could the case for moral leaders just "doing what they thought was right" really be made?[114] Would not showing the true human disaster in places like Uzbekistan undermine the "war on terror," otherwise, why undermine

Murray? In fact this takes the discussion to another level. This is not dehumanizing, this is systematic ignoring the very existence of human beings. After all, are they really there and do they really suffer and die if we don't look?

The British journalist Robert Fisk has also found out something similar on a couple of occasions. When Fisk reported Saddam's use of mustard gas in the 1980s, a Foreign Office official told Fisk's editor at the *Times* that this was "not helpful" because Saddam was, of course, a British ally then. More recently, in the Kosovo war Fisk had reported that civilian convoys had been hit by NATO after initial NATO denials. More recently still, in the 2003 Iraq war, he incurred the innuendo of the then Defence Secretary Geoff Hoon for his claims that a second marketplace had been bombed in Baghdad, killing over 60 civilians.[115] Denying deaths, it would seem, is of paramount importance rather than preventing them. Why might this be?

In the general context of the current dehumanizing in the "war on terror" at the intellectual level, an important feature that ought to be added is intentionality, or rather a lack of it. As we saw, in the aftermath of September 11, Chomsky caused some controversy when he pointed out the lack of interest in those who suffered as a result of the Clinton administration's bombing of the al-Shifa pharmaceuticals plant in Sudan, a bombing which wiped out masses of supplies in a third world country which could not be readily replaced. In a very reluctant response to Christopher Hitchens on this issue, and a response which is obviously more broadly applicable to the ideas discussed in this chapter, Chomsky points out that "to regard the comparison to September 11 as outrageous is to express extraordinary racist contempt for African victims of a shocking crime."[116] But, crucially, Chomsky additionally stresses the *unintentional* nature of this contempt: people (like Hitchens) do not realize quite what they are saying or, it might be added, just how much they are buying into, supporting and influencing the hideous effects of an emboldened Orientalism.

Concluding Remarks

Obviously, I would not deny the power of the clash of civilizations rhetoric and I would not deny that, for its many, many faults, it does help describe certain people. Tariq Ali's modified "clash of fundamentalisms" or Gilbert Achcar's modified "the clash of barbarisms," are, given the underlying diversity presented in this chapter, particularly apt.[117] Similarly, Said was clearly right when he claimed that the Huntington-style analysis of culture is "fundamentalism, not analysis of culture, which it bears repeating, is made by humankind, not decreed once and for all by an act of divine genesis... The clash of civilizations thesis is presented as if it is inevitable, whereas of course it is imposed upon a world filled with uncertainty and potential as well as discord."[118] But this "fundamentalism" in its various manifestations remains dangerous and held by far too many powerful people in the US and UK, as well as by some particularly violent people who construct "the West" as the Great Satan. Unfortunately, this ideology is profoundly embedded in the Anglo-American media and in Anglo-American academia, including issues directly relating to biblical studies. We now turn to see just how embedded such dangerous rhetoric is in the study of Christian origins.

Chapter 4

Anglo-American Power and Liberal Scholarship: Scholarly Reconstructions of the Social World of Christian Origins

literally everything imputed to the Persian or Muslim...can be applied to "the American"... Who but "the American" denies history and reality in saying unilaterally that these mean nothing to "the Persian"? Now play the following parlor game: find a major Judeo-Christian cultural and social equivalent for the traits that Laingen ascribes to "the Persian." Overriding egoism? Rousseau. Malevolence of reality? Kafka. Omnipotence of God? Old and New Testaments. Lack of causal sense? Beckett. Bazaar mentality? The New York Stock Exchange. Confusion between words and reality? Austin and Searle. But few people would construct a portrait of the essential West using only Christopher Lasch on narcissism, the words of a fundamentalism preacher, Plato's Cratylus, *an advertising jingle or two and (as a case of the West's inability to believe in a stable or beneficial reality) Ovid's* Metamorphoses *laced with choice verses from Leviticus.*

Edward W. Said[1]

In contrast to a trust in the general applicability of models such as honour and shame, both social and cultural anthropology has in light of recent developments abandoned a purely "exotic" view of culture and social life. The ethnocentric "West and the Rest" mentality, most notably challenged by Edward Said's Orientalism no longer holds persuasion in a discipline that gives greater attention to individual diversity within the field.

Louise J. Lawrence[2]

New Testament Scholarship and the Rhetoric of Grand Difference

At the most simple level, this [divine] rage [generated from Mel Gibson's *The Passion of the Christ*] will be directed at whoever our enemy of the moment might be. Given the current American and British invasions of Muslim Afghanistan and Muslim Iraq, as well as a global "war on

> (Muslim) terrorism" by the United States, the target is obvious, all the more so when the most intuitive contrast to one religious tradition will be another: Islam versus Christianity. More than this, the movie invites us to identify as the "natural" targets of (our) divine rage those who perpetrated the unasked-for violence against the innocent victim... The tropes of prejudice are easily transferable: for "Western" audiences, the dark skin, hooked noses, and inscrutable "other-ness" of the Jew of anti-Semitic propaganda (including Gibson's film) signifies the contemporary Arab more easily and directly than it does the contemporary Jew. Few people these days believe such slanders as the claim that Jews control the banks; but very many believe that Arabs, more or less indiscriminately, are terrorists.
>
> William Arnal[3]

In a Discovery documentary about the controversial James Ossuary, showered with a glittering cast of many a fine scholar of Christian origins (and other areas), the narrator takes us on a journey, and not for the first time in the documentary, into "the centre of the Israeli-Palestinian conflict." However, this time, the narrator informs us, "the centre of the Israeli-Palestinian conflict" is "a no-man's-zone outside Jerusalem where suicide bombers and soldiers clash on a daily basis."[4] The imagined edge of civilization is being drawn here. And *imagined* is a doubly right word because why are we being told about suicide bombers in a documentary about the James Ossuary and, more bizarrely, why does the narrator say that suicide bombers and soldiers *clash on a daily basis*? What are we supposed to be imagining here? Is this just an unfortunately bizarre-sounding factual error or are *any* Palestinians who happen to clash with soldiers simply to be categorized as "suicide bombers"?

Or again, we find the narrator exploiting September 11 with the documentary showing no sign of shame in its attempt at emotional manipulation of the audience:

> It would help to know how the Ossuary suddenly appeared. What is its point of origin? Is it a modern forgery executed by cynical men carving on an ancient artefact? Or is it a 2000 year old relic surfacing in a post-9/11 world to remind humanity of a man called James the Just?

What has September 11 got do to with the James Ossuary? Taking the narrator far more seriously than he deserves to be, what is he implying by a Judeo-Christian symbol bursting out of the blue after September 11? This documentary, which is armed to the teeth with *science* to prove that the inscription of the James Ossuary is genuine, then goes and gives us the two options cited. The first option is, presumably, to be discounted given the agenda of the documentary. By the process of elimination the second option could be the right one. At least, no one implies it is not. For all the science, the ultimate origin of the ossuary is mysterious, possibly miraculous, and from "our" great tradition. But, perhaps, it is here for all humanity and here to do something in this post-September 11 world. If the Ossuary is supposed to be miraculous, it has to be high on the list of the Most Disappointing Miracle Ever Recorded.

This is not the first time a documentary presentation of Christian origins has employed images, clichés and stereotypes relating to the "war on terror," the clash of civilizations and so on. One of the most obvious recent examples of this was a Christmas 2002 BBC/Discovery documentary on Mary, which also happened to boast some of New Testament studies' finest scholars.[5] The documentary has a clear distinction between "us" and "them," "west" and "Oriental." This distinction is made in several ways. There is the contrast between the traditional blue-veiled Mary and the scraggily-dressed Mary of the scholarly reconstruction. The traditional Mary is accompanied by serene music; the scholarly Mary has classic music of the Orient. The traditional Mary is accompanied by silent people; the scholarly Mary is accompanied by people speaking in a fast-paced alien tongue with arms often waving. The traditional Mary is accompanied by someone from the present telling us "what I was brought up with..." or "in the traditional Christmas story"; the contrast with the scholarly Mary is immediate, with authorities telling us what things were *really* like.

This documentary also has a participant/observer who is one of "us" and designed to make the contrast quite explicit. Like a ghost, the popular English actor, Sue Johnston, walks down the alleyways, sits on steps, and stands in the desert of ancient Palestine, looking on, usually concerned, at the culturally strange ancient action before her/our very eyes. Johnston, presumably, reacts the way "we" are supposed to react to this culturally strange world. Johnston, for instance, puzzles over what might be different about a young Mary, tentatively concluding, "D'know, I think it's her clothes." Even more ridiculously, a frightened Johnston looks into the small birthing room and at the pain Mary suffers when giving birth. When it is over, Johnston is relieved, as we should be, and walks off down a dark ancient Palestinian alley.

As with so many contemporary contrasts between "us" and "them" Semitic stereotypes are everywhere in this scholarly reconstruction of Mary and her world. There is the emphasis on sex, family, and male dominance, so typical of Orientalist scholarship.[6] In a reconstruction of Mary's pregnancy, on the occasion of her being pregnant out of wedlock and not by Joseph, there is dramatic, fast-paced music with a rotten-toothed figure, screaming and raging, frightening the poor women of the household. What is interesting about the Semitic stereotypes is that they stand in contrast to the heroes of our story, Mary, Jesus and, to a lesser extent, Joseph. And it ought to be pointed out that these Semitic stereotypes immediately recall contemporary Arab/Muslim stereotypes rather than Jewish: the headdresses, the rotten teeth, the wild hand movements, and the fast-paced alien language remains common in Western cultural portrayals of Arabs and Muslims since the 1970s, as Said pointed out long ago.[7] So, for all the good intentions of the documentary, we have to ask, why do we have so many stereotypical images of those funny Arabs? Why now? It is difficult to avoid the conclusion that, as Arnal also points out, such stereotypes occur now in popular culture precisely because the Middle East is the object of so much scrutiny and interest in Anglo-American culture and politics. As Arnal puts it with reference to the Semitic caricatures in Mel Gibson's *Passion of the Christ*, "'other-ness' of the Jew of anti-Semitic propaganda...signifies the contemporary Arab more easily and directly than it does the contemporary Jew. Few people these days believe such slanders as the claim that Jews control the banks; but very many believe that Arabs, more or less indiscriminately, are terrorists."[8]

Yet the contrasts show that the documentary cannot quite go so far as to make our heroes totally like "them." The adult Mary, in direct contrast to all other heavily covered women, lacks headwear, most notably when she is in a crowd. Similarly, in many scenes the adult Jesus conspicuously does not have a headdress or turban, in direct contrast to all of those with whom he eats and meets. He has a fine head of curly hair and he is either immaculately clean-shaven or has an immaculately trimmed beard, quite unlike those surrounding him. To make him look western-style mysterious-but-wise the only time he gets headwear is a Jedi Knight-style gown and hood, again in direct contrast to the turbans and headdresses. In Chapter 6, I will argue that Jesus is put in a context constructed by scholars as "Jewish" before being made to be different from that "Jewish" context, despite all the scholarly emphasis on Jesus" "Jewishness." I refer to this as a "Jewish...but not *that* Jewish" Jesus. The Jesus and Mary of this documentary may accordingly be called "Oriental...but not *that* Oriental."

A similar thing also happens to Joseph but Joseph has to be rescued from his Oriental context through common "western" decency, namely by becoming an ideal loving and caring husband. When Joseph is to be engaged to the child Mary, he is a seedy-looking older man. When Mary moves into Joseph's home, it is dark, shadowy and filled with formidable-looking individuals, emphasized by the narrators if we did not get the point. Joseph begins his married life as a distant figure, paying no attention to poor Mary who does the housework and looks on melancholically. But then things change. When it is acknowledged that things might have been difficult at first, Johnston then tells us that, based on nothing but a romantic imagination, "you get the impression that he was a good father," "it's easy to imagine that over the years a bond grew between them," and even "I'd like to think that eventually she grew to love him." Lo and behold, from now on Joseph is no longer the filthy misogynist paedophile but a pleasant-looking, kindly man.

This should already warn us that we are going to find stark generalizing statements on Islam and/or Arabs, of the type we saw in the previous chapter, creeping into New Testament studies. The internet has brought many things but ranking up there with its most unusual creations are, as we have seen, the bibliobloggers, professionals and amateurs blogging on anything relating to biblical studies. As we also saw, one advantage of such people blogging is that we get some very clear political views of people in New Testament studies coming through. For example, New Testament scholar Michael Bird claims, "I don't wish to invoke animosity against Muslims," followed by the inevitable "but," "but the fact is many Muslims commit acts that are despicable and do not happen in Western countries"![9]

For present purposes, one blog is of particular importance, namely, Loren Rosson's informative, liberal, secularized (in the world of blogging on the Bible this is significant), and sometimes thoughtful blog, *The Busybody*. Rosson is, effectively, the unofficial voice of the Context Group on the internet. Rosson was a student of Context Group stalwart, Richard Rohrbaugh, and regularly posts, praising and discussing the work and heroes of the Context Group, applying their theoretical models to various New Testament passages, and even criticizing those whom some of the Context Group like to criticize (e.g. J. D. Crossan). Rosson also writes on the application of the honour and shame model to New Testament texts with brutal regularity.

In the context of a forum (in this instance the blog) whereby anything is up for discussion, honour and shame as applied to Islam, Arabs and/or the Middle East right up to the present can dramatically rise to the surface. Rosson has on several occasions applied honour and shame to things Muslim and/or Arab and it highlights some important trends relating to the clash of civilizations and contemporary stereotyping about Islam. On a basic level he can talk in spectacularly general terms of "an honor-shame culture like [contemporary] Asia or the [contemporary] Middle-East," massive areas where "insults are fine and frequent arts; belligerence a commendable show of machismo; public degradation a staple of life; two-faced attacks (and backhanded compliments) prestigious displays of wit; and "treating others as if they are invisible" a proper way of snubbing inferiors and equals."[10] We will see that huge generalizations about "Islam" and "the Arab world" likewise bubble under the surface, and sometimes burst out way above the surface, of certain Context Group rhetoric. With the popularizing views of Rosson such rhetoric roars away untamed.

For example, Rosson believes that after the Crusades, Islam became "over-sensitive, defensive, intolerant, sterile – attitudes that grew steadily worse as world-wide evolution continued," modernism "became alien." This "stagnation" was due to "the *jihad* revival" which was "in reaction to the success of the First Crusade (1099)." There is, apparently, "a great irony" in that "the Muslim world" reacquired "the holy lands at the expense of its cultural sophistication, while Christendom, as it relinquished those lands, was able to take from abroad and propel itself into the Renaissance."[11] It is difficult to respond to this because we are not told much about Islamic "stagnation"[12] and its unsophisticated culture, not to mention what we do with the problematic subjective nature of such judgments. There is some mention of Islam's great intellectual tradition *prior* to the crusades but nothing about what came after. It is simply assumed that this generalization holds for a hugely diverse range of people across a range of territories with a massive range of cultural pursuits.

More significantly, Rosson makes close links between anthropological models, Islam and the contemporary rhetoric of clashing civilizations. Rosson notes that the film *300*, based on 300 Spartans fighting against the odds against the hordes of Persian soldiers led by Xerxes, caused some upset in Iran. Rosson tells us never to "underestimate the power of humiliation in shame-based cultures and Iran feels globally shamed." After citing an Iranian, Adadeh Moaveni, Rosson comments that "we" have an easier time laughing off "egregious drivel" than people like Moaveni because "nonsense" is taken "quite seriously in honor-shame societies."

First, notice the "we" contrast. And speaking of *we*, *we* are not told how Iranian global shame is measured, or indeed any evidence of it. We are not told how the vague and highly subjective category "nonsense" is to be defined. After all, one person's nonsense is another person's all. For instance, we could reasonably say that religious belief seems quite nonsensical to many people in the US and UK and there are many who cannot understand why people take such offence when a given religion is seemingly attacked. At the same time, as this already implies, religious belief is central to the lives of many people in the US and UK. So where does the nonsense lie? To take another example: if someone burned the American, British or English flag somewhere in the US, UK, or England, it would probably not be too difficult to find individuals who would shrug their shoulders in indifference or perhaps think it was a waste of energy and lighter fuel. Such individuals might be puzzled as to why emotions run so high over the issue of burning cloth. But, for many, flag-burning is, apparently, a big emotive issue. So, again, where does the nonsense lie?

In a post "The Evolution of Religious Tolerance," Rosson looks at the recent issue of the Danish cartoons of Mohammed.[13] He acknowledges, as he has done elsewhere, that there is nothing inherently good or bad in the Qur'an but asks "why hasn"t Islam done what other faiths have largely done" in moving away from intolerance? Rosson adds that religious intolerance "is more at home in honor-shame cultures than innocence-guilt cultures," and that "the code of honor-shame is largely about intolerance: not tolerating those who happen to offend you, regardless of perhaps their best intentions, irrespective of their actual innocence."

Apparently, religious tolerance "began in Europe" when it was "propelled…out of its medieval and largely honor-shame outlook." In the sixteenth and seventeenth centuries, "Christian Europe became more globalized and cosmopolitan" thereby encouraging tolerance. Quoting Robert Wright, "Modern global capitalism has its faults, but religious intolerance isn't one of them." Rosson adds that "the honor-shame outlook in general just isn't compatible with developments in Europe at this time" and was the "code of the feudal past" before Protestants began introducing "more cosmopolitan" dimensions into their theology. This "paved the way to a world in which people were expected to treat others in 'just' terms more than 'honorable' ones." Consequently, "a more tolerant morality evolved."[14]

There are serious difficulties with such a view (and note how it reflects a Sam Harris-style concept of moral evolution). To characterize religious tolerance in such terms faces the problems of well-known intolerant examples from Protestantism. I will cite just a few. John Calvin made sure Michael Servetus paid for his heresy by having him burnt to death. Martin Luther's views concerning Jews are hardly a useful template for religious tolerance. These cannot be dismissed as individual, isolated examples or hangovers from a bygone era. Post-Luther Protestantism has had a profoundly unpleasant strand of antisemitism, culminating in Nazi Christians, including those who were New Testament scholars, most infamously Walter Grundmann, K. G. Kuhn, and Gerhard Kittel. Or, to take a different example, the European Wars of Religion are called so for good reason.

More recently, the violent history in Northern Ireland has been heavily identified with profound religious intolerance and a Glasgow Celtic versus Glasgow Rangers football/soccer match could match many for religious intolerance, with the chants of Rangers supporters, including "fuck the Pope" and "Fenian bastards," currently being monitored as I write.[15] For religious intolerance in the US we could now cite the American Christian right. The Reverend Jerry Vines, pastor of First Baptist Church in Jacksonville, and a past president of the Southern Baptist Convention, called Muhammad a "demon-possessed paedophile," which is not the kind of allegation that is designed for winning awards in inter-religious harmony.[16] The Christian right, not known for their love of Islam, have been intimately involved with the Reagan and Bush Jr administrations, both of which are good representatives of modern global capitalism, and their religious form of capitalism has deep roots in seventeenth-century strands of Puritan thought.[17]

On the "Islamic side" of things there are significant examples of religious tolerance. Hugh Goddard not only shows how examples of Muslim intolerance (e.g. the Rushdie affair, reaction to September 11) have been frequently overblown and misrepresented but, with reference to medieval Islam, we can also recall the hardly uncontroversial comments cited in response to Will Cummins, "tolerance usually extended to Christians and Jews in the early Islamic empire was in marked contrast to the treatment which Jews generally received in the medieval Christian world."[18] We might also add the problem of using the classification "Islam" or "Muslim": such a label covers a massive range of people over a range of geopolitical areas. Amartya Sen has attempted to counter such grand generalizations about Islam (and other "non-Western" identities), pointing out that we can find examples of Muslim religious tolerance in figures such as the Great Mughal emperor Akbar who, at the turn of the sixteenth century, codified minority rights, including religious tolerance.[19] Rosson's view also ignores the interactions with imperialism in areas of high Muslim population, repeatedly mentioned in this book.

We can give a specific example that shows the serious problems with the kinds of massively generalizing arguments used by Rosson. Oddbjørn Leirvik points to the shift in Muslim-Christian relations in twentieth-century Muslim writers. During the 1950s, one such figure, Khalid, was writing about morality, social justice and democracy, and including arguments from an inter-religious perspective. Muhammad and Christ were seen "together on the road," two compatible religious figures for two compatible religions in the modern state. Leirvik suggests that Khalid's concern transcended the vision of a moral unity between Muslims and Christians in Egypt, but also included nation-transcending, universalistic visions. By 1981, Khalid was no longer writing about shared ethical values between Muslims and Christians and instead was writing about Islam as an all-compassing system and the future for human progress. One of the central reasons for this shift was the broader sociopolitical shift from nationalism and the importance of citizenship to the emergence of "pan-Islamic" responses in Egypt and beyond.[20] Clearly, the shift away from a more tolerant and inclusive worldview has more to do with wide-ranging religious, social and political shifts in Egypt and the Middle East in the mid- to late-*twentieth century* and little to do with the unsubstantiated generalizations provided by Rosson.

In many ways, Rosson's questioning feeds into, and assumes, that often asked post-September 11 question, in one sense re-launched by George W. Bush, "Why do they hate us?"[21] In fact issues of honour and shame have been used by some of the aggressive neo-conservative right in the US to describe the issues at the heart of the war on terror and answer why "they" hate "us."[22] Such views effectively ignore, or do not discuss in any detail, the serious impact of US foreign policy, such as the propping-up and support of Saddam, the bombing of Iraq, the destructive sanctions against Iraq, the unflinching support for Israel over against the Palestinians, the more specific context of Saudi Arabia and Wahhabism, the support of numerous oppressive regimes which have oppressed Muslims and so on and so on. As we saw, even bin Laden and his associates have used such concrete situations as a recruiting sergeant. Rosson's view also ignores the role of urbanization and slum-dwelling in Islamic countries, mixed in with the stark economic shifts brought about in oil economies. And then there is also the issue of agency, not to mention a whole range of regional, ethnic, cultural and other such differences in Iraq, Afghanistan, Saudi Arabia, Palestine, and elsewhere (see the previous chapter).[23]

More generally, on the issue of honour and shame, such related sentiments are found in public declarations in the US and UK. In a recent talk marking the twenty-fifth anniversary of the Falklands War, Margaret Thatcher said, in a radio message on the British Forces Broadcasting Service, that the war, where nearly 1000 people died, saw that "Britain's honour and interests prevailed."[24] Well that's ok then. In post-Vietnam America, Reagan could speak of America standing tall again after the days of weakness by inflicting a crushing defeat on...Grenada, hardly the biggest dog in the yard.[25] Issues echoing honour and shame are easily found on the American "side" in the "war on terror." Perhaps George W. Bush's famous comments that Saddam "tried to kill my dad" fit into the honour-shame context best. Of course, there is not a chance that this was a remotely significant reason for re-invading Iraq – for what it is worth, Bush Jr explicitly denied this too – but the fact that the media and political figures could pose questions and discuss issues relating to "vendettas," "grudges" and the like shows how issues echoing honour and shame can be found on "our" side.[26] The main and blindingly obvious reasons why it is difficult to see issues of honour and shame as having a serious role in US actions in Afghanistan and Iraq are largely related to arguments involving the broader concerns of long, medium and short term geopolitical and economic interests of American capitalism.[27] If we concede this, then it is worth thinking the same kind of way when thinking about Muslim and Arab reactions. In fact, the various international, regional and cultural differences in various contexts where Muslims and Arabs are present renders the honour and shame approach so banal as to be largely meaningless in terms of understanding present politico-religious tradition.

The above suggestions are important for present purposes because they show that the use of anthropology in the study of Christian origins has potentially intimate links with the contemporary us-them rhetoric associated with the clash of civilizations rhetoric, the present "war on terror" and the outrageous generalizations about Muslims and Arabs. Rosson may well agree with the sentiments of my argument but, to the best of my knowledge, it does not come through on his biblioblog. All we find is the grand theory of honour-shame, honour-shame, honour-shame.

Anthropology in the Study of the New Testament and Christian Origins

> *In the last forty years or so a branch of anthropology has developed devoted to analysing the culture of the Mediterranean... The principal result of this research has been the discovery of a number of features typifying Mediterranean culture from Spain in the west to Iraq in the east.*
>
> P. F. Esler[28]

> *In view of the concern to avoid objectification of individuals studied, how comfortable would a contemporary publisher in anthropology be to publish a [1958] book [by E. Banfield] entitled* The Moral Basis of a Backward Society?
>
> Louise J. Lawrence[29]

> *The Oriental world is presented as static, and incapable of any change. Biblical scholars often unconsciously replicate this notion that the non-Western nations lack vitality and creativity, living in conditions, categories, and with customs that have barely changed since biblical times...The core cultural values such as honor/shame and pollution/purity of which Osiek speaks are static, regardless of the lapse of time. The possibility of development and change are denied.*
>
> R. S. Sugirtharajah[30]

> *In the United States, [anti-Arab racism] is really the last legitimate form of racism. You don't have to try to cover it up. You may be racist toward other groups, but you have to pretend you aren't. In the case of anti-Arab racism, there's no pretense required... Distinguished Harvard professors produce statements that you would regard as hideously racist if they were aimed at any other target – Jews: impossible; Blacks, Italians, any of them: unacceptable but if you say them about Arabs, it's fine.*
>
> Noam Chomsky[31]

Criticisms of some members of the Context Group for using generalizing anthropology are hardly new and the validity of modelling and generalizing continues to be debated in detail.[32] That is not what I want to focus on here and even though some of those discussed below have got some things very wrong this does not necessarily undermine generalizing and modelling in New Testament studies and Christian origins as a methodological approach, even if more caution ought to be encouraged. What I particularly want to do is to question the morally dubious stereotyping of peoples, particularly the stereotyping which relates to the neo-Orientalism described in the previous chapter, and why we are seeing certain stereotypes at this point in the history of New Testament and Christian origins scholarship.[33]

Let's begin by looking at the systematic use of the "other" in contemporary scholarship and how it reflects contemporary attitudes to "others." Compare the following generalizations about "Mediterraneans" given by Bruce Malina, arguably still the central figure of the Context Group:

> Because one is to focus entirely on the needs of others, one begins to neglect one's own needs, and thus stifles normal individual psychological development... But persons have feelings, especially of hurt, and they are quick to learn to repress and deny those feelings. Mediterraneans... learn to lose the ability to sympathize with the pain of others and are quite willing to abuse others physically, emotionally and spiritually. They abuse those in their group "for their own good," for example, their children, spouses and elderly relatives; and they abuse those not of their group simply to underscore their own social boundaries... This

> sort of emotional stifling and constant attention to the cues of others leads to blocking one's own growth and development in the mental, emotional and spiritual aspects of one's personhood.[34]

This is a stunningly judgmental generalization about peoples, covering vast geographical and cultural areas, and which smacks of old-fashioned imperialistic anthropology and the Orientalist scholarship famously demolished by Said. No amount of resorting to "heuristic value" could ever justify such unfortunate judgments. Moreover, some of the implications for the contemporary world are pointed out by Justin Meggitt when critiquing Malina on this very issue: "Such comments would be sufficiently disturbing if they only concerned the long dead inhabitants of the first century but they are all the more so when it is realised that, by virtue of his method, Malina is also making them, however unintentionally, about *contemporary* inhabitants of the Mediterranean as well."[35] With reference to another book by Malina, but with obvious relevance to the case in hand, Markus Bockmuehl points out that "All the while, the cultural stereotypes merrily accumulate to an extent that would be unthinkable if the object were contemporary 'African' or 'native American' people groups."[36] Let's try something similar:

> Jews neglect their own needs.
>
> Jews have stifled normal individual psychological development.
>
> Jews repress feelings of hurt.
>
> Jews abuse children, spouses and the elderly "for their own good."
>
> Jews abuse others physically, emotionally, and spiritually.
>
> Jews have blocked mental, emotional and spiritual growth.

Though not the kind of "culture area" that concerns anthropological approaches to the ancient Mediterranean, this replacement ought to make many contemporary readers profoundly uncomfortable, or at least I would hope so, and it is unthinkable that this sort of racist language could find its way into the mainstream of academic studies today. Yet why can such comments about "Mediterraneans" be found in such a prominent work in New Testament and Christian origins studies?

The answer, I suspect, is when we look closely at the sorts of peoples these "Mediterraneans" might include, notably "Arabs" and "Middle Easterners," and when we recall the Orientalist tradition in Western scholarship. For example, a noticeable feature of certain works from the Context Group relating to Said's critique is the overemphasis on family and "the Arab." As Said pointed out, "Almost without exception, every contemporary work of Orientalist scholarship (especially in the social sciences) has a great deal to say about the family, its male-dominated structure, its all-pervasive influence in the society...what is really left to the Arab after all is said and done is an undifferentiated sexual drive."[37] There is little doubt that gender and family have played a central role in the social reconstructions of certain members of the Context Group using cultural anthropology.[38] Indeed, the sexual drive is important for Malina's "Mediterranean." For example he can write,

> Mediterraneans have traditionally believed that a male could not possibly suppress the strong urges that surely take possession of him every time he is alone with a pre-menopausal woman... The extreme Mediterranean emphasis on the human genitals...on sexual transgression and on the male's uncertainty of his maleness... I wish to note that focus on legitimate cohabitation and the constant threat of sexual transgression fail to create a definite self-image... Young people grow up believing that were it not for the segregation of the sexes and the vengeance that would surely be meted out on the young man if caught in a sex offence, all the prohibitions hammered into him would be unable to inhibit him from having intercourse with the first woman he encountered. Young men come to consider their own sex drive so strong that only the physical impossibility of sexual access to the women of his social circle...prevents them from satisfying their urges... Girls are brought up to believe that once they might find themselves alone with a male, they would be unable to resist his advances.[39]

Malina is careful to refer to the level of belief but the centrality of sexual drive is clear enough. This is doubly significant given that generalizations about "the Mediterranean" drift easily into generalizations about "the Arab (world)" or "the Middle East(ern)." For example, Malina argues that kinship is a "primary and focal" institution in the Mediterranean world. To show this Malina turns to a 1959 book by Edward Hall (as he does for other sexual generalizations) and his comments on revenge of the brothers as a price for seeing a woman without family permission in the *contemporary* Middle East and Arab world, a point to which we will return, and contrasted with America and Europe, another point to which we will return:

> An *American* these days will not normally consider the revenge of the brothers as a price for seeing a woman without her family's permission, nor will it cross his mind that she might lose her life if she chooses to be intimate with him... Death of the woman and revenge on the man are within the expected range of behavior in the less *Europeanized* parts of *the Arab world*... In *the Middle East* the family is important because families are tied together in a functional interlocking complex [my italics].[40]

Similar concerns with the Middle East/Arab and family are echoed in the works of other members of the Context Group and in related scholarship. Richard Rohrbaugh informs us that "Family honour determines everything...aspersions cast on lineage, that is on family honour, are the most serious insults the *Middle East* has to offer" [my italics].[41] The work of Carolyn Osiek and David Balch focused directly on families in "the New Testament world" and is much more carefully qualified with statements on the problems of using more recent evidence to illuminate the Mediterranean. They note, for instance, the various waves of migration (particularly Arab and Turk) over the past 2000 years. Yet there remain the usual close connections between a male-dominated family structure, sex, and Arabs. Those "who would maintain a common cultural heritage in Mediterranean societies" believe that "the fundamental values of these societies revolve around honor and shame especially as a way of structuring social relationships through sex and gender roles." Or again, "The surest way for a male to dishonour an individual male or family is to seduce or rape its women." Consequently, boys were socialized "to preserve the family property, protect their women, and beget sons." Of male members of the household, "Aggressiveness, virility, sexual prowess, and production of sons are important components." There is also the notable contrast with "modern Western stereotypes," in this case "women were thought in antiquity to have less ability to control their sex drive than men."[42] The endnote adds the important *contemporary* Middle Eastern connection, something we will see again with Osiek and Balch: "As is still thought in the Middle East and traditional Mediterranean societies today, women are thought to be unable to resist men's sexual advances, and must therefore be protected from them."[43]

A tendency toward merging, overlapping or blurring of the Mediterranean and the Middle East (or "the Arab"), including the *contemporary* Middle East, should now be clear from some of the above examples. Such overlapping, including mention of the *contemporary* Middle East, or simply mention of the Middle East as the culture area, is found elsewhere among the Context Group and related scholarship. In an introductory article on "kinship," K. C. Hanson informs readers that "contemporary Middle Eastern cultures...have many parallels to ancient Israelite and Judean practices" and he regularly refers to the significance of the Middle East.[44] According to Osiek and Balch, "One of the closest and most conflicted relationships in Mediterranean culture is that of mother and son..." The endnote adds, "One of the authors of the present volume, visiting an Arab family in the Middle East, witnessed a 16-year-old boy sit unashamedly – and rather awkwardly – on his mother's lap for a family photo."[45]

Some of the generalizations are milder and more aware than others in their dealings with Arabs and the Middle East, some are not *necessarily* inaccurate as generalizations, and no doubt in some or most cases a quest for knowledge is predominantly in mind. Yet, for present purposes, there is something crucial about the overlapping of *the Mediterranean* and *the Middle East* given that leading Context Group figure Philip Esler describes the cultural area of the Mediterranean as stretching "from Spain in the west to Iraq in the east,"[46] a designation that covers a massive amount of area *not* typically designated as "the Middle East." So why the big stress on the Middle East? Is it simply because Jesus lived in ancient Palestine? Then again, certainly not all the New Testament story takes place in the Middle East and certainly some New Testament documents, perhaps including more than one gospel, were not written in the Middle East. And why was this stress on the Middle East not so prominent before the 1980s? As ever, one of the primary reasons for highlighting these connections between anthropology and the (contemporary) Middle East/Arabs is to show how Arabs and the Middle East are a prominent emphasis in contemporary scholarship *now* and how anthropology in New Testament studies emerged at the same time as "the Arab" and "the Middle East" became culturally and politically significant in a major way since the 1970s. There should be little doubt that this context helps explain the major emphasis on the Middle East in contemporary New Testament and Christian origins scholarship.

Yet, on the other hand, these brief illustrations, combined with the results of the previous chapter, should already suggest that certain work from the Context Group and related scholarship stand firmly in the Orientalist tradition as critiqued by Said. As intellectually and morally dubious as some of these generalizations about "the Mediterranean," "the Arab world" and "the Middle East" are, in light of wider events of the past 40 years that have been discussed in this book a more sinister politicized edge to these generalizations emerges. Malina, for instance, throws up a stereotype that has become a modern classic, the hostage-taker: "since in *Mediterranean* perspective all Americans form an undifferentiated ethnic ego mass, it would be impossible for a *Middle Easterner* to view the kidnaping of a single American as a random act...any group member equally well represents the whole group [my italics]."[47] Though John Pilch warns readers of "mistaken American assessments of contemporary Middle Eastern personalities," he does claim when talking of "Mediterranean core cultural values of honor and shame" (and as if Said never happened) that "suppressed behavior, however, can burst out unexpectedly and uncontrollably, a common occurrence in Middle-eastern cultures."[48] Beware of the Arab!

As is already implicit in much of what we have seen, the contrast with "the West," "North America," and/or "Northern Europe" is also important. Malina comments on Hall's ideas, suggesting that to understand familism better and to develop ways of reading "Mediterranean communications" we can make contrasts with "the US central value of economic success." By way of further contrast, he adds, "For Americans and a growing number of northern Europeans, the main social institution is economics."[49] Elsewhere, Rohrbaugh shifts from the typical stark contrast of "American" and "Mediterranean"/"Middle East" to something more specified: "The Private self is an issue only for Westerners... Westerners require an account of Jesus' private self...it is this very private self that *Middle Easterners* [my italics] do not consider central, do not reveal, indeed, do not even admit to having in public."[50] These are not the only ones fond of such contrasts of course.

Like "Americans" versus "Mediterraneans," the contrast between "Westerners" and "Middle Easterners" is found regularly throughout Richard Rohrbaugh's work and, again, this involves the telling merger of imagined anthropological and geographical areas – "the Mediterranean" and "the Middle East" – as the following example shows, typical of his essay as a whole: "Luke [in Lk. 4:22] has drawn us into a *Mediterranean* melodrama that would have had every *Middle Eastern* reader clinging to the edge of the seat [my italics]."[51] According to Jerome Neyrey, another prominent member of the Context Group, "If Euro-Americans cannot understand *the modern inhabitants of the Middle East* [my italics], all the more should the peoples from these same regions in the Fourth Gospel present severe problems for understanding." Naturally, the "more sensitive, accurate interpretation" involves the "pivotal values" of honour and shame and that involves the old Orientalist themes of family and origins.[52]

According to Esler, "Foreign visitors who imagine that Arab women, at least where there has been little Western influence, might share the enthusiasm of Northern European or US mothers for proudly showing off their babies would be making a fundamental cultural error. They would be guilty of unfortunate ethnocentrism."[53] But we really have to ask ourselves, are these hypothetical foreign visitors the only ones guilty of unfortunate ethnocentrism? The generalizations and the contrasts, such as those we have seen, may seem fairly bland (though admittedly dubious) and antiquated but the repeated stress on "America," "the West" and so on, once again highlight how the interests in anthropological studies of Christian origins coincide with pronounced US/Anglo-American interests in Arabs and the Middle East in the 1970s and how "they" differ from Americans and the "West."

The following example – and note the typical shift from "the Mediterranean" to the *contemporary* Middle East – highlights this well: it is a classic Context Group tabulation by Rohrbaugh in a 2002 article with a title that could easily be counter-read, "Ethnocentrism and Historical Questions about Jesus." The following piece of classic Orientalism is not a million miles away from the listings given by people such as Sir John Keegan which we saw in the previous chapter:

> Individualist Cultures
>
> They tend to attribute actions to internal causes and to personal choices in ways that collectivists do not. They focus on personal rights, needs, and abilities. They are relentless in seeking cognitive consistency. Individualists attribute motives to internal needs and aspirations...etc. etc. This sort of individualism, however, has been rare in world culture. It is nearly absent in *the Middle East today* [my italics] and almost certainly was in antiquity as well.
>
> Collectivist Cultures
>
> Persons are defined by the groups to which they belong and do not understand themselves as having a separate identity. They are motivated by group norms rather than individual needs or aspirations, and strenuously avoid articulating personal goals or giving them priority over the goals of the group...etc. etc....the individualism-versus-collectivism distinction is a fundamental challenge to the universal applicability of Western psychological understandings.[54]

There is the ever present overarching problem of using the contemporary "Middle East" (whatever that is supposed to mean) to describe the geographical areas of Christian origins millennia earlier but there is, I think, an even more serious problem in generalizing about the contemporary Middle East, namely the striking similarities with the views of Huntington's *Clash of Civilizations*. This, it should be added, suggests just how ideologically relevant Rohrbaugh's claims are. Note Huntington's reformulation in the mid-1990s of the individualist West over the collective, unified mass that is the *Muslim* other:

> *Individualism*. Many of the above features of Western civilization contributed to the emergence of a sense of individualism and a tradition of individual rights and liberties unique among civilized societies.

> Individualism remains a distinguishing mark of the West among twentieth-century civilizations...the dominance of individualism in the West compared to the prevalence of collectivism elsewhere...the promotion of human rights and democracy also assumed a prominent role in the foreign policies of European states [!] and in the criteria used by the Western-controlled international economic institutions for loans and grants to developing countries [!]... Almost all non-Western civilizations were resistant to this pressure from the West... The greatest resistance to Western democratization efforts, however, came from Islam and Asia... While Asians became increasingly assertive as a result of economic development, Muslims in massive numbers were simultaneously turning toward Islam as a source of identity, meaning, stability, legitimacy, development, power, and hope... God, or rather Allah, has made His revenge most persuasive and fulfilling in the *ummah*, the community of Islam.[55]

The fact, as Chomsky has repeatedly shown, with masses of evidence, that democratization and human rights have been the exact opposite of most European and US foreign policy objectives is significant because clashing civilizations theory conveniently covers this up and plays into the hands of Anglo-American power and its designs on those parts of the world, particularly the Middle East, where Muslims just happen to be.

Given that one function of this book is to look at how ideology keeps certain types of scholarship buoyant, it is also important to note that there is something morally disturbing about these generalizations. Clearly Rohrbaugh has a less aggressive stance on the rights and wrongs of different cultures than proponents of the clash-thesis but if we remove the moral judgment for one moment, the same basic, structural contrast remains. In the major tabular quotation from Rohrbaugh above, notice the italicized reference to the Middle East *today* and that this is contrasted with "Westerners." The claims about "personal rights" and how they are, effectively, absent from *the Middle East today* is disturbing (and, incidentally, how does Rohrbaugh know this?), particularly in the light of well-publicized human rights abuses (based on similar assumptions – see below) in the Middle East that had happened by the time Rohrbaugh was writing his 2002 article and, more famously, since Rohrbaugh wrote. Worryingly, Rohrbaugh republished this (and several other) essays in 2007.[56] Comparing the two versions we can see that some changes were made to Rohrbaugh's article, words like "simply" added to "do not." Unfortunately, the editing of Rohrbaugh's article did not stretch too far beyond style and Rohrbaugh's dubious stereotyping of Middle Eastern culture was not deemed sufficiently problematic to be changed.

As ever, it is worth pointing out that the rhetoric concerning the Middle East, apparently being close to a "personal rights" free zone, is not far removed from some of the justifications of human rights abuses coming from Anglo-American thought. For example, we will shortly see some of the alleged impact dubious generalizing has had on elite figures in Washington and the thinking behind Abu Ghraib but we might add other general comments. The problems of imposing views of individual rights over what "they" are really like are particularly acute in war and, more sensationally, in the recent "war on terror." The indiscriminate bombing, torture and killing in war effectively has to function with a collective, dehumanized "them," something also seen in Guantánamo or the death of Baha Mousa in Basra (see previous chapter). Of course, I am not accusing Rohrbaugh of holding any of the gruesome sentiments of certain media hacks or commentators or that he personally believes that *human rights* issues are not a concern in the Middle East. But given his privileged status as a liberal academic who spends a serious amount of time thinking about such issues then more political and cultural awareness is required when generalizing about Arabs and the Middle East, especially when generalizing about the contemporary Middle East and individual rights. Recall the warning of Amartya Sen, "Cultivated theory can bolster uncomplicated bigotry."[57]

If economics has been one big feature of contemporary clash of civilizations rhetoric then the other big rhetorical feature is surely democracy, or lack of it, famously noted by Said as a major feature of traditional Orientalist scholarship. Interestingly enough this is another feature that turns up in the work of Malina in another contrast between *contemporary* Arabs and Western *civilization* where it is explicitly tied in with politics. This time the issue is personal causality and Malina cites the notorious book by Raphael Patai with the ominous title, *The Arab Mind* (originally published in 1976), which in turn is citing a 1959 book by Hans Tütsch. The following has more than a hint of racial stereotyping:

> personalization of problems goes so far in the Arab countries that even material, technical difficulties accompanying the adoption of elements of Western civilization are considered as resulting from human malevolence and felt to be a *humiliation*... Where the Arab encounters an obstacle he imagines that an enemy is hidden. Proud peoples with a weak "ego structure" tend to interpret difficulties on their life path as personal humiliations and get entangled in *endless lawsuits* or throw themselves into the arms of *extremist political movements. A defeat in elections*, a risk that every politician must face in a democracy, appears to be such a humiliation that an Arab can thereby be induced without

> further ceremony to take up arms against the victor and the legal government [italics original].[58]

Malina not only accepts this unfortunate and, frankly, absurd analysis (in contrast to Malina, even the sympathetic Patai conceded that it was "somewhat exaggerated") but he alarmingly claims that what Tütsch "says of Arabs holds for village Mediterraneans in general," adding that "the Mediterranean feels enemies and humiliations where Americans make allowances for material, objective and, in any event, impersonal difficulties."[59] We have already seen how the second use of the contemporary "Arabs" by Malina is seriously problematic in terms of politics and history by ignoring all the complex local histories, the history of democracy in the Middle East, and engagements with imperialism from "Western civilization" which have explicitly hampered democracy in the Middle East (and Mediterranean). In this instance we can see how clearly Malina's use of anthropology not only echoes the ridiculous Orientalist tradition of "the Arab mind" somehow being psychologically incapable of peace,[60] but that it also fits extremely neatly into *contemporary* clash of civilizations rhetoric, including the claim that places like Iraq and the Middle East in general are not particularly suited to democracy. Again, if there is any question about the racist implications of the above generalization cited from Malina, replace "Arab" with "Jew" or "black," read it out loud, and listen to what it sounds like.

It is also worth stressing that this idea of certain people being "not suited" to democracy was strongly put forward, for instance, in the context of the 1991 Gulf War, and has been recently reemphasized in the light of the present conflicts in Iraq. A liberal interventionist variant of this argument came from leading neoconservative, Paul Wolfowitz, who is quoted as saying, "You hear people mock it by saying that Iraq isn't ready for Jeffersonian democracy. Well, Japan isn't Jeffersonian democracy, either. I think the more we are committed to influencing the outcome, the more chance there could be that it would be something quite significant for Iraq."[61] Notice the imperialistic assumption that "our" influence is required to bring "them" to democracy: presumably those poor souls can't do it on their own. Clearly these kinds of assumptions are not only rooted in massive cultural generalizations but they are also, potentially, politically dangerous and devastating. When, in 1991, Bush Sr gave the notorious encouragement for the infamous Shia uprising before going back on his decision (and leaving those who rose up to Saddam), the logic "behind this theory," as Avi Shlaim puts it, lay in the pessimistic view that Iraq was not suited for democracy and that Sunni minority rule was the only formula capable of keeping Iraq in one piece."[62] Chomsky also points to the implementation of this view, adding that the iron-fisted ruler theory of controlling the masses (and, of course, the resources) was a standard line of intellectual thought at the time, most clearly articulated by none other than the Pulitzer Prize winning journalist and establishment figure, Thomas Friedman.[63]

We might also add that the vague idea of "humiliation" (used by both Malina and the scholarship he cites, not to mention its use by Rosson) is a regular explanation in trying to understand all those Arabs and Muslims and all the strange things they do. And, of course, this whopping great generalization covering vast geographical and cultural differences also serves the function of avoiding the blindingly obvious: the sheer amount of outside involvement in Middle Eastern (and Mediterranean) politics. With this in mind, the use of "Arab" (or "Muslim") "humiliation" is not just morally lacking but intellectually dubious when applied to the Mediterranean 2000 years ago. Put bluntly, such uses of "the Arab" or "the Middle East" are not remotely useful as a "heuristic tool" as they are grounded in a fraudulent and at times racist understanding of others.

As ever, a typical example of the use of this "humiliation" category comes from Thomas Friedman.[64] Grounding an article in a speech by the former *Malaysian* prime minister, Mahathir Mohamad, Friedman argues "humiliation" is a key to problems in/with *Palestine* and *Iraq*. One of the reasons why US forces never got a standing ovation for "liberating Iraq from Saddam's tyranny," Freidman informs us, is partly because (wait for it...) "many Iraqis feel humiliated that they didn't liberate themselves, and America's presence, even its aid, reminds them of that." Ah, so *that's* why. Let's not mention over a decade of horrific sanctions, previous US support for Saddam at his worst, the use of cluster bombs and depleted uranium, or the US pulling support on a previous uprising. No, details are presumably not important. "Humiliation," grounded in a Malaysian speech, is the key to what has happened (or not) in Iraq. Friedman's article is a classic example of how accepted ideology is particularly effective in obscuring basic facts.

And then Friedman explains the Palestinian situation. We are told that, without any attempt at analysis or presentation of detail, "one reason" why Arafat "rejected the Clinton plan for a Palestinian state" was because "he and many followers didn't want a state handed to them by the U.S. or Israel. That would be 'humiliating.' They wanted to win it in blood and fire." As Hezbollah had "bombarded Palestinians with stories of how the Lebanese drove the Israelis out," so "Palestinian militants wanted the 'dignity' of doing the same." Friedman adds that we should remember that "the Arab-Israeli conflict is about both borders and Nobel Prizes. It's about where the dividing line should be and it's about the humiliation that comes from one side succeeding at modernity and the other not." As we have seen, the situation is hardly anywhere near as simplistic as this, with Clinton's plan being extremely one-sided, but, presumably, that doesn't matter because all we really need is the generalizing rhetoric of what all those countless funny Muslims and Arabs are *really* like.

Malina, of course, quoted the "humiliation" category from some old scholarship, notably Raphael Patai. This is the kind of scholarship that ought to be immediately reminiscent of that clinically exposed in Said's *Orientalism*. As it happens, Patai's views of "the Arab mind," along with the familiar anthropological language, were given a damning critique by Said:

> Much of his paraphernalia is anthropological – he describes the Middle East as a "culture area" – but the result is to eradicate the plurality of differences among Arabs (whoever they may be in fact) in the interest of one difference, that one setting Arabs off from everyone else. As a subject matter for study and analysis, they can be controlled more readily. Moreover, thus reduced they can be made to permit, legitimate, and valorize general nonsense of the sort one finds in works such as Sania Hamady's *Temperament and Character of the Arabs*.

Said was speaking of Patai's *Golden River to Golden Road* (1962). Of Patai's later work referenced by Malina, *The Arab Mind*, Said claimed it "outstripped even his previous work" and then referred to "an *even more* racist work" [my italics] of John Laffin [*The Arab Mind Considered*].[65] Whether what Said is right or wrong, the fact that he fiercely denounced such work as racist in a highly prominent 1970s book ought to be serious cause for concern. I should add that Malina is not the only person associated with the Context Group to have cited Patai positively.[66]

Similarly others have had problems with Patai's book, not least because of its reliance on old-fashioned concepts of national and pan-national character for extreme generalizations (often sexual) about millions of people covering continents sometimes illustrated by the most bizarre examples, including handling a baby boy's genitals to make him smile, lengthy breastfeeding, masturbation rates, aversion to manual labour (grounded in a "Bedouin attitude" and supported by Gen. 3:17-19 no less!), and the tightness of figure-hugging Western trousers in a particularly homoerotic passage.[67]

Whether through interpretation or misinterpretation, Patai's work takes on an even more disturbing dimension.[68] Worryingly, there are alleged connections with contemporary political elites. In his investigation of the chain of command underlying the disastrous events of Abu Ghraib, the investigative journalist Seymour Hersh claimed that the idea of Arabs being particularly vulnerable to shame and sexual humiliation was a talking point among pro-war conservative figures in Washington in the run-up to the 2003 invasion of Iraq. This in turn would, apparently, help create a network of scared informants in contexts such as Abu Ghraib. And one book that was central to this understanding, Hersh claims, was none other than Patai's, *The Arab Mind*. Hersh's comments are worth quoting more fully:

> The book includes a twenty-five-page chapter on Arabs and sex, depicting sex as a taboo vested with shame and repression. "The segregation of the sexes, the veiling of the women . . . and all the other minute rules that govern and restrict contact between men and women, have the effect of making sex a prime mental preoccupation in the Arab world," Patai wrote. Homosexual activity, "or any indication of homosexual leanings, as with all other expressions of sexuality, is never given any publicity. These are private affairs and remain in private." The Patai book, an academic told me, was "the bible of the neocons on Arab behavior." In their discussions, he said, two themes emerged – "one, that Arabs only understand force and, two, that the biggest weakness of Arabs is shame and humiliation."... The government consultant said that there may have been a serious goal, in the beginning, behind the sexual humiliation and the posed photographs. It was thought that some prisoners would do anything – including spying on their associates – to avoid dissemination of the shameful photos to family and friends. The government consultant said, "I was told that the purpose of the photographs was to create an army of informants, people you could insert back in the population." The idea was that they would be motivated by fear of exposure, and gather information about pending insurgency action, the consultant said. If so, it wasn't effective; the insurgency continued to grow.[69]

What is also interesting is how Hersh has been received in military circles. Montgomery McFate is extremely keen to get anthropology on board for US military purposes but (via Hersh) still points to the absurdity of using Patai's book. If, McFate claims, "anthropologists refuse to contribute, how reliable will that information be? The result of using incomplete 'bad' anthropology is, invariably, failed operations and failed policy."[70] If using generalizations from Patai was bad enough then putting them into practice shows just how dangerous they can be. And, apparently, we have now seen this monstrously before our very eyes. Yet, note: Patai is a problem because his work failed in practice. Clearly, if better anthropology of those exotic cultures can be found then it can be used for the purposes of American foreign policy.

On the other hand, there are concrete examples of the "positive" significance of Patai's book in military and intelligence circles. In a review by Lloyd Jordan for the Center for the Study of Intelligence, an academic wing of the CIA no less, the book is not only regarded as "a significant contribution to the field of national character research" and "to the understanding of Arab culture" but it also "implicitly suggests the relevance of national character research to intelligence analysis." Indeed, one part of the book is contextualized and analysed for its usefulness for intelligence analysis. And useful it is deemed to be.[71] We may add to this endorsement that the foreword to the latest edition of *The Arab Mind* is by Colonel Norvell B. De Atkine who teaches at the JFK Special Warfare School and holds a graduate degree in Arab studies from the American University of Beirut.[72] De Atkine opens by stressing the importance of Patai's book for understanding September 11. In fact there is "a critical need to bring this seminal study of the modal Arab personality to the attention of policymakers, scholars, and the general public." De Atkine has already disseminated the book in his own military circles:

> This book...is essential reading. At the institution where I teach military officers, The Arab Mind forms the basis of my cultural instruction, complemented by my own experiences of some twenty-five years living in, studying, or teaching about the Middle East... Over the past twelve years, I have also briefed hundreds of military teams being deployed to the Middle East. When returning from the Middle East, my students, as well as the members of these teams, invariably comment on the paramount usefulness of the cultural instruction in their assignments. In doing so they validate the analysis and descriptions offered by Raphael Patai.

One question: does all this include comparative masturbation rates?

More generally, the discovery of implied or explicit support for governmental policy in the academic output of intellectuals is not difficult to find and, as we saw in the first chapter, Chomsky's famous *American Power and the New Mandarins* (1969) is a landmark critique here. There are also other crucial political antecedents to the kinds of anthropology and cultural generalizing used in New Testament studies. Said noted long ago that the study of the "Muslim and Arab worlds" in the US took off in the 1970s as a political enterprise, often grounded in corporate, governmental and military interests, with intellectually dubious conclusions and little interest in cultural and spiritual histories. This, of course, included those dubious analyses of "the Persian" psyche and national character (see previous chapter).[73]

In the UK the politicizing of Islamic studies has also become a controversial issue. The 2007 Siddiqui Report, commissioned by the government, claimed that Islamic studies in universities was outdated, with government ministers seeing Islamic studies as a "strategic subject" for its role "in preventing extremism."[74] It is notable that the recommendations in the report want to look at aspects of diversity in Europe, particularly with "the growing number of Muslims in this country" in mind. There should be greater focus on the "theological and civilisational aspects of Islam which are relevant to practising Muslims." Significantly, pastoral care should also be included "in the future training of future religious leaders, especially in *madrasas*, in the community."[75]

It is difficult not to read this as a partial attempt to control a controversial area in the universities. As the outgoing Prime Minister Tony Blair said of the report, "what...we need to do to encourage *the right intellectual and academic debate* [my italics] on these issues here in Britain. We intend to follow-up on many of Dr Siddiqui's recommendations and will be providing significant funding to deliver on this commitment."[76] Though Blair reassured us that "healthy rigorous debate about the controversies of foreign policy" (the recent past makes many of us ultra-sceptical that this would genuinely be one of Blair's aims), it is not difficult to see that this is clear evidence of political influence on the teaching of Islam in the universities (why else talk of "the *right* [my italics] intellectual and academic debate"?), a point not lost on observers. A quite sympathetic Ahmed Versi, editor of *Muslim News*, was present at the conference but pointed out that the pressing issue among Muslims which was radicalizing many young Muslims – namely foreign policy (especially Afghanistan and Iraq) – was not properly addressed. Labour peer Lord Ahmed of Rotherham even claimed that the conference had excluded "those Muslims who disagree with government policy."[77]

Of even more direct relevance for the approaches associated with the Context Group are the long noted links between anthropology, nationalism and imperialism – how could there not be some link with the actions of colonial powers old and new in the mid-twentieth century?[78] Anthropology has had a long history of being politicized, stretching back before the Second World War. In the Second World War and the Cold War, social sciences were part of the wide-ranging study of areas and their strategic value for the purposes of American expansionism or militarism, as David Price, Matthew Farish and others show.[79] Anthropologists such as Carlton Coon and Gregory Bateson used their skills for overseas operations in areas such as North Africa, Thailand and Burma. Bateson, for instance, believed that an American neo-colonial order should alter attitudes partly through the nurturing of indigenous culture and avoid the possible reactions of imposing external cultural models. Bateson's wife, the anthropologist Margaret Mead, was advocating an opposition to authoritarian rule while pushing other populations to democracy, though allowing the use of undemocratic means to do so. Social scientists were also seeking to establish the idea of the national character of "the Germans" and "the Japanese." Matthew Farish adds that, influenced by the War and with the support of the War Department,

> studies of other cultures, positioned next to ongoing consideration of America's unique attributes, contributed substantially to the solidification of a regionalized world with the United States at its center... In its most simplistic variants, national-character study documented the acquisition by a culture of a singular personality. To create unity and pattern...an integrated whole had to be created and bounded, at both cultural and global scales... Advocates of this approach focused on cultural anthropology and psychology...although Benedict and other innovative theorists such as Bateson were keenly aware that characters were constructed markers of difference depending on stereotypes, they defended these formulations as nonetheless significant...this long-range scrutiny aided by the compilation of various data sources and *not* by personal experience necessarily adopted a detached perspective, more prone to generalization and abstraction than even the most egregious colonial ethnographies... Individuals remained blurry and were relatively devoid of agency.[80]

The kinds of social psychology and anthropology approaches discussed would be developed by the CIA and policy after the Second World War and had a notable impact on Cold War area studies and mainstream social sciences, with the political and the academic significantly overlapping and reinforcing one another.[81] Even today Margaret Mead has been found useful in describing the present situation in Iraq. Montgomery McFate finds that Mead's analysis of "Americans" as altruistic fighters who walk away from conflict once it is completed and on to the next to be reflected in Bush Jr's administration *characterizing* Iraq as a "defensive war." The Iraq war is *characterized* as defensive because it was prompted by the "imminent threat" of weapons of mass destruction and to bring democracy to Iraq. At this point it is difficult not to cough with utter incredulity at such views given the known lies and half-truths concerning the Iraq war, not to mention the stunningly innovative concept of an altruistic war. But we should remember that we are dealing with *characterization* rather than actual reasons. Yet the level of characterization still remains culturally significant for present purposes because it shows how anthropological generalization feeds very neatly into justifying acts of aggression against a distant other.

As it happens, there has been a resurgence of interest in anthropology among military elite, as we have already seen in passing. Various figures in US military circles have been calling for greater awareness of adversaries. In 2004, the Office of Naval Research and the Defense Advanced Research Projects Agency sponsored the Adversary Cultural Knowledge and National Security Conference. This, tellingly, was the first major US Department of Defense conference on the social sciences since 1962. Coming in from a military perspective, McFate suggests that the reason for this resurgence of interest is that technologically driven and traditional methods are not wholly suitable for counterinsurgencies in Afghanistan and Iraq, where combatants are hidden among civilians, they do not abide by the Geneva Convention (!), they use improvised explosive devices, and their organizations are "not military, but tribal."

So, to counter such people, cultural and social knowledge of the adversary is required. Here anthropology can help, McFate argues. Anthropology has had a "long, fruitful relationship with various elements of national power," which ended following the "failure" in Vietnam and, apparently, due to the descent into the "abyss of postmodernism."[82] The civilizations theory lurks beneath the surface of McFate's article. In true Sir John Keegan-style, the old war with the Soviets required little cultural knowledge due to similar technology and, crucially, "two powers of European heritage" as opposed to a "non-Western" enemy of the present. Naturally, McFate points to "ethnocentrism" on the part of US in failures of detecting the seeming "irrationality" of adversaries.

Given his dislike for postmodernist anthropology and the hope for a better understanding of "Iraqi culture and mindset" to improve war plans, it is not difficult to see how much more significant anthropology of the sort that discusses broad social psychological, political and cultural tendencies would be to a figure like McFate. And we should not forget that some members of the Context Group have, rightly or wrongly, been as scathing of postmodernism and ethnocentrism as McFate. This is not, of course, to say that certain members of the Context Group would (or would not) approve of the militarization of cultural anthropology but, once again, it is quite clear that the two contemporary approaches are clearly culturally compatible. David Price rightly warns, "As the American President seems intent on committing his nation to a prolonged war against the ill-defined concept of terrorism...anthropologists have new reasons to focus on issues *embedded* [my italics] in their discipline's militaristically mobilized past."[83] And, should anyone say so, this is not scaremongering. From a military perspective McFate can say, "Despite the fact that military applications of cultural knowledge might be distasteful to ethically inclined anthropologists, their assistance is necessary."[84]

It should, therefore, be no surprise that the obviously related anthropology used in areas of Christian origins should readily lend itself to contemporary constructions involved in the clash of civilizations. Significantly, there are further indications that Malina and others are tapping into the traditions described here. He suggests, for example, that "the best we can attempt is a type of regional character study, patterned after the national character studies of the 1940s and 1950s. These studies have been picked up once again, now under the label of social psychology."[85] Elsewhere, Malina claims that if we are to understand "persons of the ancient Mediterranean world" we need "entirely new ways" of perceiving in order to understand them on their own terms. If we do not, "we will be perpetuating the long-standing problem of being 'Ugly Americans,' a phrase coined to describe the utter failure of U.S. personnel at the beginning of the Vietcong insurgency to understand the ways of that mysterious culture."[86]

Are You with Us or against Us?

> *Strong ingroup identification also leads to the view that outgroups are not like "us" and therefore a threat. Should dissimilarity be detected in the way others speak, such negative views are easily reinforced.*
>
> Richard Rohrbaugh[87]

In contemporary anthropological and social-scientific study of Christian origins, the rhetoric of dealing with, and the dismissal of, opponents has been striking, particularly as it frequently gets linked in with imperialism, empires and/or clashing civilizations, a point echoed by Said discussing related academic contexts.[88] To a fairly stunned-but-entertained audience at the November 2006 American Academy of Religion session on "The Role of Secular Viewpoints in Scriptural Studies: Past, Present, and Future," Arthur Droge openly spoke of crushing any counter-revolutionary activities aimed against views associated with new secularizing views on Christian origins before launching into a lengthy Gibbonesque speech on the benefits of the Roman Empire and how all its blessings to world history were corrupted by Christianity.[89]

Nothing quite so dramatic, as far as I am aware, has been said by anyone associated with the Context Group, or indeed anyone else associated with the secularizing views Droge spoke about. Moreover, Droge's tongue was, presumably, firmly in his cheek when using such language. More seriously though, it has been noted that there is a tendency among certain scholars associated with the Context Group to reject outsiders who do not follow their party line, with such rejections lacking sufficient detail or argument and being overly confident of their findings. David Horrell pointed out that while those like Esler are content to provide robust defences of their approaches, the heavily model-based approaches associated with the Context Group are "(sometimes) overly dismissive of work which adopts a different perspective" and seem to be over dependent on "the basic set of models" of Bruce Malina's 1981 work, "which in any case lack the reference to extra-biblical ancient sources necessary to demonstrate the models' validity as a representation of ancient Mediterranean culture." Horrell adds the question, "Have other socio-historical studies failed to find and employ the social-scientific resources which would enable them to grasp the distinctive culture reflected in the New Testament texts and hence perpetuated anachronistic and ethnocentric readings?"[90] Similarly, Justin Meggitt has criticized Malina for ascribing "to his descriptions a degree of certitude which, frankly, would seem strange to the professional practitioners of the disciplines he employs to produce his models" and for being "rather too facile in his treatment of ideas that challenge his axiomatic assumptions."[91] We might add that a search through reviews by prominent Context Group members in the widely disseminated *Review of Biblical Literature* shows some blistering attacks on people using different views (though, to be fair, these are, on occasion, in reaction to polemics aimed at the Context Group's methodology and *some* criticisms are backed up) with stunningly high praise reserved for fellow Context Group members.[92]

Crucially, the bone of contention, which is of immediate concern here, remains whether the reviewed book uses the right anthropology and generalizations. Elsewhere, in a scathing review of what has otherwise been regarded as a seminal book, Malina dismisses Rodney Stark's *The Rise of Christianity*, along with the work of other scholars, with sweeping generalization and sarcasm. And note the typical civilization distinctions:

> Stark states that his aim is "to introduce historians and biblical scholars to real social science" (p. xii). Instead, for the most part, he uses theories, models, and data from contemporary sociology of religion to describe and explain early Christianity and its development. The results are the usual ethnocentric anachronisms we have come to expect from those who have applied North American or Northern European sociology to Mediterranean antiquity (e.g., W. A. Meeks, H. C. Kee, G. Theissen,

> J. G. Gager, A. J. Blasi, R. K. Fenn)… S. does show us much of what Christians would be like and why their movements or groups would have turned in certain ways if they were twentieth-century, individualistic persons living in the industrialized West. Apart from demography based on mathematics, he tells us next to nothing new about collectivistic Mediterranean persons who lived in advanced agricultural societies… If this is real social science, then the author is to be congratulated for providing a convincing argument for the irrelevancy of sociology, especially sociology of religion, for biblical interpretation and the study of history. Rather, the *only* [my italics] real social science of value for the task of interpreting the ancient world is a consciously comparative social science (e.g., macrosociology, cross-cultural social psychology, and cultural [British: social] anthropology).[93]

Significantly, when Malina does get into details to counter Stark they are based on basic factual errors, such as the number of bishops at Nicea in 325 CE and when gladiatorial games ceased. Regrettably, there is no serious argumentation for the reader to be able to judge in the cases of the sweeping dismissals and it is apparent that clear-cut ideological and civilizational differences guide the dismissal. And who are the "we" in "we have come to expect"? If "we" are not simply Malina sympathizers, it seems that this "we" must, presumably, represent some kind of generally held view but that is certainly not the case as a wide range of scholars regard the work of some of those cited by Malina as groundbreaking, influential and highly relevant.[94]

It could be argued that the scholarship attacked by Malina shows that Malina has misrepresented his opponents. As it happens, Stark's work on networks in particular has been developed in different ways, showing how issues relating to social networks are deeply embedded in ancient ideas and social contexts.[95] But over a decade prior to Stark, and in a book also regarded as a seminal work in Christian origins, Wayne Meeks, one of those whom Malina dismisses, developed crucial insights into the application of social networks to Christian origins. Meeks showed this with reference to a range of primary sources and has been praised by another big name in non-Context Group social-scientific criticism, Jack Sanders.[96] So who is right?

Elsewhere, Meggitt points to Malina's passing comments on Judith Perkins and her views on Christian origins and the rise of subjectivity in the ancient world which, of course, differs sharply from the Mediterranean self as defined by some of the Context Group.[97] Malina speaks simply of "the unverifiable assertions of French philosophers quoted by Perkins" (and nothing more). However, Meggitt points out that Perkins' work is "highly verifiable, thoroughly (and carefully) engaged with a wide array of primary sources, as well as recent secondary literature produced by classicists and social theorists, whether French or otherwise."[98] Now what should we believe?

Firing at a certain type of psychology is by no means confined to Malina. After generalizing about Individualist/Western/American culture versus Collective/Mediterranean (/and, elsewhere, Middle Eastern) culture, Richard Rohrbaugh points out that psychology is "irrelevant" for "collective cultures" and that the "extensive psychologizing of Western biblical interpretation provides an example of ethnocentric confusion on this point." He then simply lists (wrong) works by Anthony Bash, Michael Reichardt, Martin Leiner, John A. Sanford, and Gerd Theissen, though it is Jack Dominian's *One Like Us: A Psychological Interpretation of Jesus* which "says it all."[99] That is all that is said by way of countering all these scholars. There is no attempt to show how any of the details are incorrect because, presumably, the *generalization* about other scholars shows that they are incorrect.

In his essay on the parable of the prodigal son (Lk. 15:11-32), the allegations levelled by Rohrbaugh at other scholars take on a more sinister tone. Before we move on to that, we first need to see how the argument is grounded in terms of stark civilizational difference which ignores diversity to the extent that Rohrbaugh makes basic errors. Rohrbaugh criticizes the "traditional" interpretation of the parable, namely that the parable is to be understood as a story about repentance. He points out that the term "repentance" is never mentioned before proposing that instead of coming at this story "with the usual preunderstandings of Western soteriology" we should look at a "new approach" that sets the parable "as closely as possible in the sociocultural milieu from which it came." In fact "Western exegesis" frequently overlooks that this was "a Mediterranean story told by a Mediterranean storyteller for a Mediterranean audience."[100] In other words, *our* anthropological way is virtually the *only* historical way of understanding this parable.

Yet for all the grand polarizing of views, crucial details are ignored by Rohrbaugh. The parable is quite explicitly linked in (cf. Lk. 15:1-2) to two previous parables, both of which explicitly mention repentance and use a standard word for "repentance" (μετανοέω/μετάνοια). It does not matter who was responsible for this framing and linking of themes (Jesus, early tradition, or Luke) because we are left with the very basic point that some ancient person or persons believed that this parable could concern repentance! Rohrbaugh's strict polarizing method excludes this voice almost by definition. Similarly, Rohrbaugh's method excludes other voices almost by definition. The reader is given little in the way of details of the many early Jewish discussions of repentance, such as the famous early Jewish repentance parallel to Luke 15:11-32 of the son returning to the king (*Deut. R.* 2.24). Similarly even the basic notion of the idea of "return" (*teshuvah*), something integral to repentance in Jewish texts and clearly echoed in the son returning from associating with unclean pigs in Luke 15:11-32, would contradict Rohrbaugh's overly confident views.[101] These details, grounded in *ancient* evidence, tell us something about the legitimate reasons why repentance is chosen as a legitimate context for interpreting Luke 15:11-32. No matter how much "heuristic value" is stressed, Rohrbaugh's model, to paraphrase Said, is close to a kind of "fundamentalism" rather than analysis of culture, the latter being far more diverse should the details be included.[102]

By ignoring specific arguments relating to ancient aspects of repentance, Rohrbaugh allows himself to be guided by his overall model of them versus us. But that is nothing we have not seen already. The more sinister aspect is when he takes this stark reasoning to another level, perhaps one of its logical cultural conclusions. One of Rohrbaugh's main targets is the allegorical reading of Luke 15:11-32 which has the contrast between Judaism and Christianity at its core, a view associated in particular with Heikki Räisänen. The rejection of such a view may well be reasonable enough in the abstract but a serious problem arises when the rejection relies not so much on *argument* but on one of the most loaded of contemporary *allegations*, antisemitism, an allegation hardly unrelated to issues of clashing civilizations and contemporary US and UK foreign policy issues and one that is increasingly abused in contemporary discourse (see above and Chapters 5 and 6). If Räisänen is not quite accused directly of "subtle anti-Semitism," then his supposed connections with such views are hardly removed either. Note once again how the rejection is grounded in the stark choice of alternatives:

> The typical allegory imagines the father as God incognito, the older son as a Jew (or a Jewish Christian: Räisänen) and the younger son as a Gentile Christian. *The subtle anti-Semitism of such interpretations is to be deplored.* Whatever claim to sense such a reading makes in patristic exegesis (Ambrose, Augustine, et al.) and elsewhere, it makes no sense whatever at the level of Jesus. As noted above, the recent study of Räisänen in which such allegorical speculation is *rife* is the result of pre-deciding that this is a traditional soteriological tale [my italics].[103]

The reader is given little in the way of the details of Räisänen's argument or if Räisänen might not in fact be engaging in subtle antisemitic interpretation. Conveniently enough, a well-known article by Räisänen on how secondary gospel editing is distanced from the Jewish nature of Jesus' teaching is simply not mentioned by Rohrbaugh.[104] If a contemporary scholar is guilty of subtle racism, should this individual not be hit and hit hard rather than mentioned in passing in a footnote? Given the gravity of the accusation of antisemitism against a contemporary scholar, some indication or evidence might be expected to at least allow the reader to make some kind of informed judgment. Instead, we are simply left with a particularly unsavoury image of a New Testament scholar who *has* to be wrong now.

Taking his own argument to its logical conclusion, anywhere that Rohrbaugh may think that there is a *New Testament* argument for overriding Judaism or rejecting the law and so on, or indeed whenever Rohrbaugh completely ignores contemporary Jewish evidence (and this article is hardly the only time he does so), he himself would have to be tied in with "subtle anti-Semitism." I should make it quite clear that I do not think Rohrbaugh is antisemitic; I do believe, as I have tried to imply, that his use of the term "antisemitism" is manipulative and insulting, using Jewish suffering for no reason other, it would seem, than to score points in a scholarly debate.

A brief counter-argument should show how strange all the above evidence-free attacks on scholars are. Evidence-free attacks against people who have provided plenty of evidence is, obviously, a problem for scholarly debate. Do those of us who follow the non-approved line of a particular sub-group change our minds because a famous name says we should? What does a researcher or interested layperson do in the absence of evidence: follow Meeks or Theissen because they are famous and respected scholars or follow Malina or other prominent Context Group members because they are famous and respected scholars? Or what do we do in the face of comments like the following from one relatively friendly review of honour and shame in biblical studies (including the work of members of the Context Group) by an anthropologist and from three critiques by biblical scholars?

> The papers in this volume might give the unwary reader the impression that anthropologists are largely in agreement on the meaning of honor and shame in Mediterranean contexts. This is most definitely not the case, however...most ethnographers are uneasy about the prospect of lumping all parts of the Mediterranean together in one large honor and shame complex...[the] dubious assumption that the cultures anthropologists study are categorized more by continuity than change has been increasingly called into question...as so often happens when one discipline borrows from another, the anthropology employed in

> these papers is beginning to look a bit dated... Herzfeld's admonition that blanket applications of a monolithic model of honor and shame should be avoided... Authors in this volume have not heeded Herzfeld's call: they have employed a common model and applied it to peoples diverse in time and space.[105]

> the book [Malina's, *The Social World of Jesus and the Gospels*] cannot tell us anything substantial about the subject of its title. Malina claims too much and too much of what he claims is implausible.[106]

> astounding generalizations proliferate, seemingly unsupported by evidence and reminiscent of grand anthropological theories of a bygone day... We hear about what is characteristically, and it appears timelessly, "Mediterranean" behaviour... A good many of Malina's cultural generalizations are plainly untrue for the followers of Jesus and for some or indeed most other religious Jews.[107]

> in his more ambitious aim of enabling interpreters to "fix implicit NT meanings" in a way that "heads off ethnocentrism from the very outset," Malina has been less than successful. Indeed, one may harbor the suspicion that the task so defined could in principle never be accomplished.[108]

All these quotations are from people who would also be regarded as respectable scholars. They do give arguments but I have deliberately quoted them to present their cases as opinion. If the above is read in this light how do I now decide who is the cleverest? How do I decide who is more or less right *now*? Do I try to decide who is the most famous or the one with the biggest name?

If statement is enough, then the audience is, presumably, simply left to gaze in awe at one kind of academic mindset that *must* be right. But, clearly, the view that "my academic view is right and yours is wrong because I say so" is logically problematic to say the least. While there will no doubt be no end to people uncritically following their academic heroes – whether this hero is Althusser, Bultmann, Chomsky, Derrida, Mary Douglas, Foucault, Freud, Greer, Huntington, Lacan, Bernard Lewis, Luther, Mack, Malina, Marx, Patai, Paul, N.T. Wright, Zwingli and so on – it is, obviously, difficult to see how a dogmatic, even sectarian, model of scholarship works *logically* in terms of *argument*. Few in the abstract would disagree with that statement but following constructed consensus and academic heroes over argument and engagement is extremely common in scholarship. Particularly striking for present purposes is the fact that the noted use of dismissal and non-argument is common among some of those associated with issues *directly relating to the generalizing of civilizations*. While this critique of scholarship ultimately has to be deduced from social context, and consequently cannot be shown with absolute certainty, I strongly suspect that this polarizing and dismissive rhetoric is not coincidental in the light of the other typical types of rhetoric associated with views on clashing civilizations. Its intensity and the ideological usefulness of such polarizing views are unlikely to be mere coincidence. It is to a brief analysis of the broader intellectual context of such dismissal that we now turn.

Let Us Never Speak of This Again: Ideological Significance of Dismissing Dissent without Argument

> *I have provided the above careful documentation of previous systematic U.S. abuse of international power because Elshtain's performance in her book, like many in the mainstream media today, deploys a kind of swashbuckling discourse that portrays critics of the U.S. war as "anti-American" or as "naïve pacifists" deploying specious arguments and false analogies without evidence.*
>
> Mark Lewis Taylor[109]

On March 22, 2007, the BBC's flagship political debate programme, *Question Time*, held a special edition focused on the four years since the invasion of Iraq. Various prominent figures from across the political spectrum were chosen. A notable US figure involved was John Bolton, former US Ambassador to the UN, a figure closely associated with the neo-conservative Project for the New American Century.[110] What was strange, at least from the perspective of the usual format of *Question Time*, was a point made to Bolton by the veteran socialist, Tony Benn. Benn said,

> And when the charter of the UN was read to me... "We the peoples of the United Nations are determined to save succeeding generations from the scourge of war which twice in our lifetime has caused untold suffering to mankind." That was the pledge my generation gave to the younger generation and you tore it up and it's a war crime that's been committed in Iraq because there's no moral difference between a stealth bomber and a suicide bomber, both kill innocent people for political reasons. And that's why in Britain the majority are against it, America, worldwide, there's no support for the United States in this worldwide. And you're...a declining empire as we were and you'll learn the truth. You were beaten in Vietnam. As you said yourself, That's why you didn't want to serve there, you don't want to die in a South East Asia rice paddy... And you'll be beaten in Iraq. I'm afraid that's the truth.[111]

Irrespective of the rights and wrongs of Benn's comments (and, incidentally, polls, which would almost certainly have been known to Bolton, have backed up the comments on a lack of support for the US-led invasion), it is a perfectly coherent case and one which might expect an answer. By the usual unsaid rules of *Question Time* debate, or indeed any debate, the person would respond with a counter-argument. I remember thinking at the time, "how on earth is Bolton going to get out of this one?" But Bolton did not seem to think in the ways normal human beings do. Instead of responding to any points, Bolton simply replied with a sneer, saying, "It's not worth responding to Tony Benn." That was it. End of argument.

Why might this be significant? Well, more generally, the purpose of outlining the faulty generalizations about the Middle East, Arabs, Muslims, Islam and so on and issues surrounding the "war on terror" is to counter all the morally dubious claims and to show that the rhetoric of civilizations is often empty rhetoric, ignoring – wittingly or unwittingly – cultural diversity and overlapping and changing identities. Additionally, the observation that the simple dismissing of alternative arguments focuses clearly on the issue of imperialistic difference is also significant in this context. A near inevitable tendency of hard political generalizing without due care to details involves cheerleading intellectuals dismissing dissenting views without any serious engagement, a point mentioned in the first chapter on the propaganda model and the manufacture of consent. The reason for this is, presumably, because the generalizing, ignoring and lying crumbles at the first sight of close analysis and counter-evidence. "With us or against us" hardly suggests a detailed debate is on the agenda and for good reason.

As Chomsky is arguably the most productive critic of US foreign policy it is perhaps little surprise that his arguments and the masses of evidence he collects is most conspicuously avoided through Bolton-style blanket rejection or dismissal with non-argument, if noted at all. In fact there are examples of arguments and even writings attributed to him that he neither made nor wrote![112] It is therefore fitting that we focus on some of the ways that this mass of evidence collected by Chomsky gets avoided. This could go on for a very long time so I will have to restrict the examples and I will restrict them to the more intellectual-sounding ones.[113] Still, these few examples should give some indication of my point.

On the basic level, Jean Bethke Elshtain, dismisses Chomsky's critique of US foreign policy in a footnote with a wildly misleading counter-statement,

> Anti-American diatribe along these lines is perennially provided by Noam Chomsky. In a 125-page paperback entitled *9–11*, Chomsky pieces together fragments of an argument based on interviews, e-mails, and so on. He sanitizes bin Laden's call to kill Americans, men, women, and children, wherever they may be found, as a call to the overthrow of

> "corrupt and brutal regimes of gangsters and torturers." I have not put Chomsky's outrageous and wholly irresponsible tirade in the body of this text because analyzing it is like shooting fish in a barrel – it just isn't very interesting.[114]

It is difficult not to express some despair as to how this wild distortion can be countered but let us try. Notice that there is no direct evidence from Chomsky specifically on his apparent "sanitizing" of bin Laden, something which would surely help if Elshtain wanted such absurd allegations to be taken seriously at the basic level of factually accurate argument. Whether Elshtain agrees with him or not, in *9/11* Chomsky gave several perfectly coherent arguments while beyond *9/11* Chomsky has continually provided detail after detail after detail. He is critical of the US government and I have never come across anything that is anti-American in any other sense than critical of his government and, more generally, he advocates an anarchist-style critique of the role of the state which stretches, obviously, beyond America. So what we are dealing with here is the replacement of Chomsky's arguments with something much easier to demolish: things he has never said or done. And we should notice that Elshtain describes Chomsky-style "anti-American diatribe" in this context: "Such critics argue, for example, that the attacks of September 11 are 'blowback'; a reaction brought on ourselves by being engaged with the world."[115] Notice how the debate is subtly dictated. Given the reference to Chomsky, "being engaged" is hardly as quaint as it sounds given Chomsky's repeated recording of the horrors of US foreign policy. Elshtain's formulation is also profoundly misleading if we acknowledge this. It logically follows that any criticism of US governmental actions must come perilously close to "anti-American diatribe" which starts sounding like an endorsement of a profoundly undemocratic notion of having criticism of the government being unacceptable, at least in academic argument. All too typically, once basic facts are avoided, academic arrogance, with the accompanying dismissive wave of the hand, is all that is required to get the real job done, namely slurring opponents into silence.

The pretence of interaction, while ignoring evidence put forward by Chomsky or misrepresenting his arguments through vague generalizations, is found in Charles Reed's book, *Just War?* Reed claims that the trend in recent decades has "radically changed" and moved toward "humanitarian intervention." "States," we are informed, "are now more likely to use force to punish evil and to intervene on the side of the oppressed." In fact, since the fall of the Soviet empire, the use of force has "taken the form of quasi-police action."[116] Chomsky has written huge amounts on such issues yet Reed says this of Chomsky (and John Pilger):

> They reflect a deep suspicion of the power of the state and its coercive powers both internally and externally. Taken to the extreme, seen in the writings of Noam Chomsky or, to a lesser degree, John Pilger, it can lead to a form of pacific globalism or revolutionary universalism. Their deep cynicism about the state denies the possibility that a state's action or behaviour can at any time be moral or ethical.[117]

This is the only mention of Chomsky (and Pilger for that matter) in the book. Given Reed's concern for establishing the idea of a "moral" and "ethical" Anglo-American foreign policy and given his acknowledgement of "the writings of Noam Chomsky" it is highly problematic, to say the least, that he has ignored Chomsky's (and Pilger's) relentless recording of post-Vietnam actions. "Their deep cynicism" is based on *masses* of empirical data and not merely, as the impression might be drawn from Reed's summary, a deep suspicion of state power. If Reed were to have properly acknowledged Chomsky's (and Pilger's) arguments and aims, then this would have undermined a great deal of Reed's arguments for "just wars" in Afghanistan and Iraq. Consequently, the convenient dismissal with reference to a non-referenced and extremely vague counter-argument about their ideas leading to "a form of pacific globalism or revolutionary universalism" is apparently all this tremulous heart requires.

Chomsky, particularly for his views on open scholarship and Israeli state violence, has regularly found himself at the end of painful allegations, such as those unsurprisingly thrown by the Anti-Defamation League, implying he is a self-hating Jew, antisemite, and even Holocaust denier. These lies sometimes occur in the writings of the rabid right and former leftists but they have, significantly, made their way into mainstream academia. For example, after discussing and denouncing various Holocaust deniers, Deborah Lipstadt, who was at the centre of the well-publicized legal battle with David Irving in 2000, moved on to Chomsky:

> It is this commitment to free inquiry and the power of mythical thinking that explains, at least in part, how revisionists have attracted leading figures and institutions. Noam Chomsky is probably the best known among them. Chomsky wrote the introduction to a book by French revisionist Robert Faurisson. In it Chomsky argued that scholars' ideas cannot be censored no matter how distasteful they may be. Though Alfred Kazin was right on target when he recently described Chomsky as a "dupe of intellectual pride so overweening that he is incapable of making distinctions between totalitarian and democratic societies,

> between oppressors and victims," Chomsky's argument shocked many people, including those who thought they were inured to Chomsky's antics.[118]

Lipstadt fires more at Chomsky's defence of free speech but by claiming "revisionists have attracted leading figures and institutions. Noam Chomsky is probably the best known among them" leaves the uncomfortable and obviously inaccurate impression that Chomsky is effectively a Holocaust denier, a figure little better than a David Irving. Furthermore, Lipstadt does not mention that the introduction to Faurisson's work was done *without* Chomsky's consent nor does she mention comments such as these made two years before and referring to work two decades before:

> In my own writings, from the earliest to the present, the conclusions of standard Holocaust studies are taken simply as fact, as Cohn knows perfectly well. In the introduction to my first collection of political essays, 20 years ago, I add that we have lost our humanity if we are willing to enter into debate over Nazi crimes with those who deny or defend them... Where no civil liberties issues arise, I have been quite explicit about the fact the views of Faurisson and others are diametrically opposed to my own firm conclusions about the facts.[119]

For another dubious argument, note the quotation from Kazin that Chomsky "is incapable of making distinctions between totalitarian and democratic societies, between oppressors and victims." This is either a lie or plain ignorance given that Chomsky has never, to the best of my knowledge, made such suggestions (and I'd be amazed if he ever would). As it happens, Chomsky has, on countless occasions made comments that flatly contradict such views. But to counter the allegations made against Chomsky, here are examples of how Chomsky might respond and note the working assumptions which do not reflect the way Chomsky was represented by Lipstadt:

> As we have stressed throughout this book, the U.S. media do not function in the manner of the propaganda system of a totalitarian state.[120]

> In what is nowadays called a totalitarian state, or military state, it's easy. You just hold a bludgeon over their heads, and if they get out of line you smash them over the head. But as society has become more free and democratic, you lose that capacity. Therefore you have to turn to the techniques of propaganda. The logic is clear. Propaganda is to a democracy what the bludgeon is to a totalitarian state.[121]

> in our system what you might call "state propaganda" isn't expressed as such, as it would be in a totalitarian society – rather it's implicit... In fact the nature of Western systems of indoctrination is typically not

> understood by dictators, they don't understand the utility for propaganda purposes of having "critical debate."
>
> [In response to a question about *misrepresentation* with reference to the Faurisson affair] Why is that surprising?...this is not happening in the mass media, this is happening in the intellectual journals. And intellectuals are specialists in defamation, they're basically commissars – they're the ideological managers, so they are the ones who feel the most threatened by dissidence...a lot of what I write is a critique of the American liberal intellectual establishment, and they don't like that particularly.
>
> I focus my efforts against the terror and violence of my own state for really two main reasons. First of all, in my case the actions of my state happen to make up the main component of international violence in the world. But much more importantly than that, it's because American actions are the things that I can do something about...the principle that I think we ought to follow is the principle we rightly expected Soviet dissidents to follow... Sakharov did not treat every atrocity as identical – he had nothing to say about American atrocities... And that was right – because those were the ones that he was responsible for, and that he might have been able to influence.[122]

Once more, facts matter little for such critics of Chomsky, presumably because slinging mud does the denouncing job much better.

What this suggests is a kind of intellectual imperialism which assumes that certain views are just off limits. In a similar and highly relevant way, Keith Whitelam has noted "methodological imperialism" in the humanities and in discussions of ancient Israel, designed to control contemporary power, knowledge and disciplinary space. This includes common techniques such as misleading denunciations of opponents without reference to sources coupled with authoritative claims.[123] Whitelam also ties in contemporary scholarship on ancient Israel with aims of the neo-conservative Project for the New American Century and discourse on "civilization," critiquing in particularly William Dever. Dever, for instance, felt "Western civilization" was being threatened by those who took a more minimalist stance on the historical accuracy of the history of Israel presented in the Hebrew Bible/Old Testament and yearned for a time when professional biblical scholars could provide "some sort of moral enlightenment and leadership," not to mention a time, which has apparently gone, when American scholarship dominated archaeology. Even more bizarrely, Dever believes that if the minimalist agenda could ever be carried out it would be disastrous for the present because it could lead to the conditions of despair that "have often historically led to Fascism"![124] As

Whitelam points out, "It is not ancient space which is being revealed in this narrative but a reflection of contemporary attempts to export a new imperialism."[125]

In this context, it is now perhaps less surprising that some of those associated with the Context Group have been so scathingly dismissive of opponents, particularly as the intellectual issue at hand concerns the differences in civilizations or a massive cultural area sometimes designated "the Middle East." These interests are prominent in contemporary political discourse and it is difficult to avoid the conclusion that here we have another attempt, witting or unwitting, to "export a new imperialism," both methodologically and politically. In certain cases of those associated with the Context Group, we come far too close not just to a sectarian model of scholarship but also to being told that there is a stark, absolute decision to be made: you are either with us or against us.

Conclusions

Lest I be misunderstood, I am not saying that there is no such thing as difference between now and then, here and there, and I am certainly not saying anything on the issue of whether those scholars critiqued personally agree or disagree with someone like Thomas Friedman (I have absolutely no idea). I like Derek Gregory's related formula that we can agree with L. P. Hartley that the past is a different country where they do things differently without neglecting William Faulkner's comments, with reference to the American South, that the past is not dead and it is not even past. Distance and difference, Gregory reminds us, is not absolute, fixed and given but "set in motion and made meaningful through cultural practices."[126] Gregory's formula may well be one that is agreed upon across the board in the historical study of Christian origins, but what I particularly want to stress is that the rhetorically stark contrasts between then and now, there and here, have emerged in New Testament scholarship at a notable period in recent history and – wittingly or unwittingly – buy into the rhetoric of Orientalism old and new. Given the amount of comparison with *contemporary* geographical areas and religious traditions that are loudly echoed in the clash of civilizations approach, contemporary constructions of Arabs and Muslims and certain Context Group material is particularly striking.

I would also strongly stress again that I am not challenging the use of anthropology used in New Testament studies as such, even if anthropology should be used far more carefully than it sometimes is and qualifications ought to be more clearly made. That said, I would equally stress that the old fashioned Orientalist, and at times basically racist, categories sometimes employed are of zero value for understanding the peoples studied, present or past. No matter how wrong some members of the Context Group think their opponents' use of social sciences may be, replacing opponents' models/approaches with models grounded in morally dubious categories is, quite obviously, outdated, naïve, and dangerous. Furthermore, some of the ways in which the generalizing nature of the use of anthropology in New Testament studies has been influenced by and feeds into the disturbing views surrounding the "clash of civilizations" ought to be cause for serious concern. The arguments sometimes made and categories sometimes used in New Testament studies are too similar and too contemporary to be mere coincidence. Indeed, we saw that a popular online advocate of the Context Group was more than happy to apply the approaches developed by the Context Group to Islam, Arabs and the Muslim world.

I would also stress strongly that some of the groups and individuals discussed in this chapter are not necessarily willing lackeys in US-led foreign policy and, many may well be outright hostile toward it.[127] But I would stress equally strongly that the emergence of these kinds of approaches in New Testament studies in the past three decades is, again, culturally explicable. They certainly replicate contemporary cultural and political concerns about the "Middle East." The danger of enhancing the kind of rhetoric used by the New Testament and Christian origins scholars discussed in this chapter can hardly be underestimated. Scratch beneath the surface of what we have recently seen in Afghanistan, Iraq, Guantánamo, Abu Ghraib, non-investigated deaths of "others," the death of Baha Mousa in British custody in Basra and, sadly, so on, and you will soon see advocates of a civilizations clash, civilization difference, stark human difference or something related. New Testament and Christian origins scholarship has consistently been tossed along by imperial powers of the times. The time for going well beyond mere lip service to critical self-scrutiny is long overdue in the light of hideously emboldened Orientalism.

Part III

"Jewishness," Jesus and Christian Origins since 1967

Black Sunday *was but one participant in the much larger transformation of U.S. public discourse about Israel in the 1970s. This transformation was the result of unplanned, uncoordinated, yet quite powerful conjuncture of diverse interests and images. What is perhaps most striking about this history is the remarkable differences in the institutions and practices that constituted it. American Jews, evangelical Christians, military policymakers, and traditional conservative intellectuals all developed their interests in Israel and its military for different reasons, and they did so from diverse socio-political locations, with different access to cultural capital, and varying levels of self-consciousness...What emerged at these intersections was an increased U.S. investment in an image of a militarized Israel, one that represented revitalized masculinity and restored national pride.*

M. McAlister[1]

Chapter 5

The Context: Judaism and Christianity; Israel and the West

"Jesus the Jew" since 1967

> *Having produced a book on Jesus which I thought would be judged "unorthodox" by Christians, Jews and New Testament scholars alike, I was greatly surprised by an overall lack of hostility. Of course, some unkind words were printed. A Jewish critic, violently resenting my refusal to classify Jesus as a Pharisee, put me among the anti-Semites... But on the whole the findings oscillated between warm approval and an open verdict.*
>
> Geza Vermes[1]

For this writer at least, one of the most perplexing things in historical Jesus studies is just how long the "Jewishness" of Jesus took to be widely recognized in European and North American scholarship.[2] By this I do not mean the issue of Jesus' ethnicity as such – with exceptions in Nazi scholarship virtually everyone has accepted Jesus was born Jewish – but the stress on, and debates over, Jesus' teachings as particularly *Jewish*, in contrast to the hard dissimilarity with Judaism that dominated much of twentieth-century scholarship. In 1973, Geza Vermes' ground-breaking *Jesus the Jew* would pave the way for a series of historical Jesus studies – with Jesus as Jew stressed in numerous book titles[3] – that would, with their own particular emphases, make claims about just how Jewish Jesus was. But why did it take until the 1970s? It might have been thought that the Holocaust would have prompted a more immediate rethink of the historical Jesus' attitude towards Jewish religion. But, as E. P. Sanders famously showed in 1977, anti-Jewish and antisemitic attitudes were deeply embedded in post-war New Testament scholarship, particularly, though not exclusively, in German scholarship.[4] This raises a similar issue: why did it take until the 1970s for a Sanders-like critique of scholarly portrayals of Judaism to have a significant impact on New Testament scholarship?

In a recent book on scholarly debates over the historical Jesus, William Arnal gives several plausible reasons for the emergence of the debate over Jesus' "Jewishness" since the 1970s which he could generally relate to "the postmodern condition" and a lack of socioeconomic stability, coupled with fractured cultural identities associated with "globalization." In this context, Arnal argues, the emergence of "Jesus the Jew," with a strict scholarly definition of a culturally stable "Judaism" functions as one response. Other reasons given by Arnal include a reaction against the dominance of pre-1970s German scholarship and the shifts in the geographical centre of scholarship towards the UK, Ireland and, most significantly perhaps, North America. Tied in with this is the desire for Christian scholars to show that Christianity is not antisemitic at its core, ultimately to distance Christianity from complicity in the Holocaust.[5]

I find no reason to dispute the contribution of these factors to the emergence of the strange debate over the "Jewish Jesus" and I will assume their validity. I do, however, think that there is another important factor that has not been properly noticed in the history of New Testament scholarship: Western and Christian attitudes toward Israel, particularly in the last third of the twentieth century, an issue mentioned in passing by Arnal.[6] Given that we have already seen that the interests of New Testament scholarship are deeply immersed in wider national and international political trends, the emergence and acceptance of such a politically charged statement as "Jesus the Jew" – and by implication the general acceptance of Vermes' Jesus and Sanders' critique of New Testament scholarship – is unlikely to be an exception.

The decisive moment, I would argue, was the 1967 "Six Day War" which led to the politically and religiously significant increase in Israeli territory (Sinai Peninsula, Golan Heights, West Bank, Gaza and East Jerusalem). Israel now emerged as the major political power in that part of the world. There is little doubt that this war, along with the 1973 war, signalled a dramatic shift in the attitudes of American Jews toward Israel, from a kind of indifference to high levels of staunch support,[7] with the Holocaust taking a more central role in American culture in particular. It will now be shown in some detail that it was in the post-1967 period that a staunchly pro-Israeli line is found more broadly in Western politics, culture and strands of Christian thought, and that these social and ideological conditions paved the way for the acceptance of, and emphasis on, "Jesus the Jew," along with attempts to distance Christianity from complicity in the Holocaust. Like the new post-1967 support for Israel, it is striking that "Jesus the Jew" was not vigorously developed in the immediate decades after the Holocaust.

Moreover, this general historical context can further explain why there have been such heated disputes over Jesus' "Jewishness" along with unsavoury comments made by contemporary scholars recalling the horrific events of the 1930s and 1940s when discussing the work of their opponents whose Jesus is deemed not sufficiently "Jewish."

What is also particularly noteworthy in New Testament scholarship is a major insistence on Jesus being Jewish but at the same time dropping some features deemed typically Jewish. As we will see in the next chapter, for all the pious words about making Jesus Jewish, there is not always much difference between Christian writing on Jesus before and after Vermes: more often than not Jesus still does away with key parts of the Torah, something I would argue is historically unlikely but, more importantly for present purposes, involves, ironically enough, a near systematic ignoring of contradictory Jewish sources. This too, as we will see, owes something to Western and Christian attitudes towards Israel, alongside attitudes of Christian superiority and a deep-rooted Orientalist tradition.

The Importance of Israel and Support for Israeli State Policy in Post-1967 Western Politics

> *Israel's stunning victory in the Six Day War marked the turning point in its relations with the United States. Prior to June 1967 U.S. policymakers regarded the Jewish state as a liability...*
>
> D. Little[8]

> *Coverage of Israel in the* New York Times *increased dramatically after June 1967. The 1955 and 1965 entries for Israel in the* New York Times Index *each filled 60 column inches. The entry for Israel in 1975 ran to fully 260 column inches.*
>
> Norman Finkelstein[9]

> *It has become commonplace in recent years that Israel and the Holocaust are the twin pillars of American Jewish "civil religion" – the symbols that bind together Jews in the United States whether they are believers or nonbelievers, on the political right, left, or center. But through the mid-1960s Israel, like the Holocaust, didn't loom that large in American Jewish consciousness. In the late sixties and early seventies, Israel became much more important to American Jews, and, in a set of spiraling interactions, concern with Israel was expressed in ways that evoked the Holocaust, and vice versa... As is well known, the spring of 1967 was a dramatic turning point in American Jews' relationship to Israel.*
>
> Peter Novick[10]

The not wholly unambiguous UN Security Council Resolution 242 put forward in the aftermath of the 1967 war stated that: "withdrawal of Israeli armed forces from territories occupied in the recent conflict; termination of all claims or states of belligerency and respect for and acknowledgement of the sovereignty, territorial integrity and political independence of every State in the area and their right to live in peace within secure and recognized boundaries free from threats or acts of force."[11] Israel made moves to cement its territorial dominance by establishing settlers on the newly gained territories with Palestinians under military rule. The aftermath of 1967 also led to a rise in religious nationalism and the hope for permanent control of occupied territories which were part of so-called biblical Israel.[12] In the following decades this has been accompanied by increased settlements that partially serve the function of embedding Israeli claims in occupied territories. As an Amnesty International report put it in 1999:

> Since 1967, when Israel occupied the West Bank, including East Jerusalem, and the Gaza Strip, thousands of Palestinian homes have been demolished... The demolition of Palestinian houses is inextricably linked with Israeli policy to control and colonize areas of the West Bank. There seems no doubt that the settlement project has been conceived, stimulated and implemented by the Government of Israel; colonization has not been a spontaneous popular movement taking place in the face of governmental resistance or indifference. Furthermore, this policy has been energetically followed for over 30 years by all administrations from 1967 until the present time... At the time of the 1967 war the only Jews in the West Bank were the Samaritan community in Nablus (numbering about 250). There are now well over 300,000 Jewish settlers living in new colonies (referred to as "settlements") throughout the West Bank.[13]

The post-1967 rise in US support for Israel was perceived partly as a counter to Soviet influence in the region, and was, more generally, deemed useful for US hegemonic interests (see below). General cultural and political similarities between the US and Israel may also have contributed to the relationship, along with the possibility of moving away from the increasing problems in Vietnam and some degree of "admiration" at the way Israel had dealt with the Arab world in contrast to the US handling of Vietnam.[14] There were initial disputes in US high offices between those following the William Rogers line and general international interpretation of UN 242 and those following the Henry Kissinger line of a continuing status quo, or "stalemate."[15] As Noam Chomsky points out, the eventual Kissinger line winning out meant "a major turning point in Middle East diplomacy and is of great significance today. Since that time, the United States has barred every diplomatic initiative based on UN 242 under its original meaning, in complete diplomatic isolation (along with Israel)."[16] As US-backed Israel was the most powerful local player involved in the Palestinian question there would only be one winner. The brutally honest comments of the then (May 21, 1973) leading oil expert in the Senate, Henry Jackson, give some clear reasons for US interests and why they would be so intimately tied up with the role of Israel:

> Mr President, such stability as now obtains in the Middle East is, in my view, largely the result of the strength and Western orientation of Israel on the Mediterranean and Iran [under the Shah] on the Persian Gulf. These two countries, reliable friends of the United States, together with Saudi Arabia, have served to inhibit and contain those irresponsible and radical elements in certain Arab States – such as Syria, Libya, Lebanon, and Iraq – who, were they free to do so, would pose a grave threat indeed to our principal sources of petroleum in the Persian Gulf.[17]

There were also post-1967 attitude changes in the UK. British governmental policy has consistently sided with Israel over against the Palestinians to the present. Mark Curtis has looked at previously secret government files and gives concrete examples. For instance, a 1970 Foreign Office report on future British policy in this area did not opt for an *entirely* pro-Israeli policy but simply could not endorse a pro-Arab policy, not only because of public and political support in the UK but also because of US pressure "to keep us in line in any public pronouncements or negations on the dispute."[18] The British rhetoric may not always compete with her more gung-ho US partner but the message is never too far removed. Interesting for present purposes are the assumptions underlying some of the claims of British governments: for all the acts of Israeli state aggression, Britain has not made any serious attempts to act in defence of Palestinian victims and, among other things, has provided intelligence for Israel against Palestinians and approved the continuing multi-million pounds supply of arms to Israel.[19]

While there are certainly voices in the British media critical of Israeli state policy toward the Palestinians, solutions such as those touted and put into practice against any other states that are criticized by Amnesty International for human rights abuses, breaches of international law, non-acceptance of international treaties on nuclear weapons, and the ignoring of UN resolutions, are not high on the agenda. This illustrates just how embedded pro-Israeli state policy is in Western media and culture. As Curtis points out, "Sanctions against Israel, unlike against Milosevic and Mugabe, are not even a serious option – sanctions are largely unmentionable in the mainstream media, whose framing of policy options is largely set by the priorities of the state."[20] More generally, the veteran British journalist, Robert Fisk, comments on the increasing downplaying of Israeli state aggression and after 1967 and 1973:

> Israel's "security" – or supposed lack thereof – became the yardstick for all negotiations, all military threats and all wars. The injustice done to the Palestinians, the dispossession, the massacres...the occupation of the remainder of the mandate territory and the bloody suppression of any and all manifestations of Palestinian resistance: all this had to take second place to Israel's security and the civilised values and democracy for which Israel was widely promoted. Her army, which often behaved with cruelty and indiscipline, was to be regarded as an exemplar of "purity of arms" and those of us who witnessed Israel's killing of civilians were to be abused as liars, anti-Semites or friends of "terrorism."[21]

Note here how links with antisemitism are made by critics of Israeli state actions, an allegation increasingly made in the past 30 years.[22] The implication of such antisemitism, as we will see (and have seen), is also important for understanding historical Jesus scholarship and the massive emphasis on Jesus' Jewishness.

It is not difficult and not controversial to show that there has been a broad post-1967 attitude shift heavily favouring Israel and Israeli policy in the US which has remained consistently positive to this day. The details in US politics and culture have been collected and discussed by Chomsky who comments,

> American liberalism had always been highly sympathetic to Israel, but there was a noticeable positive shift in attitudes in 1967 with the demonstration of Israel's military might. Top Israeli military commanders made it clear not long after that Israel had faced no serious military threat... But this fact was suppressed here in favor of the image of an Israeli David confronting a brutal Arab Goliath, enabling liberal humanitarians to offer their sympathy and support to the major military power of the region... Considerable effort was devoted to showing that the New Left supported Arab terrorism and the destruction of Israel, a task largely accomplished in defiance of the facts (the New Left, as the documentary record clearly shows, quite generally tended to support the position of the Israeli doves)... Now, the insistent complaint is that the media are antagonistic to Israel and subject to the baleful influence of the PLO... While this may appear ludicrous given the evident facts, neither the effort...nor its insignificant success in containing deviations towards a minimal degree of even-handedness will come as no surprise to students of twentieth century propaganda systems.[23]

The broad cultural bias in favour of Israeli state actions against the Palestinians in the US media has been shown by others. In US popular culture and television news coverage, which have been heavily pro-Israel, even to the extent of the mildest criticism of Israeli actions toward Palestinians only just recently peeking through,[24] Israel had become a model for military power and the combating of terrorism and was able to fight in a way that the US was not able to in Vietnam.[25]

Another important development involves the memorializing of the Holocaust since 1967. Norman Finkelstein has argued in some detail that this post-1967 development in the US involved increased investment in the Holocaust memorials and publicity which, he suggests, was, and continues to be, an ideological weapon that supports Israeli actions and little to do with the horrors of Jewish suffering in under the Nazis.[26] Peter Novick has similarly argued, though not without significant differences from Finkelstein, that from the end of the 1960s the Holocaust and the plight of German Jews at the turn of the twentieth century became increasingly prominent and sensitive in US culture. The cultural context of the increasing interest in the Holocaust from the end of the 1960s included American Jewish perceptions of "new antisemitism" after a "golden age," the perceived problems surrounding increasing assimilation,[27] the emergence of identity politics, and, significantly, Israel's wars of 1967 and 1973 which formed part of a heightened solidarity between American Jews and Israel, including endorsement of matters relating to Israel in US party politics.[28]

In another way, the cultural bias has been shown in detailed research carried out by the Glasgow University Media Unit.[29] Based on a study of British television news over two years and interviews with over 800 people (including senior television figures), Greg Philo and Mike Berry show that the reporting of the Israeli/Palestinian conflict works to confuse viewers and disproportionately sides with Israeli government views. Israelis get twice as much interview time as the Palestinians. US politicians who support Israeli actions feature more than politicians from any other country and twice as much as those from Britain.

In terms of viewers, the lack of historical context in television reporting had significant consequences. Most viewers did not know that Palestinians were forced from their homes in 1948 and that Israel had forcibly occupied territories where Palestinian refugees had moved. Most viewers did not know Palestinians were effectively under Israeli rule and that there was Israeli economic dominance (e.g. control of water). Not unrelated was a tendency for viewers to see Palestinian action as the cause of the problem and this was partly because Israeli actions were often explained and seen as responding to what had been done to them. For example, in the 2001 samples, Israeli action was six times more likely to be presented as retaliation and response than Palestinian action. It naturally follows, then, that there was often a stronger emphasis on Israeli casualties despite heavier Palestinian casualties. Through audience analysis, the effects of this presentation weighted in favour of Israeli state action are consequently shown, as are the ways in which this presentation can lead to a profound lack of knowledge of the history of the conflict.

Clearly, then, the argument of a pro-Israeli line in post-1967 Western thought and practice is a powerful one. We can now turn to its impact on religion and academia, both of which are crucial contexts for understanding the stress on Jesus' "Jewishness" since the 1970s.

The Rise of Christian Zionism and their Agenda in Anglo-American Political Circles

> *Now the Lord said to Abram, "Go from your country and your kindred and your father's house to the land that I will show you. I will make of you a great nation, and I will bless you, and make your name great, so that you will be a blessing. I will bless those who bless you, and the one who curses you I will curse; and in you all the families of the earth shall be blessed."*
>
> Genesis 12:1-3

> *Oh, but ready or not, Jesus is coming soon.*
>
> From the "Rapture Ready" website

With all the turmoil happening in and around Israel in the late 1960s, not to mention the widespread shifts in the Middle East from secular nationalism to more overtly Islamic identities, it is no coincidence that certain Christians began to think of end times and see divine work at hand in Israel. Indeed, we should not forget that the "biblical lands" were a prominent feature of American popular culture for decades, ranging from the nineteenth-century travelogues to the Hollywood biblical epics.[31] And so since the 1970s Christian Zionists, with many or most arguing that the Land of Israel includes the lands gained in 1967, have risen sharply in prominence, particularly among evangelicals, and have fostered close links with the Israeli nationalist party, Likkud. Many of the figures and groups have since become household names in the US and beyond. Most famously these include Pat Robertson and the Christian Coalition and Jerry Falwell and the Moral Majority. Their approach is quite explicitly in favour of

Israeli state policy. As Pat Robertson put it in a letter to Omri Sharon, "For over thirty years I have been one of the strongest supporters of the nation of Israel anywhere in the world. I have stood with the cause of Israel against all of the threats of the nation's enemies," adding – and note the typical connection made with antisemitism – "I see looming in the distance grave threats against the nation of Israel, not only from militants in Hamas and Hezbollah and the nuclear ambitions of the leaders of Iran, but also the virulent anti-Semitism which is so frequently expressed throughout the Muslim world, Europe, and the United Nations."[32]

Linked with such groups are the wide ranging hard-line pro-Israel organizations and hard-line pro-Israel church networks and organizations like Americans for a Safe Israel, Christians' Israel Public Action Campaign, Christian Friends of Israel, Christians United for Israel, the International Fellowship of Christians and Jews/Stand for Israel, and The Friends of Israel Gospel Ministry, Inc.[33] Examples of their hard pro-Israel line can range from lobbying the most senior officials in US politics for the US embassy to be moved from Tel Aviv to Jerusalem to funding Jews to emigrate from Russia, for instance, to Israel. It barely needs stating that such groups unashamedly mix religion and party politics. Christians United for Israel, for example, has the following goals:

> To develop a national Rapid Response e-mail and fax communication to Christians United for Israel members in every state and congressional district for the imperative purpose of responding immediately with broad national support in defense of Israel on biblically based issues.
>
> To continue to increase our basis of support of Israel and the Jewish people around the world through the education of the Christian Community concerning the Jewish contribution to Christianity and Israel's biblical mandate to the land through bible teachings and pilgrimages to Israel.[34]

Christians' Israel Public Action Campaign head their website with a classic "end-time" quotation from Habakkuk 2:2-3, while on the same page a picture from a meeting concerned with "the expected effects of the planned evacuation of Gaza on U.S. national interests" (May 23, 2005). This combination of party politics and evangelical Christianity is clear in the explanation of their history and typical of the details available on their website. The Campaign was developed "to speak out on behalf of Israel and the Jewish people from a biblical perspective, for Christians primarily" but they also wish to speak for "official Washington: Members of Congress, the Senators and Representatives, the President, the Secretary of State and the other officials of the executive branch." There were also concerns that "people at the grassroots across America" did not understand "Israel's serious predicament in the Middle East today." Through daily activity on Capitol Hill they claim, "we have an impact for solid policies that support Israel on biblical grounds."[35]

Educational programmes of at least one of these groups are culturally significant for present purposes because their aims are close to some of the concerns of modern scholarship on Jesus in that they highlight the importance of the Jewish roots of Christianity (see below). The Friends of Israel Christian Ministry, Inc. – whose editorial line has claimed that "Palestinians can't afford to lose Israel as a neighbor because, when all is said and done, she is a very good one"[36] – have teaching programmes designed to promote understanding of the Jewish nature of Christian origins. For example, their Institute of Jewish Studies is "a one-year program of biblical study for the committed Christian who wants his or her life to count for eternity." Moreover, "as one of the premier Bible-teaching organizations in the world today," The Friends of Israel Christian Ministry, Inc. has "a wide range of ministries to acquaint believers with the Jewish background of the Bible and with the place God's ancient people occupy in His plan."[37]

Christians of a right-wing Zionist ilk have not only made spectacular use of media resources such as television, radio, and newspapers but have produced their very own prophetic books and pioneered major developments in the millenarian novel. One landmark publication was *The Late Great Planet Earth* by Hal Lindsey, published (1970), non-coincidentally, in the aftermath of the 1967 war. In fact, the book deals with the events of 1967 and their aftermath in some detail, taking staunchly pro-Israeli and anti-Arab lines.[38] The book looks to biblical prophecies, such as those from Ezekiel, to show that Israel was prophesied to be a state in 1948 and would go on to witness a period of great prosperity prompting an attack from the far north (Gog/Russia) and, ultimately, the rapture, the second coming and end times in general. One major event that will be a sign of the time is the rebuilding of the third temple on its historic site.[39] That this might be problematic given the location of the Muslim Dome of the Rock means little: "Obstacle or no obstacle, it is certain that the Temple will be rebuilt. Prophecy demands it."[40] To highlight the popularity of this book, the staggeringly high sales it claims for itself on the cover of most editions only need be noted: "OVER 15 MILLION COPIES SOLD."[41] It was even made into a film in 1977 with Orson Welles, no less, as the narrator. Michael Northcott's comments reflect the widely-held commonsensical view that *The Late Great Planet Earth* represents a pivotal role for Christian Zionism, helping "turn dispensationalism from a minority creed of the more conservative evangelical churches and Bible Colleges into a majority faith among millions of American evangelical Christians."[42]

The years and decades following *The Late Great Planet Earth* spawned numerous books, films and videos concerning end times and the Middle East. Creating fiction out of Lindsey-style prophecy are the *Left Behind* series of novels written by Jerry Jenkins and Timothy LaHaye, two major figures of the Christian right (LaHaye, for example, was a key figure in the founding of the Moral Majority). *Left Behind* begins by describing Israel's economic miracle, attacks on Israel foiled by God (based on prophecies from Ezekiel), the rapture, the origins of the third Jerusalem temple, the rise of the antichrist through the UN, and so on. A group of intrepid converts are among those "left behind" ready to do God's work against the forces of evil amidst explosions, romance, tension and intrigue. The series is constantly reported to have sold *over 60 million copies* since the first book (a figure, naturally, heading one of their websites)[43] and the books repeatedly top US book charts. And for the younger ones (ages 10–14) there is also the *Left Behind: The Kids* series which has sold over 10 million copies, according to the Left Behind website.[44]

We can also visually follow the adventures of our post-rapture heroes in the *Left Behind* films. These may contain painful acting of the cheap soap opera variety, they may include a once z-list celebrity from the not-so-funny US sitcom *Growing Pains*, and they may not be dominating the world of Hollywood. But then the target audience may not care, as the films can premier through a massive network of churches, schools, universities and "everywhere there are projection systems and Christians with a passion for outreach."[45] The first film, *Left Behind: The Movie*, was originally released on video in 2000, sold 2.5 million copies and, after a concerted campaign, was shown at 900 cinemas by 2001. As one critic put it, this is "an extraordinary achievement for an independent film by any standards but even more remarkable for one that had sold so well on video."[46] The Left Behind team are even tapping into the lucrative computer game market with *Left Behind: Eternal Forces*, a game where the gamers can get involved with the post-rapture action. In a combination of "physical and spiritual warfare" gamers can stand firm in the tradition of Christian Zionism: they can use "the power of prayer to strengthen your troops in combat and wield modern military weaponry throughout the game world."[47]

If the numbers of books sold, films watched, and violent prayers recited do not say something about the cultural and, ultimately, political significance of these books then perhaps the fact that the authors, without any Dan Brown ambiguity, claim to believe something like what they write should. The boundaries between their fiction and what they really believe are well and truly blurred. As their website informs us with obvious relevance in terms of a post-1967 cultural shift:

> Did you know the Bible is full of prophecies that have already come true? When Jesus Christ was born in Bethlehem, he fulfilled a prophecy. The fact that his mother was a virgin fulfilled another prediction. Later when Jesus healed the blind and the crippled and fed the hungry, his actions fulfilled more prophecies. When Jesus died on the Cross, it fulfilled a prophecy. More prophecies were likely fulfilled in 1948 when Israel became an Independent nation and in 1967 when Israel regained control of Jerusalem from Jordan in the Six Day War.
>
> "They will be brutally killed by the sword or sent away as captives to all the nations of the world. And Jerusalem will be conquered and tramped down by the Gentiles until the age of the Gentiles comes to an end" (Luke 21:24).[48]

It is too easy to dismiss Christian Zionists and the Christian right as a bunch of religious extremists on the fringe because nowadays, in terms of conventional party politics, they should be taken very, *very* seriously. In other words these kinds of Christians form a significant enough group that the major US political players may feel it unwise to ignore them. Donald Wagner has given a notable statistic. In 2002, when there was strong international pressure for Ariel Sharon to withdraw from Jenin, the pro-Israel lobby and the Christian right gathered over 100,000 emails, calls and visits urging George W. Bush to avoid restraining Israel. Wagner quotes the comments of Jerry Falwell, who represented 20–25 million dispensationalist evangelicals, made on an October edition of *60 Minutes*: "I think now we can count on President Bush to do the right thing for Israel every time." Wagner also points to full-page advertisements placed in major newspapers and Christian journals under the campaign heading "Christian Call for a United Jerusalem" and including claims that Jerusalem has been "the spiritual and political capital of only the Jewish people for 3,000 years." The signatories included Pat Robertson and Jerry Falwell along with Brandt Gustafson (president of the National Religious Broadcasters) and Don Argue (president of the National Association of Evangelicals).[49]

In recent times the Christian Zionists have had their men in presidential office. Ronald Reagan, who was using the language of extreme evangelicals long before he assumed the presidential office, had wondered out loud whether biblical prophecies of Armageddon were due within a generation and seems to have viewed the Cold War and the Middle East in apocalyptic terms based on biblical prophecy of the sort that might be found in *The Late Great Planet Earth* (e.g. Gog/north=Russia), a book which Reagan had read.[50] And, at the time of writing, the Christian right once again have their man in the presidential office, George W. Bush, not to mention several of their people in key governmental positions. Among other things, Bush is the man who was *reported* to have claimed that God told him to invade Afghanistan and Iraq, the man who apparently opens his cabinet meetings with prayers, the man who conducts weekly Bible studies in the White House, the man who has presidential speeches littered with biblical allusion, the man who had the openly Islam-hating dispensationalist Reverend Franklin Graham (son of Billy) give a prayer at his inaugural address, and the man who continues Reagan's apocalyptic attitude toward Middle Eastern politics.[51] When Bush first started on his presidential campaign he went to a Christian right meeting run by the Committee to Restore American Values chaired by...none other than the co-author of the *Left Behind* series, Reverend Timothy LaHaye.[52]

It is widely acknowledged that Bush's slightly surprising electoral victory of 2004 was helped in no small part by that most Machiavellian of political movers, Karl Rove, mobilizing millions of white evangelicals who form the breeding ground of the Christian Zionists, or the Republican Party's "base" as Rove would have it.[53] The caution of Rove in carefully cultivating the Christian right is shown in the writings of the Christian Zionist group "Rapture Ready" who wait impatiently for the imminent second coming. "Rapture Ready" is a group wary of political powers and readily admits that Jesus would not have voted Republican. But ultimately the Republicans have to be the best of a bad bunch and this means certainly *not* voting Democrat:

> You can be a perfectionist and find a hundred things wrong with the Republicans. It is serious error to try compare [*sic*] a floundering friend to a deadly enemy. Human government never will be able to solve the world's problems. There never will be true peace until the Prince of Peace establishes His Millennial Kingdom. That understood, until the Lord Jesus comes for His Church in the rapture – presuming both major political parties in America continue to hold to their present party lines – it is the view of Rapture Ready that Republican values are America's best political option.[54]

It would also be a mistake to think that western-centred views on Israel were restricted to right-wing Christian extremists. From a more secular imperialistic perspective, though obviously tied in with the Bush administration and the agenda of the Christian right, are the views of those individuals associated with the neo-conservative Project for the New American Century such as William Kristol, Paul Wolfowitz, Dick Cheney, Richard Pearle, Elliott Abrams and Donald Rumsfeld, along with their surrounding advisors.[55] Away from the religious rhetoric and firmly in camp of secular state ruthlessness, Rumsfeld claimed in 2002:

> My feelings about the so-called occupied territories are that there was a war, Israel urged neighboring countries not to get involved in it once it started, they all jumped in, and they lost a lot of real estate to Israel because Israel prevailed in that conflict. In the intervening period, they've made some settlements in various parts of the so-called occupied area, which was the result of a war, which they won.[56]

Away from the conventional right wing of US politics, there have been strong overlaps in the aims of the neo-conservatives with the aims of Democrats, including the Clinton administration, and American liberalism in general.[57] On the issue of Israel, the Democrats have remained staunchly pro-Israel at the expense of Palestinians. This is perhaps best seen in Oslo II (1996) where Bill Clinton has been heavily praised for what is widely seen as the (positive) landmark of his presidency. Yet, underlying all the rhetoric, the balance of economic, material, and geographical power is overwhelmingly in favour of the state of Israel.[58] In more general terms there are few better ways of highlighting the extent of US support for Israel than the hard facts of the allocation and use of US foreign and military aid. As George Monbiot put it:

> Though Israel ranks 23rd on the global development index...it remains the world's largest recipient of US aid. The US government dispensed $11bn of civil foreign assistance in 2004. Of this, Israel received $555m; the three poorest nations on earth...were given a total of $69m. More importantly, last year Israel also received $2.2bn of military aid. It does not depend economically on this assistance. Its gross domestic product amounts to $155bn, and its military budget to $9.5bn... Most of the money given by the US foreign military financing programme – in common with all US aid disbursements – is spent in the United States.[59]

We might add that in August 2007 it was announced that Israel was to receive $30 billion dollars in military aid over the next decade, with Ehud Olmert quoted as saying that it "illustrates the depth of the relationship between the two countries and the commitment of the United States to the defense of Israel and preserving its qualitative superiority."[60] Action Aid is *reported* to have criticized this announcement in the light of the amount of aid given to third world countries.[61]

In other general contexts, there is, for all the heated disagreements, notable broad agreement between Democrats and far-right Republicans on the issue of Israel, thereby illustrating the deeply embedded pro-Israeli state policy in US politics. Hilary Clinton, who caused some controversy, including among the ranks of Democrats, for once endorsing a limited Palestinian state and kissing Suha Arafat, continues to show significant favour toward Israel. America will support Israel, she said, "to send a message to Hamas, Hezbollah, to the Syrians, to the Iranians – to all who seek death and domination instead of life and freedom – that we will not permit this to happen and we will take whatever steps are necessary." Clinton added that it "is a message that we want not only those in the Middle East to hear, but the world, because no nation is safe from these terrorist extremists," for "they do not believe in human rights, they do not believe in democracy. They are totalitarians, they are the new totalitarians of the 21st century." Clinton was supported by other Democrats. Anthony D. Weiner criticized "our feckless friends in Europe" for an apparently more nuanced and ambiguous approach and praised the Bush administration, showing the underlying unity over questions of Israel: "President Bush has been wrong about a lot of things but he's right about this – the United States stands with Israel." Clinton's remarks were even given cautionary approval by Helen Freedman, executive director of Americans for a Safe Israel, "I thought her remarks were very good, especially in light of her history, and we can't forget her kiss to Suha."[62] It is worth reporting that Americans for a Safe Israel (founded 1971) believe,

> Israel must retain possession and control of Judea, Samaria, Gaza and the Golan... AFSI believes that a strong Israel is essential to U.S. security and that the Jewish towns in these areas are the best guarantee against strategic vulnerability. Most importantly, the pioneering efforts of the residents in these areas have the potential of rejuvenating a dormant Zionism and igniting a second Zionist revolution.[63]

The Christian right not only have close connections with party politics through think tanks, pressure groups and funding agencies but they have strong links with the corporate world, so important in Republican- and Democratic-led party politics. Mark Lewis Taylor stresses that it is not a case of the Christian right simply putting Bush in power as their voting block affected only 1.6% of the Republican votes gained, important though this is in close elections. Instead, Taylor argues, it is the close ties the

Christian right have forged with the hugely influential 20% of US voters earning over $75,000 a year and who affect nearly 4% of nationwide presidential voting. Taylor notes the ways in which the Christian right makes such connections, such as through the Council for National Policy.[64] To state the obvious: this again shows just how deeply embedded in US political culture the Christian right have become.

One quirky (to those of us who are outsiders) but revealing example of just how embedded such ideas are in relation to Israel comes from the March 2004 Republican Party convention in Harris County, Texas. George Monbiot reports that – after large agreement on uncontroversial matters of homosexuality being clean contrary to divine will, gun control being wrong, the desire for the abolition of various taxes such as the corporate tax, and the benefits of electric fences in keeping out immigrants – screaming and fistfights began when Israel was discussed. This bitter feud lead to the "watering down" of the final motion which held that Israel has the rightful claim to Jerusalem and the West Bank, that Arab states should be pressured to take Palestinian refugees, and that Israel should do whatever is necessary to remove terrorism.[65] As Monbiot implies in his article, if the final motion was this pro-Israel and anti-Palestine, God and those Republicans only know what non-watered down versions might have looked like.

In British politics there is of course a long pro-Israeli tradition, most notably the Balfour Declaration of 1917, named, of course, after the Conservative politician and former Prime Minister Arthur Balfour. The support for Israel has crossed the right-left divide in British politics. The Labour Party, historically on the left of British mainstream politics, has shown steadfast support for Israeli state policy, usually over against Israel's neighbours. In the light of the 1973 conflict, the historian of British politics, David Childs, notes that "many on the Labour side still regarded Israel as an embattled socialist state."[66] The present Blair administration has continued to allow arms sales to Israel while the Labour Friends of Israel remain an influential lobby group in British politics. The blurred boundaries of the so-called left and right in British politics are shown by Mark Curtis who notes that Britain's failure to criticize Israel in 2001 by abstaining on a UN resolution (the only European Union state to do so) because the resolution did not sufficiently criticize the Palestinians is an instance of how some British policies are more pro-Israeli than under the Conservatives, who had even voted to condemn Israel in such resolutions in the past.[67] In fact, elsewhere Curtis goes as far as saying that "Blair leads the most pro-Israel government in recent British history."[68]

Christian Zionism has British antecedents stretching back through the sixteenth century all the way back to Bede and the Epistle of Gildas, and Christian Zionism was, of course, vigorously developed in nineteenth-century England through figures such as John Nelson Darby, founder of the Plymouth Brethren, and the Earl of Shaftesbury who argued for the central role of Jews in Israel/Palestine before the end times.[69] More recently, there are several British Christian Zionist organizations such as the Church's Ministry among Jewish People/Israel Trust of the Anglican Church, Christian Friends of Israel, Intercessors for Britain, Prayer Friends of Israel and the Council of Christians and Jews, all of which have wider international links and have been influential among British evangelicals.[70] For my present overall argument about the "Jewish Jesus," it is important to note some of the "aims" of the Church's Ministry among the Jewish People as described on their website:

> Intercession...for Jewish people to come to faith in Messiah and for the mission of the Society.
>
> Vision...pointing to God's continuing commitment to the Jewish people explaining how his future purposes for them (Romans 11) are an encouragement to mission.
>
> Co-operation...with Messianic believers to evangelize and disciple Jewish people.
>
> Education...*teaching the Jewish roots of our faith* as an incentive to prayer and mission.[71]

Mud Sticks: Higher Education and Discrediting, Misleading concerning and/or Lying about Nadia Abu el-Haj

> *Clearly we know from historical accounts (from Josephus's book* The Jewish Wars *for one) that the Roman Legion burned the city down, destroying the Upper City on the eighth of Elul, in the year 70 C.E.*
>
> Nadia Abu el-Haj[72]

> *She [*Nadia Abu el-Haj*] absurdly attempts to suggest that the Jews destroyed Jerusalem in the year 70 CE, in direct contradiction to the only historian [Josephus] who was there at the time.*
>
> Paula R. Stern[73]

> *In "Facts on the Ground," Ms. Abu el-Haj suggests Jerusalem was destroyed not by the Romans, but by the Jews themselves due to rising class tensions among them. Yet, the 1st-century historian and scribe Josephus described in great detail the Roman siege of Jerusalem.*
>
> Gabrielle Birkner[74]

The general post-war US Middle Eastern and foreign policies, of which Israel has played a central role, is to be seen as a part of the intertwining geopolitical, hegemonic and economic interests underlying or threatening US and Western capitalism.[75] At a more superficial or surface level, issues around the Middle East have attracted, and continue to attract, huge media attention. Given these points, and given what was discussed in Chapter 1, it is almost inconceivable that higher education would not show signs of many of its scholars flowing effortlessly in sync. And so, if biblical studies on an academic level were hardly going to be immune from the influences of international political and economic contexts, then how much greater would be the impact of international politics on the universities, theology departments and confessional colleges with studies so heavily focused on the Land at the heart of the Jewish and Christian faiths?

There is good evidence to back up such generalizations. Debates around the Israel/Palestine issue have explicitly made an impact on the universities, particularly but not exclusively in the US. Since the late 1970s, groups such as the American Israel Public Affairs Committee (AIPAC) have attempted to develop academics with a pro-Israel slant while attempting to gain information on academics deemed pro-Palestinian.[76] Various further examples could be given.[77] Obvious contemporary examples might include that present day McCarthyite Campus Watch, de Paul's controversial denial of tenure to Norman Finkelstein, or the David Horowitz's sensationalist and, frankly, utterly weird book, *The Professors: The 101 Most Dangerous Academics in America*, which includes plenty of well-known critics of Israeli state aggression such as Noam Chomsky and Norman Finkelstein.

Another recent and significant example of the impact of the Israel-Palestine issue in the universities is the sacking of Douglas Giles from Roosevelt University, Chicago, in Spring 2005. Giles was told by his head of department, Susan Weininger (an art historian), to avoid discussions of Israel and Palestine. A student asked about Palestinian rights, a complaint was lodged, and Giles was fired.[78] Giles claims that Weininger did not want him to allow Muslims to raise questions and that she said the following: "What disturbs me is that you act like the Palestinians have a side in this. They don't have a side! They are ANIMALS [emphasis hers]! They strap bombs to their bodies and blow up women and children! They are NOT CIVILIZED!"[79] *If* these details are correct then what is particularly significant here is that Giles' supposed wrongdoing concerns allowing *students* to discuss such issues: Giles himself did not even say anything about the state of Israel.[80]

Keith Whitelam is an important case in the context of academic biblical studies and the influence of the Palestine-Israel question on biblical studies, particularly concerning his 1996 book, *The Invention of Ancient Israel: The Silencing of Palestinian History*, and its reception. Whitelam gives numerous examples of how scholarly reconstructions of ancient Israel have suppressed Palestinian histories while creating ancient Israel in the image of modern Israel and the modern European nation state.[81] This book caused a bit of a politico-religious stir in the field and led to highly unprofessional (to put it extremely mildly) and factually inaccurate slurs levelled against Whitelam (and, to lesser extent, the other so-called "minimalists") by William Dever and others, some of whom did not even bother to read Whitelam's book![82] Allegations involved the ideologically convenient blurring of the categories of anti-Zionism, antisemitism, and criticisms of Israeli state policy. Whitelam can, of course, demolish slurs such as that of antisemitism with great ease; but that lies and factually groundless and hugely emotive slurs can be made by scholars illustrates the sensitivity of the Israel-Palestine issue in biblical studies and how it ties in with the various agendas we saw above and the policing of knowledge discussed in Chapter 1.[83]

Such attempts at discrediting any criticisms of the modern state of Israel in relation to biblical studies have continued with great intensity. The recent attempt to deny Nadia Abu el-Haj tenure at Barnard College over her critique of Israeli archaeology and its relationship to contemporary Israeli nationalism is the most prominent recent example.[84] It has certainly been noted in areas relating to New Testament and Christian origins, with major bloggers such as Jim West and James Davila regularly following the story while a major scholar of early Judaism and Christian origins, Alan Segal, has openly said that his Barnard colleague does not deserve tenure.[85] There has been plenty of aggressive hostility aimed at Abu el-Haj – notably the anti-Islamic rant (for some reason classed as a "review") we saw in Chapter 3 by Muslim-despising "Hugh Fitzgerald." First, I will focus on the academic hostility before moving on to the ways in which the clear misrepresentations of, and sometimes lies about, Abu el-Haj's work have developed into "facts" about Abu el-Haj's work.

In a scathing and, it would seem, influential review of Abu el-Haj's book, Aren Maeir made the following representation of Abu el-Haj on the Jewish-Roman war of 66–70 CE:

> In her discussion of the "Jewish Quarter" in Jerusalem, Abu el-Haj argues against the "standard" explanation (Roman destruction at Jerusalem in 70 C.E.); she prefers a ludicrous explanation, relating the

> archaeological evidence of wide-scale destruction in Jerusalem to internal disputes, that flies in the face of available evidence.[86]

But this is a leap from debating who burnt down buildings to something that comes close to implying that Abu el-Haj denied that Romans burnt down Jerusalem. It is important to be clear here because other critics are quite explicit in claiming that Abu el-Haj suggests that the Romans did not destroy Jerusalem. Let us start by noting that Abu el-Haj's argument *assumes* that Romans destroyed Jerusalem 70 CE and that she is actually questioning the methodology of interpreting archaeology through literary sources and pre-existing narrative. This is the context for her questioning the responsibility for the destruction of certain parts of Jerusalem. Put simply, Abu el-Haj did *not* and does *not* (I have asked her) deny the destruction of Jerusalem by the Romans. As we will return to this, and as it has been a criticism aimed at denying her tenure, it is worth quoting the relevant parts in full. I *stress*, read the key comments *in context*:

> But the assertion that either of these two sites – the Herodian Quarter or Burnt House – provide empirical evidence of the Roman destruction of the city is something that needs to be looked at more carefully. How does one determine that a specific historical event is causally linked to *physical* remnants of fire?
>
> While Avigad treated the ash as evidence that these two sites were destroyed by the Romans in 70 C.E. during the siege of the Upper City, there is no accurate means by which to date the ash, the *material* evidence of fire, to the decade, let alone to the year or to the day of its creation. Furthermore, there is no way to determine the cause of that fire without referring to textual sources, to an already known narrative. Clearly we know from historical accounts (from Josephus's book *The Jewish Wars* for one) that the Roman Legion burned the city down, destroying the Upper City on the eighth of Elul, in the year 70 C.E. It is on that basis that Avigad reached the specific dating of the destruction layer at Burnt House. This story, the Roman siege and Jerusalem's subsequent burning, is a tale of destruction much more in keeping with a nationalist historiography than are several alternative *but equally plausible* accounts. For example, at least some of the evidence of fire and destruction at both Burnt House and the Herodian Quarter could just as convincingly be read as evidence of class or sectarian conflict *within* Jewish society during the period immediately prior to its destruction at the hands of the Romans. There is ample textual evidence for that story as well... That possibility is not recognized at either Burnt House or the Herodian Mansion, however, even though the time span between these two possible kinds of fires – those set by Jewish Zealots and those by Romans – is too short for any dating of the ash itself to

> determine which event it proves. In other words, both of these stories are *under* determined by the data. Each is potentially compatible with it. The choice thus rests at the conceptual level: which interpretative framework is to be brought to bear upon the archaeological evidence... With no prior narrative at all, ash could quite simply be evidence of an accidental (or, at least, inexplicable) fire, or more accurately, of accidental (or inexplicable) fires...each of these houses could have been burned more than once, by Zealots, by Romans, and by accident.[87]

The allegations against Abu el-Haj get more serious. Maeir claimed the following about Abu el-Haj,

> Perhaps the most astonishing part of the book is a discussion on the last page of the text (p. 281). Abu el-Haj describes and condones the attack, and subsequent ransacking, by a Palestinian mob on what is known as "Jacob's Tomb" [?] in Nablus in 2001. Several people were killed as a result of this attack; the gleeful tone in which she describes this act of vandalism exemplifies how her political agenda completely overcame her duties as a social scientist.[88]

Given the gravity of the allegation, and given that it has been repeated, it is important to compare Maeir's comments with what Abu el-Haj actually said on Joseph's Tomb:

> It is within the context of that distinctive history of archaeological practice and settler nationhood that one can understand why it was "that thousands of Palestinians stormed the site" of Joseph's Tomb in the West Bank city of Nablus, looting it and setting it alight during the renewed intifada that rocked Palestine and Israel in the fall of 2000. Joseph's Tomb was not destroyed simply because of its status as a Jewish religious shrine. The symbolic resonance of its destruction reaches far deeper than that. It needs to be understood in relation to a colonial-national history in which modern political rights have been substantiated in and expanded through the material signs of historic presence. In destroying the tomb, Palestinian demonstrators eradicated one "fact on the ground." Archaeology remains salient in this world of ongoing contestation. It is a sign of colonial presence and national rights, of secularism and science, as various groups in Palestine and Israel engage in struggles to (re)configure the Israeli state and polity and to determine its territorial limits.[89]

I do not know how a "gleeful tone" can be deduced from this and I do not know how anyone who does not know Abu el-Haj could possibly work out whether or not Abu el-Haj approved of the actions. There is certainly no mention of endorsement and there is certainly no phrase that can be said to describe a "gleeful tone." It seems clear that she is trying to explain an act of violence and makes no moral judgement whatsoever. It might be comparable to me – and indeed much of the British nation according to polls – thinking that the London bombings of July 7 were acts of unjustifiable, horrific brutality yet I can still accept that one reason underlying such acts has been British foreign policy in Iraq and beyond. Violent attacks have various kinds of underlying causes and it should be obvious enough that Abu el-Haj is trying to explain the *why* questions. To be fair, it is hardly untypical of explanations of emotive issues to be misunderstood as justification by those linked with victims but, to paraphrase an old phrase, to explain does *not* necessarily mean to justify.[90]

Similarly, in a disgraceful review that relied heavily on opinion, snobbery, non-argument and name-dropping, Alexander H. Joffe claimed of Abu el-Haj on Joseph's Tomb, "Are scholars now in the business of advocating the eradication of 'facts' rather than their explanation?"[91] No, and Abu el-Haj said nothing of the sort so why does Joffe bother saying such an irrelevant thing? Joffe also criticized Abu el-Haj of suffering from too much political interference. Consequently Joffe claimed that "scholars should not act as politicians or propagandists, or make reference to their scholarship when they do so." It is even added that "politics that are liberatory, that are virtuous, are by definition immune from criticism, which makes them neither politics, nor scholarship, but articles of faith, the most dangerous thing of all." A split in our lives may be necessary, Joffe therefore concludes. Abu el-Haj has apparently "once again demonstrated, without that split, without that even quavering aspiration to self-regulation, to objectivity and truth, however vague and elusive these may be, the results may be dark indeed."[92]

Interestingly enough, Joffe allowed this review to be posted on the explicitly right-wing, anti-Muslim, anti-Palestinian, ultra-Zionist blog, Solomonia.[93] Furthermore, in 2004 Joffe was appointed director of Campus Watch, a group that, as we saw, has some explicitly anti-Muslim, anti-Arab and anti-Palestinian views at the forefront of its interference in academic practice. The press release to accompany his appointment is worth quoting given the claims to splitting our lives between scholarship and politics:

> Philadelphia – The Middle East Forum announced today the appointment of Alexander Joffe as director of Campus Watch, the Forum's project to critique Middle East studies at North American universities with a view to improving them.
>
> Mr. Joffe, an archaeologist and historian, holds degrees from Cornell University and the University of Arizona. He has participated in over a dozen field projects in Israel, Jordan, Greece and the United States. Previously, Mr. Joffe taught in the Department of Anthropology at the

> Pennsylvania State University. An associate of Global Policy Exchange of Alexandria, VA, he has also written extensively on modern history and policy, including disarmament and environmental security, intelligence reform, and the Middle East, and he contributes regularly to the *Journal of International Security Affairs.*

The Forum's director, Daniel Pipes, welcomed Mr. Joffe's appointment. "Alex emerged as the strongest candidate from an impressive field of contenders. His dedication to this important Forum project will be an asset and I'm very pleased he has sought us out to join our team."

"I am delighted to be joining the Middle East Forum as director of the Campus Watch project," said Mr. Joffe. "My goals are to expand CW's demonstrated role as a 'consumer advocate' for high standards of scholarship in Middle Eastern Studies, and, equally important, to help articulate a positive vision of what this discipline could and should be in the 21st century."[94]

In fear of understatement, the charge of too much political influence can be aimed in more than one direction. Indeed, Joffe's obvious lack of being able to split politics and scholarship could, in this instance at least, also lead to some very dark results he worries about: academic support for the vile Campus Watch.

James Davila also weighs in on the politics of Abu el-Haj's work, though with explicit attention to representing Abu el-Haj fairly.[95] What is particularly notable about Davila's more careful attempt to represent Abu el-Haj is that he has to resort to more ingenious ways of branding her work ideologically wrong. Davila's approach is to suggest that Abu el-Haj should have been more *explicit* in condemning the actions at Joseph's Tomb:

> It is possible that Abu el-Haj is simply offering a [**sic**] explanation of the mentality behind the actions of the marauders here and perhaps we should assume this more charitable interpretation. But I was struck by the fact that there is no condemnation of the desecration of this site and it is equally possible to read the passage as a justification of the actions of the mob (especially given her quoted statement from p. 255...). I wish she had helped us out a little more to read what she says in the more charitable light.

There is clearly the assumption that Abu el-Haj *might* be a supporter of extreme violence so an answer must be given by her. In fact, as it is "charitable" to suggest that she is just explaining the situation, presumably we really do have to be suspicious of this Palestinian American academic. But people have been making similar analyses in different fields for decades and in the study of early Judaism and Christian origins we often see analogous discussion of bandits. If, for instance, I analyse ancient banditry and do not condemn it, am I up for suspicion too? If someone analyses Herod the Great or Herod Antipas and does not condemn them should we be suspicious that the scholar is a supporter of tyrannical government? If I analyse September 11 or July 7 and do not explicitly condemn these acts of mass murder in print, does it somehow mean I support these acts, or at least I am only worthy of a "charitable" interpretation? Why does Abu el-Haj have to prove her credentials as "one of us"?

Davila gives similar sentiments in his assessment of Abu el-Haj's discussion of looting. Abu el-Haj comments:

> Although never argued by Ju'beh, looting could well be analyzed as a form of resistance to the Israeli state and an archaeological project, understood by many Palestinians, to stand at the very heart of Zionist historical claims to the land. In James Scott's words, looting is perhaps "a weapon of the weak."[96]

Davila claims that he "can't think of any other way to read this than as a – granted, tentatively, but still unambiguously phrased – political justification of the looting of archaeological sites," before adding, "I think this is one of the most disturbing passages in the book and I am surprised not to have encountered any other comments on it so far." But Davila's point virtually rules out the abstract analytical possibility of looting being a "weapon of the weak." This is a very misleading point by Davila because even the most hostile opponent of looting should be able to acknowledge intellectually that looting could actually be a reaction to social circumstances, just like people may analyse crime in inner-city areas, for example, without having to think that crime is the right thing to do. Again, to explain is *not* necessarily to justify. We should also add that Abu el-Haj quite explicitly uses the word, *analyzed* (qualified, incidentally, by *could well be*). Again, it seems that Abu el-Haj must to go the extra mile to prove she is not a lover of violence and theft. Again, we ought to ask ourselves: why might this be?

The downplaying of their own personal politics by critics of Abu el-Haj and critics of political influence on her work is a common feature in the review/attacks. As noted, Alan Segal has voiced his opinions against the tenure of Abu el-Haj.[97] Segal explicitly distances himself from political motivations and claims scholarly motivations:

> I have not made a secret of my opposition to this candidacy... Many have told me that I only oppose her because I am Jewish or because I feel I must represent the wishes of the Jewish community. None of

> these charges have any truth to them at all... My negative evaluation has nothing to do with her ethnic identity, her gender, *or even* [my italics] her opinions about modern Israel. Some people will disbelieve me but those people are essentializing me to dismiss the evidence without considering it.

I will take Segal at his word and assume that he genuinely believes that he is not acting from such political motivations; besides, individual belief is not necessarily the point underlying an ideological analysis of a scholarly discipline. The point is that the broader ideological context is dictating the way Segal argues against the tenure of Abu el-Haj.

For example, when Segal's arguments are particularly weak we can see ideology taking control. He points out that Abu el-Haj "makes almost exclusive use of these biblical minimalists," with the accompanying disqualifier that they constitute "no more than a handful of scholars really, out of the thousands at work in the world," though failing to mention (a) how he knows this statistic and (b) that some of the biggest named scholars in the world are labelled "minimalist," a point worth mentioning given that Segal puts weight on the importance of what scholars think. Segal adds that "Being a biblical minimalist is not a crime; but the school is often consciously infused with modern Middle Eastern politics in ways that are hard to ignore." This appears to assume that conscious acknowledgement of "modern Middle Eastern politics" is a problem (and, incidentally, why the phrase "not a crime"?). Again, so what? This does not make their arguments wrong and it does not make Abu el-Haj's arguments wrong. The debate is being framed in a way that is simply excluding Abu el-Haj from conventional scholarship by default through her associations and *not* by scholarly standards. It would seem that Segal is (wrongly) assuming that only explicit political motivations count, a point supported by Segal's defence of his own position above. Yet we should further add that the work of Keith Whitelam was explicitly designed to uncover the *implicit* political links with modern Middle Eastern politics in the study of historical Israel. In this light it is very difficult to see how politics are not involved in this case against Abu el-Haj. It is deeply regrettable that a senior scholar such as Segal has resorted to cheap political insinuation in order to discredit a career. Why would this be unless Segal too is immersed in the politics of the situation?

The academic allegations levelled at Abu el-Haj and discussed in academic reviews have now become "facts" in their own peculiar way in the campaign against her. In the *New York Sun*, Gabrielle Birkner wheeled out the counter evidence to counter a case never actually made, claiming:

> In "Facts on the Ground," Ms. Abu el-Haj suggests Jerusalem was destroyed not by the Romans, but by the Jews themselves due to rising class tensions among them. Yet, the 1st-century historian and scribe Josephus described in great detail the Roman siege of Jerusalem. Additionally, carvings in the Arch of Titus in Rome depict the Roman General Titus showing off menorahs and other objects looted from the Second Temple.[98]

As we have seen, this representation of Abu el-Haj is not true. To quote Abu el-Haj again in order for the basic point to hit home, "Clearly we know from historical accounts (from Josephus's book *The Jewish Wars* for one) that the Roman Legion burned the city down, destroying the Upper City on the eighth of Elul, in the year 70 C.E."[99] Birkner has either hastily read Abu el-Haj's book or not read her book at all, perhaps relying on or misinterpreting someone else's take. Whatever way we take it, it is very poor journalistic practice, particularly as the journalism involves criticizing someone for not knowing basic historical facts, though it does its intended job of discrediting Abu el-Haj.

On the anti-Palestinian blog Solomonia, in a slightly more nuanced but nonetheless highly polemical review, it was claimed that,

> while it is true that "these interpretive frameworks clearly rely upon an already existing story," the "story" of the Roman destruction of the city in the year 70 is a well-documented part of Roman history supported by a vast amount of evidence, much of it literally carved in stone. This is hardly a case of an archaeologist choosing a narrative on a nationalistically-inspired whim.[100]

Again, notice the edging toward an implication that Abu el-Haj denies the Roman destruction which, to stress yet again, she does *not*. It misses Abu el-Haj's point that the archaeological data does not demand destruction by the Romans in every single instance and that other options are not readily put forward. Abu el-Haj gave other options for destruction of certain parts of Jerusalem. Those options may ultimately be right or wrong but it is a perfectly legitimate practice to question why one option is heavily favoured over others, particularly when no debate is offered. The lack of basic reading of a scholarly text suggests that ideology underpinning Solomonia has got in the way too much of fairly representing an opponent.

Or again, in *Israel Insider*, Paula R. Stern, a 1982 graduate of Barnard who apparently now lives in a West Bank settlement,[101] called Abu el-Haj a "professor of questionable ethics" and a "young, clearly biased woman."[102] An observer might counter, "Aren't her opponents biased too?" Well, apparently not. Stern comments, without any prompting cited, that the "protests were not based on the fact that Abu El Haj is a Palestinian American, but on her inability to follow correct scholarly procedures and actually document anything of truth or value." This really does seem to be protesting too much in the light of the evidence we have seen. And why bother mentioning Abu el-Haj's background if her scholarship is apparently so self-evidently shoddy? We in fact see the not-too-hidden agenda coming through in Stern's article when she repeats the standard misrepresentation in her letter to the Tenure Committee: "She justifies the desecration of archaeological sites by Arabs... She absurdly attempts to suggest that the Jews destroyed Jerusalem in the year 70 CE, in direct contradiction to the only historian who was there at the time." As should now be crystal clear, none of this is true and allegations of not following correct procedures and not documenting anything of truth or value are easily turned on the accuser here. In fact Stern goes even further in her allegations against Abu el-Haj in a blog comment:

> I am against El Haj's personal politics. I find them abhorent [**sic**], based on hatred and ignorance... BUT...the reason I believe I am justified is not because she is an anti-Semite, not because she hates Israel and will do all in her power to obliterate my country...the reason is because she does not, on the basis of ONE book that was poorly researched, inaccurately documented, and whimsical in its claims and conclusions...deserve tenure at a university such as Barnard/ Columbia.[103]

Incidentally, no evidence is cited for Abu el-Haj being an antisemite who will do all in her power to obliterate Israel. In a similar evidence-free manner, the story of Stern's campaign on IsraelNationalNews.com had the headline, "Barnard Grad Heads Protest against Anti-Semitic Prof."[104] It would seem, then, that Abu el-Haj is as obviously antisemitic as she is a prof. If that is not enough, then we can see even more the naked ideology coming through in a brief piece from JTA Breaking News where, on August 13, 2007, it was pointed out that over 800 people had signed a petition seeking to deny Abu el-Haj tenure at Barnard College. The reasons were accusations of "shoddy scholarship" and "a pro-Palestinian agenda," the latter reason at least revealing some honesty in the reasons underlying the campaign against Abu el-Haj, even if unintentionally so (would a pro-Western, pro-Israeli, pro-British, pro-American, or pro-Christian agenda etc. be reported as being a so obviously self-explanatory for denial of tenure?).[105]

Conclusions

There is little doubt that 1967 saw a massive political, cultural and religious shift in Anglo-American attitudes towards Israel. These attitudes are, of course, overwhelmingly positive. This provides an important context whereby the emphasis on Jesus' "Jewishness" could emerge and the shift towards a much more positive attitude toward Judaism could take place in New Testament and Christian origins scholarship. However, the general cultural shift toward Israel has involved high sensitivity toward anything sounding like criticism of Israel and Israeli state actions. As we have already seen in Chapter 2, this attitude has made an impact on areas relating to biblical studies. The cases of Whitelam and Abu el-Haj are particularly notable. Neither has done anything like what their opponents claim of them yet it is somehow academically acceptable to accuse them of antisemitism or make related allegations despite the complete lack of evidence. As facts matter little we are again in a situation where ideology is dictating the debate too much. In related areas, the following chapter will now investigate the ways in which basic facts in Christian origins and New Testament scholarship have been avoided and the reasons why.

Chapter 6

Jewish...but Not *That* Jewish

The November 2002 convention of the Christian Coalition, held in Washington DC, was opened with a videotaped benediction that came straight from the Oval Office. The most powerful Republicans in Congress addressed the Convention (as did the Zionist mayor of Jerusalem), including Tom Delay who was then the House majority whip. We are "standing up for Jews and Jesus" he told the crowd.

Lawrence Davidson[1]

Israel, Biblical Studies and Cultural Context

With this general cultural and historical context behind us we can now see why Jesus the Jew emerges as late as the 1970s. For a start, in terms of religious context, it is well known that many scholars in the discipline work in highly conservative evangelical seminaries and Bible colleges (particularly in the US) and it would not be difficult to find staunchly pro-Israel Christian scholars. For example, after outlining the various positions of conservative Christians on end times and Israel, the well-known dispensationalist New Testament scholar, Darrell Bock, writing in the *Los Angeles Times,* adds the following "practical concerns by almost all of these groups about whether any agreement can be signed that will truly give Israel peace":

> When so many radical Muslims believe that mere Jewish presence defiles the Holy Land – and thus Israel as the Jewish state must be removed and the Palestinians liberated – then one wonders whether peace in fact would result. Some of the violence we see now is the result of those who deny Israel's right to exist.[2]

No concern about violence done the other way is expressed. It can simply be assumed, it would seem, that Israel is the only one for whom we should care when it comes to peace, not to mention these sentiments coming perilously close to an old imperialist argument that overwhelming power needs to keep the crazy natives in check. It may be that Bock has been edited but if so the editing itself remains instructive. Unedited, the evangelical New Testament scholar Michael Bird mentions Bock's article, referring to "these sound and sober reflections."[3]

Yet it also remains obvious that some biblical scholars are of a more "liberal" persuasion, theologically at least. Moreover, there are even biblical scholars, including conservative evangelicals, like N. T. Wright (and even Bird), who have been critical of some actions of Israeli state aggression and US actions in the Middle East, while there are plenty of scholars from Wright to the Jesus Seminar who openly contradict US conservative evangelical views of the end times. This is one of the key reasons for showing just how deeply embedded pro-Israel ideas and rhetoric were and are across the political divides, from Christian Zionists to American liberals. In other words, this shows how a previously controversial issue of "Jesus the Jew" could become much more palatable and something that could now be discussed from the 1970s onward. In his reflections on the reception of his 1973 book, *Jesus the Jew*, Vermes recalls that the "title enunciating what should be patent to all still sounded striking and pioneering" and yet, for the minority reactions of shock and horror, the book was well received.[4] Ever since the 1970s, there has been a constant emphasis on just how Jewish Jesus was, as William Arnal has shown (see previous chapter), to which I could add my own arguments for a Law observant Jesus who never portrayed himself as anything other than a Law observant figure.

And then there is always the example of the biblioblogers who come in from different perspectives. We have seen how James Davila has regularly blogged on issues relating to Israel and Palestine, particularly the Temple Mount, yet his reporting is heavily one-sided and there are repeated criticisms of Arab, Palestinian or Muslim propaganda. We saw how Jim West's suggestion that the first Temple might not have been an extensive Temple complex immediately turned into a highly sensitive and polemical debate relating to modern Israel with no one appearing to side with Jim West. We also saw how Chris Tilling's well-intentioned attempt to discuss Christian Zionism, including some key political issues, was soon hijacked and turned into a discussion of biblical interpretation alone. Clearly, issues relating to Israel are present among scholars in areas relating to the study of the New Testament and Christian origins.

The context of Christian-centred support for Israel and serious academic sensitivities on the Israel-Palestine issue also explains the hostile comments aimed at people with whom others disagree. Recall Orientalist Richard Rohrbaugh's unfortunate association of Räisänen's interpretation of Luke

15:11-32 with "subtle anti-Semitism" while at the same time giving the reader no indication or evidence to show if Räisänen actually is guilty of this grave insinuation, and no mention of the fact that Räisänen has actually stressed that Christian editing covered over the Jewish nature of Jesus' teaching.[5] Though not as directly as Rohrbaugh on Räisänen, perhaps none have been wrongly tainted with antisemitism in historical Jesus studies as much as those associated with the Jesus Seminar, something which has rightly troubled people like William Arnal and John Kloppenborg. What reactions might be expected from unfortunate comments such as the following which do not make a precise connection but still manage to make a general parallel with Nazi Germany?

> The Jesus of the Jesus Seminar is a non-Jewish Jesus. To put it metaphorically, the Seminar has performed a forcible epispasm on the historical Jesus, a surgical procedure for removing the marks of circumcision. The result might arouse some disquiet in the minds of people who know the history of the 30's and 40's of our century. But the Jesus of the Jesus Seminar is much too banal to cause us to think that the ideology producing him is like that which produced the "Aryan Jesus" of the 1930's.[6]

> Have the New Questers, and the advocates of the Cynic Jesus, come to terms with the problematic analogy between themselves and those German scholars who, in the 1920s and 1930s, reduced almost to nil the specific Jewishness of Jesus and his message?[7]

What is also interesting about the deeply misleading, not to say morally dubious, "parallels" is that scholars associated with the Jesus Seminar, as Arnal points out, take great pains to stress that they are also engaged in combating antisemitism and never once deny Jesus' "Jewishness" (notably, as Arnal points out, the scholarly definition of "Jewishness" virtually excludes the possibility of Jews behaving outside the scholarly definition of "Jewishness"!). Mack, for instance, not only believes Jesus was ethnically Jewish but also sees the gospel of Mark partly to *blame* for a range of atrocities aimed at Jews and culminating in the Holocaust (incidentally, clichés about Jews in New Testament scholarship are denounced by Mack).[8] Crossan wrote a book on the passion narrative to expose, as its subtitle puts it, "the roots of anti-Semitism in the Gospel story of the death of Jesus."[9] Indeed, the subtitle to his famous book on the historical Jesus stressed that Jesus was a Mediterranean *Jewish* peasant! To hammer the point home, we might add that Crossan's passion book carries an endorsement by Susannah Heschel – one of the foremost Jewish critics of antisemitism in New Testament scholarship, especially that in the Nazi period – who recommended this book to "Anyone concerned with the rising tide of anti-Semitism."

Whatever we are to make of the results of these scholars' work it is hard to deny that their intentions relating to Judaism were and are strictly honourable. Moreover, their works are, to some extent, explained by the general context of the rise of Christian pro-Jewish thought which Arnal attributes to much of modern Jesus scholarship, alongside the broader Western attitudes toward Israel from the 1970s onward discussed in the previous chapter. It would seem that this all matters little if a relatively petty scholarly argument needs to be won.

Finally, one visual example of specific evidence for changes in biblical studies tied in with the events of 1967 ought to be mentioned: the production of biblical maps. Keith Whitelam has looked at the role of cartography and here the issue of Israel's expanded territories is a particularly notable influence at the end of the 1960s. *The MacMillan Bible Atlas* was originally and significantly published one year after the 1967 war and 20 years after Israel was declared to be an independent modern state. Whitelam also points to the loaded quotation on the title page from Numbers 34:12: "This shall be your land with its boundaries all round." Whitelam also notes a variety of quotations, sometimes backed up by biblical passages concerning the land (e.g. Gen. 13:14-15; Josh. 8:14) which tie the map in with the "foundation narrative for modern Zionism and the modern state of Israel." So, for example, "To the north the...mountains of Lebanon; to the south the semiarid Negeb; to the east the wide desert; to the west the Great Sea – these are the natural borders of Palestine. Within their confines was enacted the history of Israel."[10] With events of 1967 in mind, one point we might also add to this is precisely where the boundaries are imposed on the ancient map: the land of the ancient Philistines naturally looks vaguely similar to the boundaries of modern day Gaza, as it does on other recent maps, including the Roman period,[11] and there is plenty of land for ancient Israel toward the east and beyond the Jordan. And remember, all this is representing a time when boundaries were anything but clear cut and umpteen centuries before the idea of the modern nation state. Something other than antiquarian interest in ancient geography is clearly dictating the ways in which these boundaries are drawn.

What is particularly interesting about this is that we have clear evidence of the question of Israel-Palestine profoundly embedded in the popularizing of biblical studies. It may well be the case that the writers and cartographers for the *The MacMillian Bible Atlas* and others did not consciously create modern state boundaries in their books. In fact this shows even more how big contemporary issues permeate a discipline. As we now narrow in on mainstream scholarship, we should not expect the intensive study of Jesus – a Jewish man who is recorded to have been concerned with questions of Israel and active in the territories that have been the site of so much ferocious and bloody dispute in modern times – to show no signs of being embedded in issues of Israel-Palestine.

Jesus the Jew...to an Extent

> *One should freely confess that there need be no necessary continuity between what Jesus taught about the law and what some of his followers taught about it. We cannot ascribe everything in early Christianity to its founder. We can no more praise him for all that went right than we can blame him for all that went wrong. His followers sometimes reaped where he did not sow.*
>
> Dale C. Allison[12]

> *In spite of the attempts to place Jesus in his Palestinian social world, the image that emerges is that of an isolated and autonomous figure.*
>
> R. S. Sugirtharajah[13]

Yet there is one recurring theme in the continual emphasis on Jesus the Jew in contemporary scholarship: Jesus may be Jewish but he usually, so the scholarly arguments frequently go, overrides at least one of the key symbols of Jewish identity as constructed by contemporary scholarship. Despite the acceptance of the phrase from the title of his 1973 book, Vermes' Jewish Jesus remains a problem for the Christian academic. One key reason is that Vermes' Jesus is very definitely *not* Christian and Vermes makes a very sharp distinction between the Jewish Jesus of history and the Christ of faith. This line gets developed in different ways by E. P. Sanders, Paula Fredriksen, Amy-Jill Levine, Maurice Casey, and others, including myself. Yet, it remains that one of the dominant issues in contemporary scholarship involves lip service being paid to "Jesus the Jew" (at least Jewish identity as constructed in modern scholarship). And so, Jesus is frequently seen to be "Jewish" – with book titles frequently reminding us of this – but noticeably different from his Jewish context. For all John Meier's emphasis on the Jewish Jesus, his Jesus does remain a *marginal* Jew.

Structurally some things do not in fact change from pre-Vermes times, even if the rhetoric shifts from being "radical" in terms of Law and grace to being socio-religiously "radical" but still socio-religiously radical over against the rest of Judaism. A clear example of this is the book on the historical Jesus by Gerd Theissen and Annette Merz, originally in German, and so no doubt reflecting some particularly German issues in relation to Judaism and Israel, but also reflecting scholarship that is both heavily influenced by Anglo-American scholarship and it has had some influence on Anglo-American scholarship. Theissen and Merz stress that "Jesus is understood in the context of Judaism and the local, social and political history of his time." They also bring this into line with presumably modern socio-religious sensibilities: "Thus we are convinced that through the historical Jesus one can find an approach to Judaism which is a sympathetic one, that grappling with his message sharpens the social conscience and that encounter with him changes the question one asks about God."[14] Yet, in one sense, Jesus dramatically stands out over against Judaism and forms the basis of later Christian rejection of Jewish food laws in their discussion of Mark 7:15:

> Did Jesus think only of a limited situation? For example the washing of hands addressed in Mark 7.5, which was not a universal practice in Judaism? Rather, the context of radical discipleship comes in question: on their travels the disciples may accept any food that is offered to them – regardless of whether it is clean or unclean... That is probably how Luke 10.7,8 is to be understood. Gospel of Thomas logion 14, which is about cleanness, stands in the same context... The logion about cleanness is a logion which makes a radical judgment. But we need not for that reason deny it to Jesus. Jesus was and remained a Jew when he uttered such thoughts. But he was a radical Jew... May we conclude...that Jesus forsook the limited world of Judaism by teaching a cosmopolitan ethic? Quite the contrary! Both tendencies of his ethics serve to preserve Jewish identity and make Jewish life possible.[15]

What is interesting here is that the Markan context provides us with one plausible context in first-century Galilee (a hand-washing dispute) yet Theissen and Merz downplay this and instead point to alternative later texts from Luke and Thomas. There is also the assumption that Jesus and his followers would have been given banned food (if I am reading Theissen and Merz correctly) when travelling around. But given that Jesus' activities were effectively limited to Jews then it would be exceptionally unlikely that they would even be given banned food to reject! Moreover, there is no criticism of Jesus overriding food laws elsewhere in the gospel tradition (something that might be expected if Jesus advocated something so monumental) and the earliest Christians had serious problems with the rise of non-observance, something incomprehensible if Jesus had advocated overriding food laws. Despite this we still manage to get a proto-Christian Jesus who must still be seen as Jewish...but not *that* Jewish.

Interestingly, N. T. Wright explicitly locates the writing of his 1996 book, *Jesus and the Victory of God*, in the context of the Israel-Palestine dispute and accepts that "the book inevitably carries overtones of current situations in the land where the story of Jesus is set." Wright recalls sensing "Jewish anxiety and Palestinian frustration in about equal measure" along with stories of riots and teargas while writing a chapter on the cross which, "to say the least," gave "food for thought." "The multiple ambiguities and tensions of that beautiful country," Wright adds, "are now forever bound up in my mind with the subject-matter of the book itself, as is perhaps appropriate." Wright ends with staggeringly high doses of over-optimism, self-confidence and self-importance: "If what I write could help in any way towards the establishment of justice and peace there, or indeed anywhere else, I would be deeply grateful."[16] To the best of my knowledge, Wright's book on the historical Jesus has not *yet* had any impact on the Middle-East peace process or indeed any other conflict.

Wright, perhaps more than any other Jesus scholar, relentlessly tells us how thoroughly Jewish Jesus was. Yet at the same time he consistently stresses that Jesus remained radically different from his social and theological context. Wright says that the general thrust of his argument is "of a very Jewish Jesus who was nevertheless opposed to some high-profile features of first-century Judaism, which seems to me the most viable one."[17] Many examples from Wright's work could be chosen, but I will have to restrict myself to one: family. That said, the general criticisms I will make here, as I have shown in detail elsewhere, apply more widely to the work of Wright and others.[18]

Wright stresses the importance of ethnic ties in constructing Jewish identity in early Jewish literature and makes it quite clear that views such as Ezra 10 may sound extreme to us but were fairly tame by ancient standards and were part of the self-preservation of the Jewish people. This is not, as Wright points out in his defence of Judaism, "in any way discreditable (however often people have thought so)." After pointing out the positives, Wright then says that Jesus, "to put it mildly, set a time-bomb beside this symbol...and realized that some of the symbols had now become (not wicked, or shoddy, but) redundant." He asks, what else can be concluded from passages such as Mark 3:21, 31-35 pars and Luke 11:27f./Thomas 79, particularly when compared with the comments of one recent Jewish historian (Safrai) on Jewish family? As for Matthew 8:21-22/Luke 9:59-60 Wright tells us that Jesus' comments are "quite frankly, outrageous... astonishing." But, as ever, Wright qualifies such statements to make sure Judaism does not come out too bad: "we must stress that this does not mean that Jesus thought such a symbol inherently bad, or even second rate."[19]

It is notable that Wright repeatedly tells us how Jesus works in a Jewish context yet the end results are structurally no different to the anti-Jewish results of a previous generation of Christian scholars (whom Wright correctly criticizes): the key symbols still go, irrespective of whether we call them "wicked" or "redundant." What should also be notable about such a discussion is that Wright places some weight on the *generalizations* of a modern Jewish historian (which are not necessarily inaccurate *as generalizations*) without looking at the readily available ancient *Jewish* parallels to Jesus' sayings. Is this not something we might expect given the all-new-love for all-things-Jewish?

On this point, Wright is left wide open to the same kinds of criticisms aimed at Theissen and Merz above. For example, there are sayings in early Jewish sources that place observing the commandments as more important than family ties (e.g. Josephus, *Antiquities* 3.87), views echoed among a group like the Essenes. There are passages discussing people not deemed spiritually worthy of burial (e.g. Deut. 28:26; Jer. 7:33; 22:19; Ezek. 29:5; *1 En.* 98:13; Josephus *War* 4.317-32, 359-60, 381-82).[20] Even so, the sacred text itself does not even quite say what Wright claims it says: the gospel account on burial actually suggests that the father will be buried anyway ("let the dead bury their own dead"). Moreover, ignoring the clear possibility of hyperbole in Jesus' teaching, the force of "hate" (μισέω) (Lk. 14:26; cf. Mt. 10:37) is over-emphasized and could easily be translated "love-less" (cf. Gen. 29:31ff.; Deut. 21:15ff.), perhaps with Matthew and Luke rendering a relatively weak Aramaic "hate" (שנא) in their own equally valid way, a point long noted in gospel scholarship but ignored by Wright, though he is hardly alone in this.[21] These criticisms are all complemented by the gospel contexts because there we find no criticism of Jesus, something that might be expected if his views on family were even half as shocking as Wright tells us. Set in *Jewish* cultural and theological contexts, not to mention the setting in the Christian Holy Scripture, Jesus' saying on family do not have to say anything as dramatic as Wright would have us believe.[22] So why does Wright insist on telling us how radical in relation to Judaism his Jewish Jesus would have been? Seen from the perspective of an ideological critique of the discipline, this begs the question: what drives such Jewish-but-not-that-Jewish results in scholarship?

Wright may be an extreme evangelical example – hence I also looked at the more moderate and careful work of Theissen and Merz – but it is fair to say this general view of Jesus being "very Jewish" yet still sufficiently

Christian is common enough in scholarship and many readers will no doubt be able to give their own examples. Even the Law-observant Jesus of one of the most brilliant interpreters of early Judaism, E. P. Sanders, curiously following the major Law-versus-Gospel scholar of our time, Martin Hengel, is given a get-out clause: Sanders claims, based on Matthew 8:21-22/Luke 9:59-60, that Jesus was prepared to override the Law when it came to following him.[23] Again even in the example of someone who really does have a profound knowledge of early Jewish religion, we are not far from the idea that Jesus *is* "very Jewish" but, by the measurements of the academic constructions of Jewish identity, is removed from what is deemed a major aspect of Judaism.

The same kind of comments are available from the "liberal" tradition represented by those associated with the Jesus Seminar, though here there is perhaps more a suspicion of cultural superiority in their Jesus. It is worth looking at their handling of Mark 7:15. Not only do their comments sound like a more extreme version of what Theissen and Merz argued but they also come close to making a methodological necessity out of Jesus being radically different from his contemporaries in establishing historical results:

> The aphorism...is a categorical challenge to the laws governing pollution and purity... As a simple aphorism, it may well go back to Jesus: it challenges the everyday, the inherited, the established, and erases social boundaries taken to be sacrosanct...he was undermining a whole way of life. That, in the judgment of the Fellows, sounds like Jesus.[24]

The criticisms aimed at Theissen and Merz again apply here, and recall in particular that no one in the synoptic tradition is shocked at Jesus supposedly undermining purity laws. Additionally, the Mark 7:15 saying is paralleled in early Judaism (e.g. *Aristeas* 234; cf. 170-71) and, as is often noted, can be read as more relativizing rather than as an absolute rejection. Moreover, it has also been argued that even in absolute form Jesus may be standing more in the tradition of those Jews who rejected the transmission of impurity from hands to food to eater, the very context in which this saying is placed in Mark.[25] It is only with these contexts unmentioned that Jesus can remain somehow "better," at least from a liberal western perspective, than his contemporaries.[26]

Examples could be multiplied. Two such examples which might be thought to be significant given the context outlined here are "the Temple" and "the Land of Israel." Indeed, W. D. Davies even wrote a major book on Jesus and the Land, including the subtitle, *Early Christianity and Jewish Territorial Doctrine*, a telling theme after the events of 1967 (and 1973).[27]

Of course, in certain cases, scholarship will stress the importance of the physical "the Land" or the physical Temple in the teaching of Jesus.[28] One example is particularly revealing for its assumptions concerning who is deserving of sympathy and who is not. John Elliott's much discussed article on the language of "Jew," "Judean," and "Israel," argues that "Judean" is a better translation of Ἰουδαῖος than "Jew" in that it reflects the crucial connection with the "land," adding that it was more an "outsider" term.[29] He also argues that terms such as "Israelite" and "Israel" were the preferred "insider" terms. I have argued about the ideological function of the scholarly rhetoric involved in Elliott's article and I will simply summarize here.[30] Elliott, like Philip Esler who makes a similar case, is aware of the moral issues surrounding translation and even suggests the possibility that "Judean" is a better translation over "Jew" in terms of a defence against antisemitism. Indeed, Elliott is extremely sensitive about anything relating to antisemitism throughout the article. Such concerns can only be welcomed. However, despite this, there is no sensitivity shown in dropping the term "Jew" in favour of "Israel" or the various designations tied in with *land*, a major stress in Elliot's argument.[31] Palestinian concerns are simply not an issue about which modern New Testament scholarship needs to worry, despite Elliott's concluding words ("so much is at stake"). If contemporary morality and ideology are to be brought into the equation (as is undoubtedly a reasonable thing to do), then it is particularly striking that sensitivity towards the Palestinian issue is not raised. This speaks volumes about the social location of American scholarship.[32]

However, it remains that "the Land" and "the Temple" are effectively like all the other symbols of Judaism in the hands of a Christian-dominated discipline: their symbolic function (over against physical locality) is stressed more, they become something else with which Jesus' teaching can be compared and, most crucially, contrasted, and then usually reapplied to Jesus himself or a more Christianized universalizing message.[33] In the case of the Temple, the evidence for Jesus claiming its ideal functions are redundant for the new age is exceptionally sparse (or: it does not exist) in the synoptic tradition in contrast to the explicit evidence of Jesus endorsing the functions of the physical temple (e.g. Mk 1:44, Mt. 5:23-24; 23:16-22).[34] Presumably for much of contemporary scholarship, stressing the importance of the Jewish symbolism of Temple and Land has important symbolic overtones but if Jesus maintained the validity of such physical symbols he would remain *too Jewish* by the scholarly standards of constructing of Jewish identity.

In two recent articles on "Jesus as the High Priestly Messiah," heavily tied in with the issue of the Temple, Crispin Fletcher-Louis can refer to "the behaviour of 'Jesus the Jew'"[35] and give thanks to the "leavening influence of Jewish members of the academy" for presenting priestly religion as an important part of "biblical religion."[36] There is also a very general constructing of scholars who stress "a non-apocalyptic political Jesus" who stands against the temple and priesthood and promotes a "brokerless kingdom" (presumably Crossan is in mind here) free from "institutional oppression, social hierarchies and loveless purity codes." Such a view is problematic as it paints "a not-very-Jewish portrait of Jesus."[37] After making sure, then, that his Jesus is going to be very Jewish, Fletcher-Louis presents an ambitious argument that Jesus was immersed in the priestly issues of his day. All "very Jewish," to be sure, but then we get the inevitable difference-maker: Jesus was running his own alternative Temple movement with himself as an alternative high priest. Naturally, this movement does not have to do those strange things like animal sacrifice because this alternative priestly movement is a more symbolic alternative Temple without the physical needs for a physical temple system. Conveniently enough, this allows Fletcher-Louis to explain the divinity of Christ that ties in very nicely with later Christian theology (e.g. Hebrews).[38] Throughout, it is difficult not to be suspicious that, for all the stress on "Jewishness," Fletcher-Louis is doing something remarkably similar to what he claims of his opponents by removing Jesus from the central physical features of his constructed version of priestly-centred Judaism.

Let's look at the example of Jesus and the Sabbath as presented in Jesus' defence of the disciples plucking grain on the Sabbath (Mk 2:23-28) and the ways in which Fletcher-Louis omits details and even has to construct a tradition that as far as we know did not exist. We are told that "Jesus agrees that, in principle, what his disciples do infringes the Sabbath."[39] Once Mark 2:27 has been established as being among "the text's principal difficulties" the "high priestly understanding of the Son of Man title" of 2:28 "solves" the problems. In even more elaborate theological language, we are also told that the Galilean cornfield must take on the role of the Temple to show that work is allowed. In fact Fletcher-Louis' argument is full of theological speculation:

> Jesus justifies his disciples' breach of the Sabbath because he claims to be a sacral king and high priestly Son of Man. Where he is, in that place there is the transcendent liturgical space and time of the true temple in which his disciples can legitimately act as priests for whom the Sabbath prohibition against work does not apply. The logic of Jesus' argument is

> dense and the Christological claims more veiled than they will be when Jesus stands in the Sanhedrin and claims to be both Daniel's "one like a son of man" and the priest-king of Psalm 110.[40]

Fletcher-Louis does not entirely avoid the counter-evidence, such as when Jesus sends a leper to the priests to be confirmed clean (Mk 1:44), and he comes up with this possible answer: "(Perhaps [at this stage in his developing self-consciousness?] he did not think his own priesthood need entail any conflict with the Aaronic line. Or perhaps he believed it did necessarily entail such conflict, but that the time was not yet right to openly and publicly ignore the Mosaic dispensation [which in fact he believed now to be relativized])."[41]

Even if we share Fletcher-Louis' trusting attitude towards the gospel sources and historical accuracy, we can still see how he fits perfectly in to the kind of pattern of "Jewish...but not *that* Jewish" we have seen for other scholars, perhaps even the most explicit example so far. For example, Fletcher-Louis shares with plenty of other scholars the avoidance of perfectly accessible contrary evidence. For all the rhetoric about Jesus endorsing "work" on, or a breach of, the Sabbath, Fletcher-Louis does not say which biblical Sabbath law was being breached. As it happens, there is not a single mention of prohibiting plucking of grain in biblical law and not a single mention of "plucking" (τίλλω) being banned in biblical law. We might add to this that none of the Hebrew or Aramaic equivalents of the Greek word for "plucking" (esp. the root מרט) are prohibited in biblical law. The closest we get in scholarship is mention of the prohibition of "reaping" and "harvesting" in Exodus 34:21 but this is not plucking grain to eat and the words used in the Greek and Hebrew versions of Exodus are not, unsurprisingly, equivalent to the Greek word for "plucking" in Mark 2:23-28.[42] Yet, despite these basic points, we are still told that plucking grain is a Sabbath violation.

Now certainly plenty of Jews did interpret and expand biblical prohibitions, including the famous rabbinic 39 prohibitions (*m. Shabbat* 7.2), none of which, however, include plucking. But it remains that there is a dispute over plucking grain in Mark 2:23-28 so there is the possibility that *someone* thought plucking was wrong. This is perhaps no surprise as Jews did dispute what constituted work such as in the following example: "Six rules did the men of Jericho make... For three the Sages criticised them... [2] they eat on the Sabbath fruit which had fallen under a tree" (*m. Pesahim* 4.8). Clearly these rabbis did not approve of picking fruit up from the ground on the Sabbath but equally clearly the men from Jericho did approve of it. The question is one of *perspective* and it is an obvious parallel to Mark 2:23-28 and the dispute over whether plucking grain is acceptable on the Sabbath. Yet this basic argument is ignored by Fletcher-Louis and by ignoring it grand claims of relativizing and ignoring the "Mosaic dispensation" (itself an interesting use of language) can be made.

Other parts of his reading involve some dramatic omissions of evidence. Fletcher-Louis may claim that "the son of man" is a high-priestly title but does not engage with the basic notion that the Aramaic term ("son of man" was not a Greek phrase) that would have been used by Jesus was the ordinary term for a "human being" in Aramaic (and Hebrew) and that, in all the available early Jewish interpretations, *no one* interpreted the "one like a son of man" of Daniel 7:13 as a high priest in early Judaism.[43] Why not? Also relevant in this context is Fletcher-Louis' suggestion that we have a "cryptic statement about the Sabbath being made for man and not vice versa [Mk 2:27]."[44] But this is not a "cryptic" statement. It is a basic piece of Sabbath thought. Similar sentiments are found in Hebrew Bible (e.g. Exod. 16:29) and they are found in early Judaism (e.g. *Jubilees* 2:17), including a well-known example (e.g. Mekhilta Exod. 31:12-17, "The Sabbath is delivered to you and you are not delivered to the Sabbath"). In this context, if Jesus had said something like Mark 2:27-28, the ordinary Aramaic term "son of man," which has long been known to include reference to both speaker and a broader group of individuals in early Jewish sources (e.g. 1QapGen 21.13; *Gen. Rab.* 79.6), could merely be picking up the general frame of reference in the saying about the Sabbath being made for human beings. In fact, a strong case could be made for this because Luke and Matthew, almost certainly copying Mark, both drop the general sentiment in Mark 2:27 to make "son of man" sound like a title for Jesus. But all this basic and well-known Jewish and New Testament evidence is not properly incorporated by Fletcher-Louis.

We have, of course, seen that, unlike Fletcher-Louis' speculative reading, we have clear evidence in favour of Jesus having an entirely positive attitude toward the ideal functions of the Jerusalem priesthood (e.g. Mk 1:44, Mt 5:23-24; 23:16-22). When Fletcher-Louis does come across such contrary evidence (Mk 1:44) this has to be dismissed by looking into the mind of what Jesus might have thought, namely he may not have felt the need for conflict or, most speculatively, we might be witnessing a different stage in his developing self-consciousness.[45] We are getting too close to replacing contrary evidence with inner thoughts that no one could possibly know.

What Fletcher-Louis has done, perhaps more so than most scholars of the historical Jesus mentioned here, is to invent a "Judaism" that works for his Christian theology, one aspect of which did not, as far as we know, exist, with evidence to the clear contrary simply ignored. To be sure, everything has to be represented but it is significant that Fletcher-Louis' "Jewish" can be deemed "Jewish" in the sense that it is a modern-day Christian construction of "Jewish." If Judaism really is so significant, why ignore crucial *Jewish* evidence? It is difficult not to conclude that something else is again going on here.

Christology and the Study of Christian Origins: Rescuing Judaism for Jesus

> *Jewish polemic has often suggested that the Trinity and the incarnation, those great pillars of patristic theology, are sheer paganization...this is certainly not true of the New Testament...a vigorous and very Jewish tradition took the language and imagery of Spirit, Word, Law, Presence (and/or Glory), and Wisdom and developed them in relation to Jesus of Nazareth and the Spirit... Resurrection pointed to messiahship; messiahship, to the task performed on the cross; that task, to the God who had promised to accomplish it himself. From then on it was a matter of rethinking, still very Jewishly, how these things could be... The Jesus I have described is both thoroughly credible as a first-century Jew and thoroughly comprehensible as the one to whom early, high, Jewish Christology looked back.*
>
> N. T. Wright[46]

As the mention of Sanders' critique of Pauline scholarship in the previous chapter already implied, the kind of analysis given in this section is not restricted to historical Jesus studies. The "Jewishness" of Christian origins is also an important feature of contemporary scholarship and the tension of "Jewish...but not *that* Jewish" remains. An excellent example of this tension is Larry Hurtado's massive book on Christ-devotion in the first and second centuries with an extremely confessional sounding title, *Lord Jesus Christ.*[47] Hurtado is explicit in his opposition to the over-use of non-Jewish material in reconstructing earliest Christ-devotion, particularly at the expense of Jewish material, something which is crucial for Hurtado. In explicit contrast to the use of Hellenistic material by Bousett and his associates in the reconstruction of Christology, Hurtado constructs his own associates, with the Jewish context being the major difference marker:

> If, therefore, we can speak of a new history-of-religions "school," it could be only in a much looser sense of the term, in this case connoting a group of contemporaries with a shared interest in historical investigation of early devotion to Jesus in the context of the Roman-era religious environment, and a shared conviction that the Jewish religious

> matrix of the Christian movement is more crucial than was recognized in the older *religionsgeschichtliche Schule.*[48]

This stress on Jewish material is important for Hurtado because he argues that earliest Christ-devotion is a development of Jewish monotheism: Jesus was worshipped in a way strongly reminiscent of the ways in which the Jewish God was worshipped and this was a "mutation" of Jewish devotional practice. This view, it is argued, was widespread in earliest Christianity and very early indeed, going back at least to the earliest post-resurrection communities. But then Hurtado has to make sure that this is distinctive. For all the emphasis on the "Jewishness" of earliest Christ-devotion, it is too much to have the earliest version being *too* Jewish. Consequently, not only was Christ-devotion unparalleled in the Greco-Roman world but also unparalleled in Judaism itself. In fact, Christian uniqueness is typically underscored with the following language: "Christ-devotion is an utterly remarkable phenomenon."[49]

While there is little doubt that Hurtado has described orthodox Christology accurately and that his view of Christ-devotion may well reflect certain late New Testament texts (especially John's gospel), his view dominates material where little support for his case can be given. A good example of this is his handling of some of the earliest pre-70 CE followers of Jesus where the evidence is patchy at best. Hurtado makes it clear that he is keen to distance himself from anything sounding anti-Jewish so he even criticizes Hengel's portrayal of Paul's message as "a misconstrual that shows the telltale signs of the influence of traditional Lutheran theological categories of law *versus* gospel."[50] However, it becomes clear that Hurtado has his own theological categories for dealing with differentiation from Judaism. In the following examples it is clear that Hurtado's version of the myth of "Jewish...but not *that* Jewish" is dictating the argument even when (especially when?) no serious evidence exists to support his case.

The issue of conflict is another crucial argument that needs to be made if Christ-devotion is to be shown to emerge from a Jewish context but remain radical, astonishing and unprecedented, a case that can certainly be made with the *explicit* evidence in the post-70 CE Gospel of John (Jn 5:16-18; 10:31-33; cf. Jn 1:18; 19:7-8; 20:28). Yet such conflict over Christ-devotion is anything but explicit in pre-70 material, though this does not stop Hurtado from finding examples. For instance, the persecution of the first followers of Jesus after his death by those such as the pre-Christian Paul was because these followers held a view of "Christ-devotion that is basically reflected in what he embraced and advocated after his conversion."[51] The main problem with this is that throughout Paul's letters there is much conflict over issues relating to Judaism but such conflicts usually involve issues of Law and ethics and never explicitly involve Christ-devotion. Furthermore, it is far from clear that the pre-Christian Paul persecuted the first followers of Jesus because of "high" Christological claims. Hurtado does note that the language of "zeal" in which Paul described his former life, including as a persecutor (Phil. 3:6; cf. Gal. 1:13-14), echoes Jewish defences of the Law and ethnic boundaries (cf. Genesis 34; Num. 25:11-13; 1 Kgs 19:10-14; Sir. 45:23; 48:2; 1 Macc. 2:26, 54, 58; 4 Macc. 18:12; Philo, *Special Laws* 2.253; 1QS 9.23; *m. Sanhedrin* 9.6).[52] Given this and given that we do not have any explicit reasons given for Paul's persecution, we now have one historically plausible context in which to understand Paul actions without having to resort to "Christ-devotion."

In contrast, we certainly do not have this kind of evidence to establish a plausible context for persecutions over "Christ-devotion." Hurtado does claim that the opposition to Stephen's speech was because of a Christological statement (Acts 7:55-58).[53] But even if we assume that Acts 7 is a reliable historical record, the problem can again be seen as a disagreement over the Law and not Christology, hence the problems start for Stephen after the allegations against the Temple authorities for them not obeying the Law (Acts 7:53-54; cf. 1 Kings 8; 2 Chronicles 6–7; Ps. 132[131]:12; Isa. 66:2, 5). Stephen is, of course, stoned after his Christological statement but this could quite plausibly be understood as a dispute over ultimate authority for Stephen's claims, over who was really doing the will of God and not over the details of Christ's being (cf. Mk 2:10; 2:28; 3:22-30; 14:65; Acts 4:1-22; 5:27-42). The crucial thing in all this is that none of the texts cited have anything explicit to say on the issue of Christology, "Christ-devotion" and conflict. Yet the theology of Christian orthodoxy shines through in Hurtado's interpretation with the "Jewish context" reflecting a major scholarly discourse and its extra sparkle of cultural acceptability and theological grounding in the "Old Testament."

This approach is not simply present in texts that have little to say on Christology. In Mark's gospel, where we have plenty of discussion of what might reasonably be called Christology, the model filters problematic evidence out to make it more palatable. After the obligatory claim that from the non-canonical gospel of Thomas, unlike the canonical gospels, "we would not even know that Jesus was Jewish," Hurtado pushes the idea that Mark's gospel promoted "intense" devotion to Jesus.[54] He argues that signs of strong devotion can be found in the Markan miracle stories (e.g. Mk 4:35-41; 6:30-44, 45-52; 8:1-9).[55] Yet in each case we know of similar actions attributed to non-Christian Jewish figures. First-century Jewish figures such as Theudas were believed to have performed miracles similar to those of Jesus (e.g. Josephus, *War* 2.258-63; *Antiquities* 20.97-99, 167-172). Philo claimed that the elements obeyed Moses (cf. Mk 4:41), while from rabbinic literature figures such as R. Eliezar were also said to have mastery over the elements (*b. BM* 59b). Figures such as Moses, Elisha and Hanina ben Dosa were said to perform feeding miracles. We might repeat that there is *nothing* in Mark's Gospel like the strong indications that Jesus is being equated with God in the strongest sense that we find in John's Gospel (e.g. Jn 5:16-18; 10:22-39; 20:28). Despite all this, Hurtado's divine (in the strongest sense) Jesus is again "Jewish...but not *that* Jewish" and, for all the "pro-Jewish" rhetoric, this can only be done by ignoring or downplaying important first-century evidence.[56]

The mention of John's Gospel should also indicate that I am not implying (should anyone wish to accuse me of doing so) that the early Christians could not play around with Jewish identity in similar ways to contemporary scholarship. Christianity did, after all, become a religion in its own right, often in explicit distinction from Judaism. Paul might also be an interesting example here. Like Jesus, the "Jewishness" of Paul has been increasingly emphasized since the 1970s. But unlike Jesus, there is plenty of evidence – though certainly not unambiguous – for Paul advocating an overriding or rejection of various aspects of Jewish Law. Yet, in the case of modern scholarship on Jesus and other aspects of Christian origins, the reconstruction of differentiation is often done by stressing "Jewishness," then having their Jesus (or someone or some group in Christian origins) overriding aspects of their constructed "Jewishness" without discussing powerful evidence to the contrary. We now need to explain in further detail why this tension over "Jewishness" exists.

An Asymmetrical Special Relationship

> *The question is how* plausible *it is to believe that American polity toward Israel has been shaped by the Holocaust. Not very. It was when the Holocaust was freshest in the minds of American leaders – the first twenty-five years after the end of the war – that the United States was* least *supportive of Israel and more interested in overtures to Arab states. It was not when Israel was perceived as weak and vulnerable, but after it demonstrated its strength, in the Six Day War, that American aid to Israel changed from a trickle to a flood. And the president who forged the close American alliance with Israel...was Richard Nixon, of all postwar American political leaders surely the one least likely to be moved by moral or sentimental consideration.*
>
> Peter Novick[57]

> *Basically the United States doesn't give a damn about Israel: if it goes down the drain, U.S. planners don't care one way or another, there's no moral obligation or anything else. But what they* do *care about is control of the enormous oil resources of the Middle East.*
>
> Noam Chomsky[58]

> *As I see it, God's promises to Israel were complete and fulfilled in the handing over and raising up of Jesus by God the Father. There is of course still the hope that national Israel will respond to the message of Christ (either as individuals or en masse).*
>
> Michael F. Bird[59]

While a great deal of this tension reflects both the lengthy history of the perceived cultural superiority of Western Christianity that has dominated the discipline from time immemorial, this idea of Jesus as Jewish has roots that shoot off in different directions. One particularly important consequence of Christian dominance of the discipline in a time when there is more interest in, and less hostility toward, Judaism, is the preservation of Christian superiority. Jonathan Z. Smith – and developed further by Arnal – has shown how in the scholarship of Christian origins and the move toward Jewish "backgrounds," Judaism serves a double or duplicitous function. One the one hand, Judaism has 'insulated' Christianity from outside influence while on the other hand, "it has been presented by the very same scholars as an object to be transcended by early Christianity."[60] In this context we might also recall the results of Todd Penner's argument (see Chapter 1) that contemporary New Testament scholarship is still feeling the impact of its roots in nineteenth-century nationalism and "the Jewish question" and, in the fashion of Smith, showing that this tradition developed both to distinguish Christianity from Judaism and keep Christianity "pure" from pagan influences.[61] Smith's and Penner's analyses of contemporary Christian origins study are supported by the results of this chapter.

However, if I am right that Anglo-American support for Israel has paved the way for the emphasis on Jesus' Jewishness and helped keep it buoyant, then we should also look to the context of Anglo-American support for Israel to further help explain this relationship. We should immediately be suspicious of entirely honourable scholarly intentions given the virtual absence of the often moralistic emphasis on the "Jewishness" of Jesus in the years immediately following the Holocaust. To re-emphasize, why did it take so long for this emphasis and this care to emerge? Would the timing alone not suggest that there is something other than philo-Semitism going on here? And would not the too-common avoidance of reading early Jewish texts while still getting preachy with too-common phrases such as "the Jewish view was..." or "as a good Jew would..." and the too-common contrasting of the "thoroughly Jewish" Jesus with Jewish views that too many scholars have not even *bothered* to investigate in any detail further suggest that something other than philo-Semitism is going on here?

As this already implies, and as we will see below, the myth of Jesus-superiority also reflects the cultural superiority at the heart of Western attitudes towards Israel. Again, there is an Orientialist tradition at work here. The construction of Jew and Arab – including the shift from the main recipient of antisemitism – in Orientalist discourse is easily done because, as Said points out, the figure is essentially the same. As we have seen, Said has argued that the Arab is "conceived of now as a shadow that dogs the Jew." In this shadow can be placed whatever traditional mistrust is felt toward the Oriental. Yet the Jew also shares the same history of representation: let us not forget that in this discourse both Jew and Arab are Oriental Semites.[62] As Said further puts it, "Orientalism and modern anti-Semitism have common roots."[63]

In its own particular way, what we are dealing with in Christian origins scholarship is, as we saw above more generally with Smith's and Arnal's analysis of "Judaism" and Penner's analysis of "the Jewish problem" in Chapter 1, the "Jew" and "Judaism" as a construct of Western scholarship with a long and continuing Orientalist tradition. "Jew" and "Judaism" are effectively designed to be a category with which to fill convenient western descriptions. Put more bluntly, as it indeed needs to be, "the Jew" remains a subservient construct in this discourse, no matter how positive this figure has been in relation to the anti-Jewish and antisemitic past of New Testament scholarship. Judaism is Judaism on Christianized terms.

Furthermore, there are, to put it mildly, some tensions in the various relationships with Israel which are related to religious and cultural superiority. In many ways the Christian Zionist relationship with Israel ought to be a strange one, even if it is obviously pragmatic from the perspective of some Israeli Jews and some Jewish Zionists. Ultimately, Jews have to bow down to Jesus Christ and do his work. As Hal Lindsey alarmingly asks us to imagine, in the end times there will be "144,000 Jewish Billy Grahams turned loose on this earth"![64] The relationship strains further when we realize that, according to the thought of much of the Christian right, once the Palestinians are finally kicked out then, following Armageddon, any remaining Jews will be destroyed unless they convert to the Christianity of the Christian right. As Lawrence Davidson puts this bizarre relationship:

> this whole-hearted evangelical support of Israel and Zionism does not come from any love of the Jewish people or pity for their past sufferings... In fact what the Christian Coalition et al have in mind for the Jewish people is annihilation in a fashion that makes the Holocaust look like an amateur operation... Remember, those who ardently await these events are part of Karl Rove's Republican base. The Grand Old Party turns out to be partially grounded on a movement of fanatic anti-Semites.[65]

Davidson is probably going too far because Republican Christian Zionists do not simply think (unbelieving) Jews are to be singled out but rather the target is *everyone* who does not believe. Like the defence given by the classic racist comedian, they don't just hate the Jews, blacks, Asians, and so on, they hate everyone; they do not single out one group: all the ethnic groups are fair game! Still, the general point stands and, to put it very mildly, unbelieving Jews will not feel the same love at end times as they are getting at present.

Furthermore, as the Christian Zionistic right continue to be deeply embedded in US politics and culture it should be clear that Jews and other non-Christians in the neo-conservative Bush administration accept the support of the Christian right for practical and Machiavellian reasons, following, apparently, the teaching of the intellectual fountainhead, apparently, of neo-conservative thought, Leo Strauss, the influential teacher of political philosophy at the University of Chicago.[66] In a similar way, so nationalistic Israeli politicians will, for pragmatic reasons, accept the support of Christians who believe Jews (such as Israeli politicians) will be wiped out if they do not convert.

There are plenty of high-profile examples of pre-rapture tensions in the attitudes of Christian Zionists toward Israel and/or Jewish people. In an email to *New York Times* journalist Nicholas D. Kristof – who had suggested that the *Left Behind* books involve the slaughter of non-Christians, including unconverted Jews, not to mention the wrong types of Christian – *Left Behind* co-author, Jerry Jenkins, is reported to have pointed out the following in a response to Kristof: "We can't read it some other way just because it sounds exclusivistic and not currently politically correct. That's our crucible, an offensive and divisive message in an age of plurality and tolerance."[67] Several more concrete examples of these tensions could be chosen[68] and many of them have invariably come from the mouth of Pat Robertson. Recently (2005) Robertson had been critical of Israel for withdrawing from Gaza and following Ariel Sharon's stroke, and for which he later apologized, he claimed: "He was dividing God's land, and I would say, 'Woe unto any prime minister of Israel who takes a similar course to appease the [European Union], the United Nations or the United States of America.' God says, This land belongs to me, and you'd better leave it alone."[69]

As all this would suggest, in the US party political scene it is difficult to see the official pro-Israel policy being done out of any sincere love for the Jewish people. The Project for the New American Century, which contains important and staunch supporters of Israeli actions, is, after all, an attempt to establish *American* values. Often Israel's interests overlap with those of the US and are therefore deemed useful at present. Recall Henry Jackson's 1973 comments quoted in the previous chapter where "reliable friends" such as Israel could deal with threats from "radical elements" in Arab states which, crucially "would pose a grave threat indeed to *our* principal sources of petroleum in the Persian Gulf" (italics added). It hardly needs stating that from this perspective and at this stage of US-Israeli relations self-interest was a key factor, with Israel being a mere "cop on the beat," to use the often-cited phrase from Nixon's Defense Secretary Melvin Laird. In Britain, the political powers have consistently deemed it necessary to swing on the coat-tails of the US. As we saw in the previous chapter, the 1970 Foreign Office document utilized by Mark Curtis showed that Britain could theoretically have adopted a more pro-Arab policy but could not practically because the US had to be followed. That is hardly a ringing endorsement of admiration and support for Israel and Israelis.

Conclusions

It should be stressed that nothing in the above discussion automatically makes historical Jesus scholars Christian Zionists or dispensationalists, even if there are many in the discipline who work among such types, and some are such types. Rather, it is the broader cultural and political shifts increasingly supportive of Israeli state policy since 1967 that has partially created the context in which the emphatically *Jewish* Jesus could emerge and be accepted widely in the discipline. Such a pro-Israeli line is so deeply embedded in the discourse and mechanisms of American capitalism that it is unthinkable that there would be no impact on biblical studies as a whole, including historical Jesus studies and the study of Christian origins. Yet, looking under the surface, there remains the myth of national and religious superiority over against Jewish people and Israel.

And so despite the acceptance of Jesus the Jew we have seen that there remains a thick seam of Christian and/or Western superiority. On the more "traditional" side, we may cite Wright whose Jesus is, we are repeatedly told, "thoroughly Jewish" but envisages the end of the food laws and the break with familial piety and ethnicity; on the more "liberal" side we can cite the social radical of the Jesus Seminar who still stands above his contemporaries on a wide range of issues. Much of this, I argued, represents a broader trend whereby Jesus is constructed over against his contemporaries and "Judaism" or the wider Jewish culture is constructed in contemporary scholarship not for any love of early Judaism as a religion in itself but to keep Christian claims sufficiently Jewish. This post-1967 interest reflects wider Orientalist and, most crucially in terms of historical explanation, foreign-policy themes. In a similar way to the Christian support for Israel being limited in its support for a group of people who are ultimately not Christian and are religiously "other," so Christian scholarly support for Jesus' Jewishness is a category packed with tension and ambivalence in a largely Christian discipline.

Chapter 7

Conclusion

Rip It Up and Start Again: The Intellectual and Moral Failings of Academics

> *This is happening in the intellectual journals. And intellectuals are specialists in defamation, they're basically commissars – they're the ideological managers, so they are the ones who feel the most threatened by dissidence. The mass media don't care that much, they ignore it, or say it's crazy or something like that...sure, you'll get a throwaway line saying, "this guy's an apologist for this that and the other thing," but that's just feeding off the intellectual culture. The place where it's really done is inside the intellectual journals – because that's their specialty. They're commissars; it's not fundamentally different from the Communist Party. And also, I'm a particular target for other reasons – a lot of what I write is a critique of the American liberal intellectual establishment, and they don't like that particularly.*
>
> N. Chomsky[1]

> *Respect for the concrete detail of human experience, understanding that arises from viewing the Other compassionately, knowledge gained and diffused through moral and intellectual honesty: surely these are better, if not easier, goals at present than confrontation and reductive hostility. And if in the process we can dispose finally of both the residual hatred and the offensive generality of labels like "the Muslim," "the Persian," "the Turk," "the Arab," or "the Westerner," then so much the better.*
>
> Edward W. Said[2]

One of the mains aims of this book was to highlight how New Testament and Christian origins scholarship is profoundly influenced by and supportive of contemporary Anglo-American power. We have seen how the general history of the discipline shows how New Testament and Christian origins scholarship has clearly been immersed in the politics of the day. We then focused in on the contemporary political constraints in the analysis of the "bibliobloggers" and how this apparently free, democratic and open media forum has, in fact, many striking similarities with the constraints on the mainstream mass media as analysed by Edward Herman and Noam Chomsky and their form of the propaganda model. Among the bibliobloggers there is a constant defence of Anglo-American foreign policy, hypersensitivity about any critique of Israel, implicit and explicit opposition to anything Islamic (the religion where much of contemporary media centred foreign policy is focused), and so on.

We then moved on to see just how deeply embedded the rhetoric of the "clash of civilizations" – with Islam and Arabs as the great civilizational enemy – and "war on terror" is in Anglo-American thought since the 1970s and how this is reflected, at times with some profoundly distasteful stereotypes, in contemporary scholarship, particularly that using dubious, nationalistic and, at times, racist anthropological scholarship, usually with reference to "the Middle East," "the Mediterranean," "Islamic world" and so on. Some of the language used in contemporary anthropological approaches to the New Testament and Christian origins is worryingly close to some of the language used in the justifications for torture, invasion, and old-fashioned imperialism. We then saw how trends relating to Anglo-American support for Israel since the key year 1967 have had a profound impact on mainstream Christian origins scholarship, though, like much Anglo-American support for Israel, this comes with cultural and religious superiority. Israel and Jews just so happen to be useful at present so emphasis on "Jewishness" is merely convenient for Christian scholarship with Christian origins being conspicuously "better" than anything "Judaism" (as constructed by scholarship) can muster.

One feature of this book is that it helps explain why certain movements in New Testament and Christian origins research emerged when and where they did. One of the reasons why anthropology and discussions of the "Mediterranean" and the Middle East occur by the 1980s is almost certainly due to the neo-Orientalism in Anglo-American thought since the 1970s that continues to go hand-in-hand with Anglo-American interests in the Middle East, Arabs, and Muslims since the 1970s. It is striking that there was no serious interest in such anthropology prior to the 1970s in the study of Christian origins. It is also striking that the stress on Jesus' "Jewishness," inaccurate suggestions of antisemitic interpretations, the destruction of antisemitic and anti-Jewish scholarship and so on emerged in the 1970s and continue to be prominent issues. It is further striking that such a shift did not occur in the years immediately after the Holocaust. One of the key historical reasons for this new emphasis is almost certainly related to the changing Anglo-American attitudes towards Israel after 1967.

In anticipation of possible criticisms, it should be stressed that this does not mean that it is necessarily wrong to use anthropology. While some of the uses of anthropology have brought about some extremely unfortunate comments about people in the Middle East, this in itself does not discredit the use of anthropology as methodologically useful as has been shown in the work of scholars from Philip Esler and Zeba Crook to Louise Lawrence and Justin Meggitt. I have little concern here for discussion of the details of method. On one level, I am merely explaining why an approach emerged when and where it did, not that it is necessarily wrong.

Yet, on a very basic academic level, a part of this book is trying to get people at least to check ideology with some basic facts. Ideology may convince your own or the like-minded but so what? Is that really getting us close to understanding the ancient world and Christian origins? If scholars are genuinely interested in finding out about Jesus in relation to Judaism then saying Jesus is "really Jewish," "a good Jew," "thoroughly Jewish" or whatever before telling us that he went beyond, intensified, overrode, rejected various Jewish symbols constructed by scholars, then why not *prove it* with reference to a wider range of *Jewish* evidence? If Jesus really overrode family ties in an unparalleled way then *show* that there was no parallel instead of just telling us and do not ignore available evidence. If Jesus really advocated something unparalleled in plucking grain on the Sabbath, it should not be good enough to state it as if fact and tell us how "Jewish" Jesus was without bothering to deal with parallel *Jewish* evidence.

Clearly, there needs to be some serious questioning of scholarly results. Any statement by a scholar, no matter how famous or revered, should be immediately questioned and we should be instantly suspicious (I am almost tempted to say the more famous and revered, the more doubt and the more suspicion should be cast on any unsubstantiated statement). All this should be the basis of creative and inquisitive thought. Otherwise, my suggestion is to be deeply suspicious that ideology and reputation are interfering too much and inquisitiveness is not high on the agenda.

This should be obvious enough, though, as we have seen, there are too many high profile examples of non-argument. Such non-argument becomes even more morally dubious when cultural stereotyping and related allegations fly. So let's question more. If certain scholars are really showing "subtle anti-Semitism," as we have been *told* (and nothing more than that), that is a massive allegation, so why not prove it? If they are genuinely guilty of being tainted by antisemitism, it should not be too difficult to prove, right? If, as we have been *told* (and nothing more than that), that Mediterranean people really neglect their own needs, if they really have stifled normal individual psychological development, if they really repress feelings of hurt, if they really abuse children, spouses and the elderly, if they really abuse others physically, emotionally, and spiritually, if they really have blocked mental, emotional and spiritual growth, then such serious allegations not only need some *evidence* but *serious, widespread evidence* to back it up. If, as we have been *told* (and nothing more than that), Arabs are supposedly quick to join extremist groups and are not good at coping with defeat in elections then quoting some basically racist scholarship is not really good enough. If a scholar wants to say this is so, why not try and prove it? If Middle Easterners do not value individual rights, as we have been *told* (and nothing more than that), *prove it,* now of all times. And if there is no attempt to prove these serious allegations then people might also want to ask: why should we believe you? Is a quest for academic truth really on the agenda, or something else? Incidentally, the contemporary impact of such views listed above should not need re-stating.

There is much talk in the secondary literature about self-awareness and honesty in scholarship. If academics are ignoring available evidence and if academics are making some morally dubious statements about Arabs, Muslims, the Middle East, Palestinians and so on at a time when such people have been as prominent as ever before in the western media as the recipients of Anglo-American foreign policy then I think there is legitimate reason to believe that, at best, mere lip-service is being paid to self-awareness and that there are too many less-than-honest approaches to scholarship. Most academics are extremely privileged individuals, many paid to think about these issues with a significant degree of freedom. Yet the fact that some of their ideas on, and generalizations about, other cultures are disseminated without any qualification and thought suggests to me that this is close to being an abuse of this privilege.

Students at the best of times should immediately question what their lecturers and professors tell them. So if students have any concern for justice or basic morality, when they then hear lecturers and professors talking about other ethnic, religious and national groups in broad stereotypical terms and particularly in a context when such people are being stereotyped, demonized, and lied about in the media, popular culture and beyond, it might be worth them pushing the good and the great to justify, with serious facts and evidence, how they come to such conclusions. If more academics would join in challenging the good and the great about the ethical impact of their conclusions then that might also help, though loss of privilege, jeopardizing old friendships, and career non-advancement may be incentive enough for most academics to do otherwise. But the following needs to be remembered: people among the various groups stereotyped by the scholarship critiqued in this book are dying and being tortured as I write and scholarship and intellectuals are helping to create a potentially lethal cultural context.

If New Testament academics can think twice about the ways in which they construct other groups, then this book has achieved something, no matter how small. If, however, the arguments about the dominance of the various intellectual power groups discussed in this book are anywhere near correct then it is not likely that my arguments will have any serious impact on the academic world. Academics are, after all, dependent on elite power, and some work directly for elite power. Moreover, given the attack on a broad range of scholarship in this book, it is unlikely many academics are going to accept challenges to their position and power. We saw in Chapter 4 that some of the scholars discussed dismiss opponents who do not agree with them, often without any attempt to back up their dismissal. I am realistic enough to be aware that this book may well be dismissed in intellectual biblical studies, as so many books taking dissenting views are. And then there is the old method of ignoring criticism which is often a more useful way of dismissing criticism. Yet this book should not be taken as an act of mere self-indulgence, as if wallowing in self-pity and pessimism. For all its seemingly inevitable reception, and no matter how much some people do not like what is written in it, I still hope, as I did above, that the main result this book will have is to make sure that some of the outrageous stereotypes are avoided in future, along with some self-awareness and more concern for detail when describing.

Yet still I find myself in an unusual position because this book does not have a natural supportive audience in academic biblical studies. But again, should anyone wish to suggest otherwise, this too should not necessarily imply a pessimistic conclusion. Beyond the traditional realm of academics, there is enough opposition in this world to contemporary Anglo-American power and enough people in this world are vigorously critiquing abuses of intellectual power. So if academics will not act or engage with critiques then the appeal of books like this may well have to be beyond the conventional academic boundaries where they can make a contribution. That is not necessarily a bad thing.

Notes

Preface

1. On the spelling of "antisemitism" in this book, I follow Richard Evans: "The spelling *antisemitism* is used throughout this book in preference to the conventional *anti-Semitism*. The latter is itself an antisemitic formulation; there was, and is, no such thing as 'Semitism,' except in the minds of antisemites." R. J. Evans, *In Defence of History* (2nd edn; London: Granta, 2000), p. 334, n. 7.

2. K. W. Whitelam, *The Invention of Ancient Israel: The Silencing of Palestinian History* (London: Routledge, 1996).

3. M. Casey, *An Aramaic Approach to Q* (Cambridge: Cambridge University Press, 2002), p. 50.

4. Cf. L. L. Grabbe, " 'The Comfortable Theory,' 'Maximal Conservatism' and Neo-Fundamentalism Revisited," in A. G. Hunter and P. R. Davies (eds.), *Sense and Sensitivity: Essays on Reading the Bible in Memory of Robert Carroll* (Sheffield: Sheffield Academic Press, 2002), pp. 174–93.

Part I

1. Amartya Sen, *Identity and Violence: The Illusion of Destiny* (London: Allen Lane, 2006), p. 44.

2. Arundhati Roy, "The Loneliness of Noam Chomsky," *The Hindu* (August 24, 2003).

Chapter 1

1. Ward Blanton, *Displacing Christian Origins: Philosophy, Secularity, and the New Testament* (Chicago: Chicago University Press, 2007), p. 7.

2. E. S. Herman and N. Chomsky, *Manufacturing Consent: The Political Economy of the Mass Media* (London: Vintage, 1988). Cf. also Roy, "Loneliness of Noam Chomsky." The summary in this paragraph is also based on J. G. Crossley, "Mark's Christology and a Scholarly Creation of a Non-Jewish Christ of Faith," in J. G. Crossley (ed.), *Judaism, Jewish Identities and the Gospel Tradition: Essays in Honour of Maurice Casey* (London: Equinox, forthcoming), ch. 5.

3. Crossley, "Mark's Christology"; J. G. Crossley, *Why Christianity Happened: A Sociohistorical Account of Christian Origins* (Louisville: Westminster/John Knox, 2006), ch. 1.

4. N. Chomsky, *Understanding Power* (ed. P. R. Mitchell and J. Schoeffel; New York: New Press, 2002), p. 233; N. Chomsky, *Imperial Ambitions* (London: Penguin, 2005), p. 142.

5. N. Chomsky, "Scholarship and Ideology: American Historians as 'Experts in Legitimation,' " *Social Scientist* 1 (1973), pp. 20–37.

6. Chomsky, *Understanding Power*, pp. 232–33; cf. Chomsky, "Scholarship and Ideology," pp. 21–23.

7. Chomsky, *Understanding Power*, pp. 243–44.

8. N. Chomsky, *American Power and the New Mandarins: Historical and Political Essays* (New York: Pantheon, 1969); N. Chomsky, *For Reasons of State* (New York: Pantheon, 1973); Chomsky, "Scholarship and Ideology."

9. Chomsky, *Understanding Power*, pp. 244–47.

10. Chomsky, *Understanding Power*, p. 228.

11. Chomsky, *Understanding Power*, pp. 230–31.

12. "N. Chomsky: An Interview," *Radical Philosophy* (August, 1989), p. 32, quoted in M. Rai, *Chomsky's Politics* (London & New York: Verso, 1995), p. 206.

13. Chomsky, *Understanding Power*, p. 242.

14. E. W. Said, *Orientalism* (London: Penguin, 1978, 1995, 2003), p. 25. Cf. E. W. Said, *Culture and Imperialism* (London: Vintage, 1993), pp. 347–67; E. W. Said, *Representations of the Intellectual* (London: Vintage, 1994).

15. D. Gregory, *The Colonial Present: Afghanistan, Palestine, Iraq* (Oxford: Blackwell, 2004), p. 16.

16. M. Farish, "Targeting the Inner Landscape," in D. Gregory and A. Pred (eds.), *Violent Geographies: Fear, Terror, and Political Violence* (New York & London: Routledge, 2007), pp. 255–71.

17. N. T. Wright, *The Resurrection of the Son of God* (London: SPCK, 2003), p. 737.

18. Chomsky, *Understanding Power*, p. 242.

19. I cannot find the precise origins of this saying. For an application see, e.g., A. Petridis, "In Pursuit of Outlaw Cool," *Guardian* (August 30, 2006).

20. B. J. Malina, "Dedication," in W. Stegemann, B. Malina and G. Theissen (eds.), *The Social Setting of Jesus and the Gospels* (Minneapolis: Fortress Press, 2002), pp. vii–viii.

21. J. H. Elliott, "Jesus the Israelite Was Neither a 'Jew' nor a 'Christian': On Correcting Misleading Nomenclature," *JSHJ* 5 (2007), pp. 119–54, on which see further J. G. Crossley, "Jesus the Jew since 1967," in W. Blanton, J. G. Crossley and H. Moxnes (eds.), *Jesus beyond Nationalism: Constructing the Historical Jesus in a Period of Cultural Complexity* (London: Equinox, forthcoming 2008). See also Chapter 6.

22. Giles Fraser, "Not Faith, but Fanaticism," *Guardian* (May 29, 2007).

23. M. Casey, "Who's Afraid of Jesus Christ? Some Comments on Attempts to Write a Life of Jesus," in J. G. Crossley and C. Karner (eds.), *Writing History, Constructing Religion*, (Aldershot: Ashgate, 2005), pp. 129–46.

24. Crossley, *Why Christianity Happened*, ch. 1.

25. S. Bates, "Unholy Row at Oxford's College for Clergy amid Staff Exodus and Claims of Bullying," *Guardian* (May 16, 2007).

26. M. Newman, "Faith Threat to Free Speech," *Times Higher Education Supplement* (16 March, 2007).

27. J. Taylor, "An Interview with Peter Williams," *Between Two Worlds*, http://theologica.blogspot.com/2007/08/interview-with-peter-williams.html

28. Though not a precise analogy, I am reminded of Charlie Brooker's criticisms of the recent right-wing satire that has emerged in the US in reaction to "liberal" satire. Brooker suggests that the best satire is prepared to lash out at all sides – whoever deserves it the most – and government or party approved satire most definitely does not work. Hitting those in power is the most effective, whether it is Republican or Democrat, and the best satire has done just this. As the Republicans are in power, "this makes sense comedically: there are more jokes to be had in lampooning the governing party since their actions carry more weight…it's hard to generate giggles by attacking the underdog. If Hilary Clinton were in charge, she'd be pilloried nightly. But she isn't. Bush is." C. Brooker, "Screen Burn," *Guardian* (February 24, 2007).

29. On Christian/religious dominance see now H. Avalos, *The End of Biblical Studies* (Amherst, NY: Prometheus Books, 2007).

30. Crossley, *Why Christianity Happened*, p. 23.

31. E.g. D. J. Harrington, "Sociological Concepts and the Early Church: A Decade of Research," *Theological Studies* 41 (1980), pp. 181–90 (189); J. G. Gager, "Shall We Marry our Enemies? Sociology and the New Testament," *Int.* 36 (1982), pp. 256–65 (257); B. Holmberg, *Sociology and the New Testament: An Appraisal* (Minneapolis: Fortress Press, 1990), pp. 145–50; S. C. Barton, "Historical Criticism and Social-Scientific Perspectives in New Testament Study," in J. B. Green (ed.), *Hearing the New Testament: Strategies for Interpretation* (Grand Rapids: Eerdmans, 1995). pp. 61–89 (e.g. 76); P. F. Esler, "Introduction: Models, Context and Kerygma in New Testament Interpretation," in P. F. Esler (ed.), *Modelling Early Christianity: Social-Scientific Studies of the New Testament in its Context* (London: Routledge, 1995), pp. 1–20 (3–4, 14–19); P. F. Esler, *New Testament Theology: Communion and Community* (Minneapolis: Fortress Press, 2005).

32. M. Casey, *From Jewish Prophet to Gentile God: The Origins and Development of New Testament Christology* (Louisville: Westminster John Knox; Cambridge: James Clarke, 1991), pp. 162–81; M. Casey, *Is John's Gospel True?* (London: Routledge, 1996), pp. 116–27.

33. R. Bieringer, D. Pollefeyt, F. Vandecasteele-Vanneuville (eds.), *Anti-Judaism and the Fourth Gospel: Papers of the Leuven Colloquium, 2000* (Assen: Royal Van Gorcum, 2001).

34. For an important analysis of the role of feminist criticism in relation to historical criticism and colonial structures that ought to be read in conjunction with the brief and inevitably crude comments here see C. vander Stichele and T. Penner, "Mastering the Tools or Retooling the Masters?" in C. vander Stichele and T. Penner (eds.), *Her Master's Tools? Feminist and Postcolonial Engagements*

of Historical-Critical Discourse (Atlanta, GA: SBL; Leiden: Brill, 2005), pp. 1–30.

35. E. C. Stanton, *The Woman's Bible* (New York: European Publishing Company, 1895–1898). Cf. R. Page, "Elizabeth Cady Stanton's *The Woman's Bible*," in A. Loades (ed.), *Feminist Theology: A Reader* (London: SPCK, 1990), pp. 16–22.

36. For related comments on the rescuing of God from problematic texts in critical theory and biblical studies see also, R. Boer, *Marxist Criticism of the Bible* (Sheffield: Sheffield Academic Press, 2003), e.g., pp. 133–57.

37. Blanton, *Displacing Christian Origins*, pp. 129–65.

38. H. Moxnes, "Schleiermacher's *Life of Jesus*, 19th Century Nationalism, and the Present Challenge," in W. Blanton, J. G. Crossley and H. Moxnes (eds.), *Jesus beyond Nationalism: Constructing the Historical Jesus in a Period of Cultural Complexity* (London: Equinox, forthcoming).

39. T. Penner, "*Die Judenfrage* and the Construction of Ancient Judaism: Toward a Foregrounding of the Backgrounds Approach to Early Christianity," in P. Gray and G. O'Day (eds.), *Scripture and Traditions: Essays on Early Judaism and Christianity* (Leiden: Brill, forthcoming 2008); cf. T. Penner, *In Praise of Christian Origins: Stephen and the Hellenists in Lukan Apologetic Historiography* (London & New York: T&T Clark/Continuum, 2004), pp. 1–59.

40. Theissen, *Social Reality*, pp. 3–8.

41. F. Engels, "On the History of Earliest Christianity (1894)," in K. Marx and F. Engels, *Collected Works Volume 27, Engels: 1890–95* (London: Lawrence & Wishart, 1990), pp. 447–69; K. Kautsky, *Foundations of Christianity: A Study in Christian Origins* (London: Orbach & Chambers, 1925, original German 1908).

42. For further discussion see, e.g., G. Theissen, *Social Reality and the Early Christians: Theology, Ethics and the World of the New Testament*, (Edinburgh: T&T Clark, 1993), pp. 9–13; S. J. Friesen, "Poverty in Pauline Studies: Beyond the So-called New Consensus," *JSNT* 26 (2004), pp. 323–61 (323–37); Crossley, *Why Christianity Happened*, pp. 10–11; Blanton, *Displacing Christian Origins*, pp. 107–20.

43. See, e.g., A. Deissmann, *Light from the Ancient East: The New Testament Illustrated by Recently Discovered Texts of the Graeco-Roman World* (London: Hodder & Stoughton, 1927), p. 403. See also Appendix XI in the 4th edition of *Light* for another attack on Kautsky. Cf. Blanton, *Displacing Christian Origins*, pp. 119–20.

44. Deissmann, *Light*, p. 404. See also Crossley, *Why Christianity Happened*, pp. 10–11; Blanton, *Displacing Christian Origins*, p. 110.

45. See, e.g., S. Heschel, "Nazifying Christian Theology Walter Grundmann and the Institute for the Study and Eradication of Jewish Influence on German Church Life," *Church History* 63 (1994), pp. 587–605; M. Casey, "Some Anti-Semitic Assumptions in *The Theological Dictionary of the New Testament*," *NovT* 41 (1999), pp. 280–91; P. Head, "The Nazi Quest for an Ayrian Jesus," *JSHJ* 2 (2004), pp. 55–89.

46. G. Vermes, *Jesus and the World of Judaism* (London: SCM, 1983), pp. 64–66.

47. On the following see Casey, "Some Anti-Semitic Assumptions," pp. 282–86.

48. K. G. Kuhn, *Die Judenfrage als weltgeschichtliches Problem* (Hamburg: Hanseatische Verlagsanstalt, 1939).

49. K. G. Kuhn, " 'Ισραήλ, 'Ιουδαῖος, 'Εβραῖος in Jewish Literature after the OT," *TDNT* 3:359–69.

50. E.g. J. D.G. Dunn, *The Parting of the Ways between Christianity and Judaism and their Significance for the Character of Christianity* (London: SCM, 1991), p. 154; Elliott, "Jesus the Israelite Was Neither a 'Jew' nor a 'Christian,' " pp. 119–54. Cf. Casey, "Some Anti-Semitic Assumptions," pp. 282–84.

51. H. Pyper, "Musical Analysis and Biblical Studies: Brucknerian Transpositions," unpublished paper presented at European Association of Biblical Studies/International Society of Biblical Literature conference, Vienna 2007.

52. Crossley, *Why Christianity Happened*, pp. 4–5.

53. Casey, "Who's Afraid of Jesus Christ?" p. 133.

54. E. Käsemann, *New Testament Questions of Today* (London: SCM, 1969), p. 186. This was also broadcast on radio. See further D. Boyarin, *A Radical Jew: Paul and the Politics of Identity* (Berkeley, CA: University of California Press, 1994), pp. 213–14.

55. Notably E. A. Judge, *The Social Pattern of the Christian Groups in the First Century* (London: Tyndale Press, 1960).

56. See P. Kowaliñski, "The Genesis of Christianity in the Views of Contemporary Marxist Specialists of Religion," *Antonianum* 47 (1972), pp. 541–75.

57. G. Bornkamm, *Jesus of Nazareth* (London: Hodder & Stoughton, 1960), p. 102.

58. Bornkamm, *Jesus*, p. 223.

59. G. Theissen, *Sociology of Early Palestinian Christianity* (Philadelphia: Fortress Press, 1978), p. 125, n. 40.

Chapter 2

1. Slavoj Žižek, *Welcome to the Desert of the Real! Five Essays on September 11 and Related Dates* (London & New York: Verso, 2002), p. 3.

2. Melani McAlister, *Epic Encounters: Culture, Media and US Interests in the Middle East, 1945–2000* (Berkeley, CA: University of California Press, 2001), p. 5.

3. Jacques Berlinerblau, commenting on the internet discussion group, Christian Origins, available at http://groups.yahoo.com/group/christian_origins/message/205.

4. D. Meadows, "Maybe a Rant...Megasites, Blogs, and Classics," *rogueclassicism* (January 27, 2004), http://www.atrium-media.com/rogueclassicism/2004/01/27.html; J. R. Davila, "Assimilated to the Blogosphere: Blogging Ancient Judaism," *SBL Forum*, http://www.sbl-site.org/Article.aspx?ArticleId=390

5. Despite this Bible-as-a-whole emphasis, I will focus more on biblioblogs relating more to early Judaism and Christian origins. The exceptions will be those with more "extreme" views on politics as they are useful for points of contrast.

6. The links are conveniently collected at C. Tilling, "*Jesus and the Eyewitnesses* – Outline of forthcoming posts," *Chrisendom* (November 15, 2006), available at http://www.christilling.de/blog/2006/11/jesus-and-eyewitnesses-outline-of.html

7. For the inaugural post see M. Bird, "Evangelical Exegetes Hall of Fame I: Longenecker," *Euangelion* (April 13, 2006), http://euangelizomai.blogspot.com/2006/04/evangelical-exegetes-hall-of-fame-i.html

8. N. Chomsky, *Understanding Power* (ed. P. R. Mitchell and J. Schoeffel; New York: New Press, 2002), pp. 276–77.

9. J. Davila, *PaleoJudaica* (November 27, 2006), http://paleojudaica.blogspot.com/2006_11_26_archive.html#116462469587671225

10. M. Goodacre, "The Jesus Project's Problems," *NT Gateway Weblog* (August 07, 2007), http://ntgateway.com/weblog/2007/08/jesus-projects-problems.html

11. Cf. E. S. Herman and N. Chomsky, *Manufacturing Consent: The Political Economy of the Mass Media* (London: Vintage, 1988), pp. 297–301.

12. M. Goodacre, " 'Jesus' Family Tomb': How Blogging Helps," *NT Gateway Weblog* (February 26, 2007), http://ntgateway.com/weblog/2007/02/jesus-family-tomb-how-blogging-helps.html

13. Davila, "Blogosphere."

14. See also the interview with Davila on blogging: B. Wason, "An Interview with James R. Davila" (January, 2006), http://www.biblioblogs.com/featured-blogs/200601/

15. *Earliest Christian History*, http://www.earliestchristianhistory.blogspot.com/

16. J. West, "Jim West Interviews James Crossley," biblioblogs.com (January, 2007), http://www.biblioblogs.com/featured-blogs/200701/

17. Craig Murray, *Murder in Samarkand: A British Ambassador's Controversial Defiance of Tyranny in the War on Terror* (Edinburgh & London: Mainstream Publishing, 2006), pp. 20, 27.

18. J. Cathey, "A Civil Service Message for Preparedness!" *Dr Cathey's Blog* (November 4, 2005), see Appendix.

19. K. Ristau, "RNC: Day One" (August 30, 2004), *anduril.ca*, http://anduril.ca/blog/2004/08/rnc-day-one.html; K. Ristau, "RNC: Day Two" (August 31, 2004), *anduril.ca*, http://anduril.ca/blog/2004/08/rnc-day-two.html; K. Ristau, "RNC: Day Three" (September 1, 2004), *anduril.ca*, http://anduril.ca/blog/2004/09/rnc-day-three.html; K. Ristau, "RNC: Day Four" (September 2, 2004), *anduril.ca*, http://anduril.ca/blog/2004/09/rnc-day-four.html; cf. https://www.blogger.com/comment.g?blogID=14521325&postID=112224652716300080

20. K. Ristau, "The Election of Hamas" (January 26, 2006), *anduril.ca*, http://anduril.ca/blog/2006/01/election-of-hamas.html

21. K. Ristau, "A New Day?" (November 10, 2004), *anduril.ca*, http://anduril.ca/blog/2004_11_01_archive.html

22. K. Ristau, "Iraq's Air Force: A Look in the Sands," *anduril.ca* (September 1, 2005), http://anduril.ca/blog/2005_09_01_archive.html

23. https://www.blogger.com/comment.g?blogID=7009956&postID=112554998724552413&isPopup= true

24. "Iraq and Just War Theory," (June 24, 2005), *anduril.ca*, http://anduril.ca/blog/2005_06_01_archive.html

25. E.g. C. Reed, *Just War?* (London: SPCK, 2004).

26. H. O. Kareem, "An Interview with Noam Chomsky," *ZNet* (January 02, 2004), available at http://www.zmag.org/content/showarticle.cfm?ItemID=4780

27. On US support for Equatorial Guinea, see, e.g., J. Bolender, "Blind Eye on Africa: Human Rights, Equatorial Guinea, and Oil," *ZNet* (August 16, 2003).

28. Murray, *Murder in Samarkand*, p. 112.

29. Amnesty International, "Report 2003 – Uzbekistan," http://web.amnesty.org/report2003/uzb-summary-eng

30. Human Rights Watch, "Changes to US Military Assistance after September 11," (February, 2002), http://hrw.org/reports/2002/usmil/USass0202-02.htm#P178_26449

31. D. Leigh, N. P. Walsh, and E. MacAskill, "Ambassador Accused after Criticising US," *Guardian* (October 18, 2003). Cf. J. Bolender, "Uzbekistan and the US: Sometimes It Really Is a War on Islam," *ZNet* (October 18, 2003), available at http://www.zmag.org/content/print_article.cfm?itemID=4367&sectionID=40

32. Murray, *Murder in Samarkand*, p. 366.

33. Herman and Chomsky *Manufacturing Consent*, p. 37.

34. J. Davila, *PaleoJudaica* (July 7, 2005), http://paleojudaica.blogspot.com/2005_07_03_archive.html#112073513544192484

35. M. Goodacre, "Terrorist Attack on London," *NTGateway* (July 7, 2005), http://ntgateway.com/weblog/2005/07/terrorist-attack-on-london.html

36. M. Bird, "Terrorism, Suffering and the Triumph of God's Mecy [*sic*]," *Euangelion* (July 7, 2005), http://euangelizomai.blogspot.com/2005/07/terrorism-suffering-and-triumph-of.html

37. E. Cook, "Learning in War-time," *Ralph the Sacred River* (July 7, 2005) http://ralphriver.blogspot.com/2005/07/learning-in-war-time.html

38. Available at www.liveleak.com/view?i=af8_1181469330

39. http://www.icmresearch.co.uk/pdfs/2005_july_guardian_july_poll.pdf; cf. J. Glover, "Two-thirds Believe London Bombings Are Linked to Iraq War," *Guardian* (July 19, 2005).

40. G. Achcar, *The Clash of Barbarisms: September 11 and the New World Disorder* (second edition; London: Saqi, 2002, 2006), pp. 23–38.

41. E.g. G. W. Bush, "Address to a Joint Session of Congress and the American People," (September 20, 2001), available at http://www.whitehouse.gov/news/releases/2001/09/20010920-8.html

42. Achcar, *The Clash of Barbarisms*, p. 30.

43. Herman and Chomsky, *Manufacturing Consent*, pp. 37–86.

44. Achcar, *The Clash of Barbarisms*, p. 34.

45. J. Crossley, "Iraq and Chemical Warfare," *Earliest Christian History* (November 15, 2005), http://earliestchristianhistory.blogspot.com/2005/11/

iraq-and-chemical-warfare.html; J. Crossley, "More on White Phosphorus Used in Iraq," *Earliest Christian History* (November 16, 2005), http://earliestchristianhistory.blogspot.com/2005/11/iraq-and-chemical-warfare.html. See further, "The Fight for Fallujah," *Field Artillery* (March, 2005), available at http://sill-www.army.mil/famag/2005.asp#mar-apr; G. Monbiot, "The US Used Chemical Weapons in Iraq – and Then Lied about It," *Guardian* (November 15, 2005); J. Wilson, "US Admits Using White Phosphorus in Falluja," *Guardian* (November 16, 2005); G. Monbiot, "Behind the Phosphorus Clouds Are War Crimes within War Crimes," *Guardian* (November 22, 2005). Matthew Coomber also made important comments in the comments section but his biblioblog life was extremely short.

46. J. Crossley, " 'Evil' and Terror," *Earliest Christian History* (August 13, 2005), http://earliestchristianhistory.blogspot.com/2005/08/evil-and-terror.html; J. Crossley, "How Not to Realise What You Are Arguing," *Earliest Christian History* (August 1, 2006), http://earliestchristianhistory.blogspot.com/2006/08/how-not-to-realise-what-you-are.html For further discussion see Chapter 3.

47. J. Crossley, "Christianity and Islam," *Earliest Christian History* (July 24, 2005), http://earliestchristianhistory.blogspot.com/2005/07/christianity-and-islam.html

48. Crossley, "Christianity and Islam."

49. N. Chomsky, "Reply to Hitchens' Rejoinder," *The Nation* (October 4, 2001), available at http://www.thenation.com/doc/20011015/chomsky 20011004.

50. Albright's infamous comments on the deaths of 500,000 children in Iraq are now available on YouTube: http://www.youtube.com/watch?v=lK_QshS2EW8.

51. See further, D. Gregory, *The Colonial Present: Afghanistan, Palestine, Iraq* (Oxford: Blackwell, 2004), pp. 47–75.

52. Herman and Chomsky, *Manufacturing Consent*, pp. xi, 2, 297–303.

53. Edward W. Said, *Orientalism* (London: Penguin, 1978, 1995, 2003), p. 287.

54. Joseph Cathey, "War on Terror, President Bush, and World War II," *Dr Cathey's Blog* (August 31, 2005), see Appendix.

55. S. Harris, *The End of Faith: Religion, Terror, and the Future of Reason* (London: Simon & Schuster, 2004).

56. J. Cathey, "War on Terror, President Bush, and World War II," *Dr Cathey's Blog* (August 31, 2005), see Appendix.

57. M. Bird, "Army, Al-Qaeda and Pacifism," *Euangelion* (August 12, 2005), http://euangelizomai.blogspot.com/2005/08/army-al-qaeda-and-pacifism.html

58. Crossley, " 'Evil' and Terror." Cf. S. P. Huntington, *The Clash of Civilizations and the Remaking of World Order* (New York: Simon & Schuster, 1996, p. 263, "The argument is made that Islam has from the start been a religion of the sword."

59. Bird, "Terrorism."

60. https://www.blogger.com/comment.g?blogID=14521325&postID=112389703202200498

61. M. Bird, "Religious News Service – Kevin O'Brien" (February 10, 2006), *Euangelion*, http://euangelizomai.blogspot.com/2006/02/religious-news-service-kevin-obrien.html

62. L. Rosson, "The Decline and Fall of Arab Civilization: The Influence of the Crusades and the *Jihad*," *The Busybody* (December 4, 2006), http://lorenrosson.blogspot.com/2006/12/decline-and-fall-of-arab-civilization.html.

63. Edward Said, *Orientalism*, p. 286.

64. E. W. Said, *Orientalism* (2003 edition; London: Penguin, 1978, 1995, 2003), pp. xiv–xv.

65. See, e.g., M. McAlister, *Epic Encounters: Culture, Media and US Interests in the Middle East, 1945–2000* (Berkeley, CA: University of California Press, 2001), pp. 155–59, 178–97; G. Philo and M. Berry, *Bad News from Israel* (London, Pluto, 2004).

66. Davila, "Blogosphere."

67. J. Davila, *PaleoJudaica* (October 10, 2005), http://paleojudaica.blogspot.com/2005_10_09_archive.html#112893304724034007 Davila has since read and (negatively) reviewed the book. I discuss this review in Chapter 5.

68. http://www.solomonia.com/blog/

69. J. Davila, *PaleoJudaica* (February 14, 2007), http://paleojudaica.blogspot.com/2007_02_11_archive.html; cf. J. Davila, *PaleoJudaica* (May 27, 2005), http://paleojudaica.blogspot.com/2007_02_11_archive.html#117145593350243884

70. J. Davila, *PaleoJudaica* (July 30, 2005) http://paleojudaica.blogspot.com/2005_07_24_archive.html#112271462161761419

71. K. W. Whitelam, *The Invention of Ancient Israel: The Silencing of Palestinian History* (London & New York: Routledge, 1996); N. Abu el-Haj, *Facts on the Ground: Archaeological Practice and Territorial Self-Fashioning in Israeli Society* (Chicago & London: University of Chicago Press, 2001).

72. J. Davila, *PaleoJudaica* (August 30, 2005), http://paleojudaica.blogspot.com/2005_08_28_archive.html

73. Davila, *PaleoJudaica* (November 27, 2006), http://paleojudaica.blogspot.com/2006_11_26_paleojudaica_archive.html#116462469587671225

74. Davila, *PaleoJudaica* (February 11, 2007), http://paleojudaica.blogspot.com/2007_02_11_archive.html#117118327777428718

75. J. Davila, *PaleoJudaica* (April 20, 2005), http://paleojudaica.blogspot.com/2005_04_17_archive.html#111398741615562330

76. Davila, *PaleoJudaica* (April 12, 2005), http://paleojudaica.blogspot.com/2005_04_10_archive.html

77. T. Sternthal, "The Temple Mount's Jewish History: More Than a Matter of Faith," CAMERA (April 11, 2005), http://www.camera.org/index.asp?x_context=2&x_outlet=35&x_article=879

78. Cf. P. Nikkel, "Avenge but One of my Two Eyes," *Deinde* (April 16, 2007), http://www.deinde.org/2007/04/16/

79. J. Davila, *PaleoJudaica* (July 30, 2005), http://paleojudaica.blogspot.com/2005_07_24_archive.html#112271462161761419; J. Davila, *PaleoJudaica* (July 27, 2005), http://paleojudaica.blogspot.com/2005_07_24_archive.html#

112271462161761419; J. Davila, *PaleoJudaica* (August 30, 2005), http://paleojudaica.blogspot.com/2005_08_28_archive.html#112539232819166623

80. E.g. E. Cook, "Open Studies, Peer Review, and Kuhnian Paradigms," *Ralph the Sacred River* (August 30, 2005). There were comments on Jim West's old webpage address which is no longer available as far as I know.

81. Davila, *PaleoJudaica* (August 30, 2005).

82. C. Tilling, "An Evangelical Letter to Bush about Israeli-Palestinian Peace," *Chrisendom* (August 21, 2007), http://www.christilling.de/blog/2007/08/evangelical-letter-to-bush-about.html

83. The links are helpfully collected at http://www.christilling.de/blog/2007/02/my-christian-zionism-series.html

84. C. Tilling, "The Use of Scripture in Christian Zionism: A Critical Examination. Pt. 1," *Chrisendom,* (August 29, 2006), http://www.christilling.de/blog/2006/08/use-of-scripture-in-christian-zionism.html

85. C. Tilling, "The Use of Scripture in Christian Zionism: A Critical Examination. Pt. 5" *Chrisendom* (September 15, 2006), http://www.christilling.de/blog/2006/09/use-of-scripture-in-christian-zionism_15.html

86. C. Tilling, "The Use of Scripture in Christian Zionism: A Critical Examination. Pt. 6," *Chrisendom* (September 24, 2006), http://www.christilling.de/blog/2006/09/use-of-scripture-in-christian-zionism_24.html

87. Tilling, "The Use of Scripture in Christian Zionism: A Critical Examination. Pt. 1."

88. M. Bird, "Arab Christians in Israel," *Euangelion* (October 5, 2007), http://euangelizomai.blogspot.com/2007/10/arab-christians-in-israel.html.

89. Similarly, when discussing hostility towards Arabs, Bird refers to Arab Christians. See M. Bird, "Arab Christians Rock in Egypt," *Euangelion* (December 10, 2007), http://euangelizomai.blogspot.com/2007/12/arab-christians-rock-in-egypt.html; "More on Arab Christians," *Euangelion* (December 17, 2007), http://euangelizomai.blogspot.com/2007/12/more-on-arab-christians.html

90. A message from the internet discussion group dedicated to the work of N. T. Wright, *Wrightsaid,* http://groups.yahoo.com/group/Wrightsaid/ (February 28, 2006).

91. S. du Toit, "Does Bush Exist?" *Primal Subversion* (October 1, 2005), http://primalsubversion.blogspot.com/2005/10/does-bush-exist.html

92. P. Vallely, "Tom Wright: It's Not a Question of Left and Right, Says the Combative Priest Who Opposes the War in Iraq and Gay Bishops," *Independent* (29 December, 2003); S. Hall, "Blair Acted Like a 'White Vigilante' by Invading Iraq, Says Bishop," *Guardian* (December 30, 2003).

93. K. Ristau, "Did Bush Exist? Revisited," *anduril.ca* (October 07, 2005), http://anduril.ca/blog/2005/10/did-bush-exist-revisited.html

94. https://www.blogger.com/comment.g?blogID=7009956&postID=112875066256047094&isPopup =true; cf. Davila, *PaleoJudaica* (October 10, 2005).

Part II

1. Derek Gregory, *The Colonial Present: Afghanistan, Palestine, Iraq* (Oxford: Blackwell, 2004), p. 18.

2. Edward W. Said, "Preface (2003)," in *Orientalism* (2003 edn; London: Penguin, 1978, 1995, 2003), pp. xiv-xv.

Chapter 3

1. Slavoj Žižek, *Welcome to the Desert of the Real! Five Essays on September 11 and Related Dates* (London & New York: Verso, 2002), p. 104.

2. J. G. Crossley, *Why Christianity Happened: A Sociohistorical Account of Christian Origins 26–50CE* (Louisville: Westminster/John Knox, 2006), pp. 3–22.

3. Said, *Orientalism*, pp. 284–88.

4. E.g. E. Ghareeb (ed.), *Split Vision: The Portrayal of Arabs in the American Media* (Washington, DC: American-Arab Affairs Council, 1983); J. Shaheen, *The TV Arab* (Ohio: Bowling Green State University Press, 1984); M. Suleiman, *The Arabs in the Mind of America* (Brattleboro: Amana, 1988); M. McAlister, *Epic Encounters: Culture, Media and US Interests in the Middle East, 1945–2000* (Berkeley, CA: University of California Press, 2001); J. G. Shaheen, *Reel Bad Arabs: How Hollywood Vilifies a People* (Northampton, MA Interlink, 2001); D. Little, *American Orientalism: The United States and the Middle East since 1945* (2nd edn; Chapel Hill & London: University of North Carolina Press, 2002, 2004), e.g. pp. 9–11, 31–42.

5. E. W. Said, *Covering Islam: How the Media and the Experts Determine How We See the Rest of the World* (2nd edn; London: Vintage, 1981, 1997), pp. 3–79; cf. N. Chomsky and G. Achcar, *Perilous Power: The Middle East and U.S. Foreign Policy* (ed. S. R. Shalom; Boulder & London: Paradigm, 2007), pp. 204–14.

6. For general Orientalism in New Testament and related scholarship see, e.g., R. S. Sugirtharajah, *Asian Biblical Hermeneutics and Postcolonialism: Contesting the Interpretations* (Sheffield: Sheffield Academic Press, 1998), pp. 101–11; E. Schüssler Fiorenza, *Jesus and the Politics of Interpretation* (New York and London: Continuum, 2000), pp. 21–22, 82–114.

7. See especially B. J. Malina, *The New Testament World: Insights from Cultural Anthropology* (3rd edn; Louisville: Westminster/John Knox, 1981, 2001), pp. 27–57.

8. B. Mack, *The Christian Myth: Origins, Logic, and Legacy* (New York & London: Continuum, 2001).

9. R. Cameron and M. Miller (eds.), *Redescribing Christian Origins* (Atlanta, GA: SBL, 2004).

10. J. D. Crossan, *The Historical Jesus: The Life of a Mediterranean Jewish Peasant* (New York: HarperCollins; Edinburgh: T&T Clark, 1991); J. D. Crossan, *The Birth of Christianity: Discovering What Happened in the Years Immediately after the Execution of Jesus* (New York: HarperCollins; Edinburgh: T&T Clark, 1998). Cf. B. J. Malina, "Social Scientific Methods in Historical Jesus Research,"

in W. Stegemann, B. J. Malina and G. Theissen (eds.), *The Social Setting of Jesus and the Gospels* (Minneapolis: Fortress Press, 2002), pp. 3–26 (4): "what has been done with the social sciences is significant, much of it important enough to be plagiarized by John Dominic Crossan."

11. W. R. Herzog, *Prophet and Teacher: An Introduction to the Historical Jesus* (Louisville: Westminster/John Knox, 2005).

12. J. P. Meier, *A Marginal Jew: Rethinking the Historical Jesus*, vol. 1, *The Roots of the Problem and the Person* (New York: Doubleday, 1991), pp. 10–11. Cf., e.g., J. P. Meier, *A Marginal Jew: Rethinking the Historical Jesus*, vol. 3, *Companions and Competitors* (New York: Doubleday, 2001), p. 67: "Ancient Mediterranean society was largely a society of 'dyadic personality,' where one's identity was formed and maintained in relation to other individuals in one's social unit – the usual unit being the extended family."

13. N. T. Wright, *Jesus and the Victory of God* (London: SPCK, 1996), pp. 52–53.

14. L. J. Lawrence, *An Ethnography of the Gospel of Matthew: A Critical Assessment of the Use of the Honour and Shame Model in New Testament Studies* (Tübingen: Mohr Siebeck, 2003), p. vii.

15. S. P. Huntington, "The Clash of Civilizations?" *Foreign Affairs* 72 (1993), pp. 22–49, available at http://history.club.fatih.edu.tr/103%20Huntington%20Clash%20of%20Civilizations%20full%20text. htm; B. Lewis, "The Roots of Muslim Rage," *The Atlantic* (September 1990), pp. 47–60.

16. Huntington, "Clash of Civilizations?"

17. S. P. Huntington, *The Clash of Civilizations and the Remaking of World Order* (New York: Simon & Schuster, 1996).

18. D. Harvey, *The New Imperialism* (Oxford: Oxford University Press, 2003), e.g. pp. 42–86; 137–82; cf. E. W. Said, *Culture and Imperialism* (London: Vintage, 1993), pp. 341–67.

19. Harvey, *New Imperialism*, p. 49.

20. N. Chomsky, *Understanding Power* (ed. P. R. Mitchell and J. Schoeffel; New York: New Press, 2002), pp. 167–68.

21. N. Chomsky, *Imperial Ambitions: Conversations with Noam Chomsky on the Post-9/11 World* (interviews with David Barsamian; London: Penguin, 2005), p. 148.

22. *Iraq's Weapons of Mass Destruction – The Assessment of the British Government* (September 24, 2002), available at http://www.number-10.gov.uk/output/Page271.asp

23. *London Evening Standard* (September 24, 2002).

24. *The Sun* (September 25, 2002).

25. *Star* (September 25, 2002).

26. George Monbiot, "America Is a Religion," *Guardian* (July 29, 2003).

27. Robert Fisk, *The Great War for Civilisation: The Conquest of the Middle East* (London: Fourth Estate, 2005), p. 1141.

28. See, e.g., Gregory, *Colonial Present*, pp. 47–49; G. Achcar, *The Clash of Barbarisms: September 11 and the New World Disorder* (2nd edn; London: Saqi, 2002, 2006), pp. 27–30, 89.

29. G. W. Bush, "State of the Union Address," (January 29, 2002), available at http://www.whitehouse.gov/news/releases/2002/01/20020129-11.html

30. House of Commons Debates, Session 2002–2003, "Iraq," (March 18, 2003), *Hansard*, cols. 767–68, available at http://www.parliament.uk/hansard/hansard.cfm

31. Cf. J. G. Crossley, "Defining History," in J. G. Crossley and C. Karner (eds.), *Writing History, Constructing Religion* (Aldershot: Ashgate, 2005), pp. 9–29 (15–17); R. Fisk, *The Great War for Civilisation: The Conquest of the Middle East* (London: Fourth Estate, 2005), pp. 1140–44.

32. A. Sen, *Identity and Violence: The Illusion of Destiny* (London: Allen Lane, 2006), e.g. pp. 4, 20–21, 40–58 (quote p. 44). See further Gregory, *Colonial Present*, e.g. pp. 19–29, 47–75.

33. C. Deane and D. Fears, "Negative Perception of Islam Increasing," *Washington Post* (March 9, 2006), p. A01.

34. BBC, "Poll Sees Hope in West-Islam Ties," (February 9, 2007), http://news.bbc.co.uk/1/hi/in_depth/6369529.stm

35. A. Coulter, "Why We Hate Them," in M. L. Sifry and C. Cerf (eds.), *The Iraq War Reader: History, Documents, Opinions* (New York: Touchstone, 2003), pp. 333–35.

36. A. Coulter, "This Is War," (September 12, 2001), http://www.anncoulter.org/columns/2001/091301.htm.

37. W. Cummins, "Dr Williams, Beware of False Prophets," *Sunday Telegraph* (July 4, 2004).

38. H. Goddard, "The Crisis of Representation in Islamic Studies," in Crossley and Karner (eds.), *Writing History, Constructing Religion*, pp. 85–106 (101).

39. P. Hitchens, "I'll Say It while They Still Let Me: Islam Is a Threat to Us All," *Mail on Sunday* (July 11, 2004).

40. W. Hutton, "Why the West Is Wary of Muslims," *Observer* (January 11, 2004).

41. http://bloodletting.blog-city.com/every_terrorist_they_kill_now.htm

42. This was on Cathey's old blog from which he subsequently retired and deleted (see also Appendix to Chapter 2). The fragments, as it were, of Cathey's blog on Doc Russia are to be found at: http://earliestchristianhistory.blogspot.com/2006/08/no-no-joe.html Further comments, including Cathey's qualifications, can be found at: http://earliestchristianhistory.blogspot.com/2006/08/how-not-to-realise-what-you-are.html

43. Available at http://politics.guardian.co.uk/labour2001/story/0,,562006,00.html (part 1) http://politics.guardian.co.uk/labourconference2001/story/0,1220,561988,00.html (part 2)

44. C. Reed, *Just War?* (London: SPCK, 2004). For further criticisms of Reed and those like him, including details of post-Vietnam Anglo-American foreign policy see J. G. Crossley, "Caesar's Willing Theologians; 'Just War' Theory and the Art of Justifying the Unjustifiable," *Political Theology* (forthcoming).

45. See especially J. Keegan, "In This War of Civilisations, the West Will Prevail," *Telegraph* (October 8, 2001). Cf. the not-so-subtle N. B. De Atkine, "Why Arabs Lose Wars," *Middle East Quarterly* 6 (1999), pp. 17–27.

46. Keegan, "In This War of Civilisations."

47. Sen, *Identity and Violence*, pp. 46–49. Cf. more generally C. Karner, *The Thought World of Hindu Nationalism: Analyzing a Political Ideology* (Lewistown, NY: Edwin Mellen Press, 2006).

48. K. Tomlinson, "Living Yesterday in Today and Tomorrow: Meskhetian Turks in Southern Russia," in Crossley and Karner (eds.), *Writing History, Constructing Religion*, pp. 107–28.

49. For further details on public discussion, democracy and religious tolerance in Muslim, Middle Eastern and general "non-Western" traditions in contrast to vulgarizing constructions of "non-Western" identity see, e.g., Sen, *Identity and Violence*, pp. 14–16, 51–55, 68–70. Cf. Said, *Culture and Imerialism*, pp. 359–60.

50. Noam Chomsky, *Interventions* (London: Hamish Hamilton, 2007), p. 101.

51. Cf. Said, *Covering Islam*, pp. xxxv–xxxvi.

52. See especially Gregory, *Colonial Present.*

53. J. Burke, *Al-Qaeda* (London: Penguin, 2003).

54. J. Glassman, "Imperialism Imposed and Invited: The 'War on Terror' Comes to Southeast Asia," in D. Gregory and A. Pred (eds.), *Violent Geographies: Fear, Terror, and Political Violence* (New York & London: Routledge, 2007), pp. 93–109.

55. T. Friedman, "Liberal Hawks Reconsider the Iraq War," *Slate* (January 12, 2004), http://www.slate.com/id/2093620/entry/2093763/

56. Cf. Gregory, *Colonial Present*, p. 22. For a critique of Friedman's journalistic output see, e.g., E. S. Herman, "The NYT's Thomas Friedman: The Geraldo Rivera of the NYT," *Z Magazine Online* (16 November, 2003), http://zmagsite.zmag.org/Nov2003/hermanpr1103.html

57. E.g. (among many) G. Kepel, *The War for Muslim Minds: Islam and the West* (Cambridge, MA & London: The Belknap Press of Harvard University Press, 2004); Achcar, *Clash of Barbarisms*, pp. 39–76; Chomsky and Achcar, *Perilous Power*, pp. 27–52; M. Watts, "Revolutionary Islam," in Gregory and Pred (eds.), *Violent Geographies*, pp. 175–203.

58. For summaries see, e.g., A. Hourani, *A History of the Arab Peoples with an Afterword by Malise Ruthven* (London: Faber, 1991, 2002), pp. 373–458; Watts, "Revolutionary Islam"; cf. Huntingdon, *Clash of Civilizations*, pp. 116–20, 259–61.

59. Watts, 'Revolutionary Islam', p. 194. On slums and urbanization in global context see esp. M. Davis, *Planet of Slums* (London and New York, Verso, 2006).

60. H. von Sponeck and D. Halliday, "The Hostage Nation," *Guardian* (November 29, 2001); cf. http://news.bbc.co.uk/1/hi/world/middle_east/642189.stm; H. von Sponeck, *A Different Kind of War: The UN Sanctions in Iraq* (Oxford: Berghahn, 2006).

61. T. Nagy, "The Secret behind the Sanctions: How the US Intentionally Destroyed Iraq's Water Supply," *The Progressive* (September 1–6, 2001), available at www.progressive.org/0801issue/nagy0901.html;

62. "Iraq Water Treatment Vulnerabilities," (January 22, 1991), http://www.gulflink.osd.mil/declassdocs/dia/19950901/950901_511rept_91.html;

"Disease Information,", (January 22, 1991, http://www.gulflink.osd.mil/declassdocs/dia/19950901/950901_0504rept_91.html;

"Disease Outbreaks in Iraq," (February 21, 1990), http://www.gulflink.osd.mil/declassdocs/dia/19950901/950901_0pgv072_90p.html;

"Medical Problems in Iraq," (March 15, 1991), http://www.gulflink.osd.mil/declassdocs/dia/19951016/951016_0me018_91.html;

"Status of Disease at Refugee Camps," (May 1991), http://www.gulflink.osd.mil/declassdocs/dia/19950719/950719_68980446_91z.html;

"Health Conditions in Iraq," (June 1991), http://www.gulflink.osd.mil/declassdocs/dia/19950719/950719_60500007_91r.html; "Iraq: Assessment of Current Health Threats and Capabilities," (November 15, 1991), http://www.gulflink.osd.mil/declassdocs/dia/19961031/961031_950825_0116pgv_00p.html

63. "Iraq: Assessment of Current Health Threats and Capabilities."

64. As Watts ("Revolutionary Islam," p. 196) puts it, "The stench of American complicity in the rise of Islamism is simply overpowering." Or again, Achcar, *Clash of Barbarisms*, p. 52: "The United States is thus directly responsible for the resurgence of anti-Western Islamic fundamentalism." The literature on American complicity in the rise of contemporary violent Islam is unsurprisingly vast. For helpful summaries see, e.g., Kepel, *War for Muslim Minds*, pp. 5–8, 47–69; Gregory, *Colonial Present*, pp. 30–46; Achcar, *Clash of Barbarisms*, pp. 39–76; M. Mamdani, *Good Muslim, Bad Muslim: America, the Cold War, and the Roots of Terror* (New York: Three Leaves Press, 2005); cf. Said, *Culture and Imperialism*, pp. 361–66.

65. Cf. further Gregory, *Colonial Present*, pp. 76–143.

66. See R. Fisk, *Pity the Nation: Lebanon at War* (Oxford: Oxford University Press, 1990), pp. 358–400 and Fisk, *Great War for Civilisation*, pp. 623–24, 1020–26, for Robert Fisk's reporting at the time and subsequent analysis. See also Fisk's visual report on YouTube, http://www.youtube.com/watch?v=4FGijoJ3fl0

67. Sam Harris, *The End of Faith: Religion, Terror, and the Future of Reason* (London: Simon & Schuster, 2004), p. 109.

68. Harris, *End of Faith*, pp. 109–11.

69. Harris, *End of Faith*, p. 128.

70. Harris, *End of Faith*, p. 131.

71. Harris, *End of Faith*, p. 132.

72. Harris, *End of Faith*, pp. 133–34.

73. Harris adds several sweeping and inaccurate generalizations, while others smack of cultural and economic snobbery, such as his slamming of what Iraqis (as an example of supposed Muslim stupidity) believe about Americans after the fall of Saddam (p. 254, n. 31) without any indication of his privileged position as an American intellectual which is not remotely comparable to living in Iraq at present.

74. A classic example packed full of very basic errors and confusion is from Campus Watch founder Daniel Pipes, "God and Mammon: Does Poverty Cause Militant Islam?" *The National Interest* 66 (Winter 2001–2002), also available at

http://www.danielpipes.org/article/104. For a short but firm and to-the-point debunking of Pipes see Achcar, *Clash of Barbarisms*, p. 171 n. 65.

75. Cf. K. Marx, "Eighteenth Brumaire of Louis Bonaparte," in K. Marx and F. Engels, *Collected Works Volume 11, Marx and Engels: 1851–53* (London: Lawrence & Wishart, 1979), pp. 101–97; R. H. Hilton, "Peasant Society, Peasant Movements and Feudalism in Medieval Europe," in H. A. Landsberger (ed.), *Rural Protest: Peasant Movements and Social Change* (New York: Macmillan, 1973), pp. 67–94; J. H. Kautsky, *The Politics of Aristocratic Empires* (Chapel Hill: University of North Carolina, 1982), e.g. p. 304; E. J. Hobsbawm, *Uncommon People: Resistance, Rebellion and Jazz* (London: Abacus, 1998), pp. 221–22.

76. D. Leigh and J. Wilson, "Counting Iraq's Victims," *Guardian* (October 10, 2001).

77. Available at www.liveleak.com/view?i=dc3_1181469312; www.liveleak.com/view?i=560_1181469398; www.liveleak.com/view?i=af8_1181469330

78. So Achcar, *Clash of Barbarisms*, p. 79.

79. http://www.icmresearch.co.uk/pdfs/2005_july_guardian_muslim_poll.pdf

80. http://www.icmresearch.co.uk/pdfs/2006_february_sunday_telegraph_muslims_poll.pdf; cf. M. Tran, "Poll: Government Had role in July 7 Bombings," *Guardian* (June 5, 2007).

81. Achcar, *Clash of Barbarisms*, p. 56.

82. For useful summaries with further bibliographical references see, e.g., Hourani, *History of the Arab Peoples*, pp. 373–472; Burke, *Al-Qaeda*, pp. 41–55; G. Kepel, *The Roots of Radical Islam* (London : Saqi, 2005); Watts, "Revolutionary Islam."

83. Harris, *End of Faith*, pp. 139–44.

84. From a May 2004 BBC *Newsnight* interview by Jeremy Paxman, available at http://news.bbc.co.uk/2/hi/programmes/newsnight/3732345.stm

85. From a February 2002 BBC *Hardtalk* interview by Tim Sebastian available at http://www.chomsky.info/interviews/20020227.htm

86. N. Chomsky, "Reply to Hitchens' Rejoinder," *The Nation* (October 4, 2001), available at http://www.thenation.com/doc/20011015/chomsky 20011004

87. "Hugh Fitzgerald" (Campus Watch), "Study the Threats, and the Response to Them," *Dhimmi Watch* (August 14, 2007), available at http://www.jihadwatch.org/dhimmiwatch/archives/017784.php

88. See, e.g., C. W. Ernst, "From the Heart of the Qur'an Belt," *Religious Studies News* 18 (2003), pp. 14–18; Goddard, "Islamic Studies," pp. 94–96.

89. For a list of media responses see http://www.haverford.edu/relg/sells/UNC_ApproachingTheQur'an.htm

90. W. F. Buckley, "Are We Owed an Apology?" National Review Online (August 16, 2002), http://www.nationalreview.com/buckley/buckley081602.asp

91. Editorial, "Sanitizing Islam," *Jerusalem Post* (August 26, 2003).

92. http://www.haverford.edu/relg/sells/UNC_ApproachingTheQur'an.htm

93. N. Abu el-Haj, *Facts on the Ground: Archaeological Practice and Territorial Self-Fashioning in Israeli Society* (Chicago & London: University of Chicago Press, 2001).

94. The scare quotes around the name "Hugh Fitzgerald" are because I am a little suspicious that this so-called "independent scholar of Islam" ("Hugh Fitzgerald on the Islamic Challenge," *A View from the Right*, http://www.amnation.com/vfr/archives/002373.html) might be some one or some others using a pseudonym. It is quite common on the internet for polemical types to use a pseudonym because it allows them to say almost anything about anyone. In the case of "Fitzgerald" it is possible that this is a pseudonym used to say some exceptionally hateful things about Islam. It seems I am not the only one to have such suspicions: R. Silverstein, "Barnard alumni cabal opposes tenure for Abu el-Haj," *Tikun Olam*, http://www.richardsilverstein.com/tikun_olam/2007/08/21/barnard-alumni-cabal-opposes-tenure-for-abu-el-haj/

95. "H. Fitzgerald," "Crisis at Columbia: Nadia Abu El-Haj," *FrontPage Magazine* (October 10, 2005), available at http://www.campus-watch.org/article/id/2228

96. His "introductory essay" on Columbia contains many of the same kinds of sweeping generalizations about Muslim culture. See "H. Fitzgerald," "Crisis at Columbia: That Awful Mess on Morningside Heights," *Campus Watch* (April 14, 2005), http://www.campus-watch.org/article/id/1943

97. http://www.campus-watch.org/about.php

98. K. McNeil, "The War on Academic Freedom," *The Nation* (November 11, 2002), http://www.thenation.com/doc/20021125/mcneil

99. Noam Chomsky, *Pirates and Emperors, Old and New: International Terrorism in the Real World* (London: Pluto, 2002), p. 150.

100. Julie Burchill, "I See in Those Photos Why We Are Fighting," *Times* (May 22, 2004).

101. Robert Fisk, "A Cry for Justice from a Good Man Who Expected Us to Protect His Son," *Independent on Sunday* (June 17, 2007).

102. K. Sengupta, "Iraq Abuse Case Ends with Soldiers Acquitted," *Independent* (March 14, 2007); Cf. R. Fisk, "British Soldiers 'Kicked Iraqi Prisoner to Death,' " *Independent on Sunday* (January 4, 2004); R. Fisk, "Who Killed Baha Mousa?" *Independent* (December 15, 2004); R. Fisk, "A Cry for Justice"; Leading article, "A Bloody Epitaph to Blair's War," *Independent on Sunday* (June 17, 2007).

103. Fisk, "A Cry for Justice."

104. R. Fisk, "The 'Good Guy' Who Can Do No Wrong," *Independent* (May 2, 2004).

105. N. Klein, "Children of Bush's America," *Guardian* (May 18, 2004).

106. See http://www.youtube.com/watch?v=lK_QshS2EW8

107. Nagy, "The Secret behind the Sanctions"; S. Graham, "Demodernizing by Design: Everyday Infrastructure and Political Violence," in Gregory and Pred (eds.), *Violent Geographies*, pp. 309–28 (319–20).

108. See, e.g., Gregory, *Colonial Present*, pp. 63–65.

109. Achcar, *Clash of Barbarisms*, p. 35, see also pp. 23–38 for similar discussions.

110. C. R. Browning, *Ordinary Men: Reserve Police Battalion 101 and the Final Solution in Poland* (2nd edn; London: Penguin, 1992, 1998), pp. 159–89.

111. For a selection see, e.g., C. Haney, C. Banks, and P. Zimbardo, "Interpersonal Dynamics in a Simulated Prison," *International Journal of Criminology and Penology* 1 (1973), pp. 69–97; S. Milgrom, *Obedience to Authority: An Experimental View* (London: Tavistock, 1974); J. W. Dower, *War without Mercy: Race and Power in the Pacific War* (New York: Pantheon, 1986), pp. 3–14, 33–73; J. Groebel and R. A. Hinde (eds.), *Aggression: Their Biological and Social Bases* (Cambridge: Cambridge University Press, 1989); Z. Bauman, *Modernity and the Holocaust* (Oxford: Polity Press, 1989); J. Bourke, *An Intimate History of Killing: Face to Face Killing in the Twentieth Century Warfare* (London: Granta, 1999).

112. "Speech by Ambassador Craig Murray – Freedom House, 17.10.02," www.europarl.eu.int; *Murder in Samarkand: A British Ambassador's Controversial Defiance of Tyranny in the War on Terror* (Edinburgh & London: Mainstream Publishing, 2006), pp. 108–12.

113 D. Leigh, N. P. Walsh, and E. MacAskill, "Ambassador Accused after Criticising US," *Guardian* (October 18, 2003); Murray, *Murder in Samarkand.*

114. Cf. G. Monbiot, "Tony Blair's New Friend," *Guardian* (October 28, 2003).

115. R. Fisk, "War Lords to their Critics: 'Just Shut Up,' " *Independent* (April 10, 2004).

116. N. Chomsky, "Reply to Hitchens," *The Nation* (October 1, 2001), available at http://www.thenation.com/doc/20011015/chomsky20011001 Hitchens responded back but missed Chomsky's point. See C. Hitchens, "A Rejoinder to Noam Chomsky," *The Nation* (October 4, 2001), available at http://www.thenation.com/doc/20011015/hitchens20011004; N. Chomsky, "Reply to Hitchens' Rejoinder," *The Nation* (October 4, 2001), available at http://www.thenation.com/doc/20011015/chomsky20011004

117. T. Ali, *The Clash of Fundamentalisms: Crusades, Jihads and Modernity* (London: Verso, 2002); Achcar, *Clash of Barbarisms.*

118. Said, *End of the Peace Process*, pp. 142–43.

Chapter 4

1. Edward W. Said, *Covering Islam: How the Media and the Experts Determine How We See the Rest of the World* (2nd edn; London: Vintage, 1981, 1997), p. Lxviii.

2. Louise J. Lawrence, *An Ethnography of the Gospel of Matthew: A Critical Assessment of the Use of the Honour and Shame Model in New Testament Studies* (Tübingen: Mohr Siebeck, 2003), p. 26.

3. William Arnal, *The Symbolic Jesus: Historical Scholarship, Judaism and the Construction of Contemporary Identity* (London & Oakville: Equinox, 2005), p. 3.

4. *James Brother of Jesus: Holy Relic or Hoax?* (DVD; dir. S. Jacobovici; Associated Producers/Discovery, 2004).

5. *The Virgin Mary* (BBC/Discovery documentary, first aired Christmas, 2002).

6. E.g. Said, *Orientalism*, p. 311; cf. E. Schüssler Fiorenza, *Jesus and the Politics of Interpretation* (London & New York, 2000), pp. 99–101.

7. Said, *Orientalism*, pp. 284–88.

8. Arnal, *Symbolic Jesus*, pp. 3–4, quotation p. 3.

9. https://www.blogger.com/comment.g?blogID=14521325&postID=112389703202200498

10. L. Rosson, "The 'No Asshole Rule': A Question of Ethnocentricity," *The Busybody* (February 18, 2007), http:// lorenrosson.blogspot.com/2007/02/no-asshole-rule-question-of.html

11. L. Rosson, "The Decline and Fall of Arab Civilization: The Influence of the Crusades and the Jihad," *The Busybody* (December 4, 2006), http://lorenrosson.blogspot.com/2006/12/decline-and-fall-of-arab-civilization.html

12. The phrase "Arab Stagnation" is used by Raphael Patai in his book (*The Arab Mind* [rev. edn; New York: Hatherleigh Press, 1976, 1983, 2002], pp. 261–83) full of infamous and outrageous generalizations and stereotypes about "the Arab mind," a book that has been used by military figures, condemned as racist, and referenced by some Context Group members, including Rosson's teacher Richard Rohrbaugh. We will return to the issue of Patai below.

13. L. Rosson, "The Evolution of Religious Tolerance," *The Busybody* (February 8, 2006), http://lorenrosson.blogspot.com/2006/02/evolution-of-religious-tolerance.html

14. There was disagreement with Rosson but it was merely an alarming cultural generalizing of its own: "daviv52 said... Very interesting but I think recent events have much more to do with the fact that non-Western people envy the West due to the success of its material civilization over the past 200 or so years...unless the fundamentalists are able to duplicate the material success of Western civilization they will not succeed unless, of course, they succeed in their avowed aim of destoying [sic] Western civilization."

15. E.g. A. Smith, "Rangers on Rack as Sectarian Chanting Mars Win," *Scotland on Sunday* (August 5, 2007), available at http://news.scotsman.com/topics.cfm?tid=225&id=1224312007; "Chanting Probe May Take Some Time," (August 8, 2007), BBC Sport, http://news.bbc.co.uk/sport1/hi/football/teams/r/rangers/6931472.stm; C. Swan, "Rangers Fans: Leave the Bigots to Us Gers," *Daily Record* (August 17, 2007).

16. S. Sachs, "Baptist Pastor Attacks Islam, Inciting Cries of Intolerance," *New York Times* (June 15, 2002).

17. G. Monbiot, "Puritanism of the Rich," *Guardian* (November 9, 2004).

18. H. Goddard, "The Crisis of Representation in Islamic Studies," in J. G. Crossley and C. Karner (eds.), *Writing History, Constructing Religion* (Aldershot: Ashgate, 2005), pp. 85–106 (101).

19. A. Sen, *Identity and Violence: The Illusion of Destiny* (London: Allen Lane, 2006), p. 16.

20. O. Leirvik, "Jesus in Modern Muslim Thought: From Anti-colonial Polemics to Post-colonial Dialogue?" in W. Blanton, J. G. Crossley and H. Moxnes (eds.), *Jesus beyond Nationalism: Constructing the Historical Jesus in a Period of Cultural Complexity* (London: Equinox, forthcoming).

21. G. W. Bush, "Address to a Joint Session of Congress and the American People" (September 20, 2001), available at http://www.whitehouse.gov/news/releases/2001/09

22. E.g. D. L. Guteman, "Honor, Shame and Terror in the Middle East," FrontPageMagazine.com (October 24, 2003), available at http://www.frontpagemag.com/Articles/Printable.aspx?GUID={EFD57D27-54A4-4F05-9DBC-108BE1EE5379}

23. This is shown at length, with detailed discussion of the historical contexts in Afghanistan, Iraq and Palestine in D. Gregory, *The Colonial Present: Afghanistan, Palestine, Iraq* (Oxford: Blackwell, 2004).

24. Broadcast available at http://www.telegraph.co.uk/news/main.jhtml?xml=/news/2007/06/13/nthatcher213.xml

25. See the comments in N. Chomsky, *Understanding Power* (ed. P. R. Mitchell and J. Schoeffel; New York: New Press, 2002), p. 841; N. Chomsky, *Imperial Ambitions: Conversations with Noam Chomsky on the Post-9/11 World* (interviews with David Barsamian; London: Hamish Hamilton, 2005), p. 97.

26. E.g. D. Rennie, "That Man Tried to Kill my Dad, says Bush," *Telegraph* (September 28, 2002); S. M. Powell, "Ending Iraqi Threat Is Personal for Bush," *timesunion.com* (November 10, 2002), available at http://www.timesunion.com/AspStories/story.asp?storyID=70750; P. Baker, "Conflicts Shaped Two Presidencies," *Washington Post* (December 31, 2006). There have even been attempts, though with qualifications, to analyse US military actions in terms of honour and shame! Cf. B. Wyatt-Brown, "Honor, Shame and Iraq in American Foreign Policy," Note prepared for the Workshop on Humiliation and Violent Conflict, Columbia University, New York (November 18–19, 2004), available at www.humiliationstudies.org/documents/WyattBrownNov04NYConference.pdf; Q&A with B. Wyatt-Brown, "Fighting for Honor: An Ethic as Impetus for War," College of William and Mary News, available at http://www.wm.edu/news/?id=3495

27. Cf., e.g., A. Callinicos, *The New Mandarins of American Power* (Cambridge: Polity Press, 2003); N. Chomsky, *Pirates and Emperors, Old and New: International Terrorism in the Real World* (London: Pluto, 2002); D. Harvey, *The New Imperialism* (Oxford: Oxford University Press, 2003).

28. P. F. Esler, *The First Christians in their Social Worlds: Social-Scientific Approaches to New Testament Interpretation* (London: Routledge, 1994), p. 22.

29. Lawrence, *Ethnography and the Gospel of Matthew*, p. 301.

30. R. S. Sugirtharajah, *Asian Biblical Hermeneutics and Postcolonialism: Contesting the Interpretations* (Sheffield: Sheffield Academic Press, 1998), pp. 105–106.

31. Noam Chomsky, in Noam Chomsky and Gilbert Achcar, *Perilous Power: The Middle East and U.S. Foreign Policy* (ed. S. R. Shalom; Boulder & London: Paradigm, 2007), p. 211.

32. See, e.g., the *JSNT* debates: D. G. Horrell, "Models and Methods in Social-Scientific Interpretation: A Response To Philip Esler," *JSNT* 22 (2000), pp. 83–105; P. F. Esler, "Models in New Testament Interpretation: A Reply To David Horrell," *JSNT* 22 (2000), pp. 107–13; Z. A. Crook, "Structure versus Agency in Studies of the Biblical Social World: Engaging with Louise Lawrence," *JSNT* 29 (2007), pp. 251–75; L. J. Lawrence, "Structure, Agency and Ideology: A Response to Zeba Crook," *JSNT* 29 (2007), pp. 277–86.

33. For comments on general Orientalism and scholarship associated with the Context Group see, e.g., Sugirtharajah, *Asian Biblical Hermeneutics and Postcolonialism*, pp. 105–106.

34. B. J. Malina, *The Social World of Jesus and the Gospels* (London: Routledge, 1996), p. 114; cf. B. J. Malina, *The New Testament World: Insights from Cultural Anthropology* (3rd edn; Louisville: Westminster/John Knox, 1981, 2001), pp. 54–55, 76–78.

35. J. J. Meggitt, "Review of B. J. Malina, *The Social World of Jesus and the Gospels*," *JTS* 49 (1998), pp. 215–19 (218).

36. M. Bockmuehl, "Review of Malina, *New Testament World*, third edition," *BMCR* (2002.04.19), available at http://ccat.sas.upenn.edu/bmcr/2002/2002-04-19.html

37. Said, *Orientalism*, p. 311.

38. See especially Malina, *New Testament World*, pp. 134–60.

39. Malina, *Jesus and the Gospels*, pp. 43, 49.

40. E. T. Hall, *The Silent Language* (Garden City: Doubleday, 1959), pp. 144–45, quoted in Malina, *Jesus and the Gospels*, pp. 44–45. Hall is also referenced by others, e.g. R. Rohrbaugh, *The New Testament in Cross-Cultural Perspective* (Eugene: Cascade Books, 2007), p. 8.

41. R. L. Rohrbaugh, "Legitimating Sonship – a Test of Honour: A Social-Scientific Study of Luke 4:1-30", in P. F. Esler (ed.), *Modelling Early Christianity: Social-Scientific Studies of the New Testament in its Context* (London & New York: Routledge, 1995), pp. 183–97 (186).

42. C. Osiek and D. L. Balch, *Families in the New Testament World: Households and House Churches* (Louisville: Westminster/John Knox, 1997), pp. 38–39, 42.

43. Osiek and Balch, *Families*, p. 238, n. 8.

44. K. C. Hanson, "BTB Readers Guide: Kinship," *BTB* 24 (1994), pp. 183–94.

45. Osiek and Balch, *Families*, pp. 42, 239.

46. Esler, *First Christians*, p. 22.

47. Malina, *Jesus and the Gospels*, p. 41.

48. J. J. Pilch, " 'Beat his Ribs while He Is Young' (Sir 30:12): A Window on the Mediterranean World," *BTB* 23 (1993), pp. 101–13. Cf. Sugirtharajah, *Asian Biblical Hermeneutics and Postcolonialism*, p. 105: "One of the embedded ideas of Orientalism is its perpetuation of the view that Orientals are prone to emotionalism..."

49. Malina, *Jesus and the Gospels*, p. 45.

50. R. L. Rohrbaugh, "Ethnocentrism and Historical Questions about Jesus," in W. Stegemann, B. Malina and G. Theissen (eds.), *The Social Setting of Jesus and the Gospels* (Minneapolis: Fortress Press, 2002), pp. 27–43 (37).

51. Rohrbaugh, "Legitimating Sonship," p. 195. In the same article compare the following: "In a classic *Middle Eastern* game of challenge-response he has bested an adversary that would frighten any mortal man. His honour has been vindicated in a frightening contest of wits... By now any *Middle East* reader would be awestruck Jesus has demolished a challenge of superhuman proportions... Is this not the son of the menial family we all know so well? That is the way you get someone in the *Middle East.* That is how you deflate overblown egos. That is how you cut down to size those who make claims all out of keeping with their proper place in the honour system. You remind them of where they were born... The death of challenger is sometimes a worthy response to public dishonour, though...in the *Middle East* an over-quick resort to violence is an inadvertent admission that one has lost control of the challenge situation" (my italics, pp. 192, 193, 195). For further crude "Middle East" and "Arab" stereotypes and generalizations see Rohrbaugh, *New Testament,* e.g. pp. xv, 4, 12, 15, 97, 103–105, 165, 167. One example from p. 104: "Bailey reports that the current custom in *the Middle East* [my italics] is for the oldest son to stand barefoot at the door and to greet guests. I have experienced that same phenomenon on several occasions, notably on arriving for tea at the home of the sheik of Bethany in 1986. The oldest son introduced the father to everyone present and supervised the serving and entertainment. Whether such a role pertained in antiquity is difficult to say...[!]" Irrespective of whether Rohrbaugh's generalization might happen to be true, the analysis hardly shows it and serious evidence needs to be put forward.

52. J. H. Neyrey, *The Gospel of John* (Cambridge: Cambridge University Press, 2007), pp. 15–19; cf. 309–10.

53. Esler, *First Christians,* p. 20.

54. Rohrbaugh, "Ethnocentrism and Historical Questions about Jesus", pp. 29–30.

55. S. Huntington, *The Clash of Civilizations and the Remaking of World Order* (New York: Simon & Schuster, 1996), pp. 71, 193, 109, 110 (all italics original).

56. Rohrbaugh, *New Testament,* pp. 61–76 (63–64).

57. Sen, *Identity and Violence,* p. 44.

58. R. Patai, *The Arab Mind* (rev. edn; New York: Hatherleigh Press, 1976, 1983, 2002). The version used by Malina is quoted in Malina, *Jesus and the Gospels,* p. 63.

59. Malina, *Jesus and the Gospels,* p. 63.

60. Said, *Orientalism,* pp. 307–308.

61. Quoted in an article full of gushing and misleading praise for Wolfowitz: B. Keller, "The Sunshine Warrior," *New York Times* (September 22, 2002). Cf. D. Little, *American Orientalism: The United States and the Middle East since 1945* (Chapel Hill & London: University of North Carolina Press, 2004), p. 326.

62. A. Shlaim, " 'Liberation' Is Not Freedom," *Observer* (March 30, 2003).

63. N. Chomsky, *Rogue States: The Rule of Force in World Affairs* (London: Pluto Press, 2000), p. 29; Chomsky, *Understanding Power*, p. 168. Cf. also S. Žižek, *Welcome to the Desert of the Real! Five Essays on September 11 and Related Dates* (London & New York: Verso, 2002), pp. 112–34.

64. T. L. Friedman, "The Humiliation Factor," *New York Times* (November 9, 2003).

65. Said, *Orientalism*, pp. 308–10, 375, n. 134.

66. Others positively referencing Patai include Pilch, "Beat" (who also warns readers of "mistaken American assessments of contemporary Middle Eastern personalities") and Hanson, "Kinship"; cf. Rohrbaugh, *New Testament*, p. 205, where Patai is referenced in the bibliography.

67. E.g. Patai, *Arab Mind*, pp. 31–37, 120–22, 139–44. Little wonder that Patai has been dismissed by anthropologists and scholars of Islam. In an email to Emran Qureshi, anthropologist Dale Eickelman is reported to have said, "Once only, I used it in an introductory class as an anti-text to indicate the pitfalls of using psychological projections to elicit the characteristics of society and nation." In another email to Qureshi, another anthropologist, Sondra Hale, is reported to have added that Patai "can no longer be taken seriously." See E. Qureshi, "Misreading 'the Arab Mind,' " *Boston Globe* (May 30, 2004).

68. Patai's *The Arab Mind* is loved by one particularly nasty and self-consciously anti-Islamic American web magazine, *6th Column against Jihad* ("6th Column against Jihad fights for America and against Islam"). "Review of Raphael Patai's, *The Arab Mind*; Revised Edition, 2002" is available at http://www.6thcolumnagainstjihad.com/a_gmason_p5.htm. E.g. "Three elements come together to give Americans a deep understanding of the entire problem of Islam, in every respect. The factual works of Ibn Warraq, Robert Spencer, Craig Winn, and others make up the first arm. The second arm comes from philosophy; adequate understanding of Islamic philosophy provides the ability to think about the problem of Islam in terms of principles. The third arm comes from this book by Raphael Patai. It shows how the history, facts, and philosophy produce the Arab psychology; it is the Arab mind in the Arab body killing people through jihad. If we follow all the arms, we will preserve our lives and our civilization. Once we know the Arab-Islamic mind, we can construct an effective remedy."

69. S. Hersh, "Annals of National Security: The Gray Zone – How a Secret Pentagon Program Came to Abu Ghraib," *The New Yorker* (May 15, 2004).

70. M. McFate, "Anthropology and Counterinsurgency: The Strange Story of their Curious Relationship," *Military Review* (March–April 2005), available at http://www.army.mil/professionalwriting/volumes/volume3/august_2005/7_05_2.html

71. L. F. Jordan, "Review of The Arab Mind by Raphael Patai," CIA Historical Review Program, Center for the Study of Intelligence, available at https://www.cia.gov/library/center-for-the-study-of-intelligence/kent-csi/docs/v18i3a06p_0001.htm

72. Also available on the Middle East Forum: Promoting American Interests (http://www.meforum.org/article/636), N. B. De Atkine, "The Arab Mind Revisited," *Middle East Quarterly* 11 (2004), 47–55.

73. Said, *Orientalism*, pp. 284–88; Said, *Covering Islam*, pp. lvii–lix, 12–24, 81–133.

74. BBC News, "Teaching Islam Is 'Outdated' " (June 4, 2007), available at http://news.bbc.co.uk/1/hi/education/6713373.stm

75. Ataullah Siddiqui's report, presented to Bill Rammell MP, *Islam at Universities in England: Meeting the Needs and Investing in the Future* (April 10, 2007), pp. 62–64, available at http://www.dfes.gov.uk/hegateway/uploads/DrSiddiquiReport.pdf

76. "Full Text: Blair Speech on Islam," available at http://news.bbc.co.uk/1/hi/uk_politics/6719153.stm

77. BBC News, "Blair in Moderate Muslims Appeal" (June 4, 2007), available at http://news.bbc.co.uk/1/hi/uk_politics/6718235.stm

78. E.g. K. Gough, "Anthropology and Imperialism," *Monthly Review* (April, 1968), pp. 12–27; E. R. Wolf and J. G. Jorgensen, "A Special Supplement: Anthropology on the Warpath in Thailand," *New York Review of Books* 15 (November 19, 1970); D. Hymes (ed.), *Reinventing Anthropology* (New York: Random House, 1972); G. W. Stocking (ed.), *Colonial Situations: Essays on the Contextualization of Ethnographic Knowledge* (Madison: University of Wisconsin Press, 1991); T. Asad (ed.), *Anthropology and the Colonial Encounter* (Amherst, NY: Humanity Books, 1973, 1998); Fiorenza, *Jesus and the Politics*, pp. 84–91.

79. E.g. Chomsky, *Understanding Power*, p. 85–86; V. Yans-McLaughlin, "Science, Democracy, and Ethics: Mobilizing Culture and Personality for World War II," in G. W. Stocking, *Malinowski, Rivers, Benedict and Others: Essays on Culture and Personality* (Madison: University of Wisconsin Press, 1986), pp. 184–217; D. Price, "Lessons from Second World War Anthropology: Peripheral, Persuasive and Ignored Contributions," *Anthropology Today* 18.3 (2002), pp. 14–20; D. Price, "Gregory Bateson and the OSS: World War II and Bateson's Assessment of Applied Anthropology," *Human Organization* 57.4 (1998), pp. 379–84; M. Farish, "Targeting the Inner Landscape," in D. Gregory and A. Pred (eds.), *Violent Geographies: Fear, Terror, and Political Violence* (New York & London: Routledge, 2007), pp. 255–71 (260–65). European anthropologists (e.g. Evans-Pritchard) were combining military service with anthropology but, as Price points out ("Second World War Anthropology," p. 15), the American application of anthropology as a weapon was more extensive. Cf. also Said, *Orientalism*, pp. 284–328.

80. Farish, "Inner Landscape," pp. 261–62.

81. Farish, "Inner Landscape," pp. 262–63.

82. McFate, "Anthropology and Counterinsurgency."

83. Price, "Second World War Anthropology," p. 20.

84. McFate, "Anthropology and Counterinsurgency."

85. Malina, *Jesus and the Gospels*, p. 37.

86. B. Malina and J. H. Neyrey, *Portraits of Paul: An Archaeology of Ancient Personality* (Louisville: Westminster/John Knox, 1996), pp. 2–4. Cf. J. Storey, *An Introduction to Cultural Theory and Popular Culture* (2nd edn; London: Prentice Hall, 1997) p. 99: "Hollywood – together with other discursive practices, songs, novels, TV serials, etc. – has succeeded in producing a very powerful

discourse on Vietnam: telling America and the world...that what happened, happened because Vietnam *is* like that. These different discourses are not *about* Vietnam, they increasingly constitute for many Americans the experience of Vietnam...for many Americans, 'knowledge' of the war, and the 'power-knowledge' relations which are constituted on the basis of this knowledge are discursive. Even when Hollywood appears to be critical of American involvement in Vietnam, it is always critical within a discursive practice which ultimately works to contain such criticism, to redirect it into the procedures and protocols or Orientalism."

87. Rohrbaugh, *New Testament*, p. 7.

88. E.g. Said, *Covering Islam*, pp. xxx li–lii, lxii, 10–12.

89. A. J. Droge, "What Difference Does Q Make? Or, Excavating Q Studies," unpublished paper presented at the *Society of Biblical Literature* annual meeting, Washington DC, November 2006.

90. D. G. Horrell, "Social-Scientific Interpretation of the New Testament: Retrospect and Prospect," in D. G. Horrell (ed.), *Social-Scientific Approaches to New Testament Interpretation* (Edinburgh: T&T Clark, 1999), pp. 3–27 (14, 22).

91. Meggitt, "Review," p. 219. Meggitt cites Malina's dismissal of cf. J. Perkins, "The 'Self as Sufferer,' " *HTR* 85 (1992), pp. 245–72; J. Perkins, *The Suffering Self: Pain and Narrative Representation in the Early Christian Era* (London: Routledge, 1995).

92. B. J. Malina, "Review of deSilva, *Despising Shame*," *RBL*, http://www.bookreviews.org/pdf/2177_1292.pdf; J. J. Pilch, "Review of Avalos, *Health Care and the Rise of Christianity*," *RBL*, http://www.bookreviews.org/pdf/434_539.pdf; J. J. Pilch, "Review of Keir, *Disease and Healing in the New Testament*," *RBL*, http://www.bookreviews.org/bookdetail.asp?TitleId=1502&CodePage=1502,434,4981; R. Rohrbaugh, "Review of deSilva The Hope of Glory," *RBL*, http://www.bookreviews.org/pdf/427_958.pdf; B. J. Malina, "Review of Ling, *The Judean Poor and the Fourth Gospel*," *RBL*, http://www.bookreviews.org/pdf/5587_5883.pdf. For a hugely glowing review see, e.g., J. H. Elliott, "Review of Malina and Neyrey, *Portraits of Paul*", *RBL*, http://www.bookreviews.org/pdf/2138_1165.pdf.

93. B. J. Malina, "Review of Rodney Stark, *The Rise of Christianity: A Sociologist Reconsiders History*," *CBQ* 59 (1997), pp. 593–95.

94. David Horrell also pointed out that, in Malina's article on "Understanding New Testament Persons," a number of New Testament scholars (including Meeks and Theissen!) have a mark by their names to denote "inadequate for a valid understanding" and "outdated or dead-end approaches." A surprised Horrell notes, "both of which, disagreements and criticisms notwithstanding, are generally regarded as important and valuable works" (Horrell, "Social Scientific Interpretation," p. 21, n. 36). See B. J. Malina, "Understanding New Testament Persons," in R. Rohrbaugh (ed.), *The Social Sciences and New Testament Interpretation* (Peabody: Hendrickson, 1996), pp. 41–61.

95. Among several examples see, e.g., J. T. Sanders, *Charisma, Converts, Competitors: Societal and Sociological Factors in the Success of Early Christianity* (London, SCM, 2000); J. G. Crossley, *Why Christianity Happened: A*

Sociohistorical Account of Christian Origins (Louisville: Westminster/John Knox, 2006), pp. 142–76. P. A. Harland, *Associations, Synagogues, and Congregations: Claiming a Place in Ancient Mediterranean Society* (Minneapolis: Fortress Press, 2003), e.g. pp. 137–60.

96. W. A. Meeks, *The First Urban Christians: The Social World of the Apostle Paul* (2nd edn; New Haven and London: Yale University Press, 1983, 2003). Cf. Sanders, *Charisma, Converts, Competitors*, and his referring to "Meeks' justly acclaimed study" (p. 103) and, on the issue of social networks, "We historians should have known as much all along. Wayne Meeks had already proposed it..." (p. 136).

97. Meggitt, "Review," p. 219; cf. Perkins, "The 'Self as Sufferer,' " pp. 245–72; Perkins, *The Suffering Self*.

98. Malina, *Jesus and the Gospels*, p. 83 (cf. p. 219); Meggitt, "Review," p. 219.

99. Rohrbaugh, *New Testament*, pp. 11–12.

100. Rohrbaugh, *New Testament*, pp. 89–90.

101. For examples of return-repentance in early Judaism see J. G. Crossley, "The Semitic Background to Repentance in the Teaching of John the Baptist and Jesus," *JSHJ* 2 (2004), pp. 138–57.

102. E. W. Said, *The End of the Peace Process: Oslo and After* (2nd edn; London: Granta, 2000, 2002), pp. 142–43.

103. Rohrbaugh, *New Testament*, p. 91, n. 8.

104. H. Räisänen, "Jesus and the Food Laws: Reflections on Mark 7:15," *JSNT* 6 (1982), pp. 79–100.

105. J. K. Chance, "The Anthropology of Honor and Shame: Culture, Values and Practice," *Semeia* 68 (1994), pp. 139–51.

106. Meggitt, "Review," p. 219.

107. Bockmuehl, "Review of Malina."

108. S. R. Garrett, "Review of Malina, *Christian Origins and Cultural Anthropology*," *JBL* 107 (1988), pp. 532–33.

109. Mark Lewis Taylor, *Religion, Politics, and the Christian Right: Post-9/11 Powers and American Empire* (Minneapolis: Fortress Press, 2005), p. 22.

110. Cf. http://www.newamericancentury.org/iraqclintonletter.htm

111. *Question Time*, BBC 1 (first aired: 22 March, 2007), my transcript. Available for viewing at http://news.bbc.co.uk/1/hi/programmes/question_time/classic_editions/default.stm#iraq4years

112. See M. Rai, *Chomsky's Politics* (London & New York: Verso, 1995), pp. 131–33, 200–202; cf. W. B. Sperlich, *Noam Chomsky* (London: Reaktion Books, 2006), p. 117.

113. For a ferocious and vile attack on Chomsky which invents a string of absurd charges – often not even bothering even to give the pretence of evidence – deliberately designed to manipulate see D. Horowitz, "The Sick Mind of Noam Chomsky" (26 September, 2001), FrontPageMag.com, available at http://www.frontpagemag.com/Articles/Read.aspx?GUID={19193155-11B3-4D95-BD7F-F30801D7C206}

114. J. B. Elshtain, *Just War against Terror: The Burden of American Power in a Violent World* (New York: Basic Books, 2003), p. 215, n. 17; cf. Taylor, *Religion*, p. 22.

115. Elshtain, *Just War against Terror*, p. 82.

116. C. Reed, *Just War?* (London: SPCK, 2004), p. 33.

117. Reed, *Just War?* p. 25.

118. D. E. Lipstadt, "Deniers, Relativists and Pseudo-Scholarship," *Dimensions*, 6/1 (1991), available at http://www.adl.org/Braun/dim_14_1_deniers.asp

119. A letter to the journal, *Outlook* (June 1, 1989), reprinted in Rai, *Chomsky's Politics*, pp. 200–202. This letter by Chomsky further uncovers some of the utter lies told about him on the issue of the Holocaust and shows the lengths to which his opponents will go to discredit him.

120. E. S. Herman and N. Chomsky, *Manufacturing Consent: The Political Economy of the Mass Media* (London: Vintage, 1988), p. 302.

121. N. Chomsky, *Media Control: The Spectacular Achievements of Propaganda* (New York: Seven Stories Press, 1991, 2002), pp. 20–21

122. Chomsky, *Understanding Power*, pp. 13, 206, 286–87.

123. K. W. Whitelam, "Preliminary Notes on Recent Historiography: Centralization and the New Imperialism," unpublished paper delivered at the Constructions of Ancient Space Seminar, AAR/SBL Atlanta (November, 2003).

124. W. Dever, *What Did the Biblical Writers Know, and When Did They Know It? What Archaeology Can Tell Us about the Reality of Ancient Israel* (Grand Rapids: Eerdmans, 2001), pp. 291, 292, 297.

125. Whitelam, "Preliminary Notes."

126. Gregory, *Colonial Present*, pp. 6, 18; cf. Fiorenza, *Jesus and the Politics*, pp. 100–101.

127. Cf. M. McAlister, *Epic Encounters: Culture, Media and US Interests in the Middle East, 1945–2000* (Berkeley, CA: University of California Press, 2001), p. 8.

Part III

1. M. McAlister, *Epic Encounters: Culture, Media and US Interests in the Middle East, 1945–2000* (Berkeley, CA: University of California Press, 2001), p. 197.

Chapter 5

1. Geza Vermes, *Providential Accidents: An Autobiography* (London: SCM Press, 1998), pp. 213–14.

2. For an overview of Jews and Judaism and historical Jesus scholarship see, e.g., T. Holmén, "The Jewishness of Jesus in the 'Third Quest,'" in M. Labahn and A. Schmidt (eds.), *Jesus, Mark and Q: The Teaching of Jesus and its Earliest Records* (Sheffield: Sheffield Academic Press, 2001), pp. 143–62; H. Moxnes,

"Jesus the Jew: Dilemmas of Interpretation," in I. Dunderberg, C. Tuckett and K. Syreeni (eds.), *Fair Play: Diversity and Conflicts in Early Christianity: Essays in Honour of Heikki Räisänen* (Leiden: Brill, 2002), pp. 83–103.

3. Cf. A.-J. Levine, *The Misunderstood Jew: The Church and the Scandal of the Jewish Jesus* (San Francisco: HarperCollins, 2006), p. 18.

4. E. P. Sanders, *Paul and Palestinian Judaism: A Comparison of Patterns of Religion* (Philadelphia: Fortress Press; London: SCM Press, 1977); cf. Moxnes, "Jesus the Jew."

5. W. Arnal, *The Symbolic Jesus: Historical Scholarship, Judaism and the Construction of Contemporary Identity* (London & Oakville: Equinox, 2005), pp. 39–72.

6. Arnal, *Symbolic Jesus*, pp. 53–55. Cf. P. Fredriksen, "The Birth of Christianity and the Origins of Christian Anti-Judaism," in P. Fredriksen and A. Reinhartz (eds.), *Jesus, Judaism, and Christian Anti-Judaism: Reading the New Testament after the Holocaust* (Louisville: Westminster/John Knox, 2002), pp. 8–30 (28).

7. Cf. P. Novick, *The Holocaust and Collective Memory* (London: Bloomsbury, 1999), pp. 146–61.

8. D. Little, *American Orientalism: The United States and the Middle East since 1945* (2nd edn; Chapel Hill & London: University of North Carolina Press, 2002, 2004), p. 307.

9. Norman Finkelstein, *The Holocaust Industry: Reflections on the Exploitation of Jewish Suffering* (2nd edn; London & New York: Verso, 2000, 2003), p. 22.

10. Novick, *Holocaust and Collective Memory*, pp. 146, 48.

11. Available at http://www.yale.edu/lawweb/avalon/un/un242.htm

12. See, e.g., G. Philo and M. Berry, *Bad News from Israel* (London, Pluto, 2004), pp. 36–37 for some examples.

13. Amnesty International, "Israel and the Occupied Territories. Demolition and Dispossession: The Destruction of Palestinian Homes," AI Index: MDE 15/059/1999 (December 8, 1999), available at http://web.amnesty.org/library/Index/engMDE150591999

14. For useful overviews of the political, cultural and historical issues underlying the increased US support for Israel post-1967 see, among many, Novick, *Holocaust and Collective Memory*, pp. 146–69; Little, *American Orientalism*, pp. 77–115, 267–306; D. Gregory, *The Colonial Present: Afghanistan, Palestine, Iraq* (Oxford: Blackwell, 2004), pp. 77–78.

15. For a historical overview see, e.g., A. Shlaim, *The Iron Wall: Israel and the Arab World* (London: Penguin, 2000), pp. 309–18.

16. N. Chomsky, *Middle East Illusions* (Lanham: Rowman & Littlefield, 2003), p. 182. On Rogers versus Kissinger see also pp. 43–44.

17. Congressional Record, May 21, 1973. An excerpt (pp. 16264–65); cf. N. Chomsky, *Fateful Triangle: The United States, Israel and the Palestinians* (updated edn; London: Pluto, 1999), p. 535.

18. Cited in M. Curtis, *Unpeople: Britain's Secret Human Rights Abuses* (Vintage: London: 2004), p. 155–57. See also M. Curtis, "Friendless in Gaza: Britain and Israel," *Red Pepper* (April 2004); M. Curtis, "The Myth of the 'Honest

Broker': Britain and Israel," http://www.cmyk.info/markcurtis/article26.html (31 March, 2006).

19. See, e.g., R. Norton-Taylor, "UK Equipment Being Used in Israeli Attacks," *Guardian* (May 29, 2002); M. White and R. Norton-Taylor, "Straw Provokes Row over Arms for Israel," *Guardian* (July 9, 2002); A. Barzilai, "UK Tightening Embargo on Israel," *Haaretz* (August 22, 2002); M. Curtis, *Web of Deceit: Britain's Real Role in the World* (London: Vintage, 2003), pp. 127–33; Staff and agencies, "Israel Captures Jailed Palestinian Militants," *Guardian* (March 14, 2006); B. Joffe-Walt, 'Made in the UK: Bringing Devastation to Lebanon – the British Parts in Israel's Deadly Attack Helicopters," *Guardian* (Saturday July 29, 2006); G. Monbiot, "The King of Fairyland Will Never Grasp the Realities of the Middle East," *The Guardian* (August 1, 2006).

20. Curtis, *Web*, p. 124.

21. R. Fisk, *The Great War for Civilisation: The Conquest of the Middle East* (London: Fourth Estate, 2005), pp. 463–64.

22. Cf. N. G. Finkelstein, *Beyond Chutzpah: On the Misuse of Anti-Semitism and the Abuse of History* (London: Verso, 2005); A. Cockburn and J. St Clair (eds.), *The Politics of Anti-Semitism* (Edinburgh: AK Press, 2003).

23. Chomsky, *Fateful Triangle*, pp. 28–29.

24. R. Fisk, "My Challenge for Steven Spielberg," *Independent* (September 2007).

25. See especially McAlister, *Epic Encounters*, pp. 155–59, 178–97.

26. Finkelstein, *Holocaust Industry*.

27. I use "perception" and "perceived" here without any judgment on the rights or wrongs of the cases.

28. Novick, *Holocaust and Collective Memory*, pp. 127–203.

29. Philo and Berry, *Bad News from Israel*. See also "Glasgow University Media Unit: Bad News from Israel" (http://www.gla.ac.uk/departments/sociology/units/media/israel.htm: this includes excerpts from the book); G. Philo, "Bad News from Israel: Media Coverage of the Israel/Palestine Conflict," http://www.gla.ac.uk/departments/sociology/units/media/israel.pdf

30. From the "Rapture Ready" website (http://www.raptureready.com/rap39.html).

31. McAlister, *Epic Encounters* , pp. 13–20, 43–83.

32. Letter of Pat Robertson to Omri Sharon available at http://www.patrobertson.com/images/TheHonorableOmriSharon2.jpg

33. M. L. Taylor, *Religion, Politics, and the Christian Right: Post-9/11 Powers and American Empire* (Minneapolis: Augsburg Fortress Press, 2005), pp. 59–60.

34. http://www.cufi.org/information.aspx

35. http://www.cipaconline.org/

36. E. McQuaid, "A Hand of Help for Gaza (editorial)" (July/August, 2005), http://www.foigm.org/partner/Article_Display_Page/0,,PTID306608|CHID556142|CIID2062048,00.html

37. http://www.foigm.org/CC_Content_Page/0,,PTID306608|CHID556138|CIID,00.html

38. H. Lindsey, *The Late Great Planet Earth* (Grand Rapids: Zondervan, 1970), e.g. pp. 73–77.

39. Lindsey, *Planet Earth*, pp. 50–51.

40. Lindsey, *Planet Earth*, pp. 56–57; cf. 152.

41. Estimated total sales by 1998 ranged between 18 and 28 million copies (McAlister, *Epic Encounters*, p. 165).

42. M. Northcott, *An Angel Directs the Storm: Apocalyptic Religion and American Empire* (London & New York: I. B. Tauris, 2004), p. 63.

43. http://www.leftbehindgames.com/

44. http://www.leftbehind.com/channelkids.asp?channelID=63

45. http://www.leftbehind-worldatwar.com/index.php?object=churchtheatricalrelease

46. D. Campbell, "Strong Cast, Good Book, Big Hit," *Guardian* (February 8, 2001).

47. http://www.leftbehindgames.com/pages/the_games.htm (where previews of the game can also be watched).

48. http://www.leftbehind.com/channelseekgod.asp?pageid=785&channelID=6. Similarly Joel Rosenberg, author of the end time novels *The Copper Scroll* and *The Ezekiel Option*, (Carol Stream, IL: Tyndale, 2005 and 2007), and heavily plugged on the Left Behind website, said in an interview (July 26, 2006; along with Jerry Jenkins) on CNN that he has been invited to the White House and, along with various members of Congress, Middle Eastern leaders "all want to understand the Middle East through the lens of biblical prophecies." Rosenberg believes Ezekiel 36 and 37 have already come true with the state of Israel and that the prophecies in his book may soon come true and fit in very nicely with the agenda of US imperialism: "Ezekiel 38 and 39, what my novel *The Ezekiel Option* is about, is an alliance of Islamic countries to destroy Israel and liberate Jerusalem. Are we seeing that come true yet? That's the big question. Then, Ezekiel 40 through 48, that's the rebirth of the Jewish temple, the rebuilding of it, in Jerusalem. Now, you know, if that happens in our lifetime, that alone could unleash the wrath of a billion Muslims worldwide. That's what *The Copper Scroll* is about – hunting for treasures, hunting for ancient documents, and the series of events that unfold that would lead to the Jewish temple and an apocalyptic war in the Middle East." See http://mediamatters.org/items/200607270001. Rosenberg has a non-fiction book, *Epicenter: Why the Current Rumblings in the Middle East Will Change your Future* (Carol Stream, IL: Tyndale, 2006).

49. D. E. Wagner, "Marching to Zion: The Evangelical-Jewish Alliance," *The Christian Century* (June 28, 2003), pp. 20–24.

50. See, e.g., McAlister, *Epic Encounters*, p. 177; Northcott, *An Angel Directs the Storm*, pp. 66–67. A. Lang, "Convergence: The Politics of Armageddon," at http://prop1.org/inaugur/85reagan/85rrarm.htm

51. R. Cornwell, "In God He Trusts – How George Bush Infused the White House with a Religious Spirit," *The Independent* (February 21, 2003); E. MacAskill, "George Bush: 'God Told Me to End the Tyranny in Iraq,' " *The Guardian* (October 7, 2005); Northcott, *An Angel Directs the Storm*, pp. 3, 67–68; Taylor, *Christian Right*, pp. 55–57.

52. R. Dreyfuss, "Reverend Doomsday," *Rolling Stone*, http://www.rollingstone.com/politics/story/5939999/reverend_doomsday/

53. See further L. Davidson, "Christian Zionism as a Representation of Manifest American Destiny," *Critique: Critical Middle Eastern Studies* 14 (2005), pp. 157–69 (164).

54. "Would Jesus Vote Republican?" http://www.raptureready.com/republican.html (19/7/06).

55. Wagner, "Marching to Zion." For the Project for the New American Century see www.newamericancentury.org. For an overview of the Project and Israel see, e.g., A. Callinicos, *The New Mandarins of American Power* (Cambridge: Polity Press, 2003), pp. 48–50.

56. A transcript of Rumsfeld's comments can be found at http://www.israelnewsagency.com/rumsfeld.html

57. Chomsky, *Triangle*, pp. 27–32; Taylor, *Christian Right*, pp. 63–64.

58. E.g. E. W. Said, *The End of the Peace Process: Oslo and After* (New York: Pantheon, 2000), pp. 14–26, 74–118, 132–38; Gregory, *The Colonial Present*, pp. 95–101 (with accompanying maps).

59. Monbiot, "King of Fairyland." For earlier figures see Chomsky, *Triangle*, pp. 9–11. For relevant data see, e.g., http://www.dsca.mil/programs/biz-ops/2005_facts/2005%20Facts%20Book%20Final.pdf; US Agency for Overseas Development, "U.S. Overseas Loans and Grants: Obligations and Loan Authorizations July 1, 1945 – September 30, 2004" (http://pdf.usaid.gov/pdf_docs/PNADF100.pdf).

60. J. Ferziger, "U.S. Signs Pact to Increase Aid to Israel," *New York Sun* (August 17, 2007).

61. R. McGuinness, "US Pays £15bn in Aid to Israel," *Metro* (August 17, 2007). I have not, however, been able to find a more detailed report on Action Aid's response, nor a direct source from Action Aid.

62. P. Healy, "Clinton Vows to Back Israel in Latest Mideast Conflict," *New York Times* (July 18, 2006).

63. http://www.afsi.org/who.htm

64. Taylor, *Christian Right*, p. 61–62.

65. G. Monbiot, "Apocalypse Please," *The Guardian* (April 20, 2004).

66. D. Childs, *Britain since 1945: A Political History* (5th edn; London and New York: Routledge, 2001), p. 173.

67. Curtis, *Web*, pp. 126–27.

68. Curtis, "Friendless in Gaza."

69. D. Wagner, "Christians and Zion: British Stirrings," *The Daily Star Beirut* (October 7, 2003; available at http://www.christianzionism.org/articlesN.asp on the "Challenging Christian Zionism" website); Northcott, *An Angel Directs the Storm*, pp. 58–62. Cf. Lindsey, *Planet Earth*, pp. 49–50.

70. S. R. Sizer, "Christian Zionism: A British Perspective," *Friends of al-Asqa: Defence of al-Asqa and Peace in Palestine* 1 (no year given), available at http://www.aqsa.org.uk/JournalsDetail.aspx?id=28

71. http://www.cmj.org.uk/about/aims.html (my italics).

72. Nadia Abu el-Haj, *Facts on the Ground: Archaeological Practice and Territorial Self-Fashioning in Israeli Society* (Chicago & London: University of Chicago Press, 2001), p. 144.

73. Paula R. Stern, "Barnard's Shame, Columbia's Dirty Deal," *Israel Insider* (July 27, 2007).

74. Gabrielle Birkner, "Barnard Alumnae Opposing Tenure for Anthropologist," *New York Sun* (November 16, 2006).

75. E.g. Callinicos, *New Mandarins*; Chomsky, *Triangle*, pp. 9–37; Chomsky, *Pirates and Emperors, Old and New: International Terrorism in the Real World* (London: Pluto, 2002), e.g. pp. 160–80; D. Harvey, *The New Imperialism* (Oxford: Oxford University Press, 2003), e.g. pp. 20–21, 220.

76. K. McNeil, "The War on Academic Freedom," *The Nation* (November 11, 2002).

77. Cf., e.g., A. Pred, "Situated Ignorance and State Terrorism: Silences, W.M.D., Collective Amnesia, and the Manufacture of Fear," in D. Gregory and A. Pred (eds.), *Violent Geographies: Fear, Terror, and Political Violence* (New York & London: Routledge, 2007), pp. 363–84 (373–74).

78. See, e.g., J. Wilson, "Politics and Palestinians at Roosevelt," *ZNet* (10 August, 2006; available at http://www.zmag.org/content/showarticle.cfm?SectionID=107&ItemID=10743); H. Porter, "The Land of the Free – but Free Speech Is a Rare Commodity," *Observer* (Sunday August 13, 2006).

79. D. Giles, "Professor Fired for Allowing Questions about Judaism and Islam," http://www.labournet.net/world/0607/roosevelt1.html (13/07/06)

80. In the UK there has, of course, been the infamous topic of the AUT (the main academic union in the UK, now UCU) boycott of certain Israeli universities which shows that the situation in the UK is not, as might be expected, identical to the US. But the issue has been extremely controversial. See, e.g., P. Curtis, "Lecturers Vote for Israeli Boycott," *Guardian* (April 22, 2005). The UCU leader Sally Hunt has even claimed, rightly or wrongly, "I do not believe a boycott is supported by a majority of (the 120,000) UCU members; nor do I believe that members see it as a priority for the union." See J. Meikle, "Lecturers Back Boycott of Israel," *Guardian* (May 30, 2007). See further D. Andalo, "UCU Head against Israeli Academic Boycott," *Education Guardian* (May 30, 2007). There have been major legal threats made against British universities, including those made by Alan Dershowitz. See, e.g., M. Taylor, S. Goldenberg and R. McCarthy, " 'We Will Isolate Them,' " *Guardian* (June 9, 2007). The issue has now been dropped by the UCU. See further T. Traubman, B. Ravid and S. Shamir, "British Academics Drop Planned Boycott of Israel," *Haaretz* (September 29, 2007). I have also been present when colleagues have said quite openly that they will resign from the union should a ban on Israeli academics occur, something they have not threatened, openly at least, on any other issue. Indeed, it is difficult to imagine any other subject being so emotive. While the UK may be different from the US, all this at least highlights the obvious relevance: the issue is highly sensitive in British academic culture.

81. K. W. Whitelam, *The Invention of Ancient Israel: The Silencing of Palestinian History* (London & New York: Routledge, 1996).

82. K. W. Whitelam, "Representing Minimalism: The Rhetoric and Reality of Revisionism," in A. G. Hunter and P. R. Davies (eds.), *Sense and Sensitivity: Essays on Reading the Bible in Memory of Robert Carroll* (Sheffield: Sheffield Academic Press, 2002), pp. 194–223 (212–15, 219) responding to, e.g., Jerome Berman, Frank Clancy, Frank Cross, William Dever, Kenneth Kitchen, and Gary Rendsburg. Compare also the comments on Philip Davies and Whitelam in S. C. Reif, "Jews, Hebraists and 'Old Testament' Studies," in Hunter and Davies, *Sense and Sensitivity*, pp. 224–45 (243–45).

83. Indeed, at a 2003 SBL/AAR session Whitelam showed that the agenda of someone like William Dever has much rhetorically in common with the agenda of the Project for the New American Century and its precursors. See K. W. Whitelam, "Preliminary Notes on Recent Historiography: Centralization and the New American Imperialism" discussed at the Constructions of Ancient Space Seminar SBL/AAR Atlanta, November, 2003. I am grateful to Keith Whitelam for giving me access to this paper.

84. N. Abu el-Haj, *Facts on the Ground: Archaeological Practice and Territorial Self-Fashioning in Israeli Society* (Chicago & London: University of Chicago Press, 2001).

85. K. W. Arenson, "Fracas Erupts over Book on Mideast by a Barnard Professor Seeking Tenure," *New York Times* (September 10, 2007); H. Negrin, "Prof Contests Abu el-Haj's Claims," *Columbia Spectator* (September 18, 2007), available at http://www.columbiaspectator.com/node/26749; A. F. Segal, "Some Professional Observations on the Controversy about Nadia Abu el-Haj's First Book," *Columbia Spectator* (September 21, 2007), http://www.columbia spectator.com/?q=node/26830

86. A. M. Maeir, "Review of Nadia Abu el-Haj, *Facts on the Ground*," *Isis* 95 (2004), pp. 523–24 (524). See also Maeir's highly polemical account of the tenure situation of Abu el-Haj, A. M. Maeir, "Freedom of Speech or Freedom of Slander?" *Columbia Spectator* (September 21, 2007), http://www.columbia spectator.com/?q=node/26830

87. Abu el-Haj, *Facts on the Ground*, pp. 144–46.

88. Maeir, "Review of Nadia Abu el-Haj," p. 524.

89. Abu el-Haj, *Facts on the Ground*, p. 281.

90. Compare the comments of Jonathan Burack, who gives no direct evidence: "Bizarrely, she [Abu el-Haj] then concludes her book by reversing herself on such desecration, asking us to 'understand' sympathetically the Palestinian mob that destroyed Joseph's Tomb on October 8, 2000." See J. Burack "Erasing History and Ourselves: Nadia Abu el-Haj, Israel and the Western Tradition," *Family Security Foundation* (December 28, 2006), available at http:// www.familysecuritymatters.org/homeland.php?id=537580. Where does she ask us precisely what Burack claims she asks us?

91. A. H. Joffe, "Review of Nadia Abu el-Haj, *Facts on the Ground*," *Journal of Near Eastern Studies* 64 (2005), pp. 297–304 (303).

92. Joffe, "Review of Nadia Abu el-Haj," p. 303.

93. http://www.solomonia.com/blog/archives/008510.shtml

94. http://www.meforum.org/press/644. For a selection of Campus Watch articles by Joffe see http://www.campus-watch.org/docs/author/Alexander+H.+Joffe

95. J. Davila, "Review of Nadia Abu el-Haj, *Facts on the Ground*," *PaleoJudaica* (September 27, 2007), http://paleojudaica.blogspot.com/2007_09_23_archive.html#7794082609795697575

96. Abu el-Haj, *Facts on the Ground*, p. 255.

97. Segal, "Professional Observations."

98. G. Birkner, "Barnard Alumnae Opposing Tenure for Anthropologist," *New York Sun* (November 16, 2006), available at http://www.nysun.com/article/43652

99. Abu el-Haj, *Facts on the Ground*, p. 145.

100. "Abu El Haj and the Skepticism of Fires," http://www.solomonia.com/blog/archives/009616.shtml

101. C. Slutsky, "Tenure Battle at Barnard Gains Fresh Urgency," *The Jewish Week* (September 21, 2007), available http://www.thejewishweek.com/news/newscontent.php3?artid=14546

102. P. R. Stern, "Barnard's Shame, Columbia's Dirty Deal," *Israel Insider* (July 27, 2007), available at http://web.israelinsider.com/Views/11769.htm

103. Comments made at R. Silverstein, "Origins of a Right Wing Campaign against Nadia Abu el Haj," *Tikun Olam* (August 19, 2007), http://www.richardsilverstein.com/tikun_olam/2007/08/19/origins-of-right-wing-campaign-against-nadia-abu-el-haj/#comment-37274. *IsraelNationalNews.com* were happy to give the story of Stern's campaign – without any evidence of antisemitism – the headline, "Barnard Grad Heads Protest against Anti-Semitic Prof.," *IsraelNationalNews.com* (August 9, 2007), available at http://www.israelnationalnews.com/News/Flash.aspx/131382

104. "Barnard Grad Heads Protest against Anti-Semitic Prof.," *Israel NationalNews.com* (August 9, 2007), available at http://www.israelnational news.com/News/Flash.aspx/131382

105. http://www.jta.org/cgi-bin/iowa/breaking/103596.html

Chapter 6

1. Lawrence Davidson, "Christian Zionism and American Foreign Policy: Paving the Road to Hell in Palestine," *Logos: Journal of Modern Society and Culture* 4 (2005), pp. 1–10 (6).

2. D. L. Bock, "Some Christians See a 'Road Map' to End Times," *Los Angeles Times* (June 18, 2003).

3. "Israel, Palestine, the Church, and Eschatology," *Euangelion* (June 30, 2006), http://euangelizomai.blogspot.com/2006/06/israel-palestine-church-and.html

4. G. Vermes, *Providential Accidents: An Autobiography* (London: SCM Press, 1998), pp. 213–14. It may also be significant that E. P. Sanders was studying in Israel in the late 1960s. See E. P. Sanders, "Comparing Judaism and Christianity: An Academic Autobiography" (April–May 2004), available at http://www.duke.edu/religion/home/EP/Intel%20autobiog%20rev.pdf

5. R. Rohrbaugh, *The New Testament in Cross-Cultural Perspective* (Eugene: Cascade Books, 2007), p. 91, n. 8; cf. H. Räisänen , "Jesus and the Food Laws. Reflections on Mark 7:15," *JSNT* 6 (1982), pp. 79–100.

6. B. A. Pearson, "The Gospel according to the Jesus Seminar," Occasional Papers of the Institute for Antiquity and Christianity 35 (The Claremont Graduate School, April 1996), quoted and discussed in W. Arnal, *The Symbolic Jesus: Historical Scholarship, Judaism and the Construction of Contemporary Identity* (London & Oakville: Equinox, 2005), p. 17.

7. N. T. Wright, *Jesus and the Victory of God* (London: SPCK, 1996), p. 79, n. 233, quoted and discussed in J. S. Kloppenborg, "As One Unknown, without a Name? Co-opting the Apocalyptic Jesus," in J. S. Kloppenborg with J. W. Marshall (eds.), *Apocalypticism, Anti-Semitism and the Historical Jesus: Subtexts in Criticism* (London & New York: T&T Clark/Continuum, 2005), pp. 19–21 (2, n. 3).

8. B. Mack, *The Myth of Innocence: Mark and Christian Origins* (Philadelphia: Fortress Press, 1988), pp. 375–76.

9. J. D. Crossan, *Who Killed Jesus? Exposing the Roots of Anti-Semitism in the Gospel Story of the Death of Jesus* (San Francisco: HarperSanFrancisco, 1995).

10. K. W. Whitelam, "Lines of Power: Mapping Ancient Israel," in R. B. Coote and N. K. Gottwald (eds.), *To Break Every Yoke: Essays in Honor of Marvin L. Chaney* (Sheffield: Sheffield Phoenix Press, 2007), pp. 40–79 (61). See further B. Long, *Imagining the Holy Land: Maps, Models, and Fantasy Travels* (Bloomington: Indiana University Press, 2003).

11. See, e.g., the inside opening page of J. D. Crossan and J. L. Reed, *Excavating Jesus: Beneath the Stones, behind the Texts* (New York: HarperCollins; London: SPCK, 2001).

12. Dale C. Allison, *Resurrecting Jesus: The Earliest Christian Tradition and its Interpreters* (London: T&T Clark, 2005), p. 150.

13. R. S. Sugirtharajah, *Asian Biblical Hermeneutics and Postcolonialism: Contesting the Interpretations* (Sheffield: Sheffield Academic Press, 1998), p. 118.

14. G. Theissen and A. Merz, *The Historical Jesus: A Comprehensive Guide* (London: SCM Press, 1998), p. ix.

15. Theissen and Merz, *Historical Jesus*, pp. 366–67.

16. Wright, *Victory*, p. xv.

17. Wright, *Victory*, p. 93.

18. For further criticisms and implied criticisms of Wright's views on Jesus and the law, see J. G. Crossley, *The Date of Mark's Gospel: Insight from the Law in Earliest Christianity* (London: T&T Clark/Continuum, 2004).

19. Wright, *Victory*, pp. 399–402.

20. S. C. Barton, *Discipleship and Family Ties in Mark and Matthew* (Cambridge: Cambridge University Press, 1995); M. Bockmeuhl, "Let the Dead Bury their Dead (Matt. 8:22/Luke 9:60): Jesus and the Halakah," *JTS* 49 (1998), pp. 553–81; C. H. T. Fletcher-Louis, " 'Leave the Dead to Bury their Own Dead': Q 9.60 and the Redefinition of the People of God," *JSNT* 26 (2003), pp. 39–68.

21. E.g. T. W. Manson, *The Sayings of Jesus* (London: SCM Press, 1957), p. 131.

22. This is not the only problem. For criticisms of Wright and his inaccurate generalizations of Jewish purity law see E. P. Sanders, "Jesus, Ancient Judaism, and Modern Christianity: The Quest Continues," in P. Fredriksen and A. Reinhartz (eds.), *Jesus, Judaism, and Christian Anti-Judaism: Reading the New Testament after the Holocaust* (Louisville: Westminster/John Knox, 2002), pp. 31–55 (37, 40, 55).

23. We also see the view of a tension in Jesus' view of the Law, especially on family, in the learned, well-referenced and detailed work of Dale Allison (who could never be accused of not reading a wide range of Jewish sources) but again when we get to apparently critical views of the Law, the key issues raised here are not always discussed. See Allison, *Resurrecting Jesus*, pp. 149–97. It should also be observed that Allison has a stress on Jesus as a Jew (e.g. p. 195).

24. R. W. Funk, R. W. Hoover, and the Jesus Seminar, *The Five Gospels: The Search for the Authentic Words of Jesus* (San Francisco: HarperCollins, 1993), p. 69.

25. E.g. R. P. Booth, *Jesus and the Laws of Purity: Tradition History and Legal History in Mark 7* (Sheffield: JSOT, 1986); Crossley, *Date of Mark's Gospel*, ch. 7.

26. This is not to say that Jesus could not historically have been radically different from his contemporaries but rather in the face of established parallel evidence from the same cultural milieu, the making of Jesus as radically different tells us something more, I would contend, about the social location of modern scholarship.

27. W. D. Davies, *The Gospel and the Land: Early Christianity and Jewish Territorial Doctrine* (Berkeley, CA: University of California Press, 1974).

28. E. P. Sanders, *Jesus and Judaism* (London: SCM Press, 1985); E. P. Sanders, *The Historical Figure of Jesus* (London: Penguin, 1993); K. J. Wenell, *Jesus and Land: Sacred and Social Space in Second Temple Judaism* (London & New York: Continuum/T&T Clark, 2007).

29. J. H. Elliott, "Jesus the Israelite Was Neither a 'Jew' nor a 'Christian': On Correcting Misleading Nomenclature," *JSHJ* 5 (2007), pp. 119–54.

30. J. G. Crossley, "Jesus the Jew since 1967," in W. Blanton, J. G. Crossley and H. Moxnes (eds.), *Jesus beyond Nationalism: Constructing the Historical Jesus in a Period of Cultural Complexity* (London: Equinox, forthcoming 2008).

31. Cf., e.g., Elliott, "Jesus the Israelite," p. 153: "let us refer to the ethnic entity as 'Israel,' 'House of Israel,' and to its members as 'Israelites,' 'children of Israel'... Let us refer to Jesus and his earliest followers as 'Israelites' or members of the 'House of Israel'... Let us stress their roots in Israel, not in 'Judaism.' "

32. An exception are the thoughtful comments in A.-J. Levine, *The Misunderstood Jew: The Church and the Scandal of the Jewish Jesus.* San Francisco: HarperCollins, 2006, pp. 183–85, 224–25, though it is perhaps significant that this book is more in the realm of inter-religious dialogue where such issues can hardly be ignored.

33. Wright, *Victory*, is, as ever, a particularly clear example of this.

34. For further criticisms see Crossley, *Date of Mark's Gospel*, pp. 82–124, 159–205. For an important recent book which also rejects the view of Jesus rejecting/replacing the Temple in the dramatic sense found in much of modern scholarship see D. Catchpole, *Jesus People: The Historical Jesus and the Beginnings of Community* (London: Darton, Longman & Todd; Grand Rapids: Baker, 2006).

35. C. H. T. Fletcher-Louis, "Jesus as the High Priestly Messiah: Part 2," *JSHJ* 5 (2007), pp. 57–79 (66).

36. C. H. T. Fletcher-Louis, "Jesus as the High Priestly Messiah: Part 1," *JSHJ* 4 (2006), pp. 155–75 (157).

37. Fletcher-Louis, "Part 1," p. 157.

38. Cf., e.g., C. H. T. Fletcher-Louis, "The Worship of Divine Humanity and the Worship of Jesus," in C. C. Newman, J. R. Davila and G. Lewis (eds.), *The Jewish Roots of Christological Monotheism: Papers from the St. Andrews Conference on the Historical Origins of the Worship of Jesus* (Leiden: Brill, 1999), pp. 112–28; C. H. T. Fletcher-Louis, "God's Image, His Cosmic Temple and the High Priest: Towards an Historical and Theological Account of the Incarnation," in T. D. Alexander and S. Gathercole (eds.), *Heaven on Earth: The Temple in Biblical Theology* (Carlisle: Paternoster, 2004), pp. 81–99.

39. Fletcher-Louis, "Part 2," p. 75.

40. Fletcher-Louis, "Part 2," p. 77.

41. Fletcher-Louis, "Part 2," p. 77.

42. On the linguistic background summarized here see Crossley, *Date of Mark's Gospel*, pp. 160–62.

43. For the most up-to-date and comprehensive work on the term "son of man" see now M. Casey, *The Solution to the "Son of Man" Problem* (Edinburgh: T&T Clark, 2007). For the different interpretative traditions surrounding Dan. 7:13 see M. Casey, *Son of Man: The Interpretation and Influence of Daniel 7* (London: SPCK, 1980).

44. Fletcher-Louis, "Part 2," p. 75.

45. Cf. also "Part 2," p. 64: "perhaps Jesus does, at this point, believe himself to be a priest but he is not yet happy that that be publicly known." So presumably, he acts clean contrary to running an alternative priestly system?

46. N. T. Wright, "The Divinity of Jesus," in N. T. Wright and M. J. Borg, *The Meaning of Jesus: Two Visions* (London: SPCK, 1999), pp. 157–68 (160–61, 164, 166–67).

47. L. W. Hurtado, *Lord Jesus Christ: Devotion to Jesus in Earliest Christianity* (Grand Rapids, MI & Cambridge, UK: Eerdmans, 2003).

48. Hurtado, *Lord Jesus Christ*, p. 12.

49. Hurdato, *Lord Jesus Christ*, p. 7.

50. Hurdato, *Lord Jesus Christ*, p. 209.

51. Hurdato, *Lord Jesus Christ*, p. 176.

52. Hurtado, *Lord Jesus Christ*, e.g. pp. 93–97, 175–76.

53. Hurtado, *Lord Jesus Christ*, p. 176.

54. Hurtado, *Lord Jesus Christ*, pp. 267, 346.

55. Hurtado, *Lord Jesus Christ*, p. 286, following J. Marcus, *Mark 1-8: A New Translation with Introduction and Commentary* (New York: Doubleday, 2000), pp. 404–21, 482–97.

56. See further J. G. Crossley, "Mark's Christology and a Scholarly Creation of a Non-Jewish Christ of Faith," in J. G. Crossley (ed.), *Judaism, Jewish Identities and the Gospel Tradition: Essays in Honour of Maurice Casey* (London: Equinox, 2008), ch. 5.

57. Peter Novick, *The Holocaust and Collective Memory* (London: Bloomsbury, 1999), p. 166.

58. Noam Chomsky, *Understanding Power* (ed. P. R. Mitchell and J. Schoeffel; New York: New Press, 2002), p. 125.

59. Michael F. Bird, "Israel, Palestine, the Church, and Eschatology," *Euangelion* (June 30, 2006), available at http://euangelizomai.blogspot.com/2006/06/israel-palestine-church-and.html

60. J. Z. Smith, *Drudgery Divine: On the Comparison of Early Christianities and the Religions of Late Antiquity* (Chicago: University of Chicago Press, 1990), p. 83.

61. T. Penner, "*Die Judenfrage* and the Construction of Ancient Judaism: Toward a Foregrounding of the Backgrounds Approach to Early Christianity," in P. Gray and G. O'Day (eds.), *Scripture and Traditions: Essays on Early Judaism and Christianity* (Leiden: Brill, forthcoming 2008); cf. T. Penner, *In Praise of Christian Origins: Stephen and the Hellenists in Lukan Apologetic Historiography* (London & New York: T&T Clark/Continuum, 2004), pp. 1–59.

62. E. W. Said, *Orientalism* (London: Penguin, 1978, 1995, 2003), p. 286.

63. Said, *Orientalism*, p. xviii.

64. H. Lindsey, *The Late Great Planet Earth*. Grand Rapids: Zondervan, 1970, p. 111. For more on the subordinate position of Jews see, e.g., pp. 48, 52, 139, 142, 167.

65. Davidson, "Christian Zionism," p. 6.

66. M. L. Taylor, *Religion, Politics, and the Christian Right: Post-9/11 Powers and American Empire* (Minneapolis: Fortress Press, 2005), pp. 67, 85–95.

67. N. D. Kristof, "Jesus and Jihad," *New York Times* (July 17, 2004) and "Apocalypse (Almost) Now," *New York Times* (November 24, 2004).

68. See, e.g., M. Engel, "Meet the New Zionists," *Guardian* (October 28, 2002).

69. http://www.cnn.com/2006/US/01/05/robertson.sharon/. The comments were broadcast on Robertson's "700 Club" TV show.

Conclusion

1. N. Chomsky, *Understanding Power* (ed. P. R. Mitchell and J. Schoeffel; New York: New Press, 2002), p. 206.

2. Edward W. Said, *Covering Islam: How the Media and the Experts Determine How We See the Rest of the World* (2nd edn; London: Vintage, 1981, 1997), p. Lxx.

Bibliography

Abu el-Haj, N. *Facts on the Ground: Archaeological Practice and Territorial Self-Fashioning in Israeli Society.* Chicago & London: University of Chicago Press, 2001.

Achcar, G. *The Clash of Barbarisms: September 11 and the New World Disorder.* 2nd edn; London: Saqi, 2002, 2006.

Ali, T. *The Clash of Fundamentalisms: Crusades, Jihads and Modernity.* London: Verso, 2002.

Allison, D. C. *Resurrecting Jesus: The Earliest Christian Tradition and its Interpreters.* London: T&T Clark, 2005.

Amnesty International. "Israel and the Occupied Territories. Demolition and Dispossession: The Destruction of Palestinian Homes." AI Index: MDE 15/059/1999 (December 8, 1999). Available at http://web.amnesty.org/library/Index/engMDE150591999

_______ "Report 2003 – Uzbekistan." Available at http://web.amnesty.org/report2003/uzb-summary-eng

Andalo, D. "UCU Head against Israeli Academic Boycott." *Education Guardian* (May 30, 2007).

Anonymous. "Barnard Grad Heads Protest against Anti-Semitic Prof." *IsraelNationalNews.com* (August 9, 2007). Available at http://www.israelnationalnews.com/News/Flash.aspx/131382

_______ "The Fight for Fallujah." *Field Artillery* (March, 2005). Available at http://sill-www.army.mil/famag/2005.asp#mar-apr

Arenson, K. W. "Fracas Erupts over Book on Mideast by a Barnard Professor Seeking Tenure." *New York Times* (September 10, 2007).

Arnal, W. *The Symbolic Jesus: Historical Scholarship, Judaism and the Construction of Contemporary Identity.* London & Oakville: Equinox, 2005.

Asad, T., ed. *Anthropology and the Colonial Encounter.* Amherst, NY: Humanity Books, 1973, 1998.

Avalos, H. *The End of Biblical Studies.* Amherst, NY: Prometheus Books, 2007.

Baker, P. "Conflicts Shaped Two Presidencies." *Washington Post* (December 31, 2006).

Barton, S. C. *Discipleship and Family Ties in Mark and Matthew.* Cambridge: Cambridge University Press, 1995.

_______ "Historical Criticism and Social-Scientific Perspectives in New Testament Study." In J. B. Green, ed., *Hearing the New Testament: Strategies for Interpretation*: 61-89. Grand Rapids: Eerdmans, 1995.

Barzilai, A. "UK Tightening Embargo on Israel." *Haaretz* (August 22, 2002).

Bates, S. "Unholy Row at Oxford's College for Clergy amid Staff Exodus and Claims of Bullying." *Guardian* (May 16, 2007).

Bauman, Z. *Modernity and the Holocaust.* Oxford: Polity Press, 1989.

BBC. "Poll Sees Hope in West-Islam Ties." (February 9, 2007). Available at http://news.bbc.co.uk/1/hi/in_depth/6369529.stm

_______ "Blair in Moderate Muslims Appeal." (June 4, 2007). Available at http://news.bbc.co.uk/1/hi/uk_politics/6718235.stm

_______ "Teaching Islam Is 'Outdated.' " (June 4, 2007). Available at http://news.bbc.co.uk/1/hi/education/6713373.stm

_______ "Chanting Probe May Take Some Time." (August 8, 2007). Available at http://news.bbc.co.uk/sport1/hi/football/teams/r/rangers/6931472.stm

Berlinerblau, Jacques. Comment on the internet discussion group, Christian Origins. Available at http://groups.yahoo.com/group/christian_origins/message/205.

Bieringer, R., D. Pollefeyt, F. Vandecasteele-Vanneuville, eds. *Anti-Judaism and the Fourth Gospel: Papers of the Leuven Colloquium, 2000.* Assen: Royal Van Gorcum, 2001.

Michael F. Bird. "Israel, Palestine, the Church, and Eschatology." *Euangelion* (June 30, 2006). Available at http://euangelizomai.blogspot.com/2006/06/israel-palestine-church-and.html

Birkner, G. "Barnard Alumnae Opposing Tenure for Anthropologist." *New York Sun* (November 16, 2006).

Blanton, W. *Displacing Christian Origins: Philosophy, Secularity, and the New Testament.* Chicago: Chicago University Press, 2007.

Bock, D. L. "Some Christians See a 'Road Map' to End Times." *Los Angeles Times* (June 18, 2003).

Bockmeuhl, M. "Let the Dead Bury their Dead (Matt. 8:22/Luke 9:60): Jesus and the Halakah." *JTS* 49 (1998): 553-81.

_______ "Review of Malina, *New Testament World*, third edition." *BMCR* (2002.04.19).

Boer, R. *Marxist Criticism of the Bible.* Sheffield: Sheffield Academic Press, 2003.

Bolender, J. "Blind Eye on Africa: Human Rights, Equatorial Guinea, and Oil." *ZNet* (August 16, 2003).

_______ "Uzbekistan and the US: Sometimes It Really Is a War on Islam." *ZNet* (October 18, 2003). Available at http://www.zmag.org/content/print_article.cfm?itemID=4367&sectionID=40

Booth, R. P. *Jesus and the Laws of Purity: Tradition History and Legal History in Mark 7.* Sheffield: JSOT, 1986.

Bornkamm, G. *Jesus of Nazareth.* London: Hodder & Stoughton, 1960.

Bourke, J. *An Intimate History of Killing: Face to Face Killing in the Twentieth Century Warfare.* London: Granta, 1999.

Boyarin, D. *A Radical Jew: Paul and the Politics of Identity.* Berkeley, CA: University of California Press, 1994.

Brooker, C. "Screen Burn." *Guardian* (February 24, 2007).

Browning, C. R. *Ordinary Men: Reserve Police Battalion 101 and the Final Solution in Poland.* 2nd edn; London: Penguin, 1992, 1998.

Buckley, W. F. "Are We Owed an Apology?" *National Review Online* (August 16, 2002). Available at http://www.nationalreview.com/buckley/buckley 081602.asp

Burchill, J. "I See in Those Photos Why We Are Fighting." *Times* (May 22, 2004).

Burack, J. "Erasing History and Ourselves: Nadia Abu el-Haj, Israel and the Western Tradition," *Family Security Foundation* (December 28, 2006). Available at http://www.familysecuritymatters.org/homeland.php?id=537580

Burke, J., *Al-Qaeda*. London: Penguin, 2003.

Bush, G. W. "Address to a Joint Session of Congress and the American People." (September 20, 2001). Available at http://www.whitehouse.gov/news/releases/ 2001/09/20010920-8.html

_______ "State of the Union Address." (January 29, 2002). Available at http:// www.whitehouse.gov/news/releases/2002/01/20020129-11.html

Callinicos, A. *The New Mandarins of American Power.* Cambridge: Polity Press, 2003.

Cameron, R., and Merrill Miller, eds. *Redescribing Christian Origins.* Atlanta, GA: SBL, 2004.

Campbell, D. "Strong Cast, Good Book, Big Hit." *Guardian* (February 8, 2001).

Casey, M. *Son of Man: The Interpretation and Influence of Daniel 7.* London: SPCK, 1980.

_______ *From Jewish Prophet to Gentile God: The Origins and Development of New Testament Christology.* Louisville: Westminster/John Knox; Cambridge: James Clarke, 1991.

_______ *Is John's Gospel True?* London: Routledge, 1996.

_______ "Some Anti-Semitic Assumptions in *The Theological Dictionary of the New Testament*." *NovT* 41 (1999): 280-91.

_______ *An Aramaic Approach to Q.* Cambridge: Cambridge University Press, 2002.

_______ "Who's Afraid of Jesus Christ? Some Comments on Attempts to Write a Life of Jesus." In J. G. Crossley and C. Karner, eds. *Writing History, Constructing Religion*: 129-46. Aldershot: Ashgate, 2005.

_______ *The Solution to the "Son of Man" Problem.* Edinburgh: T&T Clark, 2007.

Catchpole, D. *Jesus People: The Historical Jesus and the Beginnings of Community.* London: Darton, Longman & Todd; Grand Rapids: Baker, 2006.

Chance, J. K. "The Anthropology of Honor and Shame: Culture, Values and Practice." *Semeia* 68 (1994): 139-51.

Childs, D. *Britain since 1945: A Political History* (5th edn; London & New York: Routledge, 2001).

Chomsky, N. "The Responsibility of Intellectuals." *New York Review of Books* 8/3 (February 23, 1967).

_______ *American Power and the New Mandarins: Historical and Political Essays.* New York: Pantheon, 1969.

_______ *For Reasons of State.* New York: Pantheon, 1973.

_______ "Scholarship and Ideology: American Historians as 'Experts in Legitimation.' " *Social Scientist* 1 (1973): 20-37

_______ *Fateful Triangle: The United States, Israel and the Palestinians.* London: Pluto, 1999.

_______ *Rogue States: The Rule of Force in World Affairs.* London: Pluto Press, 2000.

_______ "Reply to Hitchens." *The Nation* (October 1, 2001).

_______ "Reply to Hitchens' Rejoinder." *The Nation* (October 4, 2001).

_______ *Media Control: The Spectacular Achievements of Propaganda.* 2nd edn; New York: Seven Stories Press, 1991, 2002.

_______ *Understanding Power.* Ed. P. R. Mitchell and J. Schoeffel; New York: New Press, 2002.

_______ *Pirates and Emperors, Old and New: International Terrorism in the Real World.* London: Pluto, 2002.

_______ *Middle East Illusions.* Lanham: Rowman & Littlefield, 2003.

_______ *Imperial Ambitions.* London: Penguin, 2005.

_______ *Interventions.* London: Hamish Hamilton, 2007.

Chomsky, N., and G. Achcar. *Perilous Power: The Middle East and U.S. Foreign Policy.* Ed. S. R. Shalom; Boulder & London: Paradigm, 2007.

Cockburn, A., and J. St Clair, eds. *The Politics of Anti-Semitism.* Edinburgh: AK Press, 2003.

Cornwell, R. "In God He Trusts – How George Bush Infused the White House with a Religious Spirit." *The Independent* (February 21, 2003).

Coulter, A. "This Is War" (September 12, 2001). Available at http://www.anncoulter.org/columns/2001/091301.htm

_______ "Why We Hate Them." In M. L. Sifry and C. Cerf, eds., *The Iraq War Reader: History, Documents, Opinions*: 333-35. New York: Touchstone, 2003.

Crook, Z. A. "Structure versus Agency in Studies of the Biblical Social World: Engaging with Louise Lawrence." *JSNT* 29 (2007): 251-75.

Crossan, J. D. *The Historical Jesus: The Life of a Mediterranean Jewish Peasant.* New York: HarperCollins; Edinburgh: T&T Clark, 1991.

_______ *Who Killed Jesus? Exposing the Roots of Anti-Semitism in the Gospel Story of the Death of Jesus.* San Francisco: HarperSanFrancisco, 1995.

_______ *The Birth of Christianity: Discovering What Happened in the Years Immediately after the Execution of Jesus.* New York: HarperCollins; Edinburgh: T&T Clark, 1998.

Crossan, J. D., and J. L. Reed. *Excavating Jesus: Beneath the Stones, behind the Texts.* New York: HarperCollins; London: SPCK, 2001.

Crossley, J. G. "The Semitic Background to Repentance in the Teaching of John the Baptist and Jesus." *JSHJ* 2 (2004): 138-57.

_______ *The Date of Mark's Gospel: Insight from the Law in Earliest Christianity.* London: T&T Clark/Continuum, 2004.

_______ "Defining History." In J. G. Crossley and C. Karner, eds. *Writing History, Constructing Religion*: 9-29. Aldershot: Ashgate, 2005.

_______ *Why Christianity Happened: A Sociohistorical Account of Christian Origins.* Louisville: Westminster/John Knox, 2006.

_______ "Mark's Christology and a Scholarly Creation of a Non-Jewish Christ of Faith." In J. G. Crossley, ed., *Judaism, Jewish Identities and the Gospel Tradition: Essays in Honour of Maurice Casey*: ch. 5. London: Equinox, forthcoming.

_______ "Jesus the Jew since 1967." In W. Blanton, J. G. Crossley and H. Moxnes, eds., *Jesus beyond Nationalism: Constructing the Historical Jesus in a Period of Cultural Complexity.* London: Equinox, forthcoming.

_______ "Caesar's Willing Theologians; 'Just War' Theory and the Art of Justifying the Unjustifiable." *Political Theology* (forthcoming).

Cummins, W. "Dr Williams, Beware of False Prophets." *Sunday Telegraph* (July 4, 2004).

Curtis, M. *Web of Deceit: Britain's Real Role in the World.* London: Vintage, 2003.

_______ *Unpeople: Britain's Secret Human Rights Abuses.* Vintage: London: 2004.

_______ "Friendless in Gaza: Britain and Israel." *Red Pepper* (April 2004).

_______ "The Myth of the 'Honest Broker': Britain and Israel." (31 March, 2006). Available at http://www.cmyk.info/markcurtis/article26.html.

Curtis, P. "Lecturers Vote for Israeli Boycott." *Guardian* (April 22, 2005).

Davidson, L. "Christian Zionism as a Representation of Manifest American Destiny." *Critique: Critical Middle Eastern Studies* 14 (2005): 157-69.

_______ "Christian Zionism and American Foreign Policy: Paving the Road to Hell in Palestine." *Logos: Journal of Modern Society and Culture* 4 (2005): 1-10.

Davies, W. D. *The Gospel and the Land: Early Christianity and Jewish Territorial Doctrine.* Berkeley, CA: University of California Press, 1974.

Davila, J. R., "Assimilated to the Blogosphere: Blogging Ancient Judaism." *SBL Forum.* Available at http://www.sbl-site.org/Article.aspx?ArticleId=390.

Davis, M. *Planet of Slums.* London & New York, Verso, 2006.

De Atkine, N. B. "Why Arabs Lose Wars." *Middle East Quarterly* 6 (1999): 17-27.

_______ "The Arab Mind Revisited." *Middle East Quarterly* 11 (2004): 47-55.

Deane, C., and D. Fears. "Negative Perception of Islam Increasing." *Washington Post* (March 9, 2006): A01.

Deissmann, A. *Light from the Ancient East: The New Testament Illustrated by Recently Discovered Texts of the Graeco-Roman World.* London: Hodder & Stoughton, 1927.

Dever, W. *What Did the Biblical Writers Know, and When Did They Know It? What Archaeology Can Tell Us about the Reality of Ancient Israel.* Grand Rapids: Eerdmans, 2001.

Dower, J. W. *War without Mercy: Race and Power in the Pacific War.* New York: Pantheon, 1986.

Dreyfuss, R. "Reverend Doomsday." *Rolling Stone*. Available at http://www.rollingstone.com/politics/story/5939999/reverend_doomsday/

Droge, A. J. "What Difference Does Q Make? Or, Excavating Q Studies." Unpublished paper presented at the *Society of Biblical Literature* annual meeting, Washington DC, November 2006.

Dunn, J. D. G. *The Parting of the Ways between Christianity and Judaism and their Significance for the Character of Christianity.* London: SCM, 1991.

Editorial. "Sanitizing Islam." *Jerusalem Post* (August 26, 2003).

Elliott, J. H. "Jesus the Israelite Was Neither a 'Jew' nor a 'Christian': On Correcting Misleading Nomenclature." *JSHJ* 5 (2007): 119-54.

_______ "Review of Malina and Neyrey, *Portraits of Paul.*" *RBL*. Available at http://www.bookreviews.org/pdf/2138_1165.pdf

Elshtain, J. B. *Just War against Terror: The Burden of American Power in a Violent World.* New York: Basic Books, 2003.

Engel, M. "Meet the New Zionists." *Guardian* (October 28, 2002).

Engels, F. "On the History of Earliest Christianity (1894)." In K. Marx and F. Engels, *Collected Works Volume 27, Engels 1890-95*: 447-69. London: Lawrence & Wishart, 1990.

Ernst, C. W. "From the Heart of the Qur'an Belt." *Religious Studies News* 18 (2003): 14-18.

Esler, P. F. *The First Christians in their Social Worlds: Social-Scientific Approaches to New Testament Interpretation.* London: Routledge, 1994.

_______ "Introduction: Models, Context and Kerygma in New Testament Interpretation." In P. F. Esler, ed., *Modelling Early Christianity: Social-Scientific Studies of the New Testament in its Context*: 1-20. London: Routledge, 1995.

_______ "Models in New Testament Interpretation: A Reply to David Horrell." *JSNT* 22 (2000): 107-13.

_______ *New Testament Theology: Communion and Community.* Minneapolis: Fortress, 2005.

Evans, R. J. *In Defence of History*. 2nd edn; London: Granta, 2000.

Farish, M. "Targeting the Inner Landscape." In D. Gregory and A. Pred, eds., *Violent Geographies: Fear, Terror, and Political Violence*: 255-71. New York & London: Routledge, 2007.

Ferziger, J. "U.S. Signs Pact to Increase Aid to Israel." *New York Sun* (August 17, 2007).

Finkelstein, N. *The Holocaust Industry: Reflections on the Exploitation of Jewish Suffering.* 2nd edn; London & New York: Verso, 2000, 2003.

_______ *Beyond Chutzpah: On the Misuse of Anti-Semitism and the Abuse of History.* London: Verso, 2005.

Fiorenza, E. Schüssler. *Jesus and the Politics of Interpretation.* New York & London: Continuum, 2000.

Fisk, R. *Pity the Nation: Lebanon at War.* Oxford: Oxford University Press, 1990.

_______ "British Soldiers 'Kicked Iraqi Prisoner to Death.' " *Independent on Sunday* (January 4, 2004).

_______ "War Lords to their Critics: Just Shut Up." *Independent* (April 10, 2004).

_______ "The 'Good Guys' Who Can Do No Wrong." *Independent* (May 2, 2004).

_______ "Who Killed Baha Mousa?" *Independent* (December 15, 2004).

_______ *The Great War for Civilisation: The Conquest of the Middle East.* London: Fourth Estate, 2005.

_______ "A Cry for Justice from a Good Man Who Expected Us to Protect his Son." *Independent on Sunday* (June 17, 2007).

_______ "My Challenge for Steven Spielberg." *Independent* (September 2007).

"Fitzgerald, H." "Crisis at Columbia: That Awful Mess on Morningside Heights." *Campus Watch* (April 14, 2005). Available at http://www.campus-watch.org/article/id/1943

_______ "Crisis at Columbia: Nadia Abu el-Haj." *FrontPage Magazine* (October 10, 2005). Available at http://www.campus-watch.org/article/id/2228

_______ "Study the Threats, and the Response to Them." *Dhimmi Watch* (August 14, 2007). Available at http://www.jihadwatch.org/dhimmiwatch/archives/017784.php

Fletcher-Louis, C. H. T. "The Worship of Divine Humanity and the Worship of Jesus." In C. C. Newman, J. R. Davila and G. Lewis, eds., *The Jewish Roots of Christological Monotheism: Papers from the St. Andrews Conference on the Historical Origins of the Worship of Jesus*: 112-28. Leiden: Brill, 1999.

_______ " 'Leave the Dead to Bury their Own Dead': Q 9.60 and the Redefinition of the People of God." *JSNT* 26 (2003): 39-68.

_______ "God's Image, His Cosmic Temple and the High Priest: Towards an Historical and Theological Account of the Incarnation." In T. D. Alexander and S. Gathercole, eds., *Heaven on Earth: The Temple in Biblical Theology*: 81-99. Carlisle: Paternoster, 2004.

_______ "Jesus as the High Priestly Messiah: Part 1." *JSHJ* 4 (2006): 155-75.

_______ "Jesus as the High Priestly Messiah: Part 2." *JSHJ* 5 (2007): 57-79.

Fraser, G., 'Not Faith, but Fanaticism', *Guardian* (May 29, 2007).

Fredriksen, P. "The Birth of Christianity and the Origins of Christian Anti-Judaism." In P. Fredriksen and A. Reinhartz, eds., *Jesus, Judaism, and Christian Anti-Judaism: Reading the New Testament after the Holocaust*: 8-30. Louisville: Westminster/John Knox, 2002.

Friedman, T. "The Humiliation Factor." *New York Times* (November 9, 2003).

_______ "Liberal Hawks Reconsider the Iraq War." *Slate* (January 12, 2004).

Friesen, S. J. "Poverty in Pauline Studies: Beyond the So-called New Consensus." *JSNT* 26 (2004): 323-61.

Funk, R. W., R. W. Hoover, and the Jesus Seminar. *The Five Gospels: The Search for the Authentic Words of Jesus.* San Francisco: HarperCollins, 1993.

Gager, J. G. "Shall We Marry Our Enemies? Sociology and the New Testament." *Int.* 36 (1982): 256-65.

Garrett, S. R. "Review of Malina, *Christian Origins and Cultural Anthropology*." *JBL* 107 (1988): 532-33.

Ghareeb E., ed. *Split Vision: The Portrayal of Arabs in the American Media.* Washington, DC: American-Arab Affairs Council, 1983.

Giles, D. "Professor Fired for Allowing Questions about Judaism and Islam." Available at http://www.labournet.net/world/0607/roosevelt1.html (13/07/06).

Glassman, J. "Imperialism Imposed and Invited: The 'War on Terror' Comes to Southeast Asi." In D. Gregory and A. Pred, eds., *Violent Geographies: Fear, Terror, and Political Violence*: 93-109. New York & London: Routledge, 2007.

Glover, J. "Two-thirds Believe London Bombings Are Linked to Iraq War." *Guardian* (July 19, 2005).

Goddard, H. "The Crisis of Representation in Islamic Studies." In J. G. Crossley and C. Karner, eds., *Writing History, Constructing Religion*: 85-106. Aldershot: Ashgate, 2005.

Gough, K. "Anthropology and Imperialism." *Monthly Review* (April, 1968): 12-27.

Grabbe, L. L., " 'The Comfortable Theory,' 'Maximal Conservatism' and Neo-Fundamentalism Revisited." In A. G. Hunter and P. R. Davies, eds., *Sense and Sensitivity: Essays on Reading the Bible in Memory of Robert Carroll*: 174-93. Sheffield: Sheffield Academic Press, 2002,

Graham, S. "Demodernizing by Design: Everyday Infrastructure and Political Violence." In D. Gregory and A. Pred, eds., *Violent Geographies: Fear, Terror, and Political Violence*: 309-28. New York & London: Routledge, 2007.

Gregory, D. *The Colonial Present: Afghanistan, Palestine, Iraq*. Oxford: Blackwell, 2004.

Groebel, J., and R. A. Hinde, eds. *Aggression: Their Biological and Social Bases.* Cambridge: Cambridge University Press, 1989.

Guteman, D. L. "Honor, Shame and Terror in the Middle East." FrontPage Magazine.com (October 24, 2003). Available at http://www.frontpagemag.com/Articles/Printable.aspx?GUID={EFD57D27-54A4-4F05-9DBC-108BE1EE5379}

Hall, E. T. *The Silent Language.* Garden City: Doubleday, 1959.

Hall, S. "Blair Acted like a 'White Vigilante' by Invading Iraq, Says Bishop." *Guardian* (December 30, 2003).

Haney, C., C. Banks, and P. Zimbardo. "Interpersonal Dynamics in a Simulated Prison." *International Journal of Criminology and Penology* 1 (1973): 69-97.

Hanson, K. C. "BTB Readers Guide: Kinship." *BTB* 24 (1994): 183-94.

Harland, P. A. *Associations, Synagogues, and Congregations: Claiming a Place in Ancient Mediterranean Society.* Minneapolis: Fortress Press, 2003.

Harrington, D. J. "Sociological Concepts and the Early Church: A Decade of Research." *Theological Studies* 41 (1980): 181-90.

Harris, S. *The End of Faith: Religion, Terror, and the Future of Reason.* London: Simon & Schuster, 2004.

Harvey, D. *The New Imperialism.* Oxford: Oxford University Press, 2003.

Head, P. "The Nazi Quest for an Ayrian Jesus." *JSHJ* 2 (2004): 55-89.

Healy, P. "Clinton Vows to Back Israel in Latest Mideast Conflict." *New York Times* (July 18, 2006).

Herman, E. S. "The NYT's Thomas Friedman: The Geraldo Rivera of the NYT." *Z Magazine Online* (16 November, 2003). Available at http://zmagsite.zmag.org/Nov2003/hermanpr1103.html

Herman, E. S., and N. Chomsky, *Manufacturing Consent: The Political Economy of the Mass Media.* London: Vintage, 1988.

Hersh, S. "Annals of National Security: The Gray Zone – How a Secret Pentagon Program Came to Abu Ghraib." *The New Yorker* (May 15, 2004).
Herzog, W. R. *Prophet and Teacher: An Introduction to the Historical Jesus.* Louisville: Westminster/John Knox, 2005.
Heschel, S. "Nazifying Christian Theology Walter Grundmann and the Institute for the Study and Eradication of Jewish Influence on German Church Life." *Church History* 63 (1994): 587-605.
Hilton, R. H. "Peasant Society, Peasant Movements and Feudalism in Medieval Europe." In H. A. Landsberger, ed., *Rural Protest: Peasant Movements and Social Change*: 67-94. New York: Macmillan, 1973.
Hitchens, C. "A Rejoinder to Noam Chomsky." *The Nation* (October 4, 2001).
Hitchens, P. "I'll Say It while They Still Let Me: Islam Is a Threat to Us All." *Mail on Sunday* (July 11, 2004).
Hobsbawm, E. J. *Uncommon People: Resistance, Rebellion and Jazz.* London: Abacus, 1998.
Holmberg, B. *Sociology and the New Testament: An Appraisal.* Minneapolis: Fortress Press, 1990.
Holmén, T. "The Jewishness of Jesus in the 'Third Quest.' " In M. Labahn and A. Schmidt, eds., *Jesus, Mark and Q: The Teaching of Jesus and its Earliest Records*: 143-62. Sheffield: Sheffield Academic Press, 2001.
Horowitz, D. "The Sick Mind of Noam Chomsky." FrontPageMag.com (26 September, 2001). Available at http://www.frontpagemag.com/Articles/Read.aspx?GUID={19193155-11B3-4D95-BD7F-F30801D7C206}
Horrell, D. G. "Social-Scientific Interpretation of the New Testament: Retrospect and Prospect." In D. G. Horrell (ed.), *Social-Scientific Approaches to New Testament Interpretation*: 3-27. Edinburgh: T&T Clark, 1999.
_______ "Models and Methods in Social-Scientific Interpretation: A Response to Philip Esler." *JSNT* 22 (2000): 83-105.
Hourani, A. *A History of the Arab Peoples with an Afterword by Malise Ruthven.* 2nd edn; London: Faber, 1991, 2002.
House of Commons Debates. Session 2002-2003. "Iraq." (March 18, 2003), *Hansard*, cols. 767-68. Available at http://www.parliament.uk/hansard/hansard.cfm
Human Rights Watch, "Changes to US Military Assistance after September 11." (February, 2002). Available at http://hrw.org/reports/2002/usmil/USass0202-02.htm#P178_26449
Huntington, S. P. "The Clash of Civilizations?" *Foreign Affairs* 72 (1993): 22-49.
_______ *The Clash of Civilizations and the Remaking of World Order.* New York: Simon & Schuster, 1996.
Hurtado, L. W. *Lord Jesus Christ: Devotion to Jesus in Earliest Christianity.* Grand Rapids, Michigan/Cambridge, UK: Eerdmans, 2003.
Hutton, W. "Why the West Is Wary of Muslims." *Observer* (January 11, 2004).
Hymes, D., ed. *Reinventing Anthropology.* New York: Random House, 1972.
Iraq's Weapons of Mass Destruction – The Assessment of the British Government. (September 24, 2002). Available at http://www.number-10.gov.uk/output/Page271.asp

Joffe, A. H. "Review of Nadia Abu el-Haj, *Facts on the Ground*." *Journal of Near Eastern Studies* 64 (2005): 297-304.

Joffe-Walt, B. "Made in the UK: Bringing Devastation to Lebanon – the British Parts in Israel's Deadly Attack Helicopters." *Guardian* (Saturday July 29, 2006).

Jordan, L. F. "Review of The Arab Mind by Raphael Patai." CIA Historical Review Program, Center for the Study of Intelligence. Available at https://www.cia.gov/library/center-for-the-study-of-intelligence/kent-csi/docs/v18i3a06p_0001.htm

Judge, E. A. *The Social Pattern of the Christian Groups in the First Century.* London: Tyndale Press, 1960.

Kareem, H. O. "An Interview with Noam Chomsky." *ZNet* (January 02, 2004). Available at http://www.zmag.org/content/showarticle.cfm?ItemID=4780

Karner, C. *The Thought World of Hindu Nationalism: Analyzing a Political Ideolog.y* Lewistown, NY: Edwin Mellen Press, 2006.

Käsemann, E. *New Testament Questions of Today.* London: SCM, 1969.

Kautsky, J. H. *The Politics of Aristocratic Empires.* Chapel Hill: University of North Carolina, 1982.

Kautsky, K. *Foundations of Christianity: A Study in Christian Origins.* London: Orbach & Chambers, 1925.

Keegan, J. "In This War of Civilisations, the West Will Prevail." *Telegraph* (October 8, 2001).

Keller, B. "The Sunshine Warrior." *New York Times* (September 22, 2002).

Kepel, G. *The War for Muslim Minds: Islam and the West.* Cambridge, MA & London: The Belknap Press of Harvard University Press, 2004.

_______ *The Roots of Radical Islam.* London: Saqi, 2005.

Klein, N. "Children of Bush's America." *Guardian* (May 18, 2004).

Kloppenborg, J. S. "As One Unknown, without a Name? Co-opting the Apocalyptic Jesus." In J. S. Kloppenborg with J. W. Marshall (eds.), *Apocalypticism, Anti-Semitism and the Historical Jesus: Subtexts in Criticism*: pp. 1-21. London & New York: T&T Clark/Continuum, 2005.

Kowaliñski, P. "The Genesis of Christianity in the Views of Contemporary Marxist Specialists of Religion." *Antonianum* 47 (1972): 541-75.

Kristof, N. D. "Jesus and Jihad." *New York Times* (July 17, 2004).

_______ "Apocalypse (Almost) Now." *New York Times* (November 24, 2004).

Kuhn, K. G. " Ἰσραήλ, Ἰουδαῖος, Ἑβραῖος in Jewish Literature after the OT." *TDNT* 3:359-69.

_______ *Die Judenfrage als weltgeschichtliches Problem.* Hamburg: Hanseatische Verlagsanstalt, 1939.

Lang, A. "Convergence: The Politics of Armageddon." Available at http://prop1.org/inaugur/85reagan/85rrarm.htm

Lawrence, L. J. *An Ethnography of the Gospel of Matthew: A Critical Assessment of the Use of the Honour and Shame Model in New Testament Studies.* Tübingen: Mohr Siebeck, 2003.

_______ "Structure, Agency and Ideology: A Response to Zeba Crook." *JSNT* 29 (2007): 277-86.

Leading Article. "A Bloody Epitaph to Blair's War." *Independent on Sunday* (June 17, 2007).

Leigh, D., N. P. Walsh, and E. MacAskill. "Ambassador Accused after Criticising US." *Guardian* (October 18, 2003).

Leigh, D., and J. Wilson. "Counting Iraq's Victims." *Guardian* (October 10, 2001).

Leirvik, O., "Jesus in Modern Muslim Thought: From Anti-colonial Polemics to Post-colonial Dialogue?" In W. Blanton, J. G. Crossley and H. Moxnes (eds.), *Jesus beyond Nationalism: Constructing the Historical Jesus in a Period of Cultural Complexity* (London: Equinox, forthcoming).

Levine, A. -J. *The Misunderstood Jew: The Church and the Scandal of the Jewish Jesus.* San Francisco: HarperCollins, 2006.

Lewis, B. "The Roots of Muslim Rage." *The Atlantic* (September 1990): 47-60.

Lindsey, H. *The Late Great Planet Earth.* Grand Rapids: Zondervan, 1970.

Lipstadt, D. E. "Deniers, Relativists and Pseudo-Scholarship." *Dimensions*, 6/1 (1991). Available at http://www.adl.org/Braun/dim_14_1_deniers.asp

Little, D. *American Orientalism: The United States and the Middle East since 1945.* 2nd edn; Chapel Hill & London: University of North Carolina Press, 2002, 2004.

Long, B. *Imagining the Holy Land: Maps, Models, and Fantasy Travels.* Bloomington: Indiana University Press, 2003.

McAlister, M. *Epic Encounters: Culture, Media and US Interests in the Middle East, 1945-2000.* Berkeley, CA: University of California Press, 2001.

McFate, M. "Anthropology and Counterinsurgency: The Strange Story of their Curious Relationship." *Military Review* (March-April 2005).

McGuinness, R. "US Pays £15bn in Aid to Israel." *Metro* (August 17, 2007).

McNeil, K. "The War on Academic Freedom." *The Nation* (November 11, 2002). Available at http://www.thenation.com/doc/20021125/mcneil

McQuaid, E. "A Hand of Help for Gaza (editorial)" (July/August, 2005). Available at http://www.foigm.org/partner/Article_Display_Page/0,,PTID306608|CHID556142|CIID2062048,00.html

MacAskill, E. "George Bush: 'God told Me to End the Tyranny in Iraq.' " *The Guardian* (October 7, 2005).

Mack, B. *The Myth of Innocence: Mark and Christian Origins.* Philadelphia: Fortress Press, 1988.

_______ *The Christian Myth: Origins, Logic, and Legacy.* New York & London: Continuum, 2001.

Maeir, A. M. "Review of Nadia Abu el-Haj, *Facts on the Ground*." *Isis* 95 (2004): 523-24.

_______ "Freedom of Speech or Freedom of Slander?" *Columbia Spectator* (September 21, 2007). Available at http://www.columbiaspectator.com/?q=node/26830

Malina, B. J. *The New Testament World: Insights from Cultural Anthropology.* 3rd edn; Louisville: Westminster/John Knox, 1981, 2001.

_______ "Review of Rodney Stark, *The Rise of Christianity: A Sociologist Reconsiders History*." *CBQ* 59 (1997): 593-95.

_______ "Understanding New Testament Persons." In R. L. Rohrbaugh, ed., *The Social Sciences and New Testament Interpretation*: pp. 41-61. Peabody: Hendrickson, 1996.

_______ *The Social World of Jesus and the Gospels.* London: Routledge, 1996.

_______ "Social Scientific Methods in Historical Jesus Research." In W. Stegemann, B. J. Malina and G. Theissen (eds.), *The Social Setting of Jesus and the Gospels*: 3-26. Minneapolis: Fortress Press, 2002.

_______ "Review of deSilva, *Despising Shame*." *RBL*. Available at http://www.bookreviews.org/pdf/2177_1292.pdf

_______ "Review of Ling, *The Judean Poor and the Fourth Gospel*." *RBL*. Available at http://www.bookreviews.org/pdf/5587_5883.pdf

Malina, B., and J. H. Neyrey. *Portraits of Paul: An Archaeology of Ancient Personality.* Louisville: Westminster/John Knox, 1996.

Mamdani, M. *Good Muslim, Bad Muslim: America, the Cold War, and the Roots of Terror.* New York: Three Leaves Press, 2005.

Manson, T. W. *The Sayings of Jesus.* London: SCM Press, 1957.

Marcus, J. *Mark 1-8: A New Translation with Introduction and Commentary.* New York: Doubleday, 2000.

Marx, K. "Eighteenth Brumaire of Louis Bonaparte." In K. Marx and F. Engels, *Collected Works Volume 11, Marx and Engels: 1851-53*: 101-97. London: Lawrence & Wishart, 1979.

Meeks, W. A. *The First Urban Christians: The Social World of the Apostle Paul* (2nd edn; New Haven & London: Yale University Press, 1983, 2003).

Meggitt, J. J. "Review of B. J. Malina, *The Social World of Jesus and the Gospels.*" *JTS* 49 (1998): -19.

Meier, J. P. *A Marginal Jew: Rethinking the Historical Jesus.* Vol. 1, *The Roots of the Problem and the Person.* New York: Doubleday, 1991.

_______ *A Marginal Jew: Rethinking the Historical Jesus.* Vol. 3, *Companions and Competitors.* New York: Doubleday, 2001.

Meikle, J. "Lecturers Back Boycott of Israel." *Guardian* (May 30, 2007).

Milgrom, S. *Obedience to Authority: An Experimental View.* London: Tavistock, 1974.

Monbiot, G. "America Is a Religion." *Guardian* (July 29, 2003).

_______ "Tony Blair's New Friend." *Guardian* (October 28, 2003).

_______ "Apocalypse Please." *The Guardian* (April 20, 2004).

_______ "Puritanism of the Rich." *Guardian* (November 9, 2004).

_______ "The US Used Chemical Weapons in Iraq - and Then Lied about It." *Guardian* November 15, 2005.

_______ "Behind the Phosphorus Clouds Are War Crimes within War Crimes." *Guardian* (November 22, 2005).

_______ "The King of Fairyland Will Never Grasp the Realities of the Middle East." *Guardian* (August 1, 2006).

Moxnes, H. "Jesus the Jew: Dilemmas of Interpretation." In I. Dunderberg, C. Tuckett and K. Syreeni, eds., *Fair Play: Diversity and Conflicts in Early Christianity: Essays in Honour of Heikki Räisänen*: 83-103. Leiden: Brill, 2002,

______ "Schleiermacher's *Life of Jesus*, 19th Century Nationalism, and the Present Challenge." In W. Blanton, J. G. Crossley and H. Moxnes, eds., *Jesus beyond Nationalism: Constructing the Historical Jesus in a Period of Cultural Complexity* (London: Equinox, forthcoming).

Murray, C. *Murder in Samarkand: A British Ambassador's Controversial Defiance of Tyranny in the War on Terror*. Edinburgh & London: Mainstream Publishing, 2006.

Nagy, T. "The Secret behind the Sanctions: How the US Intentionally Destroyed Iraq's Water Supply." *The Progressive* (September 1–6, 2001).

Negrin, H. "Prof Contests Abu el-Haj's Claims." *Columbia Spectator* (September 18, 2007). Available at http://www.columbiaspectator.com/node/26749

Newman, M. "Faith Threat to Free Speech." *Times Higher Education Supplement* (16 March 2007).

Neyrey, J. H. *The Gospel of John*. Cambridge: Cambridge University Press, 2007.

Northcott, M. *An Angel Directs the Storm: Apocalyptic Religion and American Empire*. London & New York: I. B. Tauris, 2004.

Norton-Taylor, R. "UK Equipment Being Used in Israeli Attacks." *Guardian* (May 29, 2002).

Novick, P. *The Holocaust and Collective Memory*. London: Bloomsbury, 1999.

Osiek, C., and D. L. Balch. *Families in the New Testament World: Households and House Churches*. Louisville: Westminster/John Knox, 1997.

Page, R. "Elizabeth Cady Stanton's *The Woman's Bible*." In A. Loades (ed.), *Feminist Theology: A* Reader: 16-22. London: SPCK, 1990.

Patai R. *Golden River to Golden Road*. Philadelphia: University of Pennsylvania, 1962.

______ *The Arab Mind*. Rev. edn; New York: Hatherleigh Press, 1976, 1983, 2002.

Penner, T. "*Die Judenfrage* and the Construction of Ancient Judaism: Toward a Foregrounding of the Backgrounds Approach to Early Christianity." In P. Gray and G. O'Day, eds., *Scripture and Traditions: Essays on Early Judaism and Christianity*. Leiden: Brill, forthcoming.

______ *In Praise of Christian Origins: Stephen and the Hellenists in Lukan Apologetic Historiography*. London & New York: T&T Clark/Continuum, 2004.

Perkins, J. "The 'Self as Sufferer.' " *HTR* 85 (1992): 245-72.

______ *The Suffering Self: Pain and Narrative Representation in the Early Christian Era*. London: Routledge, 1995.

______ "In Pursuit of Outlaw Cool." *Guardian* (August 30, 2006).

Philo, G. "Bad News from Israel: Media Coverage of the Israel/Palestine Conflict." Available at http://www.gla.ac.uk/departments/sociology/units/media/israel.pdf

Philo G., and M. Berry. *Bad News from Israel*. London, Pluto, 2004.

______ *"Glasgow University Media Unit: Bad News from Israel." Available at http://www.gla.ac.uk/departments/sociology/units/media/israel.htm*

Pilch, J. J. " 'Beat his Ribs while He Is Young' (Sir 30:12): A Window on the Mediterranean World." *BTB* 23 (1993): 101-13.

_______ "Review of Avalos, *Health Care and the Rise of Christianity*." *RBL*. Available at http://www.bookreviews.org/pdf/434_539.pdf

_______ "Review of Keir, *Disease and Healing in the New Testament*." *RBL*. Available at http://www.bookreviews.org/bookdetail.asp?TitleId=1502&CodePage=1502,434,4981

Pipes, D. "God and Mammon: Does Poverty Cause Militant Islam?" *The National Interest* 66 (Winter 2001–2002).

Porter, H. "The Land of the Free – but Free Speech Is a Rare Commodity." *Observer* (Sunday August 13, 2006).

Powell, S. M. "Ending Iraqi Threat Is Personal for Bush," *timesunion.com* (November 10, 2002). Available at http://www.timesunion.com/AspStories/story.asp?storyID=70750

Pred, A. "Situated Ignorance and State Terrorism: Silences, W.M.D., Collective Amnesia, and the Manufacture of Fear." In D. Gregory and A. Pred, eds., *Violent Geographies: Fear, Terror, and Political Violence*: 363-84. New York & London: Routledge, 2007.

Price, D. "Gregory Bateson and the OSS: World War II and Bateson's Assessment of Applied Anthropology." *Human Organization* 57.4 (1998): 379-84.

_______ "Lessons from Second World War Anthropology: Peripheral, Persuasive and Ignored Contributions." *Anthropology Today* 18.3 (2002): 14-20.

Pyper, H. "Musical Analysis and Biblical Studies: Brucknerian Transpositions." Unpublished paper presented at European Association of Biblical Studies/International Society of Biblical Literature conference, Vienna 2007.

Qureshi, E. "Misreading 'the Arab Mind.' " *Boston Globe* (May 30, 2004).

Rapture Ready. "Would Jesus Vote Republican?" (19/7/06). Available at http://www.raptureready.com/republican.html

Rai, M. *Chomsky's Politics*. London & New York: Verso, 1995.

Räisänen, H. "Jesus and the Food Laws: Reflections on Mark 7:15." *JSNT* 6 (1982): 79-100.

Reed, C. *Just War?* London: SPCK, 2004.

Reif, S. C. "Jews, Hebraists and 'Old Testament' Studies." In A. G. Hunter and P. R. Davies, eds., *Sense and Sensitivity: Essays on Reading the Bible in Memory of Robert Carroll*: 224-45. Sheffield: Sheffield Academic Press, 2002.

Rennie, D. "That Man Tried to Kill my Dad, Says Bush." *Telegraph* (September 28, 2002).

Rohrbaugh, R. L. "Legitimating Sonship – a Test of Honour: A Social-Scientific Study of Luke 4:1-30." In P. F. Esler (ed.), *Modelling Early Christianity: Social-Scientific Studies of the New Testament in its Context*: 183-97. London & New York: Routledge, 1995.

_______ "Ethnocentrism and Historical Questions about Jesus." In W. Stegemann, B. Malina and G. Theissen, eds., *The Social Setting of Jesus and the Gospels*: 27-43. Minneapolis: Fortress Press, 2002.

_______ *The New Testament in Cross-Cultural Perspective*. Eugene: Cascade Books, 2007.

_______ "Review of deSilva The Hope of Glory." *RBL*. Available at http://www.bookreviews.org/pdf/427_958.pdf

Rosenberg, J. C. *The Ezekiel Option.* Carol Stream, IL: Tyndale, 2005.
_______ *Epicenter: Why the Current Rumblings in the Middle East Will Change your Future.* Carol Stream, IL: Tyndale, 2006.
_______ *Copper Scroll.* Carol Stream, IL: Tyndale, 2007.
Roy, A. "The Loneliness of Noam Chomsky." *The Hindu.* (August 24, 2003).
Sachs, S. "Baptist Pastor Attacks Islam, Inciting Cries of Intolerance." *New York Times* (June 15, 2002).
Said, E. W. *Orientalism.* London: Penguin, 3rd edn, 1978, 1995, 2003.
_______ *Covering Islam: How the Media and the Experts Determine How We See the Rest of the World.* 2nd edn; London: Vintage, 1981, 1997.
_______ *Culture and Imperialism.* London: Vintage, 1993.
_______ *Representations of the Intellectual.* London: Vintage, 1994.
_______ *The End of the Peace Process: Oslo and After.* 2nd edn; London: Granta, 2000, 2002.
Sanders, E. P. *Paul and Palestinian Judaism: A Comparison of Patterns of Religion.* Philadelphia: Fortress Press; London: SCM Press, 1977.
_______ *Jesus and Judaism.* London: SCM Press, 1985.
_______ *The Historical Figure of Jesus.* London: Penguin, 1993.
_______ "Jesus, Ancient Judaism, and Modern Christianity: The Quest Continues." In P. Fredriksen and A. Reinhartz, eds., *Jesus, Judaism, and Christian Anti-Judaism: Reading the New Testament after the Holocaust*: 31-55. Louisville: Westminster/John Knox, 2002).
_______ "Comparing Judaism and Christianity: An Academic Autobiography" (April-May 2004). Available at http://www.duke.edu/religion/home/EP/Intel%20autobiog%20rev.pdf
Sanders, J. T. *Charisma, Converts, Competitors: Societal and Sociological Factors in the Success of Early Christianity.* London, SCM, 2000.
Segal, A. F. "Some Professional Observations on the Controversy about Nadia Abu el-Haj's First Book." *Columbia Spectator* (September 21, 2007). Available at http://www.columbiaspectator.com/?q=node/26830
Sen, A. *Identity and Violence: The Illusion of Destiny.* London: Allen Lane, 2006.
Sengupta, K. "Iraq Abuse Case Ends with Soldiers Acquitted." *Independent* (March 14, 2007).
Shaheen, J. *The TV Arab.* Ohio: Bowling Green State University Press, 1984.
_______ *Reel Bad Arabs: How Hollywood Vilifies a People.* Northampton, MA: Interlink, 2001.
Shlaim, A. *The Iron Wall: Israel and the Arab World.* London: Penguin, 2000.
_______ " 'Liberation' Is Not Freedom," *Observer* (March 30, 2003).
Siddiqui, A. *Islam at Universities in England: Meeting the Needs and Investing in the Future.* (April 10, 2007). Available at
http://www.dfes.gov.uk/hegateway/uploads/DrSiddiquiReport.pdf
Silverstein, R. "Origins of a Right Wing Campaign against Nadia Abu el-Haj." *Tikun Olam.* Available at http://www.richardsilverstein.com/tikun_olam/2007/08/19/origins-of-right-wing-campaign-against-nadia-abu-el-haj/#comment-37274

______ "Barnard Alumni Cabal Opposes Tenure for Abu el-Haj." *Tikun Olam.* Available at http://www.richardsilverstein.com/tikun_olam/2007/08/21/barnard-alumni-cabal-opposes-tenure-for-abu-el-haj/

Sizer, S. R. "Christian Zionism: A British Perspective." *Friends of al-Asqa: Defence of al-Asqa and Peace in Palestine* 1 (no year given). Available at http://www.aqsa.org.uk/JournalsDetail.aspx?id=28

Slutsky, C. "Tenure Battle at Barnard Gains Fresh Urgency." *The Jewish Week* (September 21, 2007).

Smith, A. "Rangers on Rack as Sectarian Chanting Mars Win." *Scotland on Sunday* (August 5, 2007).

Smith, J. Z. *Drudgery Divine: On the Comparison of Early Christianities and the Religions of Late Antiquity.* Chicago: University of Chicago Press, 1990.

Sperlich, W. B. *Noam Chomsky.* London: Reaktion Books, 2006.

Staff and Agencies. "Israel Captures Jailed Palestinian Militants." *Guardian* (March 14, 2006).

Stanton, E. C., *The Woman's Bible* (New York: European Publishing Company, 1895-1898).

Stegemann, W., B. Malina and G. Theissen, eds., *The Social Setting of Jesus and the Gospels.* Minneapolis: Fortress Press, 2002.

Stern, P. R. "Barnard's Shame, Columbia's Dirty Deal." *Israel Insider* (July 27, 2007).

Sternthal, T. "The Temple Mount's Jewish History: More Than a Matter of Faith." CAMERA (April 11, 2005). Available at http://www.camera.org/index.asp?x_context=2&x_outlet=35&x_article=879

Stocking, G. W., ed. *Colonial Situations: Essays on the Contextualization of Ethnographic Knowledge.* Madison: University of Wisconsin Press, 1991.

Storey, J. *An Introduction to Cultural Theory and Popular Culture.* 2nd edn; London: Prentice Hall, 1997.

Sugirtharajah, R. S. *Asian Biblical Hermeneutics and Postcolonialism: Contesting the Interpretations.* Sheffield: Sheffield Academic Press, 1998.

Suleiman, M. *The Arabs in the Mind of America.* Brattleboro: Amana, 1988.

Swan, C. "Rangers Fans: Leave the Bigots to Us Gers.' *Daily Record* (August 17, 2007).

Taylor, J. "An interview with Peter Williams." *Between Two Worlds.* Available at http://theologica.blogspot.com/2007/08/interview-with-peter-williams.html

Taylor, M., S. Goldenberg and R. McCarthy. " 'We Will Isolate Them.' " *Guardian (June 9, 2007).*

Taylor, M. L. *Religion, Politics, and the Christian Right: Post-9/11 Powers and American Empire.* Minneapolis: Fortress Press, 2005.

Theissen, G. *Sociology of Early Palestinian Christianity* (Philadelphia: Fortress Press, 1978).

______ *Social Reality and the Early Christians: Theology, Ethics and the World of the New Testament.* Edinburgh: T&T Clark, 1993.

Theissen, G., and A. Merz. *The Historical Jesus: A Comprehensive Guide.* London: SCM Press, 1998.

Tomlinson, K. "Living Yesterday in Today and Tomorrow: Meskhetian Turks in Southern Russia." In J. G. Crossley and C. Karner, eds., *Writing History, Constructing Religion*: pp. 107-28. Aldershot: Ashgate, 2005.

Tran, M. "Poll: Government Had Role in July 7 Bombings." *Guardian* (June 5, 2007).

Traubman, T., B. Ravid and S. Shamir. "British Academics Drop Planned Boycott of Israel." *Haaretz* (September 29, 2007).

Vallely, P. "Tom Wright: It's Not a Question of Left and Right, Says the Combative Priest Who Opposes the War in Iraq and Gay Bishops." *Independent* (29 December, 2003).

vander Stichele, C., and T. Penner. "Mastering the Tools or Retooling the Masters?" In C.

vander Stichele and T. Penner, eds., *Her Master's Tools? Feminist and Postcolonial Engagements of Historical-Critical Discourse*: 1-30. Atlanta: SBL; Leiden: Brill, 2005.

Vermes, G. *Jesus the Jew.* London: SCM Press, 1973.

_______ *Jesus and the World of Judaism* (London: SCM Press, 1983).

_______ *Providential Accidents: An Autobiography.* London: SCM Press, 1998.

von Sponeck, H. *A Different Kind of War: The UN Sanctions in Iraq.* Oxford: Berghahn, 2006.

von Sponeck, H., and D. Halliday. "The Hostage Nation."' *Guardian* (November 29, 2001).

Wagner, D. "Marching to Zion: The Evangelical-Jewish Alliance." *The Christian Century* (June 28, 2003): 20-24.

_______ "Christians and Zion: British Stirrings." *The Daily Star Beirut* (October 7, 2003).

Watts, M. "Revolutionary Islam." In D. Gregory and A. Pred, eds., *Violent Geographies: Fear, Terror, and Political Violence*: 175-203. New York & London: Routledge, 2007.

Wenell, K. J. *Jesus and Land: Sacred and Social Space in Second Temple Judaism.* London & New York: Continuum/T&T Clark, 2007.

White, M., and R. Norton-Taylor. "Straw Provokes Row over Arms for Israel." *Guardian* (July 9, 2002).

Whitelam, K. W. *The Invention of Ancient Israel: The Silencing of Palestinian History*. London: Routledge, 1996.

_______ "Representing Minimalism: The Rhetoric and Reality of Revisionism." In A. G. Hunter and P. R. Davies, eds., *Sense and Sensitivity: Essays on Reading the Bible in Memory of Robert Carroll*: 194-223. Sheffield: Sheffield Academic Press, 2002.

_______ "Preliminary Notes on Recent Historiography: Centralization and the New Imperialism." Unpublished paper delivered at the Constructions of Ancient Space Seminar, AAR/SBL Atlanta (November, 2003).

_______ "Lines of Power: Mapping Ancient Israel." In R. B. Coote and N. K. Gottwald, eds., *To Break Every Yoke: Essays in Honor of Marvin L. Chaney*: 40-79. Sheffield: Sheffield Phoenix Press, 2007.

Wilson, J. "US Admits Using White Phosphorus in Falluja." *Guardian* (November 16, 2005).

_______ "Politics and Palestinians at Roosevelt." *ZNet* (10 August, 2006). Available at http://www.zmag.org/content/showarticle.cfm?SectionID=107&ItemID=10743

Wolf, E. R., and J. G. Jorgensen "A Special Supplement: Anthropology on the Warpath in Thailand." *New York Review of Books* 15 (November 19, 1970).

Wright, N. T. *Jesus and the Victory of God.* London: SPCK, 1996.

_______ *The Resurrection of the Son of God.* London: SPCK, 2003.

_______ "The Divinity of Jesus." In N. T. Wright and M. J. Borg, *The Meaning of Jesus: Two Visions*: 157-68. London: SPCK, 1999.

Wright, N. T., and M. J. Borg. *The Meaning of Jesus: Two Visions.* London: SPCK, 1999.

Wyatt-Brown, B. "Honor, Shame and Iraq in American Foreign Policy." Note prepared for the Workshop on Humiliation and Violent Conflict, Columbia University, New York (November 18-19, 2004). Available at www.humiliationstudies.org/documents/WyattBrownNov04NY Conference.pdf

Yans-McLaughlin, V. "Science, Democracy, and Ethics: Mobilizing Culture and Personality for World War II." In G. W. Stocking, *Malinowski, Rivers, Benedict and Others: Essays on Culture and Personality*: 184-217. Madison: University of Wisconsin Press, 1986.

Žižek, S. *Welcome to the Desert of the Real! Five Essays on September 11 and Related Dates.* London & New York: Verso, 2002.

Select blogs

Anonymous. *Solomonia*. Available at http://www.solomonia.com/blog

Bird, M., and J. Willitts. *Euangelion*. Available at http://euangelizomai.blogspot.com

Cathey, J. *Dr Cathey's Blog*, see Chapter 2 Appendix

Cook, E. *Ralph the Sacred River*. Available at http://ralphriver.blogspot.com

Crossley, J. G. *Earliest Christian History*. Available at http://www.earliestchristianhistory.blogspot.com/

Davila, J. *PaleoJudaica*. Available at http://paleojudaica.blogspot.com

Doc Russia. *Bloodletting*. Available at http://bloodletting.blog-city.com

du Toit, S. *Primal Subversion*. Available at http://primalsubversion.blogspot.com

Goodacre, M. *NT Gateway Weblog*. Available at http://ntgateway.com/weblog

Meadows, D. *Rogueclassicism*. Available at http://www.atrium-media.com/rogueclassicism

Nikkel, P., and D. Zacharias. *Deinde*. Available at http://www.deinde.org

Ristau, K. *anduril.ca*. Available at http://anduril.ca/blog

Rosson, L. *The Busybody*. Available at http://lorenrosson.blogspot.com

Tilling, C. *Chrisendom*. Available at http://www.christilling.de/blog

West, J., and B. Wason. *Biblioblogs*. Available at http://www.biblioblogs.com

Index of References

Index of Names

Made in the USA
Monee, IL
13 May 2025

17404246R00155